THE AGE O

THE AGE OF
INDUSTRIALISM
IN AMERICA

INDUSTRIALISM IN AMERICA

ESSAYS IN SOCIAL STRUCTURE AND CULTURAL VALUES

Edited by **FREDERIC COPLE JAHER**

The Free Press   NEW YORK
Collier-Macmillan Limited   LONDON

Preface

The nature of historical scholarship is such that the more significant the subject the more improbable the appearance of any definitive treatment. Exhaustive explanations have not yet emerged to terminate historiographical controversies that range from the formation of the Early Kingdom in Egypt to the origins of the cold war. Greater understanding of the crucial issues of the past seems to involve the discovery of unforeseen ramifications and the challenging of established interpretations. The spirit of incisive and continual inquiry defines the purpose of these essays. They do not "cover the field" of American industrialism, but seek to uncover portions of it by evaluating and communicating aspects of this experience.

Contributors

Howard N. Ross *Assistant Professor of Economics, Baruch School, The City College, The City University of New York*

Ari Hoogenboom *Professor of American History, Pennsylvania State University*

Michael Parenti *Professor of Political Science, Sarah Lawrence College*

Ann Lane *Former Instructor in the History Departments of Brooklyn College, Hunter College, and Sarah Lawrence College*

Leonard Dinnerstein *Assistant Professor of American History, Department of Social Sciences, Fairleigh Dickinson University*

Gunther Barth *Associate Professor, Department of History, University of California at Berkeley*

Frederic Cople Jaher *Assistant Professor of History and Social Sciences, University of Chicago*

Herbert G. Gutman *Professor of History, The University of Rochester*

David Brody *Professor of History, University of California at Davis*

Richard Weiss *Assistant Professor, Department of History, University of California at Los Angeles*

John G. Cawelti *Associate Professor of English and Humanities, University of Chicago*

David Reimers *Associate Professor of History, New York University*

CONTENTS

Contents

ix

THE AGE OF
INDUSTRIALISM
IN AMERICA

Introduction

By 1850 the destiny of a united America became manifest. Transcontinental transport would supply the sinews for a national economy; the peopling of a huge and mighty land, the westward surge of settlement, and the unearthing of mineral riches gave substance to a vision of virtually boundless natural and human resources; from new factories would come quantities of goods barely imagined by the most extravagant enthusiasts. Unless thwarted by secession, the United States was building to a future unprecedented in wealth and power.

The fruition of these expectations (investigated by Howard Ross in the first essay in this volume) required economic and cultural adjustments that disrupted tradition, dislocated groups and individuals, and caused conflicts in interests and values. Society grew more powerful, but also more frightening. Promise was fulfilled at the expense of cherished beliefs and institutions; some people won immense victories while others suffered defeats. Colossal wealth and

1

power were created, but toil, pain, and sacrifice too often went unrewarded. Industrial development attracted masses of immigrants, built great cities, raised living standards and social status for millions, and thrust America to the pinnacle of world power. Some felt, however, that riches and power were controlled by narrow and ruthless groups of railroad barons, corporate magnates, and investment bankers, thereby setting East against West, country against city, individual against community, labor against capital, change against continuity, and wealth against conscience. The gains made by industrialization did not still the dissent of farmers, artisans, and shopkeepers who considered it a weapon aimed at the agrarian heartland of White Anglo-Saxon Protestant America. Miracles of mechanized production did not halt the confusion and fear of ghetto inhabitants who apprehensively regarded new industrial processes as a menace to residual family, community, and culture comforts rescued from the arduous journey out of the old world or the spent farm. Customs and relationships weakened by the shock of being uprooted and then transplanted at best provided fragile protection for newcomers, those unable to comprehend the rhythms of city life or easily endure the discipline of the factory. Nor could the aloof contempt of the Main Line or Beacon Street conceal anxiety over departures from the past which made the old upper class vulnerable to parvenu challenges.

By 1910, the physical and corporate organization of industrial capitalism were essentially complete. Funds flowing from investment banking houses grouped the nation's heavy industry and transportation systems into mammoth trusts. Technological advances, cheap labor, centralized administration, efficient factory organization, and abundant financing enabled the production of huge quantities of standardized goods. After World War I, the American economy perceptibly shifted concentration from producers' goods to accommodate the new mass market for consumer goods and services. For a decade, consumer demand was assiduously nurtured by advertising, installment buying, and planned obsolescence. Luxury and leisure, once considered the guilty privileges of an anachronistic aristocracy or the earned reward of the successful entrepreneur, were now claimed in the name of the average man. While the traditional virtues of thrift, prudence, and hard labor had spurred the effort and gathered the capital that industrialized the United States, they loomed less significant in a landscape illuminated with Hollywood stars, athletes, and frenzied good times. The figures of the heroic age of American industrialism vanished as these virtues faded. People no longer marvelled at the commercial conquests once known as the Vanderbilt railroad, Carnegie steel, or Rockefeller oil. Massive agglomerations of capital absorbed many productive and distributive functions formerly organized independently. These annexations and integrations had grown too large and complex to be assimilated, let alone dominated, by a single personality. Specialists manned posts in the new corporate empire while managers, serving as brokers among the diffuse functions and interests, strove to coordinate the whole.

Another decade, the 1930s, found America gripped by a savage depression whose mockery of the national shibboleths of progress, production and prosperity quickly made the 1920s half memory and half fantasy. Retention and recovery were at the helm and for the first time in its history the country, becalmed in the eye of an immense storm, no longer surged ahead. Economic disaster spurred radical changes in the social system. The gigantic achievements of industrial capitalism had formerly canonized the rights of private ownership and free enterprise. Dwarfed by the esteem accorded to successful businessmen, the government had been deemed the proper repository for those who lacked the intelligence or character to survive in commerce, or for businessmen and their agents who sought to use politics to facilitate commercial triumphs. With the notable exceptions of tariff protection and aid to railroads, the post-Civil War political system had been largely confined by this laissez-faire philosophy to the role of protecting property, policing violence, and mediating the demands of contending business interests. Only against the background of delimited government operations could the flurry of moderate reforms and the few feeble gestures at regulation during the Progressive period have aroused such excitement. The Great Depression collapsed the colossal stature of business magnates and reversed the roles of commerce and politics. For the first time in the history of the nation, society turned primarily to the federal government for relief, regulation, and rejuvenation. Personal development, social welfare, and economic stability, traditionally the province of unfettered competition, voluntary association, and individual capacity, became an obligation of the political system. After World War II, America returned to the pattern of affluent expenditure, that had permeated the 1920s. However, unlike that era, the postwar years retained and even broadened the public role in providing for economic stability and expansion and in enabling the dispossessed to enter that struggle for success known as the American way of life.

Social change and the search for community frame the dimensions of these studies in the experience of America in the industrial era. Movement from Europe to America, from East to West, from farm to factory, from country to city, and from class to class created the aspirations and disappointments, the conflicts and associations, and the perceptions and prejudices discussed in the following essays. Old communities rallying around antiquated values broke down or at the very least were challenged and modified by the impact of industrialism upon the full range of human activity from family relations to foreign involvements. Michael Parenti's "Immigration and Political Life", Ann Lane's "The Negro Response: A Study in Desperation" and Leonard Dinnerstein's "Atlanta in The Progressive Era: A Dreyfus Affair in Georgia" illustrate the experience of ethnic and immigrant enclaves in the upheavals that uprooted traditional ways of life and thought. Gunther Barth analyzes the attempts of emergent elites in the young cities of Denver and San Francisco to consolidate their newly won status. Frederic Cople Jaher focuses on an antipodal situation when he describes the tribulations of the Boston Brahmins trying to overcome an *arriviste* challenge. Herbert G. Gutman and David Brody, investigating another sector of society, comment respectively on the influence of industrial capitalism upon the relationship between the worker and his community, and upon the structure of union leadership. A similar confrontation of social change with community value systems is the central concern of those authors who deal with the cultural impact of industrialism. Richard Weiss, in an essay on Horatio Alger, Jr., discusses the poignant obsolescence of the pre-industrial moral code. John G. Cawelti traces the attempt to make industrialism esthetically meaningful through the Philadelphia and the two Chicago World's Fairs. David Reimers shows how Protestantism tried to come to terms with the problems raised by modern times.

Transformation and upheaval notwithstanding, American industrialism involved no abrupt end to established institutions and ideas. The nature and pace of mechanization varied. In some areas of the social system, gradual transition permitted graceful and meaningful union between the old and the new. Even more important, much of the traditional creed and social structure remained relevant. Traits vital to contemporary success—productive labor, prudent venture, practical ingenuity, and propensity to wealth—had been considered virtues in colonial America. Beliefs and attitudes which seemed less useful as the economy grew in size and complexity also remained influential. The transformation of America into the world's foremost industrial society took place in the context of a formidable if diminishing attachment to laissez-faire capitalism. Similar continuity, existing in community organization, is indicated by Ari Hoogenboom's findings that through the mercantile and industrial eras, the social origins of United States senators remained remarkably constant.

Important phases of American industrialism have now been completed and perhaps now, as cities disperse and blue-collar workers disappear, we are already in the initial stages of a new era. Whatever shape the future assumes, short of global holocaust, it will retain the bountiful production and bureaucratic organization bequeathed by the mechanized civilization. Hopefully the next age will build on the accomplishments but eliminate the brutalities that permeated the industrial process.

1

Economic Growth and Change in the United States Under Laissez Faire: 1870–1929

by **HOWARD N. ROSS***

I. Introduction—Growth and Cycles

Between 1870 and 1929, aggregate income, or the net output of goods and services (Net National Product) of the United States, when measured in 1929 prices, increased about tenfold while population only trebled. The result was a rise in income per capita—a signal indicator of economic progress—of about three and a half times. (More precise estimates and their derivation are given in Table 3.) The record is remarkable by any standard. It should be especially remarkable to the contemporary observer inclined toward the necessity of government planning for growth. For this historical achievement was sustained under conditions of sharp and recurrent recessions and a virtual absence of government policies to control the business cycle and promote growth.

During the first half of our period, 1870–1900, downswings were so prolonged that the economy contracted for as many months as it

* I am indebted to Philip Friedman for conscientious research assistance.

expanded; in other words, on an average of one out of every two months, economic activity was declining, according to the business cycle chronology of the National Bureau for Economic Research. In this respect, the succeeding period was not much better. Between 1900 and 1927, all recessions accounted for 136 months or 42 per cent of the total period.[1] This chronic instability, unparalleled in our history, was a heavy drag on the rate of growth. If the economy can be viewed as traveling along a rising path of maximum output—a path of natural growth at full employment determined by population increases and technological progress—recessions will wrench the economy off its path as output and employment decline. A resumption of natural growth will take time, the time necessary to absorb the slack in unemployed manpower, capital, and other resources. What has been lost, meanwhile, is a necessary ingredient to growth. That essential ingredient is investment, or capital goods, which as traditionally defined by the Department of Commerce for the purposes of measuring economy-wide production—there are other useful definitions— includes plant and equipment, residential and nonresidential construction, inventories, and exports net of imports. Each of these capital goods is capable of providing additional output and employment in the future. As the population and the labor force increase, growth of the total capital stock is a prerequisite for merely maintaining a given standard of living or real income per capita, let alone raising the standard, as economic growth usually implies. During mild recessions the stock of some of these capital goods will fall, particularly inventories and occasionally exports, while the stocks of the other capital goods will either remain stationary or rise less than they would have. As recessions deepen into depressions, the stock of all capital goods is likely to fall. Although recessions are less severe in their impact on the capital stock, they will nevertheless stunt its growth, and an economic policy permissive of only mild recessions will set the economy to drift below its path of natural growth. The price is always a lower observed rate of growth, for movements along the path have already been defined as states of maximum growth.

So far this crude picture does scant justice to the complex problems of growth. It is presented more as a heuristic device for setting growth in perspective than as an analytical model with specified characteristics of behavior. At some later point the device will be given more analytical content, but not enough to make it really tick. What has been said so far may leave the impression that irrational policies were the sole cause of cycles. The laissez-faire policy of the government during our period meant a passive posture toward the cycle; to the extent that the policy intensified cycles or was a proximate cause, it contributed to instability, but it is difficult to argue that the policy was a major cause. Economists have produced many competing explanations for the recurrence of cycles. If their very proliferation attests to a lack of persuasion, there has been some clarification in the modern view that the etiology of cycles is bound up with the growth process. Predictably, this too has stimulated a number of theories of varying generality, but a common feature of all is the inevitability of cycles in a growing capitalist economy. The forces responsible for growth also generate cycles through a multiplicity of economic mechanisms, all of which involve in an essential way investment (changes in the capital stock) and its relation to income. The rate of investment or changes in the rate of investment thus appears and reappears as a strategic variable both in the joint and independent analyses of growth and cycle. The superiority of those theories that conceive of growth and cycles as interdependent—theories of cyclical growth—over those that do not lies in their greater realism and therein a greater relevance to history. History supports neither the vision of steady development nor that of stationary cycles, i.e., cycles without trends, implicit in the constructs that ignore interdependence. Theories that explain economic progress as a rising trend of output around which cycles dance have caught something essential to the world for which they were devised.[2]

An interesting example of the foregoing is R. M. Goodwin's model, arranged with great skill and simplicity, in which cycles are not possible without growth. The model is inspired by Schumpeterian insight: "The recurring periods of prosperity of the cyclical movement are the form progress takes in a capitalist society."[3] Investment is the focal variable and responds to two stimuli: innovation and changes in output. The latter is the famous "accelerator" principle and is prominent in all cycle-growth theories. The model also exhibits shorter contractions than expansions, said by Goodwin to be "one of the most firmly established generalizations about business cycles."[4] In a strongly expansionist economy this might be expected, and over a long run it is true for the United States. For the lengthy period 1870–1900, however, contractions and expansions were of equal duration.[5]

With the conviction that growth is really cyclical in nature, our crude picture of the developing American economy can be enhanced with more substance:

(1) Cycles and the growth process are mutually determining and unique for time and place. Just as agrarian and industrial economies are expected to differ in their growth profiles and sources of growth, so will the character and causes of their business cycles differ. By the same token, the U.S. economies in 1870 and 1929 were two quite different animals, but do we want one, two, or ten theories to explain the evolutionary links between them and their cyclical history? Attempts to bridge these discontinuities have been made in the stage of development approaches of Colin Clark and W. W. Rostow[6]—we exclude the awesome doctrines of Marx and Schumpeter, in which capitalism is but a temporary stage of development—these attempts have failed to uncover the mechanisms of growth, and for all their ad hoc theorizing, they are essentially descriptive. The claim has been made that a single theory, simple and broad, should serve the purpose despite profound changes in structure and institutions that are and must be ignored if the theory is to remain general and manageable. The claim for simplification rests on the central importance of capital accumulation for growth; increases in capital, and what is even more critical, technological innovation, embodied in an updated capital stock. The claim has been fruitful. Advances in our knowledge about capital have fertilized and clarified what we know about growth.

(2) The path of natural growth is an artifice, a bench mark for indicating maximum growth. As defined, it highlights the major exogenous forces of economic progress: technological innovation and population increases operating in a full employment environment.

Recently, an approximation of the path has been ingeniously measured for the U.S. in the present decade by projecting Gross National Product at a post-Korean War growth rate adjusted for full employment, i.e., an unemployment level of 4 per cent. This path of "potential GNP" assumes that post-Korean War rates of technological improvements and labor force increases will continue into the extrapolated future.[7] Unfortunately, no such measures exist for our period, but the record of recessions assures us that the economy rarely traveled its path of natural growth. The longevity and frequency of these adversities probably exerted a depressive influence on the path itself. Not only is growth slowed by the underutilization of existing resources, but a potent and durable effect could result from a "depression psychology" inhibiting long-run decisions to spend by individuals and business. Consumption statistics are not kind to this proposition, perhaps because shifts in the consumption function over time have hidden the effect. Surely one of the casualties of the Great Depression was investment in education, not an easily reversible decision, and one that reduced the natural growth rate for succeeding generations. Inventions lost, not merely delayed, are not likely to come to our attention. We may be convinced from personal experience that built-in and unmanaged economic contractions have a far-reaching influence beyond their time, sufficient to dampen the long-term growth rate. Empirical research has yet to vouchsafe these convictions, which may be its limitation rather than ours.

(3) Convenient and conventional ways of measuring growth, whether or not it be maximum growth, are by flows of aggregate income or output (the two are equal by definition) and by aggregate income per capita. Frequently these magnitudes are GNP or NNP (Net National Product), the latter being less by an amount of depreciation supposed to represent the use of fixed capital in the production process. Available depreciation figures are arbitrary, and as a guide to actual capital consumption they are unreliable. This makes estimates of NNP suspicious, but to include depreciation (GNP) distorts what factors of production are earning, since depreciation is income to no one. Fortunately, the two measures move closely together in time, and I have selected NNP as an approximation of factor income at market prices. Income statistics are never as good as they should be, but they tell a reasonable story of growth even though they are subject to doubt.

Price changes confuse movements in output; growth means higher output, and a comparison of annual money incomes will reflect that as well as price fluctuations. To remove this distortion, to allow comparisons between real output in different years, output must be expressed in prices of a given base year. Here the base year will usually be 1929.

Net National Product is a less sensitive criterion for evaluating growth than NNP per capita. To grow by the latter index means NNP must rise faster than the population and this generally occurs when productivity (output per unit of input) is also rising. By the former index, any rise in NNP will be counted as growth; this could happen because more capital and labor are employed, or the productivity of those inputs is increasing, or both. When the indexes diverge, when NNP is growing faster than NNP per capita, productivity increases are dependably low. Since this has been the case in some periods of our economic history we can expect to find in general more rapid rises in NNP. Other standards have been proposed for judging growth; of particular current interest is consumption per capita. Since the utility of expanded production ultimately lies in greater consumption, the golden rule of capital accumulation dictates a maximization of consumption per capita for optimal growth, under certain constraints.[8] However, the data are not available to forge this policy prescription into an interpretative tool for our purposes.

Finally, our picture tells us to measure growth over the cycle: data in any one year will reflect a growth component and some phase of the cycle. To isolate the growth component and screen out the impact of the cycle, most observations for any bench-mark year in this paper will be an average of five years, with the bench mark as the middle year. This technique relies on the National Bureau's chronology of business cycles, the average duration of which between 1854 and 1954 has been estimated as slightly over four years.[9]

(4) Policy implications can be read into our picture. Within the context of the era under review they serve to put laissez faire in perspective, the more clearly to see it and the economic record it produced. A policy for growth should aim at keeping the economy as close as possible to the natural growth rate. This involves a two-fold effort: (a) to minimize cyclical departures from the path of growth—or what is thought of as stabilization policy, and (b) to push the economy deliberately along its path of growth at some

socially desirable rate—or growth policy, a thoroughly contemporary innovation in American policy making.

Laissez faire in this country sought, so it seems, a single objective in the minimization of government influence in the conduct of economic affairs. It was more by inference than by conscious design— for example, Adam Smith's articulated scheme for a self-regulating economy under competition—that the private sector was left to determine the direction of the economy. The only way that determination could be made was through the medium of the market and the price mechanism. The lack of principles of how and to what ends the market should work was inevitably matched by a lack of policy to preserve the freedom of the market. An awareness that business could be a "malefactor" and subvert the public's interest was recorded in the passage of the Sherman Antitrust Act of 1890. This was a notable event, but one which would hardly stand as a bulwark against the waves of mergers in the nineteenth and twentieth centuries that permanently altered the structure of many industries towards monopoly. The utter absence of an economic rationale for a market-governed economy perhaps is no surprise; the evolution of laissez faire seems in retrospect to have been more political than economic doctrine. The problems of stabilization and growth were presumably to be solved by the movements of prices, particularly by key relative prices, money wages in relation to the price of output, and the interest rate.

The United States economy could have grown faster and could have grown with greater stability. This thesis would probably win universal agreement among both advocates of laissez faire and those who see virtue in extensive government planning. It is as true as it is naive. Historical realism might permit speculation on the possibility of expanded government powers to encourage competition and consequently to improve the performance of the economy. Even this requires a substantial modification of laissez-faire policy, more radical than all the antitrust legislation enacted up to 1929 and certainly more effective than its execution. This is speculation on a colossal scale, but one can go no further. What we have come to think of as the tools of stabilization were simply unavailable, and were not to be discovered until after the close of our period. They grew out of a theory proposed by J. M. Keynes in *The General Theory of Employment, Interest, and Money*, (London : The Macmillan Co., 1936), and they still owe their being more to his original formulation than to either the amendments of his disciples and critics or to glimmers in the work of his predecessors. Keynes challenged neoclassical economics at its very core, namely, its assumption that full employment was a normal state for a competitive economy. Lapses from full employment were regarded as temporary and, if prolonged, could be rationalized by the imperfections of competition in practice. The Keynesian challenge took the form of Aggregate Demand, a theoretical tool that determined what would be purchased from the economy's output. To stabilize at full employment or somewhere on the path of natural growth, Aggregate Demand had to be sufficient to absorb what the economy produced when resources were fully employed. Keynes argued that this could only be fortuitous under laissez faire. To ensure the condition required deliberate government action : emphatic fiscal policy; the manipulation of the government budget and, to a lesser extent, monetary policy; changes in the money supply and interest rates. Beyond that, Keynes intended the private sector to make its decisions and to preserve the essential character of a capitalist system. Concern for cyclical falls from full employment income was not matched with a concern for long-run income over the cycle. The regulation of Aggregate Demand is the proper objective of stabilization policy, but growth policy looks primarily toward enlarging the supply of output, something Keynes took as given. Major stress in growth policy inevitably is laid on investment either through direct stimulus or indirectly through overall measures to raise income, which tend to induce further investment. Monetary policy is given important leverage as a proximate determinant of investment; Keynes' denigration of monetary action has been largely ignored in this context. New and experimental, growth policy has yet to meet the test of time.[10]

This brief detour into stabilization and growth policies was meant to give some perspective to laissez faire. I have chosen more or less consistently to look back from a vantage point in the present. It makes better economics than it does history, but after all, the subject of this essay is progress, and there is always the nagging question—progress toward what? It was made clear from the beginning that society did not have a real choice between laissez faire and "managed capitalism" until the advent of Keynesian thought. Some perspective can be acquired from the statistics on business cycle contractions within our period and after the Full Employment Act of 1946, an avowal of government responsibility for stabilizing the economy at high employment. In its short career, the Act has been implemented with the inconsistency of the political climate. Earlier references have been made to the source of the data in Table 1.

Table I—U.S. Business Cycle Contractions, 1870–1927, 1945–1961[11]

Trough TOTAL CYCLE Trough	Interval (months)	Number of Contractions	All Contractions (months)	Months per Contraction (Average)	Contractions as per cent of Interval
Dec., 1870-Dec., 1900	360	7	179	25.6	49.7
Dec., 1900-Nov., 1927	323	8	136	17.0	42.1
Post-Full Employment Act					
Oct., 1945–Feb., 1961	184	4	42	10.5	22.8

The most recent trough is 1961, and 1945 is the closest trough to the passage of the Act. Had the interval been stretched to February, 1967, or a total of 256 months, the absolute months of contractions would have remained the same and contractions as a percentage of the interval would have fallen to 16.4 per cent. The efforts at stabilization have paid off with fewer downswings of shorter duration; after 1961, sporadic policies for growth form part of the policy mix. Between the two earlier subperiods, arbitrarily defined by century, the earliest period is marked by fewer contractions of much longer span. Students of business cycles ascribe this to the financial panics of 1873 and 1893 and the several disruptions of railroad expansion, all of which seriously hampered industry output and long-run investment opportunities.[12] On the amplitude of the contractions and the steepness of the declines, Achinstein has averaged some familiar indexes of business activity.[13] The average amplitudes per contraction are 21.8 and 20.9 per cent respectively for the subperiods in chronological order. Data are available only to the trough in August 1954, and between 1945 and 1954 the rate of decline per contraction is 15.9 per cent. Achinstein ranked the six severest peacetime contractions by the dual criteria of duration and amplitude: 1929–33, 1873–79, 1882–85, 1920–21, 1893–94, 1937–38. Crowded within the final quarter of the last century—a relatively brief historical period—are three of the harshest contractions known to American business.

II. The Setting: Laissez Faire

The thread that binds 1870 and 1929 in a continuum is the passive attitude of the federal government toward the course of the general economy—the very essence of a laissez-faire policy. During almost two generations of drastic and widespread change, nothing remains as consistent. The size and composition of the federal budget will provide instruction on this point. The trend values of federal expenditures indicate about a tenfold increase over the period; as percentages of GNP, they exhibit a moderate decline from 4.4 per cent to 3.6 per cent from the beginning to the end of the period (see Table 4). The almost proportionate growth in federal expenditures still consigned government to a minor share of income, and to what certainly follows, a minor influence on the determination of income. The impact of expenditures, small as they were, could have been greater had they been used as an active counter-cyclical weapon. As one could have anticipated, this was not the case: the budget was never intended as a stabilizer. Firestone's study reveals a general counter-cyclical pattern of budgetary surpluses and deficits in our period, expansion generating surpluses and contractions generating either smaller surpluses or deficits.[14] Notable exceptions are the depressions of 1873–79 (the longest on record) and 1882–85, and the recession of 1887–88, when the Treasury ran persistent surpluses.[15] Any similarity to a real compensatory fiscal policy is purely illusory; conscious stabilization requires purposive changes in the level of expenditures and tax rates depending on the phase of the cycle. What Firestone observed was produced by expenditures that were random over the cycle (subject to a rising trend), and by receipts that were sensitive to the direction of the cycle. Nevertheless, the pattern is correct for stabilization. But this is not the whole story. Before 1914, the bulk of federal receipts came from customs duties and excise taxes (consumption taxes); after the enactment of the sixteenth amendment, permitting the federal government a direct levy on income without apportionment among the states, the major source of revenues was the income tax. This institutional change may very well have raised consumption permanently. The shift from consumption taxes to income taxes may have altered the burden of global taxes from regressive (a proportionately larger share borne by lower income groups) to proportional—the early income tax was only weakly progressive. If so, consumption would have increased by more than it would have under the pre-1914 tax structure.

Firestone also examined the timing of tax legislation and arrives at a rather startling conclusion. "Indeed, until the 1930s, tax rates and tariffs, more often than not, were lowered during prosperity and raised during depression."[16] When a surplus prompted a tax decrease and a deficit, a tax increase, the imbalanced budget was of necessity destabilizing, driving income in the direction in which it was moving and, perversely, reenforcing the imbalance in the budget. The difficult task of relating tax rate changes to subsequent income and budget balances was not pursued by the author. The conclusion is less startling if one recalls that the major business of the Treasury was to balance its budget; deficit financing was a bitter experience made unavoidable by wars. A broader truth lurks behind this example of fiscal policy under laissez faire: There is no necessary equation between a passive policy and one that is neutral in its economic effects. One fault of laissez faire was that its advocates and practitioners neither anticipated nor understood its non-neutrality. Its ultimate fault lies in the policy itself, narrowly conceived to optimize efficiency under full employment. The full employment bias of the theoreticians was unfortunately not shared by the real world, and without this bias, Adam Smith's Invisible Hand could work wonders and could also strangle.

Laissez faire's resistance against controls and its reckoning with the economic consequences of its practices was one face of policy, and was understandable. The other face, the less understandable, was its conservation of institutions in view of their sometimes disastrous performance. There is no a priori reason for the laissez-faire policymaker to be less of a reformer than anyone else in serving the objectives of his policy—especially if he studies Adam Smith. And perhaps he isn't, but this does not explain the marked inertia of laissez-faire policy toward certain institutions badly in need of change. A prominent instance was the National Banking System, established in 1863 and displaced in 1914 by the Federal Reserve System, our first authentic central bank. The National Banking System fulfilled its initial purposes of providing a demand for government securities (originally Civil War debt) and replacing the heterogeneous and occasionally worthless state bank note issues with a uniform national bank currency (the result of a penalty tax on state notes in 1866). In its principal and continuing function of supplying money, the system was dangerously inadequate. Locked in by inflexible requirements, the supply of money turned rigid in the face of a high and rising demand, and if at the same time currency was drained from the banks, the supply of money contracted. Consequently there were recurrent periods of astronomical interest rates (120 per cent on call loans in New York in 1893) and banking panics, the most severe in 1873, 1884, 1890, 1893, and 1907. These caused wholesale bank failures and at times the suspension of convertibility of bank deposits into currency. The banking crises of 1873, 1890, 1893, and 1907 are also associated with cyclical downswings that developed in the same years. These episodes and the monetary history of which they form a part have been interpreted with great mastery by Friedman.[17] It took eighty years to reform the National Banking System by eliminating it; in a regime where policy was more responsive to the economic climate, such longevity would seem incredible.

Limits to the economic powers of the central authority under laissez faire were sharp and, it has been argued, entailed a cost in growth and stability. Constitutional restrictions proved to be less onerous than those that grew out of a political tradition of federalism in this country. The tradition kept alive a constant struggle for fiscal domination by the states, a struggle in which the federal government offered more succor than resistance. The founding fathers saw the necessity of giving Congress what appeared to be broad prerogatives of taxation: exclusive rights over customs duties and concurrent jurisdiction with the states over internal taxes. No prescriptions were made for the scope of federal expenditures, and it was here that the greatest restraint eventually fell. Public spending for "internal improvements" was largely deferred to the states in strict regard to their constitutional authority. As the Treasury accumulated budget surpluses with nothing to spend them on, decisions to distribute the excess to the states met with repeated presidential disfavor—from Jackson, Pierce, and Buchanan—lest the federal government control the states through purse strings.[18]

> Beginning in 1866 and stretching to 1893, the Treasury had a long series of surpluses, broken only by a small deficit in 1875. In 1882 The Secretary of the Treasury was making the same complaint as had his predecessors in the 1820s and 1830s: he had too great an annual revenue. Congress required his advice not to get revenue into, but to get it out of the Treasury.[19]

Combined state and local expenditures exceeded federal expenditures by a substantial margin in all peacetime years. Federal spending accelerated during the later 1930s, and after World War II the relationship between the two classes of government spending was completely reversed. For selected years, the percentage of federal to state and local expenditure is shown in Table 2.

Table 2—Proportion of Federal to State and Local Expenditures, Selected Years[20]

Year	Per cent
1902	52.2
1913	43.0
1927	45.2
1936	107.8
1948	167.4

Another tradition was evolving at about the same time we were fighting to become a republic. Its spokesman was Adam Smith. Constructing a beautifully reasoned argument, Smith demonstrated the superiority of competition to private monopoly as a means of achieving social welfare. His famous attack on mercantilism was only part of this; the mercantilist trade policy of the state had encouraged monopolies under a shelter of tariffs and subsidies. Given the alternatives as Smith puts them: competition or monopoly, a market free of state interferences or one distorted toward monopoly by the crown's pursuit of gold, Smith's intellectual defense of laissez faire is irresistible. In a passage of great eloquence, Smith sets down at once a philosophy of laissez faire and a practical guide for government: [21]

> Every man, as long as he does not violate the laws of justice, is left perfectly free to pursue his own interest in his own way, and to bring both his industry and capital into competition with those of any other man, or order of men. The sovereign is completely discharged from a duty, in the attempting to perform which he must always be exposed to innumerable delusions, and for the proper performance of which no human wisdom or knowledge could ever be sufficient; the duty of superintending the industry of private people, and of directing it towards the employments most suitable to the interest of the society. According to the system of natural liberty, the sovereign has only three duties to attend to; three duties of great importance, indeed, but plain and intelligible to common understandings: first, the duty of protecting the society from the violence and invasion of other independent societies; secondly, the duty of protecting, as far as possible, every member of the society from the injustice or oppression of every other member of it, or the duty of establishing an exact administration of justice; and, thirdly, the duty of erecting and maintaining certain public works and certain public institutions, which it can never be for the interest of any individual, or small number of individuals, to erect and maintain; because the profit could never repay the expence to any individual or small number of individuals, though it may frequently do much more than repay it to a great society.

Smith's rules for ideal government would in practice determine the size of government expenditures and their functional allocation. In peacetime the size would be relatively small (as we have already seen) and the allocation would invariably be dictated by the Smithian concept of the State's responsibilities. With regard to the administration of justice and public works, jurisdictions overlap between the states and the federal government in our political system so that federal expenditures would tend to be concentrated on defense and its incidental expenses and restricted to public investment of a nonlocal nature. A comparison of the distribution of federal spending (inclusive of government upkeep) in 1900, the earliest available year, and in 1929 bears this out; the years 1939 and 1949 make the comparison even more pointed. All figures in Table 3 are percentages of total expenditure.

Table 3—Allocation of Federal Expenditures to Various Functions, Selected Years[22]

	1900 Per cent	1929 Per cent	1939 Per cent	1949 Per cent
National defense	32.1	23.1	12.2	33.0
Veterans' services and benefits	27.4	26.2	6.3	18.5
Postal service	20.4	26.5	8.9	6.0
Transportation and communication, other	4.7	9.0	5.2	3.2
General government	11.0	7.8	6.3	3.0
Total	95.6	92.6	38.9	63.7

Provision for navigation aids and facilities is almost all of transportation in 1900; in 1929 this is still as large, high-ways accounting for most of the rise in the entire item. Over this period, the steepest increase in relative expenditures beyond those already cited was for agricultural subsidies—a rise from 0.6 to 2.1 per cent. Spending on health and welfare remained predictably low but showed a moderate growth from 0.9 to 1.6 per cent; the proportion devoted to education and research was constant at 0.6 per cent. The great similarity in the distribution of federal spending in 1900 and 1929 is evidence of the continuity of a laissez-faire policy. It is also consistent with Adam Smith's program for a well-behaved government. To conclude that Smithian notions shaped the policy is attractive but facile. The bridge between theory and policy in history has proved much too elusive; this case seems to be no exception.

There is yet another way—perhaps the most telling of all—to evaluate laissez faire in the United States. Let us ask what influence the government sector had on determining the magnitude of total income, and further, let us compare its influence with that of the private sector. The modern theory of income determination tells us that the size of a sector's expenditure will generate income by some multiple greater than the expenditure; concomitantly, employment of resources will expand. It then follows that variations in expenditures will lead to variations of income by some multiple. However, concern here is not with the business cycle, a short-run phenomenon, but rather with the long-term trend. We already know that the government budget was a passive reflection of the business cycle at best, revenues being the sole reactor to changing business conditions. At worst, the budget destabilized when autonomous decisions were made to raise or lower taxes at the wrong times. Here we will focus on the longer term position of the budget and ask what importance it had in providing income and employment through time. The thesis is that under laissez faire the federal budget was immune to the course of the economy both with respect to the cycle and growth. Our attention narrows now to the growth aspect. To give relative weight to the government's contribution, a comparison is made to the income-producing power of gross investment or the expenditures of the business sector. The other component of private expenditures, consumption, is excluded on the grounds that its trend was probably stable—more stable at least than either government or business spending—and that in history as in theory, investment is the more potent growth variable. Table 4 presents the relevant data. All observations are five-year averages in current prices centered on the given year.

Table 4—The Federal Budget and Gross Investment, Trend Values for Selected Years, 1871–1949[23]

| | FEDERAL EXPENDITURES | | FEDERAL BUDGET
Surplus (+) or Deficit (−)
(3) | GROSS INVESTMENT | |
	(1) $ Billion	(2) Per cent of GNP	per cent of Federal Expenditures	(4) $ Billion	(5) Per cent GNP
1871	0.298	4.4	(+)25.5	1.34	20.0
1880	0.262	2.6	(+)24.4	2.01	20.3
1890	0.319	2.5	(+)20.1	2.92	23.0
1900	0.516	2.9	(+) 2.3	4.23	23.4
1910	0.686	2.2	(−) 4.4	6.48	20.4
1920	9.220	12.4	(−)44.8	16.7	22.5
1929	3.279	3.6	(+)18.9	16.8	18.7
		Post-Full Employment Act (1946)			
1949	39.057	15.9	(+) 4.0	55.5	22.6

During most of the nineteenth century, the budget surplus was a substantial fraction of expenditures. The decline in the surplus at the turn of the century is reversed in 1929 which, it will be recalled, includes observations for 1930 and 1931 in the method of finding trend values. The ratio of federal expenditures to GNP is small throughout, except for 1920 when, also due to war financing in 1918 and 1919, a large deficit was run. The higher ratio in 1949 denotes a change in policy, and is free of the bulge in Korean war expenditures that occurred in fiscal 1952. Gross investment is a reasonably stable proportion of NNP; as a proportion of federal expenditure, it ranges from a high of 920 per cent to a low of 455 per cent, with the exception of 1920. In 1949, the expansion in government activity reduced the relative size of investment to 142 per cent.

With the data of Table 4 it is possible to gauge the relative effects of the federal budget and gross investment on the production of income. Since the precise value of the multiplier—the link between expenditures and income—is unknown, a hypothetical value will be substituted. Even if the true multiplier were known it would not disturb the basic conclusion, viz., the contribution of the business sector to income far exceeded that of government not only for the obvious reason of differences in the size of expenditures but also because of the secular propensity of the budget to accumulate large surpluses. In other words, had the Treasury adopted the principle of a balanced budget in the long run, a principle entirely consistent with laissez faire policy, its contribution to income growth would have been substantially greater.

The "pure consumption" multiplier rests on a simple division of income (disposable income) to the household between consumption and saving. A rise in government or investment expenditures will cause an initial rise in income, part of which is spent on consumption. This consumption expenditure is in turn income to other recipients who likewise spend a fraction of it on consumption, and so on. The spending and respending of the initial expenditure on consumption creates a succession of incomes, the sum of which in a sufficiently long period, say a year or two, will be larger than the initial expenditure by some multiple. A decrease in expenditures stimulates a parallel downward reaction. That multiple or multiplier has been estimated in econometric models for more recent history under varied conditions of economic activity and with varied allowances for government tax yields. There seems to be a general agreement on valuing the "pure consumption" multiplier on GNP somewhere between one and two on an annual scale; a "super multiplier" including induced inventory spending in addition to consumption has been measured at 2.72.[24] We will assume the effective multiplier on GNP is two for the entire span of our period. The assumption is highly conservative. The estimates of contemporary multipliers are derived for a time when taxes and depreciation allowances are a greater proportion of GNP, and the "automatic stabilizers" of progressive income tax rates, undistributed profits, government transfers, and others operate to subdue fluctuations in GNP resulting from fluctuations in expenditures.

Table 5—Income (GNP) Derived from the Federal Budget and Gross Investment, Trend Values for Selected Years, 1871–1949

	Y(G) $ Billion (1)	Y(I) $ Billion (2)	Y(I)/Y(G) (3)	I/G (4)	Y(I)/Y(G) with Balanced Budget (5)
1871	0.222	2.68	12.07	4.55	9.10
1880	0.198	4.02	20.30	7.81	15.62
1890	0.255	5.84	22.98	9.20	18.40
1900	0.504	8.46	16.79	8.07	16.14
1910	0.716	12.96	18.10	9.27	18.54
1920	13.351	33.40	2.51	1.81	3.62
1929	2.659	33.60	12.64	5.19	10.38
Post-Full Employment Act (1946)					
1949	37.495	111.00	2.96	1.42	2.84

SOURCE: Table 4 and the above equations.

Significant changes in the relationship between disposable income (the determinant of consumption) and GNP over time have all reduced the multiplier from what it would have been in the past. There is no telling here how much higher the multiplier was, nor is there any way of finding other disparities that might crop up if the multiplier were adjusted for induced investment and imports. What does seem most probable is that a multiplier of two is low for the era 1870–1929.

Given the multiplier, the federal budget will add to income—symbolized by Y(G)—according to the amount of government expenditures (G) and the size of the budget surplus (+S) or deficit (−D). The relationship is expressed in the equation: $Y(G) = G [1 − S/G (k−1)]$ where k is the multiplier, and S and D enter with their respective algebraic signs; the equation was written to make use of the data in Table 4. The income attributed to gross investment, Y(I), is simply related to investment (I) by: $Y(I) = I \cdot k$, where again k is the multiplier. In this view, both G and I are exogenous, meaning that they are not determined by income. If the budget was balanced at the prevailing G, Y(G) would equal G, since there would be neither a surplus nor a deficit, i.e., $S/G = 0$. With $k = 2$, values are calculated from the above equations in Table 5. Column 4 indicates the proportion of I to G and column 5 shows what the ratio of Y(I) to Y(G) would have been under a balanced budget.

In 1890, investment added about twenty-three times more to income than government operations; this ratio would have dropped to eighteen had the budget been balanced. It is important to notice what is going on in this comparison. Under the balanced budget assumption, government expenditures remain unchanged, but the $64 million surplus run in 1890 (see Table 4) is assumed to be either taxes never collected or else taxes rebated. If the surplus had not accumulated, government would have donated 26 per cent more to GNP, or the percentage difference between Y(G) and G. A surplus will diminish the impact of G on income just as a deficit will enhance it—compare columns 3 and 5 in 1910 and 1920, when deficits were incurred. If taxes had been raised to cover expenditures, income derived from G would have been lower. All of this springs from the essential structure of the budget, consisting of G, which raises income by a multiple (k), and of taxes, which diminish income by a multiple (k−1).

The ratio of Y(I) to Y(G) or column 3 is bound to exceed one under the most likely conditions. If I and G were just equal, and the budget was balanced, the ratio would be two or the value of the multiplier. For all the years documented, however, I was larger than G. A focus on income formation conveys a keener and more complete sense of laissez faire in the United States than any comparable series of expenditure ratios. The preeminence of the business sector is perhaps familiar knowledge; the same could not be said about how restricted a role the government played. The division of income implied in column 3 reveals a dwindling role in the nineteenth century as investment increased faster than federal expenditures. This increase continued into the first decade of the twentieth century, but the budget was now in deficit, raising the government's share in income formation. Thereafter, federal expenditures rose more rapidly, but in 1929 a large surplus reappeared in the budget. The flowering of peacetime government activity after World War II and a relatively small surplus reduced the ratio in 1949 to a figure approaching the multiplier.

If the multiplier were greater than two or if the multiplier were larger in the earlier than in the later years—either proposition seems plausible—the story told in column 3 would be more dramatic still. A multiplier of five would mean that in 1871, the government added nothing to GNP—indeed, it would have been faintly contractionary on income—in 1880, the same multiplier would mean the government added to income next to nothing. So far the discussion has devolved on the trend in the federal budget and its implications for the composition of income formation, and to a much lesser extent, for income growth. There are strong hints that fiscal policy was inhibitory on the growth rate, but that remains a question for more systematic treatment.

III. The Growth Record

In 1870, agriculture employed 52.5 per cent of the labor force, and 74.3 per cent of the population lived in towns and villages with fewer than 2,500 inhabitants. Growth radically transformed this structure so that by 1930, agriculture claimed 21.6 per cent of total employment and the influx to urban centers reduced the rural population to 43.8 per cent. Eighteen-seventy is an important date for economists: almost all statistical series of relevant growth variables have been painstakingly constructed back to that year. Before, the picture is dim and incomplete, although this too has yielded somewhat to the probing of diligent researchers.[25] Our initial year occurs sometime after entry into sustained industrialization, although precise dating of this complex and cumulative process as if it were an event, is very misleading. Kuznets calls the turning point at about 1840. Real GNP (1879 prices) in the succeeding decade grew by nearly 4.2 per cent a year, manufacturing employment increased by 65 per cent, and labor in agriculture decreased by 13 per cent. Rostow's "take-off into self-sustained growth" is placed between 1843 and 1860 caused by the widespread economic effects of railroad construction and replacement. Fogel makes a strong case for looking at the long period 1807–1900 as the industrialization phase, no shorter period being sufficiently unique to be so designated.[26] Our terminal year occurs when the magnificent machine was about to falter into a full decade of depression. Table 6 records the chronicle of growth in terms of output,

Table 6—Economic Growth in the United States, 1871–1929[27]

	1871 (1)	1929 (2)	1929/1871 (3)
Output:			
(1) NNP ($ billions)	8.30	82.6	9.95
(2) NNP per capita ($)	197	677	3.44
(3) NNP per member of labor force ($)	613	1710	2.79
Input:			
(4) Population (millions, excluding armed forces overseas)	42.0	122.0	2.90
(5) Labor force (millions, excluding armed forces overseas)	13.50	48.24	3.57
(6) Employment (millions, civilian)	12.61	45.34	3.59
(7) Manhours (billions, civilian)	35.22	113.83	3.23
(8) Average work week (hours)	53.7	48.3	0.90
(9) Manhours per capita	839	933	1.11
(10) Real capital stock (domestic including government, $ billions)	51.18	362.69	7.09
(11) Real capital stock per capita ($)	1219	2973	2.44
(12) Capital-Labor ratio (per employed worker, $)	4058	7999	1.97
Efficiency:			
(13) Output (NNP) per manhour ($)	0.236	0.726	3.08
(14) Output (NNP) per unit of capital ($)	0.162	0.228	1.41

input, and efficiency or productivity. All figures are trend values with 1871 as the earliest possible five-year average; all dollar magnitudes are in constant 1929 prices.

The tenfold rise in aggregate NNP implies a growth rate of 4 per cent per annum; at the same time, NNP per capita, which will serve as an index for the standard of living, grew at an average annual rate of 2.1 per cent. The entries in Table 6 can be arranged into an explanation for this growth of real income. Three facets of American growth, all interrelated, stand out clearly. First, the tangible capital stock, estimated to include equipment, inventories, structures, land, and the stock of monetary gold and silver, increased more rapidly than the labor force or each of the two measures of labor input, employment or manhours.

Manhours rose more slowly than employment because of the reduced work week. In more formal language, production became more capital intensive in the economy as witnessed by the near doubling of the capital-labor ratio. Second, NNP grew faster than either resource input, labor or capital, or any combination of these inputs however weighted (a weighted index of these inputs will be specified shortly). At this point, it is sufficient to notice that the higher growth in real income relative to input can be justified only by a rise in factor productivity. This is the third prominent feature of the growth record : factor productivity did increase but labor productivity (output per manhour) increased much more than capital productivity (output per unit of capital). According to Table 6, as labor productivity trebled, capital productivity rose only 41 per cent. This substantial differential in efficiency helps to understand a phenomenon not directly confronted in the table : why, in fact, the average earnings of labor grew at a faster pace than those of capital. The usual comparison is carried out between real wages and interest to capital, but this requires an elaborate functional distribution of income and is easier done in principle than in practice. Instead, Kendrick's estimates of real income per unit of input can be used to establish the point. Over a somewhat shorter period, 1899–1929, and for the domestic economy excluding government, average labor income in 1929 prices advanced by 70 per cent while the average return to capital increased by 18 per cent.[28] There is little question but that this spread would widen if the initial year were pushed back to 1871. That differences in productivity should lead to differences in income is just what economic theory would have us expect. The theory of how society's product is distributed among the factors of production is still firmly wedded to the tenet that productivity is a prime determinant of income. The conformity between observation and theory is surely very superficial here, and at some later point it will be submitted to a more searching test. However, it still remains to extract meaning from the facts, and for this, the theory offers the only plausible interpretation.

Table 6 may appear to have inconsistencies; it unquestionably has limitations. The population and labor force figures include military forces stationed domestically, while employment and manhours relate to the civilian population. Upward adjustment of either measure of labor input for the military is of the order of one half of one per cent. The limitations are not so trivial nor so easy to adjust for. The income estimates reflect only transactions that move through the market; they fail to make allowances for production and consumption, which originated strictly within the household and on which the market never conferred a value. At the beginning of our period these internal household activities were more important in generating income than they were later on when, as it is commonly and reasonably assumed, more of them were shifted to the expanding market. To the extent this occurred, income growth over the period is overstated. A comparison of real incomes over a relatively short period will automatically raise reservations; when the comparison is made between incomes in constant prices separated by nearly sixty years, reservations will be magnified to suspicions or even disbelief. The problem is serious simply because there is no alternative to measuring output. For one thing, the choice of 1929 prices was arbitrary, and were prices of another year selected, the calculated growth rates would have varied. Kuznets has remarked that economic history could be rewritten—many times, apparently—just by changing the price weights in which real income is expressed. Moreover, the price index used to convert money to real income is blind to the quality changes that certainly took place since 1871 and to the disappearance and appearance of commodities and services between the bench-mark years. There is at best a tenuous connection between the horse and buggy and the automobile, but the price index will not allow that a dollar's worth of transportation in 1929 was superior in most ways that count. The cost of living was higher in 1929 than in 1871, but if the market basket of goods was richer, more varied, and of higher quality in the later year—and we like to think it was—then the rise in the cost of living has a large element of illusion. Consequently, the inflating of 1871 output by 1929 prices would tend to understate real income growth. Two biases in measuring income over our lengthy period have been noted, each going in a different direction. There are others,[29] but not much can be said of the sum total of their influence on the estimates. Such ignorance is and should be less of a discouragement than an open invitation to improve and refine what we think we know so far.

There are two additional aspects of the growth record which, by virtue of being shortcomings in the statistics, also steer us to the heart of the growth issue. They concern the quantities of labor and capital input and what meaning can be attached to these quantities in a context of formidable changes in production techniques and organization and in the skills and requirements of labor. The quantities are confounded by qualitative improvements which themselves have contributed to growth and productivity, in some instances as much as or more than the increase in physical inputs. This discovery, originally made by empirical analysis and then successfully conceptualized by the theorists, has within the last decade created the new frontiers of growth and capital theory. The labor force, and, by implication, labor input not only increased over the period, but was also improved by better health, more education and on-the-job training, more leisure, and a higher standard of living. The reported increase in the table belies these changes; if the statistic in 1929 could be measured in terms of labor quality in 1871, it would be much higher. The intangible dimensions of labor services will show up in greater labor productivity, although the problems of measurement here are unusually difficult. The new view of labor as a stock of human capital to which investment in quality will pay off in income premiums to the individual and growth premiums to the economy is still young.[30] Denison has devised some intriguing estimates of the effects of education on growth. In his subperiod 1909–29, which conforms closest to ours, he claims an increase in labor quality of about 11 per cent as a result of more schooling. This in turn has contributed 11–12 per cent to the growth of total real national income and 23–29 per cent to the growth in real national income per person employed.[31] These percentages are half of what they were in the succeeding period, 1929–57, but they are still very large. Compared to the allocation given to capital in the growth of real income per employed person, 22–29 per cent, they are extraordinary.[32] The traditional theory had no place for human capital; to be told that it is of equal importance in growth to nonhuman capital—after 1929 it becomes much more important—is a rude awakening to what may well be the facts of life. Denison was forced to miss the full impact of labor's quality improvement since he was restricted to formal education. Mincer has shown that lifetime investment in on-the-job training including the informal "learning from experience" was larger than in schooling in 1939 and selected years thereafter.[33] If this type of investment could be duplicated for earlier periods, it is more than likely that human capital's share of the growth dividend would be even larger.

The challenge to the traditional theory is not yet complete. If human capital has quality dimensions that are valuable inputs to the production process, certainly the same, and probably much more, can be said about nonhuman capital. The least subtle transformations have occurred in technology and economic organization; it is precisely these that capture our attention, transmit a sense of cultural changes, and give substance to the abstract notion of progress. Most of the time we are talking about the changing quality of capital, whether it be a modern high-rise building that replaced a group of brown-stones or a high-speed computer that replaced an office full of clerks and hand calculators. These examples hardly do justice to the capital stock in our period, nor do they suggest enough of the attributes of quality improvement, but they can serve to indicate that, just as in the case of labor, the estimates in the table tell us only by how much capital increased, not the many ways in which it was improved. As it turns out, the improvements to capital were much more significant for growth in per capita income than the actual physical increase. Similarly with labor, they surface through the productivity estimates. If we could imagine a capital stock with invariant quality, say, vintage 1871, then we could reenter the world of the traditional theory. The observed increase in the capital stock would be a fairly unambiguous measure of capital services. The "widening" of capital, simply an increase in capital sufficient to keep labor fully employed, would raise the capacity of the economy to produce and yield higher aggregate income but not necessarily higher per capita income. In order to raise per capita income, aggregate income would have to climb faster than the population, and to do this both capital and labor would have to increase faster than the population. This actually happened in the economy: Table 6 shows that both manhours and capital per capita rose over the period. All this could take place without any noticeable increase in productivity; if inputs are doubled, output doubles. This is a costly way to grow, and one fortunately that does not characterize the American experience. The traditional theory was far more imaginative than to envision a mere "widening" of capital. It foresaw a "deepening" of capital as typical of growth; in other words, an increasing capital-labor ratio that furnished labor with higher productivity. A vital principle here is the law of diminishing returns, which goes at least as far back as the Reverend Malthus, and which dominated the theoretical approach to growth for a long time.[34] This is not to say that traditional theory ignored the force of technology—it could not, if only because capital deepening without technological progress would erode the profit rate and consequently, future capital accumulation. Yet it failed to recognize how powerful this force was. Research in the past decade has revolutionized thinking with its findings that those inputs that have been referred to as qualitative dimensions of the capital stock, expanded to embrace human capital, have been the mainsprings of growth.

IV. Productivity and Its Sources

Quality improvements and increases in the capital-labor ratio will reveal themselves in productivity; productivity plus additional resources per capita together exhaust the possibilities for explaining the growth in real income per capita. A simple estimating procedure will allocate to productivity and resources their respective shares in income growth. For this we require an index of total resources per capita corrected as nearly as possible for quality improvements and changes in the capital-labor ratio. It is desirable to screen out any productivity change trapped in the input data, instead to be reflected in the measure of productivity itself. The actual adjustment to the data must be crude and imperfect; the individual indexes of manhours per capita and capital per capita are added with weights proportional to their average returns in 1919–29.[35] If these returns are also proportional to the marginal productivities of the inputs—in theory, they will be—then the resulting index has been standardized to show how inputs would have changed if constant 1919–29 productivities ruled throughout the period. Such an index of total inputs per capita registers a 51 per cent rise between the terminal years. From the relationships that exist between real income per capita and its components, the numbers tell us "total factor productivity" increased 128 per cent. Total factor productivity is measured for all cooperating inputs and will be sensitive to changes in the input mix; since these have been significant, it is a preferred indicator of overall efficiency, free of some severe limitations that plague the estimates of partial productivities of inputs taken separately.

Empirically, however, total factor productivity and output per weighted manhour are found to be close substitutes in size and movement, due in great part to the relatively large average returns consistently earned by labor.[36]

According to percentage increases in the components of real income per capita, fully 67 per cent of the growth in income is attributable to total factor productivity; the remainder is explained by increases in inputs per capita.[37] This and similar results for different and longer periods have been the most singularly impressive findings about the growth record. They dispel any notion that the major source of growth was additional inputs; instead, the American tradition was to grow by raising productivity, if not deliberately by policy, then by the grace of good fortune. Abramovitz, in one of the earliest papers on the subject, found total factor productivity's share in per capita income growth from 1869–78 to 1944–53 to vary from 73 per cent to 91 per cent, depending on the choice of the base year.[38] Kendrick, employing a different and somewhat arbitrary method of allocation, ascribes to total factor productivity a 76 per cent share in the rise of real income per capita from 1889 to 1953.[39] Despite variations in data, terminal years, and even methodology, the conclusion that productivity increases were primarily responsible for progress in the standard of living is confirmed. The conclusion is strengthened for the years after 1909, for although there appears to be a retardation in the rate of growth of real NNP per capita, there is no diminution in the growth rate of total factor productivity.

Kendrick's estimates portray a decline in the growth in real income per capita from 2.6 per cent in 1889–99 to 2.3 per cent in 1909–19 to a sharply lower 1.6 per cent in 1919–29[40]. The decline is due entirely to smaller increments in inputs, both labor and capital, but particularly labor, which decreased absolutely during 1919–29 in per capita terms.[41] Meanwhile, the growth in total factor productivity fluctuated narrowly between 1.5 and 1.4 per cent throughout 1889–1929, and its contribution to the rise in real income per capita was 58, 65, and 88 per cent respectively in the three subperiods.[42] What these data suggest and what is especially noteworthy is that productivity apparently grew independently of inputs and independently of a substantial slowdown in the rise of the capital labor ratio.[43]

This point returns us again to the sources of productivity, some of which have already been mentioned. It has been shown that capital accumulation per se played a subsidiary role in growth, but how important was the deepening of capital in enhancing productivity? If pushing up the capital-labor ratio is a strong determinant of productivity, we are left with a conclusion that still emphasizes the size of capital accumulation rather than its quality. Solow has given an answer to this question in a sophisticated and ingenious essay.[44] Manipulating a thoroughly familiar tool of production theory in the untried context of history, he has managed to distill out of real GNP per man-hour its component elements. Between 1909 and 1949, the increase in the capital-labor ratio accounted for only 13 per cent of the rise in his measure of labor productivity, while the factor he calls technical change was responsible for the remainder.[45] Between 1909 and 1929, the technical factor is more subdued, contributing only about 66 per cent to the total rise.[46] In a closer examination of the trend, Solow draws our attention to what is an apparent acceleration in technical change after 1929. There may be other explanations, one of which will be ventured below.

Solow's technical change is a broad box containing improvements in the nonhuman and human capital stock indiscriminately. Improvements by type cannot be identified; all we are able to say is that technical change can be reconciled with higher labor quality, technological innovation, and external economies, which may subsume the effects of the other two as well as a host of other changes. Another improvement, associated with the tangible capital stock, is assumed away in Solow's technique, economies of scale. Their importance is minimized by no one, least of all by Solow, and one could argue that they were of considerable importance to the American economy in our period. They will find their way into technical change, and once accounted for, could reduce the value of technical change (Solow's definition) by a substantial margin.[47]

Technological innovation is capable of raising productivity in an industry regardless of the size of the producer, usually by a greater degree of mechanization and specialization of labor. Economies of scale, on the other hand, although similar in character and effect, are customarily enjoyed by the relatively large producer in an industry, and their incidence is more clearly evident in only certain industries. This efficiency of size is a static concept, defined for a given state of the arts. Let the world revolve, and progress in the state of the arts more closely resembles what is meant by technological innovation. There is no point in drawing a hard and fast distinction between the two economies, because in a historical perspective none exists. Technological innovation can create new efficiencies of size, destroy old ones, and conceivably eliminate advantages of size altogether. We can, however, single out certain industries where economies of scale are overwhelming both at a point in time and through time. Also, as the economy and markets developed, the growth in the average size producer was probably as much in response to economies of scale to be found in all industries beyond the very small unit as to anything else.

External economies are another long-run force, but one that increases productivity across the economy. Where technological innovations and economies of scale are thought of as specific and internal to an industry, external economies are closely connected with growth and often with the early stages of economic development, and they modify production costs of many industries. As a prerequisite for industrialization, emphasis is laid on investment in social overhead: transportation, communication, power sources, health, education, and so on.[48] It is precisely these investments that initially furnish the greatest external economies, affecting both supply and demand, and at the same time giving breadth to the market.

Table 7—Relative Industry Growth, Capital, and Labor Productivity, 1899-1929[49]

Industry	Output (1)	Capital Input (2)	Output per Manhour (3)
Electric Utilities	5,000.0	1,265.8	537.6
Rubber Products	2,325.6	1,219.5	609.8
Transportation Equipment	1,369.9	518.1	568.2
Electrical Machinery	1,298.7	1,204.8	167.5
Telephone	1,250.0	450.5	189.0
Petroleum and Coal Products	1,149.4	787.4	381.7
Crude Petroleum and Natural Gas	980.4	917.4	286.5
Manufactured and Natural Gas Utilities	632.9	421.9	300.3
Paper and Allied Products	546.4	487.8	232.0
Chemical and Allied Products	537.6	389.1	243.3
Printing and Publishing	526.3	248.8	295.0
Fabricated Metal Products	485.4	387.6	266.7
Primary Metal Industries	458.7	389.1	245.7
Nonmetallic Mining and Quarrying	418.4	287.4	268.8
Local Railways and Bus Lines	387.9	145.1	207.0
Nonelectric Machinery	355.9	301.2	171.5
Miscellaneous and Instruments	341.3	393.7	178.9
Tobacco Products	335.6	478.5	431.0
Stone, Clay, and Glass Products	334.4	342.5	269.5
Food and Kindred Products	330.0	284.9	179.2
Apparel and Related Products	328.9	340.1	224.7
Railroads	301.2	155.8	204.1
Local Electric Railways	289.0	139.9	177.3
Bituminous Coal Mining	277.0	298.5	173.9
Furniture and Fixtures	272.5	337.8	137.4
Metal Mining	255.6	156.3	256.4
Textile Mill Products	245.1	201.6	173.9
Leather and Leather Products	156.3	153.4	147.7
Pennsylvania Anthracite Mining	122.2	137.9	101.4
Lumber Products, except Furniture	110.4	228.3	119.0
Beverages	33.8	58.6	62.4

In Table 7, thirty-one industries are ranked by output growth in the latter half of our period. The sample is drawn from manufacturing, mining, transportation, communication, and utilities. Data limitations restrict the sample size and the years covered. Among the fastest growth industries are three utilities: electricity, telephone, and gas. We know that economies of scale are especially strong in these industries, and it is easy to imagine the savings reaped by their inception in every quarter of the economy. These industries continued to provide external economies as the real prices of their services declined, as they did in a number of instances. The spectacular growth of motor vehicles explains the position of the transportation equipment industry in the table, and here too, economies of scale are prominent, if we could borrow on Bain's evidence for a much later date.[50] According to Bain, the same could not be said of tires and inner tubes (rubber products) and petroleum refining (petroleum and coal products), although he admits these conclusions would be upset in markets smaller than those he observed.[51] This introduces an important point: we are likely to underestimate the strength of scale economies in all industries as the market expanded. As firms grew from small to medium size (in some absolute sense), scale economies were significant; as firms advanced from medium to large size (still in some absolute sense), scale economies dwindled. This generally agrees with what many believe to be the relevant cost behavior of firms in the long run.

The relationships that exist between output, capital input, and labor productivity in the table can be summarized in correlation coefficients. Between output and capital, the correlation coefficient is +.80, and between output and productivity, the coefficient is +.69. Both indicate a statistically significant association between the related variables, and what follows, between capital and output per manhour, for which no measure was taken. These are routine results. Should we have expected otherwise? If technical change was strongly correlated with output, as it should be with real income per capita (that correlation has not been established), we might have anticipated a lower correlation between output and capital. That it isn't so is no repudiation of Solow. Still, Solow's contention that technical change was slower prior to 1929 might now be due to more potent economies of scale in the total mix of technical changes which required relatively more capital to be realized than pure technological innovations.

V. Productivity, Real Wages, and Income Distribution

Between 1889 and 1929, real hourly earnings for all labor in the private domestic economy rose at an average annual rate of 1.9 per cent, while the corresponding rise in output per weighted manhour (weighted by wage and salary differentials among industries) was close to 1.8 per cent.[52] The results conform nicely to the theory with two exceptions: the theory predicts identical rates and is couched in terms of marginal rather than average products. We can excuse the imperfections of the real world, and we do not know whether marginal and average products are in fact equal, for which no excuse is made. During the same period, output per unit of weighted tangible capital (weighted by differences in average returns among industries) increased by a little more than .7 per cent a year.[53] As remarked before, the rise in the capital-labor ratio is responsible for this. The reasons for the steady rise in the capital-labor ratio may be stated here succinctly and without explanation. First, the substitution of capital for labor as the price of labor increased relative to capital; second, under the impact of labor-saving technology; and third, the shift in the composition of output toward capital intensive industries. The many growth factors that impinge on the capital-labor ratio have made it a prime subject of discussion.[54] Not only were average returns to capital lower than labor's but following the divergence in productivity rates, they fell relative to labor earnings, although not absolutely over the period. There was a stretch of years when capital productivity was falling absolutely. Between 1890 and 1900, output per unit of weighted tangible capital declined erratically, so that the values in the two years are almost the same.[55] This trend set in earlier, and although the productivity data are not accommodating, five-year average yields on common stocks may serve as a proxy for return to capital. The average yield in 1871–75 was 6.2 per cent. Thereafter it fell almost without interruption to a low of 3.9 per cent in 1896–1900.[56]

The correlated movement between real hourly earnings and labor productivity observed for the economy breaks down at the industry level. Earnings in individual industries appeared tied to the national trend despite sizable differences in productivity change. This has been explained by the theory that under competition, resources are mobile and will flow into the higher paying occupations out of the lower paying occupations and consequently will mitigate the disparity in earnings trends.[57] Productivity can work itself into higher earnings or lower product prices or some combination. Kendrick has found that industries with relatively higher productivity increases tend to show greater decreases in relative prices; his correlations for industries at various levels of aggregation are statistically significant, although not particularly high.[58] All these results are intriguing but subject to reservation because of the data and the methodology employed.

The period 1890–1914 was a mystery to students of wages. Productivity had grown in manufacturing, but real wages appeared almost stationary. In a careful job of reconstruction, Rees discovered that real hourly earnings in manufacturing had actually risen over the period by as much as 37 per cent, but this time by less than the rise in output per manhour. He explains these events by the closing of the geographical frontier and the large influx of immigrants during those years.[59] When Rees's new index of real hourly earnings is correlated with Kendrick's index of output per manhour in manufacturing the correlation coefficient is $+.90$—inevitably high.[60] Instead of disclosing a relationship, it merely reenforces what we already know—that the two variables had positive time trends. We can circumvent this difficulty by taking first differences in the data, i.e., subtracting the index in one year from the index in the succeeding year. This gives us a new hypothesis: first differences of an index measure percentage change. We are now asking whether there are equal percentage changes year to year between real earnings and output per manhour. The answer lies in a negligible and slightly negative correlation coefficient of $-.09$. We could have foreseen this result because labor productivity moved up more rapidly than real earnings. This hypothesis, however, insists on a simultaneous adjustment between earnings and productivity. Suppose the rise in productivity in one year is better reflected in next year's earnings. This third hypothesis tests the relationship between the percentage rise in real earnings and the percentage rise in output per manhour lagged by one year. The correlation coefficient is now +.48 and high enough so that chance alone explains it less than once in a hundred times. Again we have a confirmation of the theory, this time in a more dynamic context. One can wonder whether the introduction of lags and other adjustments might not improve and perhaps illuminate some of the other relationships mentioned above.

The radical changes wrought by growth on the size, proportion, and quality of factor inputs and their respective compensation seem not to have significantly altered the functional distribution of income. The stability of income shares to capital and labor is remarkable and not easily explained in relation to the other facts of growth and to the kind of technology that governed production; yet a growth theory must do just this. Kuznets' distribution data represent shares in aggregate payments to individuals, flows which are less than the more familiar concept of national income by the amounts of government and corporate savings, both considered small for these years. The percentage shares in Table 8 are averaged for overlapping decades and fall within a shorter period than we would like.

Table 8—Functional Distribution of Income
1909–18 to 1924–33[61]

Years	Employee Compensation (1) Per cent	Entrepreneurial Income (2) Per cent	Service Income (3) Per cent	Property Income (4) Per cent
1909–18	56.2	24.6	80.8	19.2
1914–23	59.2	22.5	81.7	18.3
1919–28	61.7	19.5	81.2	18.8
1924–33	63.1	16.6	79.7	20.3

Service income is the sum of employee and entrepreneurial income. A comparison between it and property income shows a constancy from which small departures are trivial. Not so constant are the subclasses of service income. Employee compensation comprises wages and salaries in money and kind including those to corporate executives. Entrepreneurial income is the sum of net returns to individual businessmen: proprietors, partnerships, farmers, doctors, and the like. The secular fall in the share of entrepreneurial income and the concomitant rise in employee compensation are primarily the result of the shrinking relative importance of the unincorporated business as the agricultural sector lost ground and the corporate enterprise gained ascendancy. Between 1909–18 and 1924–33, although the number of entrepreneurs increased, their proportion of the labor force fell from 23.5 to 20.3 per cent, the difference being absorbed in the class of employees.[62] This does not fully explain the decline in the entrepreneurial share of income. In addition, the average income of entrepreneurs did not rise as rapidly as that of employees: the ratio of average entrepreneurial income to average employee income was 142 per cent in the first decade of our period and fell steeply thereafter to 103 per cent in 1924–33. This terminal decade includes four depression years, yet in the previous decade, 1919–28, the proportion was only 115 per cent.[63] These results are due in part to the way Kuznets defines entrepreneurial income, and in part to real differences in the dispersion of entrepreneurial and employee incomes.

On the distribution of income by size in our period, nothing can be said. In the early days of the federal income tax, available data only approximates the distribution among the upper income groups. Information on the complete range of income size was not forthcoming until the mid-1930s. Kuznets' wry comment is worthy of citation: "The scarcity of data would seem to be due to lack of attention to the problem in the past, reflecting lack of public concern—which in turn may have been due to the belief that the key economic problem was production, and that with assurance of rapid growth in the nation's output there was no need for concern with the distribution of income, i.e., of claims to output."[64]

VI. The Rise of Monopoly

Monopoly in the product and factor markets deserves more attention than it will receive here. The subject has been treated extensively by economists and historians, and in the predepression years was the leading economic issue in public policy. Longevity and the engagement of professional interest and talent have not been impressively productive of firm conclusions about the effects of monopoly on prices, employment, profits, technological innovation, and growth. It is easy and partially justified to blame data inadequacy. Prices are a prime variable in the study of monopoly, and yet available price data may often be deficient indicators of actual prices. This is one example among many, but data problems are universal in economics, and they have rarely proved insuperable. There is another weakness in the evolution of the subject which is more serious, and that is the failure to develop testable hypotheses concerning the behavior of industries and firms. This has been remedied in recent years, but for too long, inquiry has been guided by neoclassical price theory, the price theories of competition and monopoly, which have gradually taken on more normative than descriptive content.

The pure theory's indictment of monopoly lies in a misallocation of resources, an underemployment of resources, which under a full employment assumption reduces the value of total output. If with a given input and the presence of monopoly the value of output is less than it would be under competition, we speak of monopoly as socially inefficient. Monopoly profits have brought this social inefficiency and will alter the optimal distribution of income as well. This holds in the static world of no change, but in the dynamic world of constant change, the role of monopoly becomes uncertain and controversial. Does it contribute more to capital accumulation, price stability, cyclical stability, the production of knowledge, the use of knowledge, technical change and growth in general than do industries that are competitively organized? We don't know yet if monopoly is dynamically more efficient than competition, but these clearly are the important questions about monopoly in a growing economy.[65]

The single most important force for the creation of monopoly in our period was the merger wave of 1898–1902, dated at its peak by Nelson in his comprehensive study.[66] As a result, a number of industries in manufacturing and mining were restructured toward monopoly. In 1899 alone, Nelson reports that 1,028 viable firms disappeared through consolidations and acquisitions, more than all firm disappearances in the decade 1905–14. During 1895–1904, U.S. Steel replaced 170 firms and controlled 65 per cent of the market; American Tobacco absorbed 162 firms and subsequently gained 90 per cent of the market. Firms bred out of the merger activity in these years and through which monopoly power was acquired compose a long list of durable giants. To mention but a small sample: E. I. DuPont de Nemours, American Can, Diamond Match, U.S. Gypsum, National Biscuit, International Harvester, International Paper, General Electric and Westinghouse, Borden, International Nickel, National Lead, and United Shoe Machinery.[67] Those firms that achieved market domination through mergers account for 48.6 per cent of all firm disappearances and 70.4 per cent of total merger capital in this period.[68] It is no extravagance to characterize this merger wave as a purposeful effort towards monopolization. Another period of intense merging occurred in 1926–30, and although it produced a spate of large enterprises, it had considerably less effect in altering the structure of industries.

Concluding Note

During 1870–1929. The United States had the fastest growing economy in the world.[69] Richly endowed with resources and blessed with political stability, the country developed by creating and exploiting opportunities. An abundant supply of capital and land, an expanding population, technical ingenuity and skills, knowledge and adaptation, and good luck were all inputs to the massive process; the output grew and improved. The market solved the economic problems of production and distribution, and provided vigorous incentives to capital accumulation and technical progress. Improvements in the quality of the human and non-human capital stock were the most potent source of productivity increases. The system that allowed and encouraged all this deserves admiration if not praise. And yet that same system was also enormously inefficient and more inequitable than we would tolerate. The model is unique, and like the society it helped to create, imperfect.

NOTES

1. U.S. Department of Commerce, *Business Cycle Developments*, Sept., 1966, p. 65.

2. For a lucid treatment of business-cycle theories and the growth-cycle issue, and an admirable job of substituting words for symbols, see R. C. O. Matthews, *The Business Cycle* (Chicago: The University of Chicago Press, 1959).

3. R. M. Goodwin, "A Model of Cyclical Growth," Erik Lundberg (ed.), *The Business Cycle in the Post-War World* (London: Macmillan, 1955) reprinted in Gordon and Klein (eds.), American Economic Association, *Readings in Business Cycles* (Homewood: Richard Irwin, 1965).

4. *Ibid.*, p. 21 (reprinted version).

5. The lack of uniformity in business cycles is well known and this contradiction has been resolved by distinguishing between major and minor cycles. See Robert A. Gordon, *Business Fluctuations* (New York: Harper and Row, 1961).

6. Colin Clark, *Conditions of Economic Progress*, 3rd ed. (London: Macmillan, 1957). W. W. Rostow, *The Stages of Economic Growth* (London: Cambridge University Press, 1960).

7. Mid-1955 was the pivot of the projection, since unemployment was then at about 4 per cent; the average growth rate in GNP was 3.5 per cent per year. The gap between "potential" and actual output has become a standard by which to judge the performance of the economy. The first appearance of this helpful tool is in *Economic Report of the President* (Washington: U.S. Government Printing Office, 1962). Subsequent reports makes steady use of it.

8. James Tobin, "Economic Growth as an Objective of Government Policy," *American Economic Review*, Papers and Proceedings, Vol. LIV, No. 3 (May, 1964), pp. 1–20.

9. Asher Achinstein, "Economic Fluctuations," Seymour Harris (ed.), *American Economic History* (New York: McGraw-Hill Book Co., 1961), pp. 162–80.

10. A penetrating analysis of the meaning of growth as policy and the choices open to society is in Tobin, *Economic Growth.*

11. Source: *Business Cycle Developments*, p. 65.

12. Rendigs Fels, *American Business Cycles 1865–1897* (Chapel Hill: The University of North Carolina Press, 1959).

13. Achinstein, *Fluctuations*, pp. 166–67.

14. John M. Firestone, *Federal Receipts and Expenditures During Business Cycles, 1879–1958*, National Bureau of Economic Research (Princeton: Princeton University Press, 1960).

15. For 1873–79, see U.S. Department of Commerce, Bureau of the Census, *Historical Statistics of the United States and Colonial Times to 1957* (Washington, D.C.: U.S. Government Printing Office, 1961), p. 711. Data for the Treasury balances in the other contractions are in Firestone, *Receipts*, Table A-3.

16. Firestone, *Federal Receipts*, p. 9; see also pp. 20–21, as well as pp. 88–91.

17. Milton Friedman and Anna Jacobson Schwartz, *A Monetary History of the United States 1867–1960*, National Bureau of Economic Research (Princeton: Princeton University Press, 1963).

18. James A. Maxwell, *The Fiscal Impact of Federalism in the United States* (Cambridge: Harvard University Press, 1946), pp. 3–28.

19. *Ibid.*, pp. 21–2.

20. Source: *Historical Statistics of the United States*, pp. 724, 726.

21. Adam Smith, *An Inquiry into the Nature and Causes of the Wealth of Nations* (New York: The Modern Library, 1937), p. 651.

22. Solomon Fabricant, *The Trend of Government Activity in the United States since 1900* (New York: National Bureau of Economic Research, 1952), pp. 62–3.

23. Columns 1 and 3 are in *Historical Statistics of the United States*, p. 711. The data are subject to minor qualifications which do not seem to alter their usefulness, see *ibid.*, pp. 687–88. Col 4 is from Simon Kuznets, *Capital in the American Economy, Its Formation and Financing*, National Bureau of Economic Research (Princeton: Princeton University Press, 1961), Table R-29, as are the figures for GNP, Table R-25, Kuznets Variant III. The budget data are for fiscal years and GNP and investment are for calendar years. The averaging over five years would tend to eliminate a good deal of the discrepancy for any one year due to differences in the time periods.

24. James S. Dusenberry, Otto Eckstein, and Gary Fromm, "A Simulation of the United States Economy in Recession." *Econometrica* (October, 1960) reprinted in Gordon and Klein, *Readings in Business Cycles*, pp. 245–47 (reprinted version). Other estimates of the multiplier have been made involving different time periods and functional relationships, see L. R. Klein and A. S. Goldberger, *An Econometric Model of the United States, 1929–1952* (Amsterdam: North-Holland Publishing Co., 1955), pp. 111–14; and Lawrence R. Klein, *Economic Fluctuations in the United States, 1921–1941*, Cowles Commission for Research in Economics, Monograph No. 11 (New York: John Wiley & Sons, 1950), pp. 76 ff. The findings of these works place a ceiling of two on the "pure consumption" multiplier.

25. See National Bureau of Economic Research, *Output, Employment and Productivity in the United States after 1800*, Studies in Income and Wealth, No. 30 (New York: National Bureau of Economic Research, 1966) and *Trends in the American Economy in the Nineteenth Century*, Studies in Income and Wealth, No. 24 (Princeton: Princeton University Press, 1960).

26. Simon Kuznets, *Economic Growth and Structure* (New York: W. W. Norton & Co., 1965), pp. 304–305. Stanley Lebergott, "Labor Force and Employment, 1800–1960" in *Output, Employment and Productivity in the U.S. after 1800*, Table 2. Robert William Fogel, *Railroads and American Economic Growth: Essays in Econometric History* (Baltimore: The Johns Hopkins Press, 1964), Chapter IV. Fogel presents and then effectively repudiates the Rostow thesis.

27. Line 1, Kuznets' estimates of NNP Variant III in *Capital in the American Economy, Its Formation and Financing*, Table R-26, p. 563; line 4, *ibid.*, Table R-37, p. 624; line 5, *ibid.*, Table R-39, p. 630; lines 2 and 3, derived from the above data; line 6, John W. Kendrick, *Productivity Trends in the United States*, National Bureau of Economic Research (Princeton: Princeton University Press, 1961). Table A-VI, pp. 305–307; line 7, *ibid.*; Table A-X, pp. 311–13; line 8 derived from line 7 ÷ line 6 ÷ 52; line 9 derived from line 7 ÷ line 4; line 10 *ibid.* Table A-XV, p. 320, line 11 derived from line 10 ÷ line 4; line 12 derived from line 10 ÷ line 6; line 13 derived from line 1 ÷ line 7; line 14 derived from line 1 ÷ line 10.

28. Kendrick, *Productivity*, p. 125.

29. Simon Kuznets, "Quantitative Aspects of the Economic Growth of Nations," *Economic Development and Cultural Change*, Vol. V, No. 1, October 1956.

30. See Gary S. Becker, *Human Capital* (New York: National Bureau of Economic Research, 1964). The applications of the theory so far have been largely directed to the microeconomics of income distribution.

31. Edward F. Denison, *The Sources of Economic Growth in the United States and the Alternatives Before Us*, Supplementary Paper No. 13 (New York: Committee for Economic Development, 1962), pp. 85, 266, 270, and 67-79.

32. *Ibid.*, p. 270.

33. Jacob Mincer, "On-the-Job Training: Costs, Returns, and Some Implications," *The Journal of Political Economy*, Vol. LXX, Supplement (October, 1962) p. 55.

34. Bert F. Hoselitz, (ed.), *Theories of Economic Growth* (New York: The Free Press, 1960), especially Erskine McKinley, "The Theory of Economic Growth in the English Classical School" and Henry J. Burton "Contemporary Theorizing on Economic Growth."

35. The weights applied to manhours and capital are 70:30 respectively. As the capital-labor ratio rose, the return to capital fell and that of labor rose in absolute terms; the corresponding weights in 1889–99 were 64:36. See Kendrick, *Productivity*, Table 9, p. 85.

36. For a discussion of this and the meaning of productivity estimates, see

Solomon Fabricant, *Basic Facts on Productivity Change*, Occasional Paper 63 (New York: National Bureau of Economic Research, 1959), pp. 3–10 and Table 1.

37. Real NNP in any year is determined by,

$$\text{NNP} = \text{Total Input} \cdot \text{Output per unit of Input}$$

Since Total Input includes labor and capital, and ideally should include all inputs, raw materials, education, etc., we can substitute for Output per unit of Input the measure of productivity that accounts for all inputs, or Total Factor Productivity. Divide through by population to get a per capita expression,

$$\text{NNP/capita} = \text{Total Input/capita} \cdot \text{TFP}$$

To measure the separate effects of the two terms on the right hand side of the equation, take logarithms of both sides,

$$\log (\text{NNP/capita}) = \log (\text{Total Input/capita}) + \log (\text{TFP})$$

If instead of values for any one year, we insert relative values, or more specifically, 1929 values on a 1871 base, the equality is not disturbed, and the actual estimating equation is,

$$\log (3.44) = \log (1.51) + \log (2.28)$$

38. Moses Abramovitz, *Resources and Output Trends in the United States since 1870*, Occasional Paper 52 (New York: National Bureau of Economic Research, 1956), pp. 10–11 and Table 1. The percentages are derived from his figures on p. 11.

39. Kendrick, *Productivity*, pp. 78–84 and Table 8.

40. *Ibid.*, p. 84, Table 8, col. 1.

41. *Ibid.*, p. 85, Table 9, cols. 1, 2, and 3.

42. *Ibid.*, p. 84, Table 8, col. 4, wtih percentages derived from cols. 4 and 1.

43. *Ibid.*. p. 85, Table 9, col. 6.

44. Robert M. Solow, "Technical Change and the Aggregate Production Function," *The Review of Economics and Statistics*, Vol. 39 (August 1957) pp. 312–20.

45. *Ibid.*, p. 316.

46. *Ibid.*, p. 315, Table 1.

47. George J. Stigler, "Economic Problems in Measuring Changes in Productivity," and Comments, Conference on Research in Income and Wealth, *Output, Input, and Productivity Measurement*, National Bureau of Economic Research (Princeton: Princeton University Press, 1961), pp. 47–77.

48. See for example, "The Economic Requirements of Modern Industrialization," in Simon Kuznets, *Economic Growth and Structure*, pp. 194–212.

49. Kendrick, *Productivity*, mining industries in Table C-III, pp. 399 ff.; manufacturing industries in Table D-IV, pp. 468 ff.; transportation industries in Tables G-III—VI, pp. 543 ff.; cmmunications an public utilities in Tables H-IV–IX, pp. 585 ff. Output and capital are measured in 1929 prices.

50. Joe S. Bain, *Barriers to New Competition* (Cambridge: Harvard University Press, 1956), pp. 68–93.

51. *Ibid.*, p. 82.

52. Solomon Fabricant, *Basic Facts on Productivity Change*, Table A, pp. 43–44 and Table C, p. 48.

53. *Ibid.*, Table A.

54. See for example the excellent essays in F. A. Lutz and D. C. Hague (eds.), International Economic Association, *The Theory of Capital* (New York: St. Martin's Press, 1961).

55. Fabricant, *Basic Facts*, Table A.

56. *Historical Statistics of the United States, Colonial Times to 1957*, p. 656.

57. Kendrick, *Productivity*, pp. 196–203.

58. *Ibid.*, Table 57, p. 201.

59. Albert Rees, *Real Wages in Manufacturing 1890–1914*, National Bureau of Economic Research (Princeton: Princeton University Press, 1961), p. 5.

60. *Ibid.*, p. 120 and Kendrick, *Productivity*, p. 465.

61. Simon Kuznets, "Long-Term Changes in the National Income of the United States of America since 1870," International Association for Research in Income and Wealth, *Income and Wealth of the United States*, Income and Wealth Series II (Baltimore: The Johns Hopkins Press, 1952), Table 27, p. 136.

62. *Ibid.*, Table 28, p. 139.

63. *Ibid.*, derived from cols. 6 and 7 in Table 28.

64. *Ibid.*, p. 141.

65. In this connection, see Kenneth J. Arrow, "Economic Welfare and the Allocation of Resources for Invention," A Conference of the Universities— National Bureau Committee for Economic Research, *The Rate and Direction of Inventive Activity: Economic and Social Factors*, National Bureau of Economic Research (Princeton: Princeton University Press, 1962), pp. 619–25.

66. Ralph L. Nelson, *Merger Movements in American Industry 1895–1956*,

National Bureau of Economic Research (Princeton: Princeton University Press, 1959).

67. *Ibid.*, Table C, pp. 161–62.

68. *Ibid.*, p. 102.

69. Simon Kuznets, "Quantitative Aspects of The Economic Growth of Nations," *Economic Development*, see appendix tables.

2

Industrialism and Political Leadership: A Case Study of the United States Senate

by ARI HOOGENBOOM

A basic ingredient both in the problems political leaders face and in the solutions they attempt, industrialism has had a profound impact on public policy. It has also changed political leaders, but few scholars agree on the nature and the extent of the changes.[1] To measure industrialism's impact on American political leaders certain questions must be answered. Who are the leaders? Has the leadership changed? If it has, why? With leadership diffused and fluctuating, with the media and political interest groups as well as government and party officials exercising political power, measuring change is difficult and perhaps impossible. If one applies a yardstick to a specific area of political leadership, however, measurement becomes feasible. The United States Senate combines relatively significant and consistent political leadership with measurability. Senators control legislation, treaties, appointments, and state parties, and constitute a group large enough for comparative purposes and prominent enough to make biographical data readily available. The *Biographical Directory of Congress*, the *Dictionary of American Biography*, and *The National Cyclopaedia of American Biography* present a convenient though spare record from which conclusions—albeit tentative—may be drawn.

A collective biography of the preindustrial-revolution Senate of 1820 and the succeeding Senates at forty-year intervals indicates changes in backgrounds and careers.[2] But these changes are surprisingly and disproportionately small when compared with industrialism's impact upon society. Since the value added to products by manufacture multiplied fifty-three times from 1849 to 1939 and the population in cities over 100,000 increased 307 times from 1820 to 1940,[3] one might expect a great increase in the number of urban businessmen in each succeeding Senate. The political careers, social origins, and class membership of senators, however, have remained relatively stable since 1820 and remarkably stable since 1860.*

In 1820 Democratic-Republican or, if you wish, Jeffersonian senators outnumbered Federalists four to one; in 1860 Democrats held a majority of twelve over the challenging Republicans; in 1900 the Republicans held a two to one edge on the Democrats; but by 1940 there were three Democratic senators for every one Republican (see Table 1).

All four of these Senates—1820, 1860, 1900, and 1940—reflect a degree of stability; none was the immediate product of a political upheaval. Though a unique set of circumstances produces each Senate, continuity with the past and the future is assured since only one-third of the seats are contested every two years.

Several generalizations are obvious. Senators constantly grow older and more experienced. The average senator was forty-six in 1820, fifty in 1860, fifty-seven in 1900, and fifty-eight in 1940. He entered the Senate at the age of forty-two if he served in 1820 and at the age of forty-nine if he served in 1940. Senators in 1940 had served that body almost three times longer than their colleagues in 1820, and

---

* The data for the ensuing analysis was drawn from the following sources: *Biographical Directory of the American Congress, 1774–1961* (Washington: Government Printing Office, 1961); *Dictionary of American Biography* (22 vols., New York: Charles Scribner's Sons, 1928–1958), cited as *DAB; The National Cyclopaedia of American Biography* ... (48 plus 10 current vols., New York: James T. White & Company, 1898–1965), cited as *NCAB*. The senators analyzed were in office on January 1, 1820, 1860, 1900, and 1940. If a seat was vacant, the incoming senator was analyzed. One seat, however, belonging to Delaware, remained vacant during the entire Fifty-sixth Congress.

their average senatorial term was more than double the eight and one half year career of the average 1820 senator. A longer period of dependence upon parents helps explain why later senators were older. The increased time allotted to formal education during these years delayed careers. Although the sharp increase in male life expectancy may seem a likely explanation for the older senators, life expectancy increased only 1.4 years for forty-year-old males and declined 1.15 years for sixty-year-old males from 1850 to 1940.[4]

Table I—Political Affiliation of Senators*

PARTY	SENATE			
	16th (44)	36th (66)	56th (89)	76th (96)
Federalist	20% (9)			
Democratic-Republican	80% (35)			
Whig-Unionist		3% (2)		
Democratic		58% (38)	30% (27)	72% (69)
Republican		39% (26)	64% (57)	24% (23)
Populist			3% (3)	
Fusionist			2% (2)	
Farmer-Labor				2% (2)
Progressive				1% (1)
Independent Republican				1% (1)

* Numeral in parentheses indicate the number of Senators involved.

While the senator's growing maturity clearly evidences change, the number of his apprenticeship years in lesser offices has varied only slightly. In 1820 the average senator had more than ten years of office-holding experience before entering the Senate, while in 1940 he had almost eleven. Presenatorial office-holding experience declined in 1900 to a low point of eight years. A number of senators then had little or no previous office-holding experience. Prowess in business or military affairs enabled some to avoid a lengthy apprenticeship, while the Populist revolt accounted for the quick rise of a few senators. Many of the 1900 senators who were new to public office had served on state party committees and were at least partially prepared for political life in Washington.

For the office-holding, or professional, politician there have been two major alternate routes to the Senate—the legislative and the judicial. These routes have not been mutually exclusive, and many politicians have traveled both the law-making and the law-enforcing roads. The law-making, though still the main road, has declined in popularity. Through the years the men who ultimately become

Table 2—Political Careers of Senators

				SENATE				
	16th (44)		36th (66)		56th (89)		76th (96)	
	Per cent of Senators	Average for Senate in years	Per cent of Senators	Average for Senate in years	Per cent of Senators	Average for Senate in years	Per cent of Senators	Average for Senate in years
Age on January 1	100	45.7	100	50.4	100	56.5	100	58.2
Age on entering Senate	100	41.6	100	43.7	100	48.4	100	49.0
Experience in Senate by January 1	100	3.3	100	5.7	100	7.8	100	9.3
Total service in Senate	100	8.5	100	9.9	100	15.1	100	17.2*
Prior service in House of Representatives	34	2.0	42	1.9	35	1.7	31	2.5
Total service in House of Representatives	36	2.2	45	2.0	35	1.7	31	2.5
Prior service in state legislatures	82	4.4	65	3.2	58	2.6	38	1.7
Total service in state legislatures	86	5.2	65	3.4	58	2.6	39	1.8
Prior service in law-enforcement posts	50	2.8	39	1.9	37	1.7	42	3.1
Total service in law-enforcement posts	55	3.4	45	3.1	38	2.0	42	3.7*
Total pre-senatorial political career	98	10.25	97	10.0	89	8.0	93	10.8
Post-senatorial political career	57	4.0	27	1.5	14	1.1	27	1.9*

* Figure is apt to increase since a few members of the Seventy-sixth Senate are still politically active.

senators have spent less and less time in state legislatures, but have averaged about two years' service in the United States House of Representatives. Combining the average previous service in both the House and the state legislatures reveals a steady drop from 6.4 years for the 1820 Senate to 4.2 years for that of 1940. Since 1900, the House has increased as a training ground for senators, while state legislatures have continued to decline. By 1940, only 38 per cent of the senators had served in a state legislature, as compared to 82 per cent in 1820. The fact that state legislators no longer elected senators seems more reflective of than responsible for the decline, which was influenced by the waning importance of states, and has been noticeable since 1820.

The length of judiciary service before entering the Senate (including minor offices, such as district attorney and marshal) has fluctuated around two and three years for all these Senates. In 1820 half of the senators had served in some law-enforcing capacity before entering the Senate; 39 per cent had served in 1860; 37 per cent, in 1900; and 42 per cent, in 1940.

The social backgrounds as well as the political careers of senators are important. Some political scientists insist that the politician's social background influences his voting more than political pressure.[5] Of primary importance is a man's occupation. Senators have been drawn from the elite of our labor force.[6] Although lawyers were only 4/10 of a per cent of the economically active population in 1940, 80 per cent of the Senate in 1820 and 69 per cent in 1940 were lawyers. Many of these lawyer-senators had special interests; they were lawyer-planters or railroad lawyers or were deeply involved in other pursuits. Adjusting occupations to count them as part of the planting, railroad, or other interest groups instead of as lawyers alters the occupational pattern of these Senates, but lawyers still remain the largest group, oscillating from 41 per cent in 1820 to 43 per cent in 1940.

Despite the continuity of lawyer strength, a significant change took place in the occupational composition of the Senate between 1820 and 1860 when business interests grew from 9 to 27 per cent. From then on, occupational classifications remained stable; senators with business interests reached 34 per cent in 1900 only to revert back to 27 per cent in 1940. Lumped together as "managers, officials, and proprietors," businessmen formed only 6 per cent of the nation's working population in 1900 and 7 per cent in 1940. A X^2 theoretical distribution substantiates the conclusion that the occupational differences between 1820 and 1860 senators are highly significant, but that after 1860 occupational classifications were highly stable.

Businessmen differ from one another in interest, wealth, power, and politics. Merchants and manufacturers, miners and lumbermen, railroad executives and bankers are all businessmen, as is the proprietor of the corner grocery store and the president of General Motors. Many businessmen-senators in this analysis neither have been identified with the leading corporations nor involved in the most dynamic sector of the economy, nor have they come from the most industrialized states,[7]

Table 3—Nonpolitical Occupations of Senators

Occupations	SENATE			
	16th (44)	36th (66)	56th (89)	76th (96)
Lawyers	80% (35)	79% (52)	74% (66)	69% (66)
Businessmen		15% (10)	18% (16)	10% (10)
Farmers	14% (6)	2% (1)	4% (4)	5% (5)
Mass Media	2% (1)	2% (1)	1% (1)	8% (8)
Doctors	2% (1)	3% (2)	1% (1)	1% (1)
Professors				3% (3)
Minister			1% (1)	
Laborers				2% (2)
Housewife				1% (1)
Unknown	2% (1)			
Adjusted Occupations				
Lawyers	41% (18)	38% (25)	42% (37)	41% (39)
Business Interests	9% (4)	27% (18)	34% (30)	27% (26)
Landed Interests	43% (19)	24% (16)	11% (10)	10% (10)
Mass Media	2% (1)	6% (4)	7% (6)	10% (10)
Doctors	2% (1)	3% (2)	2% (2)	1% (1)
Professors		2% (1)	1% (1)	5% (5)
Minister			1% (1)	
Historians			2% (2)	
Labor Interests				4% (4)
Housewife				1% (1)
Unknown	2% (1)			

but most of them have preferred the Republican party. Three of the four businessmen-senators in 1820 were from the frontier states of Illinois and Indiana, with interests in milling, wool-carding, ferrying, and banking. The interests of the fourth, Mahlon Dickerson of New Jersey, whom Martin Van Buren later labeled an"ultra-protectionist" and who owned and managed the Succasunna Iron Works,[8] were more closely attuned to the forthcoming industrial transformation of the United States.

The interests of the 1860 businessmen-senators, many of whom were involved in a variety of enterprises, reflect changes in the economy. Nine were identified with railroads as president, director, counsel, or contractor; four were identified with manufacturers; three, with the extractive industries of lumbering and fur trading; and three, with banking and finance. These businessmen-senators preferred the Republican party, but they were not conspicuously from the leading industrial states. With 58 per cent of the Senate Democratic and 39 per cent Republican, only 44 per cent of the businessmen-senators were Democrats while 56 per cent were Republicans. Although two of these senators were from the industrial state of Pennsylvania, there were also two from Ohio, Maine, and Oregon. The industrial states of Massachusetts and Rhode Island each boasted one businessman-senator but so did many nonindustrial states, such as Florida, Tennessee, Wisconsin, and Minnesota.

Though the overall occupational patterns of the Senate changed little between 1860 and 1900, the multifarious interests of businessmen senators in 1900 continued to reflect industrial changes. Fifteen were involved in railroads (an additional three were in other transportation ventures), fifteen in extracting minerals, lumber, and oil, nine were bankers and financiers, six were merchants, and three were manufacturers. Forty-four per cent of the senators from the nine industrial states were businessmen as compared to 31 per cent from the remaining states. The Senate in 1900 was 64 per cent Republican and 30 per cent Democratic, but 90 per cent of the businessmen-senators were Republicans while only 7 per cent were Democrats.

Although businessmen-senators in 1940 decreased merely 7 per cent, their multiple interests differed considerably from 1900 senators. Bankers, manufacturers, and insurance men increased while the number of senators involved in extractive industries declined. No senator had appreciable railroad interests. Fifteen 1940 senators were in banking, nine in manufacturing, five in mercantile pursuits, five in insurance, and four in extractive industries. While these changes reflect to a degree the nation's shifting economic interests, they fail to register the fantastic growth of individual firms. The increase of banker-senators, for example, does not reflect the growing importance of gigantic financial institutions; senatorial bankers were almost invariably local lawyers who became officers of local banks.[9] As in previous Senates, the more industrialized states did not choose an overwhelming number of businessmen-senators, but senators with business interests frequently chose the Republican party. Twenty-nine per cent of the senators from the twelve most industrialized states were businessmen as compared to 26 per cent from the remaining thirty-six states. Though the Senate in 1940 was disproportionately Democratic (72 per cent to 24 per cent Republican), only 62 per cent of the businessmen-senators were Democrats while 38 per cent were Republicans.

By 1940, senators were less involved with the nation's leading businesses than they had been in 1900. Despite the increased national outlook of the country's main industries by 1940, senators' economic interests remained regional. As long as industry was primarily local, senatorial businessmen reflected the dominant American industrial focus, but when in the twentieth century industry became national and even world-wide in scope, senators continued to represent the limited economic interests of their states. The election of senators directly by the people, whose vision was narrower than that of the average legislator who formerly elected senators, favored candidates with local economic interests over those with national interests. Furthermore, the Republican party not only attracted more business-men than the Democratic party, it attracted larger businessmen. This factor coupled with the great Democratic majority in 1940 partly accounts for the failure of Senate business interests to reflect national business trends. But this is only part of the answer; though involved in some substantial industries, Republican businessmen-senators in 1940 were relatively more provincial than their 1900 counterparts.

The vast number of farmers, including individuals of all social levels and conditions, have been significantly but not proportionately represented in the Senate. In 1820, 72 per cent of the nation's gainful workers were farmers while 43 per cent of the Senate farmed or speculated in land. By 1940 this landed interest group had declined to 10 per cent while 17 per cent of the nation's working population were farmers. Rural areas (including villages with fewer than 2,500 people) have not produced their share of senators. In 1790, 95 per cent of the American people were rural while 86 per cent of the 1820

Table 4—Population of Senators' Birthplaces Compared with Nation as a Whole[a]

	16th Senate (44)	Nation in 1790[b]	36th Senate (66)	Nation in 1810	56th Senate (89)	Nation in 1840	76th Senate (96)	Nation in 1880
Farm	55% (24)		29% (19)		37% (33)		21% (20)	
0–2,500	32% (14)		52% (34)		40% (36)		43% (41)	
Subtotal Rural	86% (38)	95%	80% (53)	93%	78% (69)	89%	64% (61)	72%
2,500–10,000	9% (4)	2%	8% (5)	3%	11% (10)	3%	13% (12)	7%
10,000–25,000	2% (1)	1%		2%		2%	13% (12)	4%
25,000–50,000		2%	6% (4)	1%		1%	2% (2)	3%
50,000–100,000				2%		1%	2% (2)	2%
Over 100,000					3% (3)	3%	4% (4)	12%
Foreign born[c]	2% (1)		6% (4)		8% (7)		3% (3)	

a. For a summary table of rural and urban population, see *Historical Statistics*, p. 14. For the population of towns and cities, see Evarts B. Greene and Virginia Harrington, *American Population Before the Federal Census of 1790* (New York: Columbia University Press, 1932), *passim*; *Return of the Whole Number of Persons Within the Several Districts of the United States* . . . (Philadelphia: Childs and Swaine, 1791), *passim*; George Tucker, *Progress of the United States in Population and Wealth in Fifty Years, as Exhibited by the Decennial Census from 1790 to 1840* . . . *with an Appendix, containing an Abstract of the Census of 1850* (New York: Hunt's Merchant's Magazine, 1855), pp. 128–32, Appendix, pp. 37–42; J. D. B. DeBow, *Statistical View of the United States* . . . *Being a Compendium of the Seventh Census* . . . (Washington: A. O. P. Nicholson, Public Printer, 1854), pp. 338–93; Joseph C. G. Kennedy, *Population of the United States in 1860: Compiled from the Original Returns of the Eigth Census* . . . (Washington: Government Printing Office, 1864), *passim*; United States Census Office, *Statistics of the Population of the United States at the Tenth Census (June 1, 1880)* . . . (Washington: Government Printing Office, 1883), pp. 93–375; United States Bureau of the Census, *Abstract of the Twelfth Census of the United States: 1900* (Washington: Government Printing Office, 1904), pp. 136–49; United States Bureau of the Census, *Sixteenth Census of the United States: 1940, Population* (Washington: Government Printing Office, 1942), I, *passim*.

b. 1790 figures are used in the absence of statistics for 1774.

c. The percentage of foreign-born senators reflects dimly the proportion of immigrants in the United States. In 1820, 2 per cent of the Senate were foreign-born; in 1860, 6 per cent of the Senate were as compared to 13 per cent of the population. In 1900, 7 per cent of the Senate and 14 per cent of the population were immigrants; in 1940 immigrants comprised 3 per cent of the Senate and 9 per cent of the population. The percentages of foreign-born in the population as a whole are derived from tables in *Historical Statistics*, pp. 8, 66.

senators were born in rural areas. In 1880, 72 per cent of the people were rural while only 64 per cent of the 1940 senators were of rural birth.[10]

Nor have large urban areas been good spawning grounds for senators. In 1820, 9 per cent of all senators were born in towns of from 2,500 to 10,000 people and 2 per cent in cities of more than 10,000. By 1940 the figures reflect an urban trend with 13 per cent born in towns, 15 per cent in small cities of from 10,000 to 50,000 people, and 6 per cent in cities larger than 50,000. Despite population trends, only 4 per cent of the 1940 senators were born in cities larger than 100,000. Around the time of their birth (approximately 1880), 12 per cent of the people lived in these large metropolitan areas. It is towns and small cities that have been the most successful producers of senators.[11]

Senatorial residences also favor towns and small cities, although the national trend toward larger population centers is exhibited by members of these Senates. The most striking change in residence occurred between 1820 and 1860. In the earlier Senate, 64 per cent of the members still lived on farms or in villages with fewer than 2,500 people, while 23 per cent lived in towns of up to 10,000, and 14 per cent lived in urban centers of more than 10,000. By 1860, only

Table 5—Population of Senators' Residences Compared with Nation as a Whole*

	16th Senate (44)	Nation in 1820	36th Senate (66)	Nation in 1860	56th Senate (89)	Nation in 1900	76th Senate (96)	Nation in 1940
0–2,500	64% (28)	93%	35% (23)	80%	30% (27)	60%	16% (15)	44%
2,500–10,000	23% (10)	3%	36% (24)	5%	17% (15)	8%	19% (18)	9%
10,000–25,000	2% (1)	1%	9% (6)	3%	19% (17)	6%	16% (15)	8%
25,000–50,000	5% (2)	1%	5% (3)	2%	9% (8)	4%	19% (18)	6%
50,000–100,000	2% (1)	1%	5% (3)	1%	8% (7)	4%	8% (8)	6%
Over 100,000	5% (2)	1%	11% (7)	8%	17% (15)	19%	23% (22)	29%

* For sources on population data, see Table 4, note a.

35 per cent lived on farms or in villages, while 36 per cent lived in towns, and 29 per cent lived in urban centers of more than 10,000. Forty-four per cent of the population as compared with 16 per cent of the Senate was rural in 1940, while 29 per cent of the people as compared with 23 per cent of the Senate lived in large metropolitan areas of 100,000 or more.[12]

Senatorial birthplaces and residences vary with political affiliation. The differences are most striking in the Sixteenth Senate, with 95 per cent of the Democratic-Republicans born on farms or in villages and 44 per cent of the Federalists born in towns. Seventy-seven per cent of the Democratic-Republicans resided in rural areas, while 89 per cent of the Federalists lived in towns and cities larger than 2,500. Differences between Republican and Democratic senators in 1860, 1900, and 1940 were less pronounced, but Democrats tended to be more rural in birth and residence. Based in the Northeast and Middle West, Federalists and Republicans were naturally more urban than their opponents, whose stronghold was the South.

There is a marked continuity in the occupations of senators' fathers when one considers the changes in occupations that occurred in this period. At the time of the American Revolution, when the average 1820 senator was born, it is commonly estimated that 90 per cent of the people farmed; 50 per cent of the fathers of the 1820 senators were farmers. In 1820, ten years after the average 1860 senator was born, 72 per cent of the working force farmed while 33 per cent of the fathers of the 1860 senators were farmers. In 1840, three years before the average 1900 senator was born, 69 per cent of the working

Table 6—Senators' Fathers' Occupations

Occupations	SENATE			
	16th (44)	36th (66)	56th (89)	76th (96)
Lawyers		9% (6)	10% (9)	18% (17)
Farmers	50% (22)	33% (22)	39% (35)	34% (33)
Businessmen	9% (4)	8% (5)	6% (5)	4% (4)
Ministers	9% (4)	5% (3)	6% (5)	3% (3)
Doctors	5% (2)	6% (4)	3% (3)	2% (2)
Editors and Publishers				2% (2)
Engineers		1% (1)		
Teachers		1% (1)		
Skilled Laborers		3% (2)	2% (2)	1% (1)
Common Laborers		1% (1)		3% (3)
Poets				1% (1)
Unknown	27% (12)	32% (21)	34% (30)	31% (30)

population farmed compared to 39 per cent of the fathers of the 1900 senators. In 1880, two years before the average 1940 senator was born, 50 per cent of the working force farmed while 34 per cent of the fathers of the 1940 senators were farmers.[13] Despite the industrial revolution, businessmen-fathers steadily declined from 9 per cent in 1820 to 4 per cent in 1940. Ministers also declined from 9 per cent in 1820 to 3 per cent in 1940; while doctors dropped from 5 per cent in 1820 to 2 per cent in 1940. Though no 1820 senator seemed to have had a lawyer for a father, 9 per cent of the senators in 1860, 10 per cent in 1900, and 18 per cent in 1940 had fathers who were lawyers. Few fathers were skilled or unskilled laborers, though their ranks might be increased if the unknown occupations could be classified.

Nevertheless, the growing labor force is poorly represented while the diminishing farm population has virtually held its own.

Officeholders frequently beget officeholders. The fathers of 16 per cent of the 1820 senators held political office; 8 per cent of the 1860; 12 per cent of the 1900, and 19 per cent of the 1940.

A survey of senators whose blood relatives served in Congress shows that 27 per cent of the 1820 senators were related to one or more previous or subsequent congressmen, 23 per cent, in 1860, and 19 per cent, in both 1900 and 1940. Delaware boasts the best example of a

Table 7—Highest Political Office Held by Senators' Fathers

Office	SENATE			
	16th (44)	36th (66)	56th (89)	76th (96)
President				1% (1)c
Governor	2% (1)a			1% (1)
Senator		3% (2)b	1% (1)	3% (3)b
Representative	7% (3)		3% (3)	5% (5)
Legislator	2% (1)	1% (1)	2% (2)	
Judge	2% (1)		2% (2)	2% (2)
Asst. At. Gen. US				1% (1)
State officer				1% (1)
Local officer	2% (1)	3% (2)	3% (3)	4% (4)
Total officeholders	16% (7)	8% (5)	12% (11)	19% (18)

a. Also served as U.S. Representative, but not counted in this table.
b. One also served as Governor, but not counted in this table.
c. Also served as Chief Justice of the U.S. Supreme Court, but not counted in this table.

political dynasty. The grandfather, father, brother, son, and grandson of Senator James A. Bayard, Jr. of the Thirty-sixth Senate were also senators from Delaware.

Senators have always been well educated, and the majority of them have been trained as lawyers. Seventy-three per cent of the 1820 senators had read law in a lawyer's office and 7 per cent had attended law school; in 1860 these percentages changed only slightly. The development of law schools and higher professional standards is reflected by senators' legal training in 1900, and even more by 1940, when only 17 per cent studied law in a private office and 54 per cent attended law school. Fifty-two per cent of the 1820 Senate attended college

Table 8—Education of Senators

	SENATE			
	16th (44)	36th (66)	56th (89)	76th (96)
Very Limited		8% (5)	6% (5)	
Common School	25% (11)	11% (7)	11% (10)	9% (9)
High School	23% (10)	20% (13)	13% (12)	10% (10)
College:	52% (23)	62% (41)	70% (62)	80% (77)
Some	11% (5)	9% (6)	22% (20)	14% (13)
Graduate	41% (18)	53% (35)	47% (42)	67% (64)

and 41 per cent graduated from college. By 1940, 80 per cent of the senators had been to college and 67 per cent of them had graduated. This percentage was much larger than the total percentage of college-educated American men in their generation. In 1870, a few years after 47 per cent of the 1900 senators graduated from college, only 2 per cent of the twenty-one year old males in the United States graduated from college. In 1903, roughly the year 67 per cent of the 1940 senators graduated, only 3 per cent of the twenty-one year old American males graduated.[14] In the 1820 Senate, twice as many Federalists had attended college as Democratic-Republicans. Democratic senators, however, were consistently better educated than their Republican colleagues. In the 1860 Senate, 68 per cent of the Democrats and 54 per cent of the Republicans had been to college; by 1940, 84 per cent of the Democratic senators and 65 per cent of the Republican ones had some college training. While no senator in either 1820 or 1940 was handicapped by very limited schooling, 8 per cent were so handicapped in 1860 and 6 per cent in 1900.

Table 9—Professional or Graduate Education of Senators

	SENATE			
	16th (44)	36th (66)	56th (89)	76th (96)
Read Law	73% (32)	70% (46)	48% (43)	17% (16)
Law School	7% (3)	11% (7)	27% (24)	54% (52)
Medical Training	5% (2)	6% (4)	2% (2)	1% (1)
Theological Training			1% (1)	
M.A.	2% (1)		1% (1)	2% (2)
Ph.D.			1% (1)	

The class origins of many senators are difficult to ascertain. Drawing precise lines between upper, middle, and lower classes in America is impossible. With the importance of material possessions and education varying with localities, wealth and schooling do not always reflect an individual's standing in a community. Though a slaveowner able to provide secondary schooling for his children, Thomas Bragg's father was counted but a "plebian" in the pretentious antebellum society of Warrenton, North Carolina.[15] Standards vary not merely from section to section but from decade to decade, and it is necessary to use loose classifications because of the paucity of precise information. Despite these difficulties in classification, we do know the education and fathers' occupations of most senators and can with reasonable accuracy determine whether they had elite, substantial, or subsistence backgrounds. In placing individuals in these categories, the advantages parents could give their children were stressed rather then class distinctions. The scale used was that employed by David J. Rothman in his book on the Senate. The elite designation was used for prominent figures in American business, politics, and professions; the substantial category was typified by town lawyers, doctors, and small merchants who assisted their children in obtaining an education but were not members of a national elite; and the subsistence category was used for fathers whose earnings barely fed and clothed their families.[16] Pending an exhaustive search of census materials, figures on socioeconomic backgrounds represent a blend of hard data and soft impressions and are tentative.

The backgrounds of each Senate suggest that a major democratic shift occurred from 1820 to 1860. Though the trend continued through 1900, it had leveled off and even reversed itself slightly by 1940. Sixty-eight per cent of the 1820 senators were born into the elite, 18 per cent into substantial homes, and 7 per cent into subsistence homes. The class origins of 7 per cent were unknown. Forty years later only 33 per cent of the senators could boast an elite background, 42 per cent came from substantial families and 18 per cent sprang from subsistence backgrounds. The backgrounds of 6 per cent were unknown. By 1900, 22 per cent of the senators were of elite backgrounds, 49 per cent still were of substantial families, while 24 per cent came up from poverty, and 4 per cent were of unknown backgrounds. Both the upper- and the middle-class backgrounds made slight gains among 1940 senators, while lower-class backgrounds correspondingly declined. The Senate in 1860, and even more in 1900 and 1940, reflected much more social mobility than it did in 1820. There were class differences between senators of different parties. The Federalists were elite to the core, while the Democratic-Republicans reflected more social mobility. The percentage of Democratic senators with elite origins declined from 45 per cent in 1860 to 20 per cent in 1940, while the percentage of Republican senators with elite origins

Table 10—Social Origins of Senators

	SENATE			
	16th (44)	36th (66)	56th (89)	76th (96)
Elite	68% (30)	33% (22)	22% (20)	23% (22)
Substantial	18% (8)	42% (28)	49% (44)	51% (49)
Subsistence	7% (3)	18% (12)	24% (21)	22% (21)
Unknown	7% (3)	6% (4)	4% (4)	4% (4)

grew from 12 per cent in 1860 to 30 per cent in 1940. At the opposite end of the social scale, a similar reversal occurred. In 1860, 13 per cent of the Democrats came up from poverty; in 1900, 15 per cent; and in 1940, 23 per cent. In contrast, 27 per cent of the 1860 Republicans were born in poverty, as compared to 26 per cent of those in 1900 and 17 per cent of those in 1940. Though the class origins of Democratic senators declined while those of Republican senators rose, such changes in political leadership do not necessarily reflect changes in party membership. Nevertheless, the leaders of our two major parties have differed in social backgrounds; and those parties, through their leadership, have projected both changing and differing images.

There are regional differences in class origin. Except for 1860, the East (the New England and Middle Atlantic states) has tended to choose senators with elite backgrounds, while in the South (states south of the Mason-Dixon Line, the Ohio River, and 36° 30″, and west to Oklahoma and Texas), there has been a trend away from such senators (from 82 per cent in 1820 to 19 per cent in 1940). The most significant shift in that southern trend (from 61 per cent to 21 per cent) occurred between 1860 and 1900. Fewer midwestern and western senators had elite backgrounds. The Midwest states north and west of the Ohio River to Kansas, Nebraska, and the Dakotas chose only 17 per cent of their senators from the elite in 1820, 19 per cent in 1860, 21 per cent in 1900, and 13 per cent in 1940. The West (the Mountain and Pacific states) chose none of their senators from the elite in 1860, 6 per cent in 1900, and 18 per cent in 1940. Forty-four per cent of western senators in 1900, 31 per cent of midwestern senators in 1860 and 27 per cent of western senators in 1940 were born in poverty. Evidently the admission of new western states with

Table II—Senators' Social Origins by Party

Senate	Party	Elite	Substantial	Subsistence	Unknown
16th	Federalist (9)	100% (9)			
„	Democratic Republican (35)	60% (21)	23% (8)	9% (3)	9% (3)
„	Total 44	68% (30)	18% (8)	7% (3)	7% (3)
36th	Democratic (38)	45% (17)	34% (13)	13% (5)	8% (3)
„	Republican (26)	12% (3)	58% (15)	27% (7)	4% (1)
„	Whig-Unionist (2)	100% (2)			
„	Total 66	33% (22)	42% (28)	18% (12)	6% (4)
56th	Democratic (27)	26% (7)	52% (14)	15% (4)	7% (2)
„	Republican (57)	21% (12)	49% (28)	26% (15)	4% (2)
„	Populist (3)		67% (2)	33% (1)	
„	Fusionist (2)	50% (1)		50% (1)	
„	Total 89	22% (20)	49% (44)	24% (21)	4% (4)
76th	Democratic (69)	20% (14)	51% (35)	23% (16)	6% (4)
„	Republican (23)	30% (7)	52% (12)	17% (4)	
„	Farmer-Labor (2)		100% (2)		
„	Progressive (1)	100% (1)			
„	Independent Republican (1)			100% (1)	
„	Total 96	23% (22)	51% (49)	22% (21)	4% (4)

their fluid class structure contributed to the shift in social backgrounds between 1820 and 1860 and helped continue the trend toward more humble social backgrounds, until 1900. By 1940 these societies were relatively stable and the Senate of that year reflected less mobility than that of 1900. The move West, however, was not the only impetus toward a Senate less aristocratic in background. The great shift in backgrounds occurred between 1820 and 1860 and the greatest change occurred in the East. In 1820, 69 per cent of eastern senators were elite in background, compared to only 11 per cent in 1860. But the eastern elite made a strong comeback. By 1900, 44 per cent and by 1940, 50 per cent of eastern senators had elite backgrounds. To a degree these figures represent the rise, progress, and prosperity of the Republican party.

Though some changes, particularly before 1860, are apparent, the main thrust of the foregoing figures is continuity; unquantifiable impressions confirm this emphasis. Many significant characteristics of

Table 12—Senators' Social Origins by Region

Senate	Region	Elite	Substantial	Subsistence	Unknown
16th	East (16)	69% (11)	19% (3)	13% (2)	
,,	Midwest (6)	17% (1)	67% (4)		17% (1)
,,	South (22)	82% (18)	5% (1)	5% (1)	9% (2)
,,	Total 44	68% (30)	18% (8)	7% (3)	7% (3)
36th	East (18)	11% (2)	56% (10)	22% (4)	11% (2)
,,	Midwest (16)	19% (3)	50% (8)	31% (5)	
,,	South (28)	61% (17)	29% (8)	7% (2)	4% (1)
,,	West (4)		50% (2)	25% (1)	25% (1)
,,	Total 66	33% (22)	42% (28)	18% (12)	6% (4)
56th	East (18)	44% (8)	39% (7)	17% (3)	
,,	Midwest (24)	21% (5)	58% (14)	17% (4)	4% (1)
,,	South (29)	21% (6)	48% (14)	21% (6)	10% (3)
,,	West (18)	6% (1)	50% (9)	44% (8)	
,,	Total 89	22% (20)	49% (44)	24% (21)	4% (4)
76th	East (18)	50% (9)	28% (5)	22% (4)	
,,	Midwest (24)	13% (3)	63% (15)	21% (5)	4% (1)
,,	South (32)	19% (6)	56% (18)	19% (6)	6% (2)
,,	West (22)	18% (4)	50% (11)	27% (6)	5% (1)
,,	Total 96	23% (22)	51% (49)	22% (21)	4% (4)

the Senate cannot be quantified but can be observed. From wide reading, extensive interviews, and careful scrutiny, Donald R. Matthews was able to discern the post-World War II Senate's power centers and folkways and to delineate the senator's way of life and his relations with lobbyists, reporters, and constituents.[17] While it would be absurd to argue that all of the senatorial characteristics

Matthews observed were present by 1820, many of them, in varying degrees, were present by 1860. Those relating to campaigns, folkways, and leadership are particularly apparent. Sticklers for stability and tradition, members of the Senate cherish its deeply rooted customs and power structure.

Most senators campaigned long and hard for many years and offices with techniques developed well before 1860. Irrational voters were appealed to by Indian fighter Richard M. Johnson of the Sixteenth Senate, who ran for the vice-presidency in 1836 on the jingle "Rumpsey, Dumpsey, Colonel Johnson killed Tecumpseh." Stephen A. Douglas of the 1860 Senate, understanding that party discipline and money won elections, organized county and state nominating conventions and contributed liberally to party campaign funds. Smears were regularly employed during campaigns: swarthy Hannibal Hamlin of Maine was rumored to be partly Negro; James H. Hammond of South Carolina lost his initial bid for a Senate seat when his enemies threatened to expose an earlier "grave indiscretion"; and Andrew Johnson of Tennessee was falsely proclaimed both as bastard and an infidel.[18]

By 1900 campaign funds had increased in volume and importance. William A. Clark of Montana spent $140,000 on his campaign in 1899, only to have the Senate Committee on Elections conclude he was "not duly and legally elected." Thomas C. Platt was particularly adept at collecting and disbursing secret campaign contributions from large corporations, in this way obligating numerous legislators to him and obligating himself to large-scale business interests. The classic fund-raising example is the three and a half million dollars raised primarily by Mark Hanna's assessment of banks, corporations, and other business institutions for McKinley's 1896 campaign.[19]

Having been around since the adoption of the Constitution and boasting great continuity, the Senate has certain patterns of behavior. Though many of these folkways date from the earliest days, they grow more pronounced as senators' tenures lengthen. All freshmen senators, for example, are expected to serve an apprenticeship. Harry S. Truman played this freshman role beautifully. He was modest, studious, and industrious. He rarely spoke on the floor and he consistently supported the policies of Franklin D. Roosevelt. Rare exceptions to the apprentice rule are made for unusual men or for unusual times —Stephen A. Douglas immediately became chairman of the important Committee on Territories, and William Pitt Fessenden opposed the Kansas-Nebraska bill with a great speech ten days after entering the Senate. It is hard for freshmen senators—particularly those from genuine two party states who must build a reputation to maintain their seats—to be seen and not be heard. Occasional concessions by seniors and defiance by freshmen have modified but have not killed this Senate equivalent of college Hell Week.[20]

Senators respect their "work horses" far more than their famous "show horses." The industrious Ohioan Benjamin Ruggles of the Sixteenth Senate was called the "wheelhorse [sic] of the Senate" and Speaker of the House Joseph G. ("Uncle Joe") Cannon paid Michigan's Julius C. Burrows of the Fifty-sixth Senate the highest possible compliment when he said, "You always found Burrows nearest the load." Eugene Hale of the same Senate typified the effective work horse senator. "Always a laborious and painstaking legislator, Sen. Hale through his intellectual attainments, ripe experience, iron determination, and strength of character was practically the dictator of national legislation during his years in the senate. He did not take a prominent part in discussions on the floor but in committee rooms his personality and influence were felt with forceful effect."[21]

Hale was in direct contrast to the show horse William E. Borah of the Seventy-sixth Senate. William E. Leuchtenburg writes:

Borah was a magnificent orator in an age when the art of oratory had gone into eclipse. A superb actor, his effect came from the richness of his voice, the simplicity of his approach, and his marvelous command of language. He never resorted to personal attacks, and even his opponents liked and admired him for his kindliness and sincerity.... He was not an effective leader in the Senate; he lacked the temperament for routine, shirked committee work, and sometimes left it to others to follow through on projects he had initiated. Senator George Norris was once reported to have said: "Borah always shoots until he sees the whites of their eyes." ... Yet for all his limitations, few equaled Borah in his ability to arouse the country on a public question. When Borah spoke, the country listened.[22]

A senator can be and often is both a show and work horse. Charles Sumner was diligent in routine work and he commanded respect in the discussion of foreign affairs, money, finance, and the tariff, in addition to kindling moral wrath against slavery.[23]

Most senators, unlike the versatile Sumner, tended to specialize. James Barbour was war governor of Virginia from 1812 to 1814, specialized in military matters as a senator, and later was John Quincy Adams' Secretary of War. With the growing complexity of issues before the Senate, specialization became more pronounced. By 1900, Stephen B. Elkins of West Virginia specialized not simply in business affairs but in railroad matters, and in 1940 Robert F. Wagner of New York was the Senate's leading authority on industrial relations.[24]

The elaborate courtesy with which senators treat each other is of early origin, and their loyalty to the Senate as an institution is scarcely less venerable. Though before the Civil War James Hammond wrote off his fellow senators as a "vulgar set of sharpshooters—county court lawyers and newspaper politicians," Henry Clay earlier compared the Senate favorably "with any legislative assembly, either in ancient or modern times, whether I look to its dignity, the extent and importance of its powers, the ability by which its individual members have been distinguished, or its organic constitution."[25]

Not all senators adhere to their folkways. In 1902 Benjamin ("Pitchfork Ben") Tillman and the other senator from South Carolina, John R. McLaurin, had a fist fight on the Senate floor.[26] Some freshmen senators will be heard; and there will always be show horses, but senators who consistently flout the folkways rarely become powerful leaders.

Chairmen of important Senate committees did not differ appreciably in social backgrounds, fathers' occupations, and birthplaces from their fellow senators. The norm of the Sixteenth, Thirty-sixth, Fifty-sixth, and Seventy-sixth Senates was compared with the chairmen of the following committees in each of these Senates: Foreign Relations, Finance, Commerce, Military Affairs, Naval Affairs, and Judiciary. In addition, the norm was compared with Public Lands in the Sixteenth and Thirty-sixth Senates; Territories in the Thirty-sixth; Agriculture, Appropriations, and Interstate Commerce in the Fifty-sixth and Seventy-sixth Senates; and Banking and Currency in the Seventy-sixth Senate. Chairmen of these important committees usually were older, more experienced, better educated and more likely to be lawyers than their colleagues. If Democrats were in power, they resided in the South or perhaps the West; and if Republicans controlled the Senate, they were New Englanders or perhaps Midwesterners. Further reflecting their parties, Democratic chairmen tended to be more and Republican chairmen less rural than the norm.

Effective senatorial leadership appears early. John Gaillard of South Carolina "developed almost as firm a hold upon the Senate as upon his state." From 1814 until his death in 1826 he was almost always president pro tempore of the Senate. The main source of Gaillard's power is obvious; he had served longer than any other senator. In 1900 Nelson Aldrich and William B. Allison, whom Aldrich called "a master of the arts of conciliation and construction," led "the big four or five" who dominated the Senate. The "sage" of this group was Orville H. Platt, a man of "untiring industry, honesty, and sound judgment," while the "brilliant" John C. Spooner lent his counsel. The work horse Eugene Hale was the fifth and perhaps the peripheral member of the group. The economic importance of a senator's state has little to do with his leadership, but Senate leaders usually represent one-party or modified one-party states. The big five represented Iowa, Rhode Island, Connecticut, Wisconsin, and Maine. More important than state represented was length of service, chairmanship of important committees, capacity for leadership, and industry. Though the Seventy-sixth Senate, like all Senates, had its leaders—Alben W. Barkley and James F. Byrnes, for example—it is doubtful that they exceeded the power of the big five. Another source of senatorial power, particularly in the twentieth century, is intimate friendship with the President. The relationship of Henry Cabot Lodge with Theodore Roosevelt and James F. Byrnes with Franklin Roosevelt enhanced their ability to lead.[27]

Most senators never become leaders within the Senate. The average senator is content to do committee work, take care of his constituents, and keep state party machinery in running order. Indeed, with some senators state affairs assume primary importance. Boies Penrose and Thomas C. Platt of the Fifty-sixth Senate serve as examples. Although well qualified to be a statesman, Penrose was so absorbed in machine politics that he never devoted himself to broad national questions. Platt was so concerned with New York state affairs that he almost never spoke, "never offered an important bill, never voted except with the party regulars, and never expressed an opinion on national issues which carried any weight." On the other hand, statesmanship can endanger one's position back home. Porter J. McCumber became so "engrossed" with national politics that he "lost touch" with local North Dakota politics and was defeated in the 1922 primary.[28]

Even in the area of individual personality and behavior, one discerns continuity. By 1820 many behavioral characteristics had appeared; succeeding senators added refinements but few new traits. There was "able, industrious, fearless," "opinionated and prejudiced" William Smith of South Carolina; the popular, ambitious, political opportunist James Noble of Indiana; "tricky" Jesse B. Thomas of Illinois; Isaac Tichenor of Vermont whose "charming manners" won him the nickname "Jersey Slick"; James Pleasants of Virginia who, true to his name, "never made an enemy or lost a friend"; and the tactful, able, and eloquent William Hunter of Rhode Island. In the Thirty-sixth Senate these traits were combined with some new and more democratic ones. There was the "subtle intrigue" of William M. Gwin of California, who had "determined not to make money, but to devote all his energies to obtaining and maintaining political power"; the convivial temperament, "salty comments," and "hearty laughter" of Robert Toombs of Georgia; and the "rough" manners and "coarse and vituperative" speech of Benjamin F. Wade of Ohio. By 1900 several senators in addition to those above possessed managerial talents. There was Thomas C. Platt's "business-like instinct for detail"; Samuel. D. McEnery's "ability to handle men"; Francis E. Warren's "keen judgement" and "executive ability"; and Nelson W. Aldrich's shrewd assessment of human nature. On the negative side, Ernest Lundeen of the Seventy-sixth Senate "lacked conviviality" and was always "at loggerheads with the leaders of his own party." "Heavy set, humorless" and a "lone wolf," Lundeen commanded admiration but not affection.[29]

Intellectually, most senators, like William Bigler of Pennsylvania, could be described as "wise rather than brilliant." But there were exceptions, such as William Pitt Fessenden of Maine and John C. Spooner of Wisconsin, who was called "the most brilliant man in Congress." Few, however, could equal the praise earned by William Pinkney of Maryland, whom Chief Justice John Marshall declared "the greatest man I ever saw in a Court of justice."[30]

There is no typical senator, each is unique in some way. But James Brown of Louisiana approximated the hypothetical average. John Quincy Adams described him as "a man of large fortune, respectable talents, handsome person, polished manners, and elegant deportment." Most senators were members of "the Middle Ground" Washington aristocracy which Mark Twain and Charles Dudley Warner describe in their book The Gilded Age:

> It was made up of the families of public men from nearly every state in the Union—men who held positions in both executive and legislative branches of the government, and whose characters had been for years blemishless, both at home and at the capital. These gentlemen and their households were unostentatious people; they were educated and refined; they troubled themselves but little about the two other orders of nobility [the Antiques and the Parvenus], but moved serenely in their wide orbit, confident in their own strength and well aware of the potency of their influence.[31]

Statistical and impressionistic evidence indicate that the Senate has changed during the period studied, but that in a revolutionary world it has remained remarkably stable. Senators have entered the Senate at older ages and have served increasingly longer terms, but training previous to their election has varied little over this 120-year period. The Senate has been dominated by lawyers, although its membership has reflected the growth of big business and the decline of agriculture. Senators have remained primarily town and country in background and residence. As our major cities grow larger, their percentage of senators in residence declines. Senators prefer a "Main Street" address to a "Broadway" number or an R. F. D. route.[32] Their fathers tend to be farmers, though by 1940, lawyers' sons had increased significantly. No matter how productive wage-earners may be, they have not produced senators. Though a significant number of senators sprang from lower-class origins, senators have been well educated and have often been impressive in appearance and personality. Their campaigns for office have long necessitated both elaborate organization and substantial funds and have been characterized by the frequent use of smears. Senators' behavior is so rooted in the past and changes so little that we speak of Senate folkways. Through the years the way to senatorial leadership has remained long service, committee chairmanships, ability, and diligence. Though the social background of senators changed rapidly from 1820 to 1860, there are no great differences between the senators of 1860, 1900, and 1940.

What impact has the industrial revolution had on senators as political leaders? Indirectly it may be responsible for making senators older, better educated, and more specialized; leadership better organized and more stable; businessmen-politicians and political amateurs more common; and federal offices more prestigious than state offices. Yet the impact of industrialism has been remarkably small.

The preponderance of underdeveloped states with representation equal to that of New York only partially accounts for that small impact. Not all businessmen-senators were from industrial states; nor were all senators from industrial states businessmen. Senators from the more industrialized states usually did not differ greatly from the norm. It is true that more of them were Republican, older at their first election to the Senate, urban in birthplace and in residence, apt to have lawyers, doctors, businessmen, and laborers for fathers, and more involved vocationally with business, mass media, and labor than other senators. But some of these deviations were not great and others were not consistent. For example, senators from industrial states in 1860, 1900, and 1940 entered the Senate 8/10, 9/10, and 4/10 of a year older than the average senator. Senators from industrial states with businessmen-fathers fluctuated from 10 per cent in 1860 to 22 per cent in 1900 to 4 per cent in 1940, as compared with the norm of 8 per cent, 6 per cent, and 4 per cent. Perhaps political affiliation was the most distinguishing characteristic of senators from industrial states. They were 90 per cent Republican in 1860, 100 per cent in 1900, and 28 per cent in 1940 (the norms for these years were 39 per cent, 65 per cent, and 24 per cent respectively). Republicans consistently did better in industrial states than in the nation as a whole. In all the other points considered (including experience, education, percentage of lawyers, and social origins), senators from industrial states were not very different from all other senators.

The greatest changes in the Senate occurred from 1820 to 1860. Many economists theorize an industrial take-off around 1840, but industrialism has continued to transform society even to our day. If accelerating industrialization caused the changes from 1820 to 1860, it should have caused far greater subsequent changes. But no major subsequent changes occurred. It seems logical to suggest that factors other than industrialization account for the changes between 1820 and 1860.

It could be hypothesized that the shift to industrial leadership had occurred by 1860 and that subsequent changes were qualitative rather than quantitative. For example, the percentage of businessmen and lawyers in the Senate could remain the same, but there could be vast differences in their commitment to large scale corporate enterprise. The Senate's stability has been qualitative as well as quantitative, however, and has actually widened the gap between today's industrial leaders and senators. The evolution of industrial leadership from local and regional to national outlook has not been matched by political leadership. Most senators have remained provincial and Andrew Hacker reports, they "have little appreciation of the national outlook of the large firm." Their world of business is the "realm of small locally owned enterprise," they focus on economic problems "through a provincial lens rather than a metropolitan compass." Misunderstandings and the inability of political and industrial elites to communicate has produced "serious tensions." Based on an analysis of the 1959 Senate and one hundred industrial leaders, Hacker's conclusion indicates that the Senate is not plugged into the industrial circuit and that political leadership is relatively undisturbed by industrialism.[33]

The simultaneous rise of both lobbying and industry further suggests the lack of rapport between industrial and political leaders. Representing economic pressure groups in particular, lobbies exist not to bribe nor even to press congressmen, but rather to educate and to brief them.[34] Though commonly considered evidence of congressional domination by powerful pressure groups, lobbies basically reflect the inability of Congress to comprehend the growing complexity of our society. Attempting to transcend the barriers between urban industrial leaders and provincial political leaders, corporations use interpreters. Former senators and congressmen, as well as retired generals and admirals, are hired to explain to their former colleagues the ways and needs of an industrialized society.

Perhaps industrialism's greatest impact has been on the ruled. While the Senate has remained relatively stable since 1820, American society has made great socioeconomic gains. This conclusion is emphasized by comparing contemporary political elites of industrial and nonindustrial societies. There is a similarity between the socioeconomic and personality traits of the political leaders of preindustrial African and Asian states and of their counterparts in the Western industrialized states. But there is an immense gulf between the political leader and the average citizen of the emerging state. In the industrialized state the gulf becomes relatively narrow. Industrialism closes the distance, in affluence and socioeconomic variables, between the political leaders and the society as a whole. But industrialism does not alter appreciably the characteristics and behavior of the leaders themselves.[35]

One hundred years of industrial revolution had wrought changes in policy by 1940. Acknowledging the growing social responsibility and the changing role of the federal government, most senators abandoned laissez faire and embraced the welfare state. But though their social outlook was transformed, the source, selection, personality, and behavior of senators remained relatively unchanged. Even methods of formulating policy and making decisions, though growing in complexity and sophistication, remained the same. Power was lodged particularly with the experienced, the able, and the diligent senator; and all senators were responsible to the electorate. The implication of the foregoing empirical and impressionistic evidence concerning one area of political leadership is that industrialism—like its chief symbol, the machine—is a neutral instrument. It ensures neither the triumph nor the failure of any class, system, or idea. An engine of oppression in a closed society, industrialism may expand man's freedom of thought and action in an open society. While industrialism supplies the politician with increasingly elaborate tools, political leadership remains relatively undisturbed.

NOTES

1. An excellent brief introduction to several hypotheses on the impact of industrialism on political elites is Donald R. Matthews, *The Social Background of Political Decision-Makers* (New York: Random House, 1954), pp. 6–19.

2. Although historians have exhaustively studied individual political leaders, they have generally avoided collective and comparative studies of leadership. An exception is David J. Rothman, *Politics and Power: The United States Senate, 1869–1901* (Cambridge: Harvard University Press, 1966). Political scientists, such as Madge M. McKinney, Donald R. Matthews, and Andrew Hacker, have analyzed contemporary political leadership since the 1940s. Madge M. McKinney, "The Personnel of the Seventy-seventh Congress," *The American Political Science Review*, 36, No. 1 (February, 1942), 67–75; Andrew Hacker, "The Elected and the Anointed: Two American Elites," *ibid.*, 60, No. 3 (September, 1961), 539–49; Donald R. Matthews, *U.S. Senators and Their World* (Chapel Hill: The University of North Carolina Press, 1960). I am indebted to Matthews for much of the methodology used in this study.

3. U.S. Bureau of the Census, *Historical Statistics of the United States: Colonial Times to 1957* (Washington: Government Printing Office, 1960), pp. 14, 409. Hereafter cited as *Historical Statistics*.

4. In Massachusetts male life expectancy in 1850 was 38.3 years at birth; at the age of 40 it was 27.9 years; and at 60, 15.6 years. Ninety years later (1939–41) male life expectancy was 63.25 at birth; 29.30 at 40; and 14.45 at 60. *Historical Statistics*, p. 24.

5. S. K. Bailey, *Congress Makes a Law* (New York: Columbia University Press, 1950), p. 190, quoted by Matthews, *Social Background*, p. 3.

6. The comparisons with the nation's working population are based on tables in *Historical Statistics*, pp. 74–75.

7. In 1860, with annual manufactures valued at more than $250,000,000 each, New York, Pennsylvania, and Massachusetts were conspicuously devoted to industrial pursuits, as were Rhode Island and Connecticut each with at least 14 per cent of its population earning wages in manufacturing. By 1900 the above states were joined by Illinois, Ohio, and New Jersey, the gross value of whose manufactured products exceeded $600,000,000, and by New Hampshire, with 17 per cent of its population employed as wage earners in manufacturing. In 1940, with manufactures valued at more than $2,225,000,000, Michigan, California, and Indiana entered the ranks of the more conspicuously

industrial states. The selection of states with substantial industrial interests was based on data found in U.S. Census Office, *Manufactures of the United States in 1860; Compiled from the Original Returns of the Eighth Census under the Direction of the Secretary of the Interior* (Washington: Government Printing Office, 1865), p. 729; U.S. Census Office, *Twelfth Census of the United States Taken in the Year 1900* (Washington: Government Printing Office, 1902), VII, *Manufactures*, Part I, *United States by Industries*, pp. CVII, CLXXXII; U.S. Bureau of the Census, *Sixteenth Census of the United States: 1940, Manufactures: 1939* (Washington: Government Printing Office, 1942), III, *Reports for States and Outlying Areas*, p. 42 and *passim; Historical Statistics*, p. 13.

8. Charles R. Erdman, Jr., "Mahlon Dickerson," DAB, V, 289.

9. McKinney, "Seventy-seventh Congress," p. 73, minimizes her discovery that one out of six congressmen were or had been bank officers by observing: "Directors of banks are not always so closely associated with banking operations that they are aware of the technical problems or of the monetary considerations involved in sound banking, but their official connection with banks should make them sensitive to the pressures of financial organizations."

10. *Historical Statistics*, pp. 74–75.

11. Matthews, *U.S. Senators*, 14–16, finds smaller towns and cities "peculiarly fecund" in the production of post-World War II senators; and Hacker, "The Elected and the Anointed," pp. 540–41, reports that 1959 senators were "preponderantly provincial in origin."

12. Matthews, *U.S. Senators*, pp. 16–17, finds the same overrepresentation of small towns and cities, while Hacker, "The Elected and the Anointed," pp. 544–45, discovers that 1959 senators were relatively immobile (having moved a median distance of only twenty-two miles from their home-towns), tended to pursue their careers in their home-towns and, remained provincial in outlook.

13. *Historical Statistics*, p. 74.

14. The percentages are derived from tables in *Historical Statistics*, pp. 8, 10, 212. The number of college graduates before 1870 is not available.

15. David Outlaw to his wife, August 1, 1848, David Outlaw Papers, Southern Historical Collection, University of North Carolina. I am indebted to Grady McWhiney of the University of British Columbia for this citation.

16. Rothman, *Politics and Power*, p. 272. Employing these categories, I classified Thomas Bragg as coming from a substantial background.

17. Matthews, *U.S. Senators*, pp. 68 ff.

18. Quoted by Thomas P. Abernethy, "Richard Mentor Johnson," DAB,

X, 115. Allen Johnson,"Stephen Arnold Douglas,"*DAB*, V, 397–98, 401. William A. Robinson, "Hannibal Hamlin," *DAB*, VIII, 197. J. G. deR. Hamilton, "James Henry Hammond," *DAB*, VIII, 208. St.George L. Sioussat, "Andrew Johnson," *DAB*, X, 81–82.

19. Paul C. Phillips, "William Andrews Clark," *DAB*, IV, 145. Allan Nevins, "Thomas Collier Platt," *DAB*, XV, 5. Arthur C. Cole, "Marcus Alonzo Hanna," *DAB*, VIII, 227.

20. "Harry S Truman," *NCAB*, Current Vol. H, 2. Allen Johnson, "Stephen Arnold Douglas," *DAB*, V, 398. William A. Robinson, "William Pitt Fessenden," *DAB*, VI, 348. Matthews, *U.S. Senators*, pp. 92–94.

21. "Benjamin Ruggles," *NCAB*, XIII, 163. Quoted by Charles Moore, "Julius Caesar Burrows," *DAB*, III, 337. "Eugene Hale," *NCAB*, XX, 220. "Practically the dictator" is perhaps an exaggeration, but Hale was a member of the big 5 who ran the Fifty-sixth Senate.

22. William E. Leuchtenburg, "William Edgar Borah," *DAB*, XXII, 52.

23. George H. Haynes, "Charles Sumner," *DAB*, XVIII, 213.

24. Dumas Malone, "James Barbour," *DAB*, 1, 591. James M. Callahan, "Stephen Benton Elkins," *DAB*, VI, 84. "Robert Ferdinand Wagner," *NCAB*, 48, 5.

25. Quoted by J. G. deR. Hamilton, "James Henry Hammond," *DAB*, VIII, 208. Henry Clay, "Valedictory to the Senate: In Senate, March 31, 1842," in Calvin Colton, ed., *The Works of Henry Clay* ... (10 vols., New York: G. P. Putnam's Sons, 1904), IX, 353.

26. Francis Butler Simkins, "Benjamin Ryan Tillman," *DAB*, XVIII, 548.

27. Robert L. Meriwether, "John Gaillard," *DAB*, VII, 90–91. Quoted by Jeanette P. Nichols, "William Boyd Allison," *DAB*, 1, 221. Leo J. Meyer, "Orville Hitchcock Platt," *DAB*, XV, 2—3. Frederick Logan Paxson,"John Coit Spooner," *DAB*, XVII, 465–66. "Alben William Barkley," *NCAB*, 52, 688–89. "James Francis Byrnes," *NCAB*, Current Vol. G, 8–9. William B. Munro, "Henry Cabot Lodge," *DAB*, XI, 348.

28. Robert C. Brooks, "Boies Penrose," *DAB*, XIV, 449. Allan Nevins, "Thomas Collier Platt," *DAB*, XV, 6. W. C. Hunter, "Porter James McCumber," *DAB*, XXI, 526.

29. J. G. deR. Hamilton, "William Smith," *DAB*, XVII, 360. Joe L. Norris, "James Noble," *DAB*, XIII, 538. Elizabeth Breckenridge Ellis, "Jesse Burgess Thomas," *DAB*, XVIII, 437. William A. Robinson, "Isaac Tichenor," *DAB*, XVIII, 523. Quoted by Thomas P. Abernethy, "James Pleasants," *DAB*, XV, 7. Edith R. Blanchard, "William Hunter," *DAB*, IX, 407. Quoted by John D. Wade, "William McKendree Gwin, *DAB*, VIII, 65. Ulrich B. Phillips, "Robert Augustus

Toombs," *DAB*, XVIII, 590. A. Howard Meneely, "Benjamin Franklin Wade," *DAB*, XIX, 304. Allan Nevins, "Thomas Collier Platt," *DAB*, XV, 4. Melvin J. White, "Samuel Douglas McEnery," *DAB*, XII, 39. Henry J. Peterson, "Francis Emroy Warren," *DAB*, XIX, 472. Nathaniel Wright Stephenson, "Nelson Wilmarth Aldrich," *DAB*, I, 152. G. H. Mayer, "Ernest Lundeen," *DAB*, XXII, 395.

30. Roy F. Nichols, "William Bigler," *DAB*, II, 264. William A. Robinson, "William Pitt Fessenden," *DAB*, VI, 349. Quoted by Frederick Logan Paxson, "John Coit Spooner," *DAB*, XVII, 466. Quoted by John J. Dolan, "William Pinkney," *DAB*, XIV, 628.

31. Quoted by Melvin Johnson White, "James Brown," *DAB*, III, 126. Mark Twain (Samuel L. Clemens) and Charles Dudley Warner, *The Gilded Age: A Tale of Today* (New York: Harper and Row, 1929), pp. 28–29.

32. For the terms "Main Street" and "Broadway," I am indebted to Matthews, *U.S. Senators*, pp. 14–17.

33. Hacker, "The Elected and the Anointed," pp. 545–49.

34. Matthews, *U.S. Senators*, pp. 176–96.

35. For this idea and much of its phraseology, I am indebted to Bernard C. Hennessy of the Political Science Department of The Pennsylvania State University.

3

Immigration and Political Life

by **MICHAEL PARENTI**

The Reception

There are few nations that do not experience conflicts in their belief systems or disparity between a professed ideal and existing practice. The reception the United States historically has accorded the newcomer is a case in point. From its earliest days, America never quite succeeded in making up its mind about the immigrant. Writing to a group of Irish immigrants in 1783, George Washington articulated the humane sentiment: "The bosom of America is open to receive not only the Opulent and respectable Stranger, but the oppressed and persecuted of all Nations and Religions . . ."[1] Yet Washington proved less than consistent when he wrote to Adams: "My opinion, with respect to immigration, is that except of useful mechanics and some particular descriptions of men or professions, there is no need of encouragement . . . for [immigrants settled in a group] retain the language, habits and principles (good or bad) which they bring with them."[2] A similar ambivalence was betrayed by Jefferson who on one occasion spoke of "a home for the oppressed" and another time, in far less sanguine spirit, argued that immigrants would become "a

79

heterogeneous, incoherent, distracted mob," ready either to support despotic rulers or "imbibe principles of extreme licentiousness."[3]

For the next century and a half, America remained the asylum for "the huddled masses" and at the same time, the breeding ground for xenophobic diatribes and exclusionist agitation. In retrospect, the virulent nativist pressures of the nineteenth century accomplished surprisingly little. A sparsely populated country, seeking fulfillment of its manifest destiny through territorial expansion and industrial production, was not yet prepared to deny itself this ready and necessary supply of manpower. Free immigration, a practice existing since the beginning of the nation's history, was not easily discarded. But before the turn of the century, as an omen of things to come, Congress had restricted Chinese laborers. By the eve of World War I, the deep South and far West had become the most vociferous restrictionist regions. The twentieth century began with eugenics and the Nordic cult very much in vogue. Racist apprehensions had spread and the South and West felt no desire to contend with large masses of immigrant voters. Southeastern Europeans, often considered less than white, were seen as only adding to the threat already posed by Japanese, Chinese, and Negroes.[4]

Much of America found itself recoiling before the forces of a raw industrialism typified by the growth of trusts and giant corporations, the amassing of great fortunes for the few amidst continuing hardship for the many, and the spread of squalor, congestion, and poverty in old cities and new factory towns. The very tone and texture of community living, all that made life seem worthwhile, appeared to be threatened.

Well before the census of 1920 revealed that city-dwellers were the new majority, rural-white-Protestant America sought to maintain its superiority in race, religion, and politics. Highly visible because of their foreign attributes and vast numbers, the immigrants became the target for much of the rural resentment against the harsh and mindless upheavals of industrial America. Minority groups were undesirable, first, because of their alien qualities and, second, because they added to the size and power of the city and allegedly aggravated its worse features, viz., crime, corruption, and Catholicism.[5] Within the city, itself, the immigrant's presence only seemed to increase the survival hazards faced by urban workers. The American worker, too often finding himself odd man out in a tight job market "could see alien labor, content with a lower standard of living, taking over more and more of the work which American hands had formerly performed."[6] The immigration laws of 1921 and 1924 marked a decisive victory for exclusionist forces; the "national origins quota system" incorporated into law the popular myth of Anglo-Teutonic supremacy and southeastern European and nonwhite inferiority, reaffirmed and codified over a generation later in the McCarran-Walter Act. The floodgates were locked but the problems faced by the millions of newcomers who had already entered the United States were not as simply resolved.

Ethnic Consciousness

During the era of the great migrations, over 25 million people settled in this country, more than half of whom arrived between 1900 and 1914. By the end of World War I, immigrants and their children composed 38.4 per cent of the population, or more than one out of every three residents of the United States. About three-fourths of them lived in urban areas.[7] Preemption of the land by earlier nineteenth-century settlers is the reason usually offered to explain why millions of former peasants settled in cities rather than on farms. More likely, the immigrants chose the cities because they had little liking for the land, many of them having fled the oppressive, impoverished rural life of the old world to find fortune in the great cities across the ocean. For most, the very strangeness of their new surroundings caused them to huddle together, and out of necessity and desire, they chose the urban ghettoes. Of those who had the interest, the fortitude, and the capital needed for an agrarian venture, many found the isolated life of American farms, so different from the village life of European peasantry, to be insufferable. They soon returned to the initial urban settlement.[8]

During the early years in America, the first generation was without any real national identity, the predominant in-group feeling being *campanilismo* or provincialism. The Poznaniskers and Mazhevoers did not consider themselves natives of Poland. The Calabresians,

Neapolitans, and Sicilians were more cognizant of their provincial antagonisms than of a national bond. German Jews stood aloof from the Sephardim and from the Ashkenazim who, themselves, were subdivided by various regional Yiddish identities. Provincialism was the spirit among those who came from Greece, Albania, Syria, Lithuania, Portugal, Estonia, Armenia, Serbia, Bohemia, and almost all other regions in Europe.[9] Neighborhoods and fraternal societies were organized along lines of provincial consanguinity. Writing of the Greeks, Theodor Saloutos describes a situation characteristic of most immigrant groups: "It appeared that every village and minute parish in Greece was represented in the United States by a society with an impressive array of banners, lengthy constitutions and high sounding names. . . . This plethora of organizations unfortunately tended to breed suspicion, mutual antagonism, aloofness, stubbornness, and 'do it alone' attitude. They helped to isolate members from strangers and to divide Greek from Greek."[10]

With the passage of time, regional prejudices were slowly submerged in the common problems of acculturation. Thrown together in crowded urban neighborhoods, the former provincials experienced a degree of intermingling unknown in the far-flung regions of the old world. Foreign language newspapers appeared written in the national tongue rather than in some regional dialect. Contacts with the American world emphasized to the immigrant his kinship with compatriots who, regardless of provincial differences, were in many ways closer to him than were other people. Defamatory epithets and discriminatory practices were applied democratically to all the group's members by a host society indifferent to provincial distinctions.

While ethnic identity expanded to include broader reference groups, ethnic subculture shrank in the face of new world conditions and exigencies. The immigrant cultures are said to have become part of a unique American blend. If, in fact, there was a "melting pot," it more often was intended to operate as a "smelting furnace . . . to burn out the alien culture elements like slag from the pure metal of American culture."[11] The contributions of the newcomers were substantial when measured in terms of manpower, talent, and occupational skills, but there seems little reason to assume they contributed greatly of their original cultures. A distinction should be drawn between the considerable impact made by ethnics as individuals and the extremely modest impact of minority cultures on established Anglo-American norms. Since the early days of the Republic, the dominion of Anglo-American cultural styles, roles, values, law, and language has never seriously been threatened. Certainly a structured, ongoing American culture was clearly visible to de Tocqueville in the 1830s. With few exceptions, as the immigrants and their children made their contributions as laborers, farmers, doctors, lawyers, and educators, they did so on terms set by the dominant culture. The inability to acculturate, that is, to adopt the necessary social and linguistic skills of the Anglo-American world, severely limited any advancement or participation within that world.[12]

Not only were the immigrants unable to exert substantial influence on American culture, they failed to preserve their own cultures. America has never been a patchwork of autonomous cultural enclaves.[13] Nearly every group arriving in this country attempted to reconstruct their old-world communities. With the exception of a few isolated sectarian groups, such as the Amish they failed.[14] If culture is to be represented as the accumulated styles, solutions, and practices that represent a society's total adjustment to its physical and social environment, then it would follow that no specific cultural system can be uprooted and transplanted to another environment without some substantial change. After the shock of departing from old world communities immigrants were confronted with an established American culture possessing indigenous forms differing in many respects from their own.[15] The newcomers faced heavy social pressure to conform, the instruments of conformity becoming ever more efficient with the growth of industrialization, mass communication, and public education. Some in-group norms and residual subcultural patterns have survived, but immigrant cultures as self-contained systemic entities began to disintegrate soon after the initial settlement. Certainly by the second generation, valuations, work habits, family life, consumption and recreational patterns, material goals, language and political loyalties assumed an unmistakably American stamp, reflecting the new-world diversity of class, income, and locale more faithfully than the old-world diversity of cultures.

If the national minorities were unable to preserve their respective cultural autonomies, does this mean they were indistinguishably absorbed into American society? Were such the case, ethnic groups would have hardly earned the attention accorded them by historians, sociologists, and politicians. Industrialization, the mass media, public education, urbanization, and suburbanization imposed a uniform imprint on the lives of nationality groups, but ethnic feelings persisted. Thus half a century after immigration, distinct minority ecological and identificational patterns are still discernible. The national minorities may have adapted themselves to the American practices available to them within the boundaries of their class and locale, but they usually have remained in close associational and social contact with others of their kind. In neighborhood, marriage, extended kinship relations, recreational and peer group activities, church and formal organizations, even at work or school or in the sectarian hospital, old age home and, finally, the sectarian cemetery, the ethnic could live and die within the confines of his group, and many of them did.[16] Whereas acculturation moved rapidly toward American norms, assimilation—that is, actual interpersonal social integration—developed much less certainly.[17]

There are several explanations for the tenacity of in-group awareness. The limitations of social distance and the natural range of interpersonal exposure inevitably brought the immigrant and the second-generation offspring into closer and more frequent contact with other group members. Early life experiences and contacts with the wider world often left ethnics with a preference for those of similar backgrounds. Frequently the group, itself, as personified by family and friends, discouraged intimate associations with people of different stock. At one time or another, spokesmen for most minority groups have expressed their fear of extinction through assimilation. Frequently, even the socially mobile member, because of family attachments and other such positive sentiments, preserved a strong identification with his group even though he had no contact with, and little knowledge of, the old culture. In a mass society often described as threatened by a "lack of belongingness" and "alienation," an ethnic identity, something larger than the self yet smaller than the nation, is not without its attractions. Finally, and most importantly, the native population, whilst insisting that nationality groups "Americanize," a process entailing the destruction of customs and appearances offensive to native sensibilities, never manifested an equally persistent desire to see the ethnics enter Anglo-American primary group life. And few things so effectively assured the persistency of in-group awareness as out-group rejection. "When the natives combined to crush what they considered the undue influence of alien groups," Hansen observes, "they committed a tactical error, for the newcomers, far from being crushed, were prompted to consolidate their hitherto scattered forces."[18]

Frequently the intolerant host society was not composed of native white Protestants but of another ethnic group, especially in the urban centers. Generally the old-stock Yankee opinion of the Irish became very much the Irish opinion of the Italians and the Italian opinion of the Puerto Ricans. Each group saw the succeeding newcomers as "trying to take over," "lowering our standards," and "refusing to Americanize." This willingness to embrace the conventional discriminatory attitudes toward other groups is partly an expected consequence of becoming American, or wanting to become American by assuming the posture of the dominant culture and identifying with those who "belong," even at the expense of less fortunate groups. Bigotry among minorities reflected with disheartening accuracy an awareness of the pecking order accorded minority groups in American society.[19] In their treatment of each other, minorities proved themselves to be no more virtuous and no less American than the native-born.

Class Consciousness

The immigrants and their children provided much of the market and the labor for the increasing services, trades, and crafts and for the titanic industrial growth America has experienced since the late nineteenth century. "We built this country" has been claimed, at one time or another, by almost every group of substantial size, and perhaps with good cause. For those who crossed the Atlantic soon became grist for the industrial mill, paying more than their full measure of misery and deprivation. Crowded into filthy and dilapidated tenements, living without privacy, sunlight, or elemental sanitary conditions, the immigrant and his children toiled from dawn to dusk in sweatshops, "crouched over their work, in a fetid air . . . hunger-hollowed faces" and "shoulders narrowed with consumption, girls of fifteen as old as grandmothers, who had never eaten a bit of meat in their lives;" ". . . heavy brooding men, tired anxious women, thinly dressed, unkempt little girls, and frail, joyless lads passed along, half awake, not uttering a word, as they hurried to the factories."[20] The work was filthy, exhausting, noisy, mindless, endless and often dangerous; rarely a day passed in large factories when a man was not killed or severely maimed because of inadequate safety conditions.

Yet if proletariat misery was the lot of most, a militant proletariat consciousness was not the corresponding ideological response. Nor was there much trace of reforming zeal in the ethnic population. The same barriers that made the native-born eschew contacts with the immigrants left the latter indifferent to social action programs. Indeed, the immigrants were more often the victims than the benefactors, more often the targets than the allies of reform movements. Middle-class reformers concerned with moral uplifting of public and private life, the abolition of corruption, the extension of civil service, and the destruction of the urban party machine offered little to the nationality groups. The immigrant communities and most of the foreign language press were lukewarm or even hostile toward Populism, urban Progressivism, women's suffrage, Negro rights, Prohibition, and in many instances, trade unionism.[21]

Even when, as with socialism, intentions were of the best and protest directed itself to the objective material conditions of urban workers, other sociocultural and psychological forces militated against change. The socialist movement of the early twentieth century, a melange of reformers, muckrackers, populists, Marxists, syndical-ists, and a handful of Social Gospel Christians and millionaire converts, was brought to the height of its appeal—and 897,000 votes—in 1912 by Eugene Victor Debs. "Far from being an exotic aberration or an imported disease like parrot fever," socialism was an indigenous movement.[22] There is no denying that some immigrants played a prominent role in the radical protest. Of the socialist publications before World War I, there were five English and eight foreign-language dailies, 262 English weeklies, and thirty-six foreign-language weeklies.

The left wing of the movement found much of its support in the Bolshevik-oriented foreign language federation, especially among coteries of Jews, Russians, and other Slavs.

But those who did respond to the left were a minority of the great mass of immigrants and their children. The linguistic, ethnic, and social distances between the native-born socialist and the ghetto worker were not easily overcome. While pertinent to the ethnic's class condition, the ideology of the left did not easily fit into his *Weltanschauung*. Suspicious of much beyond the home or beyond the ethnic community, tradition-bound and fearful of authority, sometimes entreprenurial in his aspirations if proletariat in his predicament, longing for security, stability, and gain rather than sacrifice and agitation, the immigrant peasant from Europe was not the best political material.

Furthermore, the immigrants, largely Catholic, often shared the hierarchy's suspicion and hostility toward all workers' movements. "Several bishops grew to think of labor unions as socialistic and therefore to be condemned as subversive of the Church and society."[23] While the Church eventually did condone membership in nonsocialistic trade unions, Catholic thought at the turn of the century reflected a "great terror of socialism."[24] Far from intensifying class consciousness with injections of alien radicalism, a favorite xenophobic nightmare of the native stock, the minorities gave the American left little cause for its earlier high anticipations. The failure of American working-class radicalism is at least partly ascribable to the unresponsiveness of the ethnic masses.

According to Marxist theory, the necessary prerequisite of a proletariat movement is some sense of class interest and identification, which eventually leads to cohesive and militant class action. But such a theory anticipates a working class enjoying a common national culture and common history. In the pluralistic cacophany that developed in America, nativist workers opposed immigrants, and immigrants opposed other immigrants. Just as warfare in Europe turned more on struggles between nations and between national groups than upon a class conflict transcending national boundaries, so in America, more thought and energy were expended on divisive interethnic competitions for jobs, neighborhoods, social standing, and group recognition than was ever directed toward the development of a common class identity. Another man was more likely to be seen as a Polack, kike, dago, mick, or hunkie than as a fellow worker in the proletariat cause. (It might be noted parenthetically that in the nativist South, relatively untouched by immigration, racial animosities served a similar and perhaps even more decisive regressive function by playing off lower class whites against blacks, thereby aborting Southern Populism.)[25]

Not only did the various national groups conflict with each other, but, as noted earlier, the provincial segmentations that obtained with any one group through much of the first generation made concerted effort that much more unlikely.[26] Old world animosities were reenacted on the new soil, newly developed intergroup bigotries arose, and ethnic associational differences persisted making for a highly vertically stratified urban population. Under such conditions of intra- and inter-ethnic cleavage, the forces of industrialization, urbanization, and political protest were not sufficiently potent to achieve a militant class consciousness. Indeed, to the extent that the minorities Americanized, it was in the direction of American bourgeois standards and valuations.[27]

Finally, to borrow a phrase from psychology, it might be said that the immigrant worker lacked a sufficient "future-orientation." Under the socialist state to come, social equality and material well-being would be secured, but meanwhile, who would alleviate the urgent plight of the immigrant family? Who would give a helping hand now? It may be for this reason alone that the minorities bypassed the future glories of the Internationale for the more immediate emoluments of Tammany Hall.

Political Life

In the period from 1875 to 1940, millions migrated to these shores, became regular voters, and raised millions of children who also became regular voters. In this same period the urban political machine flourished as never before, or since. "Once the immigrant base finally began to disappear," Cornwell observes, "so did most of the bosses of the dependent upon the other."[28] Immigration is not the sole factor in classic model. In a very real sense, then, the one phenomenon was the rise and decline of urban political machines but it is doubtful that the old-style bosses, dependent as they were on an acquiescent and pliable mass base, could have prevailed for so long without a supply of succeeding waves of impoverished culturally alienated, socially unequipped, nonideological—but swiftly enfranchised—immigrants.

Although most students of urban politics recognize the contributions made by the city machines, popular perception to this day is still largely colored by the excoriations of muckrakers and early civic reformers.[29] In E. E. Schattschneider's words "power, patronage and plunder" were the boss's exclusive *raison d'être*.[30] Proponents of this view either pity the nationality groups for being dupes or chastise them for being the accomplices of a corrupt system. Moral judgments, however, should not preclude analytic explanations. That the immigrant became the boss's ready collaborator was due less to venality than to necessity. We must remind ourselves of that extraordinary time in American history, when millions of indigent aliens were literally dumped onto our city streets without the barest provision made for their settlement, employment, or survival. Inadequate or, more often, nonexistent public services and chaotic antiquated governmental structure were the most distinguishing features of earlier municipalities.

In an era of ruthless, boundless capitalism, enfeebled unionism, limited and often discriminatory private charity,[31] and indifferent and insufficient government, the only social agency that filled the vacuum and answered to the pressing needs of a large dependent population was the political machine. Jobs, housing, emergency relief, minor welfare services, personal favors, outings and other recreational activities, and instant naturalization were among the services performed by the party organization.[32] In return the immigrant only too gratefully lent his support to organization candidates. In terms of the services performed, the fee exacted was not an unreasonable one. The relationship was more symbiotic than exploitative.

If the party's voting resources came from the ethnic population, its financial resources were siphoned from the public treasury and from the sale of municipal properties, permits, licenses, and contracts to the business community for a variety of legal and sometimes illegal enterprises. As broker for the businessman and patron of the ethnic, the political machine used its political power to extract financial support, and its financial power to win political support.[33] It was probably this system that prompted Frederic Schuman to describe politics as that process whereby the politician gets money from the rich and votes from the poor on the promise that he will protect each from the other.

The result was a crude, inefficient, and frequently corrupt improvization of a social welfare system, involving a minor redistribution of income. As in most welfare systems, the lower-strata groups paid a good part of the expenses in the form of widely diffused taxes and in the costs that business passed on to the consumer. But such cost was not readily discernible, whereas the particular and personalized benefits allocated by the district captain were highly visible and readily appreciated.

To treat only the material services, however, is to overlook other important functions performed by the local political system. In a world of threatening, faceless forces, the political club was a friend. Even for those individuals who did not materially benefit, and even in instances when the local politician could not perform a miracle, the fact that there was someone to go to who cared enough to listen and "look into it" was no small comfort. Most of the activities that district leaders considered of the utmost importance, such as attending funerals, putting in a good word with the judge, offering moral support, knowing people personally, complimenting people, inquiring about family illnesses, reminding constituents that you are available if ever needed and keeping "your door open at all times," were explicitly designed to maximize this sheltering, comforting role of the politico.[34] Many social institutions afford a sense of security by "just being there" and enjoy a good portion of their support on this account; the political club was—and in some areas still is—a case in point.

Furthermore, in facilitating naturalization, inducing electoral participation, and conferring a citizen's identity upon the immigrant and his children, the party hastened political acculturation. The politico, himself, was sometimes aware of this function, as erstwhile Tammany chieftain, Richard Crocker, testified:

> More than one half [of the people of New York] are of foreign birth. . . . They do not speak our language, they do not know our laws, they are the raw material with which we have to build up the state. . . . There is no denying the service which Tammany has rendered to the Republic. There is no such organization for taking hold of the untrained, friendless man and converting him into a citizen. Who else would do it if we did not? . . . There is not a mugwump in the city who would shake hands with him.[35]

Election campaigns, voting, and friendly contacts with the political club gave the ethnic some small sense of participation and practice as an American, some tenuous feeling that his voice counted with the powers that be, and some claim to legitimacy and equal status.

For over a century, nativists' anxieties rested on the unexamined presumption that immigrants and their offspring would be slow to discard foreign loyalties and unwilling to attach themselves to American symbols and institutions. As late as 1914, there were officials who believed that the United States could never intervene in the European conflict without bringing on a civil war between the large German and English elements in our population.[36] In war or peace, the minorities were suspect. The danger of contamination and subversion from alien ideologies remained an historical preoccupation. Palmer raids, alien deportation, denaturalization, surveillance, detention, and culturally intolerant federal, state, and local programs for the propagation of "100 per cent Americanism" were symptomatic of this phobia.[37] Yet, ironically enough, no other nation has ever absorbed such a vast number of foreigners and their children with so little challenge to its basic unity. The ethnics internalized a loyalty to the core political symbols, values, and institutions of the American polity. One of the factors determining the positive identification to the political system was the political system itself. Political life is seldom a merely dependent variable. Without the grass roots, egalitarian, and inclusive features of American politics it is difficult to imagine what course minority loyalties and political activity might have taken.

As part of its assimilative function, the political club served as an avenue of upward mobility for some of the more ambitious sons of immigrants.[38] Andrew Hacker reminds us that "it is only since 1940 that banks, investment houses, the diplomatic service and established industries and universities have opened their positions of power and responsibility to others than those of old American antecedents. Twenty years ago Americans of Irish, Italian, Slav and Jewish antecedents were simply not recruited, admitted or welcomed."[39] Until these new social areas were opened, opportunities for ethnic upward mobility were largely confined to the worlds of sports, entertainment, marginal service trades, the rackets, and politics. Seen in this light, the "balanced ticket," so often bemoaned as un-American because it gave more weight to the candidate's tribal identity than to his other qualifications, could not have been more American. What better way of getting ahead? And what firmer assurance of the group's Americanism, social respectability, legitimacy, and worth than acession to positions of power, prominence, and public responsibility. If the old stock did not see it that way, at least the nationality groups did.

An analysis of immigrant political life usually begins and ends with a discussion of the big-city machine. Nationality groups, however, played a crucial role in national politics by lending massive support to federal decision-makers who were more responsive to the problems of an urban industrialized society than to the images and myths of an agrarian or laissez-faire past. The 1928 election gave the first clear sign that something new was happening in national politics. The defeat, in the Democratic party, of the forces of prohibitionism, western ruralism, and Protestant old-stock respectability, and fundamentalist bigotry, by the big-city, wet, Irish-Catholic Al Smith, a lower East Side emissary of the sidewalk masses, was symbolic of the emergence of a new generation, and was the inevitable reflection of "a little matter of birth rates."[40]

The thirteen million foreigners who arrived in America between 1900 and 1914 began their political participation in growing numbers after the first world war. Their children, whose numbers were substantially greater, were to reach voting age in full force between 1930 and 1940. Smith gleaned the early benefits of this demographic upsurge.

He laid the foundation for a new coalition within the Democratic party, shifting the center of gravity from the rural South and West to the big cities of the industrial North.[41] Until 1928, the Northeast had the most consistent Republican record and the greatest number of foreign-born. After 1928, this same region harbored many of the most heavily concentrated Democratic counties in the nation. Smith was a catalyst for that "other half" of America. His emergence as a presidential candidate stirred a new sense of political consciousness in millions of minority-group members, and was for them a symbolic affirmation of their own personal worth and a refutation of their marginal status.

If the personal appeal of Al Smith was not enough in 1928, the expanding ranks of second-generation voters and a catastrophic depression were sufficient to bring the Democratic party to power four years later. The New Deal era saw a changing social temper in the nation : a new class militancy born of despair and depression coupled with a widespread hostility toward the financial-industrial powers that seemed to have brought America to ruin. It was during this time that the first significant steps were taken toward ending the long-standing ethnic divisions among American workers.[42] The day was passing when mining companies could place groups of different nationalities in each mine in the correct assumption that a work force segmented along ethnic lines would be difficult to organize. "Much of the A. F. of L.'s reluctance to embark on a real organizing drive in the mass production industries," Lubell notes, "reflected the dislike of the 'aristocrats of labor' in the skilled crafts for the immigrant 'rubbish'."[43] With the encouragement of a friendly Administration in Washington, and the passage of the NRA, particularly section 7a recognizing the workers' right to organize, industry-wide unionization of unskilled workers began. The conservative craft unions, which had so long monopolized and constricted the field of organized labor, now had to contend with an industrial unionism that brought large numbers of native and ethnic workers under the same banner. The acculturated second generation was coming into its own; in earlier years immigrants might have been used as strikebreakers, but more and more of their American-born sons were joining the CIO.

The regional and ethnic considerations of previous elections now shared the political stage with a growing class feeling. The 1936 election saw a realignment in both parties. Always more favorably disposed toward the party of Coolidge and Hoover, large propertied and financial interests moved with even greater solidarity than usual into the Republican camp, while urban workers of all regions and ethnic identities rallied in still greater numbers to Roosevelt's support. But the heavy pluralities of the urban-ethnic masses in the great cities formed the center phalanx of the Democratic coalition. In retrospect, the year 1928 marks the last victory of small-town, old-stock Protestant America.

Conclusion

This essay has attempted to investigate the ways in which the late immigration was and was not consequential to American life. Here we might summarize some of the central propositions:

Contrary to popular thought, immigrants contributed only a negligible element of their original cultures to an ongoing cultural system established well before their arrival. There is little evidence to support the myth of a "melting pot." The "alien cultural challenge" existed more in the fearful anticipations of the native population than in reality. By the same token, contrary to nativist phobic preoccupations, the newcomers did not contaminate America with alien political radicalism. During their acculturation, they developed a positive identity to American core political symbols and institutions, and a loyalty to the American nation, demonstrated in both war and peace. Their general political orientation betrayed a marked social conservatism. While popular anxiety has concentrated on the potentially centrifugal effects of aliens and alien loyalties, the remarkable fact is that this nation did absorb so many millions in the span of a generation with no serious challenge to its basic unity.

Although the old world cultures did not survive as systemic entities much beyond the immigrant first generation, identificational pluralism persisted into the second and even the third generations. Even as the minorities considered themselves loyal Americans, they retained their ethnic identifications with a tenacity that may be as much attributable to the bigotry encountered beyond the group as to the attachments and enjoyments experienced within the group. At the very time exploitation of immigrant labor was most ruthlessly practiced, intergroup conflicts with the native-born or with other minority groups had the effect of retarding the ethnic's class consciousness and class protest. In short, ethnic in-group attachments and intergroup rivalries worked to the detriment of lower-strata material interests.

The popular view that the nationality groups were to blame for the political strength of urban political machines is correct insofar as any group might be "blamed" for lending massive support to the one agency that performed a variety of material and psychological functions on its behalf. The view that the city machines retarded the Americanization of the nationality groups seems to have little basis in fact and rests mainly on unexamined moral judgments. What evidence we have indicates that the local clubs fostered the political acculturation of minority groups in a variety of ways.[44] The political parties hastened the political education and experience of the minorities, while the political system in general became an arena for the maximization of ethnic interests, and the realm in which the marginal minorities could challenge the hegemony of established Protestant America.

We are left with the conclusion that the major impact the immigrants and their children have had on American life is to be measured in terms of their numbers, labor, and votes rather than in terms of their alleged old world ideologies or new world corruptions. As workers, consumers, and city-dwellers, the minorities contributed massively to an industrialization that transformed America from a rural to an urban civilization. As voters they gave strategic support to an era of federal activism, thereby helping to move the nation toward new public commitments. The transition from antiquated laissez faire capitalism to the reality of social welfare programs is not over; in many ways it is only beginning.

NOTES

1. Quoted in Maldwyn Allen Jones, *American Immigration* (Chicago: University of Chicago Press, 1960), p. 79.

2. *The Writings of George Washington*, W. C. Ford (ed.) (vol. 12, New York: Putnam, 1889), p. 489.

3. Jones, *American Immigration*, pp. 80–81.

4. See John Higham, *Strangers in the Land: Patterns of American Nativism 1860–1925* (New Brunswick: Rutgers University Press, 1955); "American Immigration Policy in Historical Perspective," *Law and Contemporary Problems*, 21, 1956, 213–35. See also Ray Allen Billington, *The Protestant Crusade, 1800–1860* (Chicago: Quadrangle Books, 1964), Chap. 16. Oscar Handlin, however, suggests that the South's failure to attract the new immigrants to buttress its white population and diminish its dependency on black labor is what turned the region against immigration. See *The American People in the Twentieth Century* (rev. ed., Boston: Beacon Press, 1963), p. 102.

5. For a discussion of such sentiments during the Populist and Progressive eras, see Richard Hofstadter, *The Age of Reform, From Bryan to F.D.R.* (New York: Random House, 1955). For other analyses of the anti-urban, anti-immigrant sentiment see Alan P. Grimes, *Equality in America: Religion, Race and the Urban Majority* (New York: Oxford University Press, 1964), pp. 89–129. Numerous present-day community studies have noted the persistence of this conviction that cities were un-American, corrupt, and foreign. See for instance, A. J. Vidich and J. Bensman, *Small Town in Mass Society* (Garden City: Doubleday, 1960), Chap. 2.

6. Billington, *Crusade*, p. 322.

7. E. P. Hutchinson, *Immigrants and Their Children, 1850–1950* (New York: John Wiley, 1956), Chaps. 1, 2. In some of the northeastern cities, first and second generation ethnics composed anywhere from 60 to 75 per cent of the population.

8. Cf. Federal Writers Project, *The Italians of New York* (New York: Random House, 1938). Theodore Saloutos, *The Greeks in the United States* (Cambridge: Harvard University Press, 1964).

9. Handlin, *American People*, Chap. 10. Jones, *American Immigration*, pp. 135–36. W. I. Thomas and F. Zananiecki, *The Polish Peasant in Europe and America* (Boston: Badger, 1918–1920), vol. 2. Nathan Glazer, *American Judaism* (Chicago: University of Chicago Press, 1957).

10. Saloutos, *The Greeks*, pp. 75–76. See also W. L. Warner and Leo Srole, *The Social System of American Ethnic Groups* (New Haven: Yale University Press, 1945), p. 165.

11. Peter Munch, "Social Adjustments Among Wisconsin Norwegians," *American Sociological Review*, 14 (December, 1949), 780.

12. See Milton M. Gordon, *Assimilation in American Life* (New York: Oxford University Press, 1964). For an impressive listing of immigrants and their children who have made notable contributions to American science, medicine,

letters, music, and art see John H. Burma, "Some Cultural Aspects of Immigration," *Law and Contemporary Problems*, 21 (1956), 213–35.

13. See Gordon, *Assimilation*.

14. Even the Amish, for all their extraordinary measures to insulate themselves, are not free from the wider forces of cultural diffusion and change. See John A. Hostetter, *Amish Society* (Baltimore: John Hopkins Press, 1963), pp. 284–325.

15. In one way or another, all major historical and sociological studies of immigration and ethnicity document or take account of the existence of a dominant American core culture. To cite but a few: Oscar Handlin, *Boston's Immigrants, A Study in Acculturation* (Cambridge: Harvard University Press, rev. ed., 1959); E. V. Stonequist, *The Marginal Man, A Study in Personality and Culture Conflict* (New York: Scribners, 1937); Thomas and Zananiecki, *Polish Peasant*; Warner and Srole, *Social System*; a recent work, which demonstrates the remarkable degree of historical continuity in American culture since the Revolution is Seymour M. Lipset, *The First New Nation* (New York: Basic Books, 1963).

16. Gordon, *Assimilation*, esp, Chaps. 2 and 7. August B. Hollingshead, "Trends in Social Stratification: A Case Study," *American Sociological Review*, 17 (1952), 685*f*. Stanley Lieberson, "Suburbs and Ethnic Residential Patterns," *American Journal of Sociology*, 67 (1962), 673–81.

17. The analytic importance of differentiating between changes in cultural systems and changes in social systems has been discussed by Talcott Parsons, *The Social System* (New York: The Free Press, 1951). For its application to the study of ethnic groups see Eric Rosenthal, "Acculturation without Assimilation?" *American Journal of Sociology* (November, 1960), 275–88; also Gordon, *Assimilation*.

18. Marcus Lee Hansen, *The Immigrant in American History* (New York: Harper and Row, 1964 ed.), p. 136.

19. Cf. Samuel Tenebaum, *Why Men Hate* (New York: Beechhurst Press, 1947), pp. 169–76. Handlin, *The American People*, pp. 104–105.

20. From eye-witness descriptions of Jewish, Italian and Polish immigrants quoted in Frederick Lewis Allen, *The Big Change* (New York: Bantam Books, 1961), pp. 51–55. See also the contemporary report provided in Oscar Handlin (ed.), *Immigration as a Factor in American History* (Englewood Cliffs: Prentice Hall, 1959), pp. 64–65.

21. Hansen, *Immigrant*, pp. 80–92. Jones, *American Immigration*, pp. 230–33, 314–15.

22. See Irving Howe and Lewis Coser, *The American Communist Party, A*

Critical History (New York: Praeger, 1962), chap. 1; the quotation is from p. 1. See also Ray Ginger, *The Bending Cross* (New Brunswick: Rutgers University Press, 1949).

23. Henry J. Browne, "Catholicism," in James Ward Smith and A. Leland Jameson (eds.), *The Shaping of American Religion* (Princeton: Princeton University Press, 1961), pp. 72–121.

24. *Ibid.*, pp. 98–99.

25. C. Van Woodward, *The Strange Career of Jim Crow* (New York: Oxford University Press, 1957).

26. Cf. John S. MacDonald and Leatrice D. MacDonald, "Urbanization, Ethnic Groups, and Social Segmentation," *Social Research*, 29 (1962), 433–48.

27. Cf. Nathan Glazer and Daniel P. Moynihan, *Beyond the Melting Pot* (Cambridge: M. I. T. Press, 1963), *passim*.

28. Elmer E. Cornwell, Jr., "Bosses, Machines and Ethnic Groups," *The Annals of the American Academy of Political and Social Science*, 353 (May, 1964), 28.

29. Journalists still fall back on the most stereotyped notions of "machine bosses"; see Theodore White, *The Making of A President, 1960* (New York: Pocket Books, 1961). Even scholars cannot always hide their moral disapproval when discussing political machines and their relationships with ethnic groups; see Louis L. Gerson, *The Hyphenate in Recent American Politics and Diplomacy* (Lawrence: University of Kansas Press, 1964), esp. the foreword by G. Lowell Field.

30. E. E. Schattschneider, *Party Government* (New York: Holt, Rinehart and Winston, 1942), Chaps. 7, 8.

31. Cf. Marvin E. Gettleman, "Charity and Social Classes in the United States, 1874–1900," *The American Journal of Economics and Sociology*, 22 (April and July, 1963), 313–29, 417–26.

32. The classic description of this role is by Tammany Hall's self-styled philosopher, George Washington Plunkitt. See William L. Riordan, *Plunkitt of Tammany Hall* (New York: E. P. Dutton, 1963). For an excellent, if brief, description of the social functions of the urban machine see Fred I. Greenstein, *The American Party System and the American People* (Englewood Cliffs: Prentice-Hall, 1963), Chap. 4.

33. Greenstein, *ibid.* See also William C. Harvard, "From Bossism to Cosmopolitanism: Changes in the Relation of Urban Leadership to State Politics," *The Annals of the American Academy of Political and Social Science*, 353 (May, 1964), 84–94.

34. Cf. Riordan, *Plunkitt.* For depth studies of second-generation individuals

see Michael Parenti, "Ethnic and Political Attitudes, A Depth Study of Italian Americans," (Ph.D. dissertation, Yale University, 1962).

35. Quoted by Arthur Mann in his introduction to Riordan, "Attitudes," p. xix.

36. Ernest R. May, *The World War and American Isolation, 1914–1917* (Cambridge: Harvard University Press, 1959). Woodrow Wilson is quoted as saying: "We definitely have to be neutral since otherwise our mixed populations would wage war on each other." Gerson, *Hyphenate*, p. 51.

37. See Robert K. Murray, *Red Scare, A Study in National Hysteria 1919–1920* (New York: McGraw-Hill, 1964 ed.). Milton R. Konitz, *Civil Rights in Immigration* (Ithaca: Cornell University Press, 1953); and Jack Wasserman, "Some Defects in the Administration of Our Immigration Laws," *Law and Contemporary Problems*, 21 (1956), 376–81.

38. Elmer E. Cornwell, "Party Absorption of Ethnic Groups: The Case of Providence, Rhode Island," *Social Forces*, 38 (1960), 205–10. "Bosses, Machines," *Annals*, for data on the political mobility of New York's ethnic groups. Samuel Lubell, *The Future of American Politics* (Garden City: Doubleday, 1956, rev. ed.), Chap. 4.

39. Andrew Hacker, "Liberal Democracy and Social Control," in L. J. Fein (ed.), *American Democracy, Essays on Image and Realities* (New York: Holt, Rinehart and Winston, 1964), p. 116, originally published in the *American Political Science Review*, December, 1957.

40. Lubell, *American Politics*, pp. 29–43.

41. Despite his defeat, Smith broke the Republican hold on the cities, swinging 122 northern counties out of the GOP column, 77 of which were predominantly urban Catholic. *Ibid.*, pp. 35–37.

42. For an analysis of the electoral results of the 1932 contest see Roy V. Peel and Thomas C. Donnelly, *The 1932 Campaign* (New York: Holt, Rinehart and Winston, 1935); and Harold F. Gosnell, *Champion Campaigner: Franklin D. Roosevelt* (New York: MacMillan, 1952).

43. Lubell, *American Politics*, p. 49. Jones, *Immigration*, pp 236 ff. It should be noted that the native born who made up the AFL membership were not exclusively Anglo-Saxon. The rank and file was often composed of ethnics of an earlier immigrant stock who wished to avoid association with those still further down the ladder.

44. At present, this task of political acculturation is still being carried on by urban politicians among recent southern Negro and Puerto Rican migrants in northern cities. See Robert A. Low, "A Councilman Serves His Constituents," unpublished monograph. Low is Democrat-Liberal Councilman of the twenty-second district in Manhattan.

4

The Negro's Response: A Study in Desperation

by **ANN LANE**

All social systems create elaborate and often tortured justifications of their least justifiable features, but the American creed and myths seem further removed from reality than most. While most ideologies juggle the truth, ours often appears to turn it upside down. Not surprisingly, the most oppressed portions of our society are frequently among the most deceived, that is, among the most willing to accept with passion all the myths that least apply to them. The economically secure Negro is still reeling from the incisive characterization by E. Franklin Frazier in *Black Bourgeoisie*.[1] Frazier's evaluation is clear in the very organization of the book: the position of the Negro middle class is discussed under the rubric "The World of Reality;" the middle-class view of itself and the world is discussed under the rubric "The World of Make-Believe." The Negro college student, the Negro journalist, even the Negro worker have been acidly sketched by critical viewers as being largely committed to, as well as products and victims of, the American dream. The less the American dream applies, the more it is defended by the very persons to whom it least applies.[2]

Much has been said, and said so often that everyone knows it to be

100

true, that with the great migration from the farm to the city, the American Negro joined industrial America. With that important move he began the slow but assuredly constant climb up the ladder of success. If he had more obstacles than others to overcome, he now, with the aid of a sympathetic federal government and a nation growing in compassion and intelligence, is on his way to sharing in the Great Society, the current and democratized version of Mark Twain's Great Barbecue.

This evaluation does, in fact have some truth. The great migration did occur. Within a period of less than one lifetime, from 1910 to 1960, the Negro has been transformed from a largely rural to a largely urban resident. In 1960 Negroes were more highly urbanized than whites. Such a change is of great moment. Even the isolation of a ghetto existence is a significant improvement over the isolation imposed by a rural life. Before 1915 the Negroes' thinking had little connection with politics. After entering the industrial world, they were able to make contact with the political one.[3] Even after the urbanization of the Negro had begun, W. E. B. Du Bois accurately claimed, in 1935,: "... There is not another group of twelve million people in the midst of a modern culture who has been so widely inhibited and mentally confined" as the American Negro.[4]

The significance of the urbanization of the American Negro is that it provided the possibility for him to see the world as it really is: not a particularly better world than it had been before, but a more truthful one. And with that perspective it is possible to build a better world. With the urbanization of the Negro came the potentiality for recognizing the depth of his conflicts with white America. While he was so far away from testing the American dream, he clung to it. Now that he can see it close up, he is beginning to recoil.

The recently published study, The Negro American,[5] the most comprehensive work of its type since Gunnar Myrdal's An American Dilemma, which was published in 1944, provides many valuable insights. It has been criticized as being "limited to the establishment,"[6] which much of it is. For instance, Lyndon B. Johnson provides an introductory statement. But much of the material speaks its own tongue.

The economist Rashi Fein, for example, in an imaginative essay,[7] calculates a time-lag statistic: how many years earlier did the white American—with the full range of opportunity open to him—attain the particular level, say of health, education, income, occupation that the Negro—so long denied that opportunity—has reached only today. He also asks whether that gap in years is greater or lesser at earlier times, that is, was the Negro more years behind in some earlier period. He thus compares the relative speed of movement over the same range of experience. The change in the length of the gap depends upon the relative rates of change of white and Negro indicators over time. The results are disturbing: in a number of cases the time gap has been widening rather than narrowing. Today the Negro is further behind the whites in years than he once was.

What is of additional importance is that if the Negro is in 1965 where the white was in 1945 this does not mean that the Negro considers himself as well off as the white did twenty years ago. The Negro is aware that a substantial majority of the nation has higher income, more education, better health. In a psychological sense, the Negro is even further behind than the data shows.

The Negro male child is born into a world in which, in 1962, his chance of reaching age twenty was about the same as that of the white's reaching thirty-seven. Negro unemployment rates are higher than white rates at the same moment in time, and the Negro has continued to face unemployment rates which would be considered a national scandal if white workers were subjected to them. Whites fluctuate between prosperity and recession, but Negroes fluctuate between depression and great depression.[8]

It should be unnecessary to continue with the dismal health records, mortality figures, occupation statistics. The Negro child grows up in a world in which opportunity is severely circumscribed. Education, moreover, is clearly not the whole answer, as it largely was for the European immigrant. The difference in earnings of whites and non-whites increases as the educational level increases.[9] In 1963 the Negro family had a median income of $4,530 if the family head completed high school. A comparable white family had $6,997, almost 55 per cent higher. The Negro who had attended, but not completed, college earns less than the white with only eight years of elementary school.

If we use a poverty standard—families with incomes under $3,000—

the chances in 1963 were 43 in 100 that a Negro child was born into a family of poverty. It is true that a large majority of impoverished families are white, but the Negro has a far greater chance, almost three times as great, of being in poverty than does the white. Even as late as 1963, the number of Negro families in poverty was 50 per cent higher than the white level had been sixteen years earlier.

Bayard Rustin, in spite of a prevailing optimism concerning the long-range future of the Negro, recognizes that "Negroes today are in worse economic shape, live in worse slums, and attend more highly segregated schools than in 1954." Further, "the day-to-day lot of the ghetto Negro has not been improved by the various judicial and legislative measures of the past decade."[10]

To whom, then, can the Negro compare himself if he is to have some hope? Apparently to himself in some earlier period—in 1947 two thirds of Negro families were poor—but not to the rest of America, which already in 1947 was better off than the Negro was in 1963 and which, since 1947, had a decline of 30 per cent in the number of poor families. The number of poor Negro families (in part a result of the increase in the absolute number of families) has, since 1947, *increased* by 2 per cent.[11]

In many respects the Negro is today living in a world the white has long since left behind. His waiting for time to bring improvement inevitably means indulging in unreal optimism. Many of the non-white indicators have not been advancing as rapidly as did the white indicators when they were at comparable levels. It often takes the Negro longer to achieve a higher social and economic position than it did the white. In many cases the narrowing of present differentials results from a redistribution of Negro population. That is, moderate upgrading of the Negro occupational pattern in past decades is largely a result of redistribution of Negro population through internal migration. White rates of progress tend to reach a plateau at a certain point, and so Negro rates, even if advancing slowly, somewhat close the gap. But this leveling off could also occur for nonwhites.

Daniel Patrick Moynihan draws attention to another set of disturbing data: "After an extended period of unprecedented economic growth, the Negro experience in the labor market remains hazardous and intermittent in the extreme."[12] Negro income has risen substantially in recent years, as has Negro employment. Yet the gap between Negro and white income is not closing; it is widening. And this in spite of the employment of Negro women, which has no doubt minimized the gap. The problems that follow are made more savage by a soaring population.

If Negroes are not able to cite statistics, they are familiar in life terms with the meaning of these figures. White Americans are living better and they are perplexed and annoyed at what they consider unreal and disproportionate demands from the Negro community. "Give them an inch," is their feeling. Their failure to face reality is an indication of national myopia and constitutes the price the Negro community at home and the world at large is forced to pay to maintain the white American's high living standard.

The psychic cost of being a Negro American is incalculable. Philip Hauser estimates $1,000 as the market price for being a Negro, that is, the median amount lost annually.[13] The price paid by Negroes in human terms is more devastating. Who can calculate the horrible self destructiveness that drives a young Negro school child to turn in hatred upon his white teacher and call him the worst epithet he could imagine: Nigger. A measure of the distress of the adult Negro is that Negro men in their prime years vanish from their families and from the job market, almost literally living out the theme of Ralph Ellison's The Invisible Man. They begin to reappear in middle age. The effect on the family (and unemployment figures if these men were to be included) of such a disappearance is immense.

The suffering to which Negroes are subjected is often reflected in the disrupted family structure. The victimization process toughens its members to function in the ghetto world, but at the same time it seriously interferes with their ability to operate in any other world.[14] In a curious way, Negroes have been granted the freedom to fashion their own adaptations within their separate world. They have created a culture that has some valuable elements and many more elements that are highly destructive to the people who must live in it. Although this strange freedom (resulting from disinterest on the part of the white world) provides some breathing space for the Negro, it also has meant that many of the protections offered by white institutions stop at the edge of the Negro ghetto: schooling, medical service, enforcement of civil and political rights.

Gunnar Myrdal suggests that the United States, among the great nations, has the most explicitly expressed creed. This may account for our unusual degree of hypocrisy, for when the creed is violated we feel the need to defend its violation in some way. We could not, as other peoples had, justify slavery on the grounds of the convenience and desire of the slaveowners. We had to be convinced that slavery was good, not only for the slaveowner but for the slave as well, or, alternatively, unspeakably evil; in either case it was solely a moral issue. The United States demands that its citizenry view it only as right. To take the once high-minded Puritan ethic and subject it to hypocritical and self-righteous standards requires a heavy price from the population and a particularly heavy one from those in the most oppressed portions of it. Their insecure positions tend to pressure them into accepting the dominant myths, in spite of the fact that the reality does not correspond. They thus often suffer from greater perceptual distortions than other members of society, who are both psychically freer to dissent from the creed, and to whom the creed more readily applies.[15]

One of the most objective appraisals one can make of American society is that it is now, and has always been a racist society; that for periods of time we have been tormented by that reality; and that there have been rare times when we were willing to cope with it at its root. Yet it is one of the truths we are unwilling to admit about ourselves. U. B. Phillips, the noted historian of the old South, was a Georgian who identified with the white South. He was able, because of this identification, to recognize that the central theme of southern history is the white South's commitment to white supremacy. There is no comparable historian of note to speak of the theme in relation to the nation as a whole. Historians and social scientists who write of American character and myth are without Phillips' racist complacency and therefore are too committed to the American ethos to see so clearly.

These commentators argue that racial discrimination is an aberration in American society and that society would benefit by its elimination—by being freed to better use its resources. While this may be true for the people involved, it is my contention that racial discrimination is at this point an integral part of the American social system and that its destruction is not possible until the social system is basically altered. Paul A. Baran and Paul M. Sweezy, both economists, have offered three sets of data to support such a claim.[16]

First they point to a formidable array of private interests that benefit, in the most direct and immediate sense, from the existence of a "segregated subproletariat." Employers benefit from divisions in the labor force that enable them to play one group off against another. Owners of ghetto real estate are able to overcharge. Middle- and upper-income groups benefit from having at their disposal a large supply of cheap domestic labor. Many small, marginal businesses, especially in the service trades, can operate profitably only if cheap labor is available to them. White workers benefit by being protected from Negro competition for the more desirable jobs. These groups taken together "constitute a vast majority of the white population."[17]

Secondly, sociopsychological pressures generated by the social system intensify rather than alleviate existing racial prejudice. If race prejudice was originally cultivated to justify the exploitation of colored labor, it now has come to serve other purposes as well. As the social system has become more complicated, and as pressures upon the individual for psychological survival intensify, we have witnessed a proliferation of status groups. People have become preoccupied with status and are strongly motivated by ambitions to move up and fears of moving down. "A special pariah group at the bottom acts as a kind of lighting rod for the frustrations and hostilities of all the higher groups, the more so nearer they are to the bottom.... It may even be said that the very existence of the pariah group is a kind of harmonizer and stabilizer of the social system—so long as the pariahs play their role passively."[18]

And finally there is the economic limitation imposed by mechanization, automation, and cybernation. Since this technological revolution has hardly run its course, the job situation, particularly for unskilled and semiskilled labor, is likely to go on deteriorating. So long as the unemployment problem can be largely confined to Negroes, the rest of the working population has some kind of protection.

Through it all, through the psychic and social emasculation of the Negro man, through the defeminization of the Negro wife and mother, through the corruption of the Negro youth, the Negro American has remained, not only a faithful American, but a super-American.

Whatever white Americans have believed in, he has believed in more. When the Negro turned to his middle class for support, it provided no substantive answers. It rarely could offer even temporary answers, as the middle class does in colonial countries, for it was tied to the power system here and did not see the white world as the "enemy," as the colonial middle class has been able to view its metropolitan country.

Is not the distorted and ironic super-Americanism of Adam Clayton Powell the reason both for the incredible popularity and respect he receives in Harlem and the hatred and fury he engenders outside of it. The qualities the white world will not tolerate and will disgracefully persecute even to the point of political foolhardiness are the very qualities his followers admire : his uppitiness; his flamboyance; the cheerful directness with which he flaunts his contempt for the "game." That it also reflects personal corruption and political irresponsibility seems irrelevant to the Negro community, which sees only that Adam is in the big time and living out all the fantasies of the ghetto dweller.

The anomalous position of the Negro in American society is illustrated by his being at the same time of old native stock and an immigrant. Until fairly recently it was possible to discover the Negro sections of Northern cities from the census by looking up those sections with very high proportions of the population native-born of native-born parents. Negroes are old Americans, a characteristic that ordinarily earns one prestige. They are almost WASPs. If only they were not black, many would be eligible for the Daughters of the American Revolution.

In another sense, the Negro American is truly an immigrant. A share in the American dream has been dangled in front of him, as it has with all immigrant groups. However, as each wave of immigrants is incorporated within the society, the Negro continues to be left behind. Negroes found themselves herded into ghettoes, as had white immigrants before them. The Negroes, though, have faced several important differences. First, they are more highly segregated than white ethnic groups; and second, Negro segregation has, in general, increased rather than decreased over time. Third, the influx of immigrants came at a time when there was a market for agricultural labor and unskilled work, and mobility through these avenues was still possible. Negroes arrived in cities at a time when opportunities for unskilled jobs as well as for small businesses were declining. And finally, ethnic minorities, other than Asians, have previously looked forward to eventual assimilation, for their distinguishing characteristics were cultural and not genetic.

Most of the socially rooted psychological difficulties within the Negro communities can be traced to these sources. As one social scientist said of the Negro: "He has come to the foot of the ladder only to find the bottom rungs gone."[19]

Much has been made of the matriarchal family structure inherited from slavery, and while this cannot be overlooked, it is equally important to note that this tradition has been reinforced by the continued inability of the Negro male to assume the role of provider and protector of the family, in accordance with the prevailing definitions of husband and father.

Much has also been made of the lack of motivation and incentive in the Negro community, as opposed to the high degree of motivation, for education, for example, within other ethnic groups. Two notable differences between the Negro community and others certainly account for most, if not all, of the explanation. The new metropolitan setting has often possessed negative incentives for education to the Negro. He knows that the acquisition of an education by an occasional Negro has not opened the doors to economic and social advance. A recent, as yet unpublished, paper by two economists deals with the implications of the continuing overrepresentation of the Negro mass in the less skilled occupations. They indicate that the low average productivity of the Negro mass is associated in the white mind with all Negroes, even those whose social and economic status is above average. Therefore a necessary, if not sufficient, condition to the elimination of prejudice against all Negroes, including middle-class Negroes, is the elevation of the lower-class Negro to a position of equality vis-a-vis the lower-class white. "The Negro problem," the economists conclude, "must be viewed and analyzed in terms of the status of the whole Negro population and not in terms of the fate of individual Negroes."[20]

Of more profound significance for the immediate internal needs of the Negro community is the absence of a cohesive communal set of values and disciplines. Other ethnic groups, which had a well-defined and clearly remembered cultural heritage to sustain their members, suffered less from the exclusion from the community at large than does the Negro, whose African culture was destroyed many generations ago and who has more or less adopted the cultural heritage of the group that excludes him.

While all newly urbanized groups faced similar problems, most of the immigrants brought with them a tradition of solidarity and discipline that regulated their members. Their families were encased in social and cultural institutions that offered restraint to stubborn individuals. Negroes have been slower to develop these institutions, first, because the ones they had were destroyed, and second, because they were not rewarded by the society at large for developing them. The early chapters in the *Autobiography of Malcolm X* show how his criminal activities serviced and were rewarded by certain portions of white society and therefore by certain portions of Negro society.

The ambiguous position of being simultaneously an old American and an immigrant can produce something akin to social schizophrenia. Where other immigrant groups have had a homeland to which they could return, physically and culturally, the Negro did not. At the same time, he could not feel this land was his home.

The fact that the Negro has never had any real alternative is the only context in which his history, his ideology, his leaders, his institutions can be understood. Myrdal's word, *dilemma*, was more accurate than he knew. It is a truth perhaps too horrible to comprehend or cope with. What can one do if the horror of the present seems to have no end? The life of the Negro in America is dotted with such stories involving groups and individuals. Each reenacts the whole.

Consider the story of the Negroes living in Okfuskee County, Oklahoma, at the turn of the century, which is poignant not because it is unique in Negro history, but because it is so representative. In the early part of the century anti-Negro sentiment was consolidating throughout the nation accompanied by violence and the establishment of Jim Crow patterns. A new resolution of the racial problem was attempted by the establishment of politically and socially free all-Negro communities. There is grim irony in the disagreement among historians as to what date marks the lowest point in Negro history. Rayford Logan's description of the nadir as the period 1877–1901 has provoked discussion as to whether indeed a later date marks the lowest point. Most agree that the point falls somewhere in the first decade and a half of this century, just preceding the great migration.[21]

It was with the vision of a new city on a hill, black, not Puritan, that the city of Boley came into existence. The inhabitants of Boley had taken seriously the American creed, and it was a long and painful process by which they learned that it was not meant to apply to them. When the whites in the surrounding territory realized that the Negro settlement, united and disciplined, held the key to political power in the area, the vision was destined to be shattered. What happened to the Boley Negroes occurred, in one form or another, throughout the nation. Their political power was broken, first indirectly by gerrymandering, and then frontally with the adoption of the "grandfather clause." The Oklahoma Negroes, still clinging to their hopes, went through all the legal forms of protest, but slowly their hopes, based as they were upon expectations of legal justice, were relinquished. Ultimately disillusionment came, and it was followed by the only natural, though not possible, alternative—the emigration to a distant and fictionalized homeland in Africa. After great opposition from the American and British governments a ship with fleeing Oklahoma Negroes landed in British West Africa. At this point only the outlines of the final despair exist. "They did not want to be Americans, but now they found that they did not want to be Africans either." These Negroes had truly lived the torments of their dilemma. The brief life of this experiment attests to what Gunnar Myrdal has called " a dissatisfaction so deep that it amounts to a hopelessness of ever gaining full life in America."[22]

In a traditional American manner, Negro ideologies are heavily pragmatic and have taken the path at any given time, as in the case of the Boley settlement, that seems most likely to eliminate, or at least minimize, discrimination and racism. In the process Negro leaders and groups have been faced with a paradox. They were fundamentally struggling for integration into American society. But by racial organizations, which many deemed necessary for effective action for their rights, they appear to be creating a segregated movement in itself, to be fostering the very thing they were attacking. In this way the Negro community has vacillated from integration to racial solidarity. Which tactic was followed, often was the product of the response of white society. During Reconstruction, for example, the outlook within the Negro world was largely integrationist, for there was much sympathy from whites. As conditions worsened, the theme of self-help and solidarity assumed a major role. Self-help, racial solidarity, emphasis on economic and moral development—all came in the wake of disfranchisement and disillusionment. The assumption was that by acquiring wealth and morality—by their own efforts—Negroes would gain the respect of white men and be accorded their rights as citizens. With the demise of the Knights of Labor, the failure of southern Populists to wipe out the color line, and a parallel decline of radicalism in the country at large, the Negro community retrenched even more. By the end of the nineteenth century and throughout the early part of the twentieth, the main themes in Negro thinking were that Negroes must work out their own salvation in a hostile environment and that they must be united in their efforts at racial elevation. This emphasis on self-help and solidarity stressed the economic approach, but it was also applied to efforts of protest and agitation. Frequently, as in Booker T. Washington's case, this philosophy was associated with a flattering approach to the white South. But always it expressed—implicitly or explicitly—a determination to succeed in the "promise of American life."

World War I aroused new hope in Negroes that the rights removed at the turn of the century would be restored, but again the expectations were smashed. Faith in integration collapsed, a collapse reflected by the mass support given Marcus Garvey's Back to Africa movement and the success of "Buy Black" slogans in the nation's ghettoes. Old dreams reappeared during the New Deal and World War II periods. CORE (Congress of Racial Equality) was born in 1942, and with it the nonviolent sit-in technique. The National Association for the Advancement of Colored Peoples led the struggle that ended the white primaries. In the 1950s and 1960s the civil rights movement achieved desegregation of public accommodations and established the right to vote. Yet at the end of this long fight, "the Southern Negro is too poor to use those integrated facilities and too intimidated and disorganized to use the vote to maximum advantage, while the economic position of the Northern Negro deteriorates rapidly."[23] "Buy Black," has changed into the more militant "Black Power," whatever it means.

A cursory view of the events that directly affected the history of the Negro in the United States from Reconstruction to the present will corroborate the motivation and justification for the frequently changing tactics.

The overthrow of Reconstruction governments in the South was slow, but it was always accompanied by intimidation. Negroes' were destroyed, their houses burned, and they and their families were whipped and lynched for voting Republican. Corruption discredited Radical Reconstruction, and with the loss of conscientious but disillusioned support from the North, white home rule could be restored. The North had grown weary of the crusade, so that before a new century began there was complete recognition in law what the South had itself accomplished in fact before the election of 1876.[24] After the Democrats returned to power in the South, they found ways to nullify the strength of the Negroes or to disfranchise them altogether.

Strangely enough, the elimination of the Negro from the political picture created circumstances that brought him back once again. The coalition of classes, which had united only to oppose another race, began to disintegrate as the poor whites came to distrust the Bourbons for legitimate economic and political reasons. As the program of radical agrarianism evolved during the last two decades of the century, Negro and white farmers in the South drifted closer together and white solidarity became more difficult to maintain. Said Tom Watson, the Georgia Populist leader, to his black and white followers: "You are made to hate each other because upon that hatred is rested the keystone of the arch of financial despotism which enslaves you both. You are deceived and blinded that you may not see how this race antagonism perpetuates a monetary system that beggars you both."[25]

As promising as this Negro-white coalition seemed at the time, it could not withstand the ultimate call to white supremacy, and the poor white farmers reverted to old, established patterns, comforted in their poverty by Conservative assurances that Negro rule must be avoided at any cost. When it became evident that white factions would compete with one another for the Negro vote, it was time for the complete disfranchisement of the Negro, the fifteenth amendment notwithstanding. On this the white South agreed.

Once the Negro was disfranchised, everything else necessary for white supremacy could be done. Laws for racial segregation had made a brief appearance during Reconstruction, only to disappear by 1868. In 1875 Tennessee adopted the first Jim Crow law and soon the rest of the South followed. Negroes and whites were separated on trains and in depots. By the end of the century the Negro was banned from white hotels, barber shops, restaurants, and theaters. The racial ostracism extended to churches and schools, to housing and jobs, to eating and drinking.

The South's adoption of extreme racism was due not so much to a conversion as it was to a relaxation of the opposition.[26] The restraining forces had included not only northern liberal opinion, but also internal checks imposed by the prestige of the southern conservatives and the idealism of the southern radicals. Toward the end of the century there was an almost simultaneous decline in the effectiveness of the restraint that these three forces had exerted. As C. Vann Woodward has indicated, as the United States undertook its imperialist activities and shouldered the white man's burden, she took up at the same time many southern attitudes on the subject of race. As the long southern agricultural depression went unrelieved, the Negro became the scapegoat to reunite the white South.

Throughout this period the vast majority of Negroes were facing the hard task of making a living on the farm. It was difficult for Negroes to purchase desirable farm lands even if they had the capital, because whites were reluctant to sell to them, land remaining the only important and prestigious investment. The return of ex-Confederates to power, intermittent agricultural depressions, discriminatory treatment by landlords and merchants, and rumors of rich opportunities in the cities and in other parts of the country stimulated an exodus of Negroes from the rural South that began as early as 1880. Thousands of Negroes left their homes; there was a virtual stampede to Kansas, so great that the whites in the South became alarmed at the number fleeing. Negro leaders were themselves in disagreement over whether or not the Negroes should leave the South.

In the last two decades of the nineteenth century, the South began to feel the impact of the economic revolution that had already enveloped the North. The iron industry was growing in Tennessee and Alabama, cloth was being manufactured in the Carolinas, and the business of transporting manufactured goods to the consumer was growing. In 1898 southern cities employed 7,395 Negroes in industry; by 1910 they employed 350,000. But everywhere there was strong objection to hiring Negroes for jobs that had even the hint of respectability, so that Negroes fleeing to southern cities soon learned that urban life could be as frustrating as rural life. As unions came more and more to affect the industrial scene dissatisfactions increased, for only the short-lived Knights of Labor showed any enthusiasm for organizing Negro workers.

As the new century wore on, Negroes learned that it had brought with it all the difficulties of the previous one and some new ones of its own. In the search for better economic opportunities Negroes, like their white neighbors, continued to move into urban areas of both North and South. Employment opportunities were fewer than the number of people coming to urban areas, and Negroes found great difficulty in securing anything except the more onerous jobs. They continued to exist around the "ragged edge of industry" with organized labor envincing a pronounced hostility. Coincident with the rise of the city in American life was the rise of the Negro community within the city.

Violence and hostility to Negroes North and South was certainly not new. But soon everyone was to realize that for the Negro, the new century meant considerably more violence and more bloodshed. In the first year of the twentieth century more than one hundred Negroes were lynched, and before the outbreak of World War I, the number for the century had soared to more than eleven hundred. It was, though, the epidemic of race riots that swept the country that aroused the greatest Negro anxiety. Such riots increased rapidly in number and barbarity, from the Wilmington, North Carolina riot in 1898 and the New York riot in 1900 to a bloody climax in the Atlanta holocaust in 1906 and the Springfield riot of 1908.

The sordid picture of Negro life in America moved a group of young Negroes, under the leadership of W. E. B. Du Bois, to draw up a platform for aggressive action. Incorporating themselves as the Niagara Movement, they met in 1905 to demand freedom of speech, manhood suffrage, abolition of discrimination based on race, and the recognition of the basic principles of human brotherhood. In 1908 the Springfield, Illinois race riot, erupting near Lincoln's home, shocked many leading, liberal whites, who met to form the NAACP and to pledge themselves to work for abolition of all forced segregation, enfranchisement of the Negro, and enforcement of the fourteenth and fifteenth amendments.

In the early years of the administration of Woodrow Wilson, Negroes were largely preoccupied with their own domestic problems. Wilson's promise of "New Freedom" had focused attention on the economic and social maladjustments that were the legacies of the industrial upheaval of the previous generation. What the Negroes received, to their horror, from the first Congress of Wilson's administration, was the greatest flood of bills proposing discriminatory legislation against them that has ever been introduced into an American Congress.

But when the war came, the Negroes "closed ranks"[27] and eagerly participated in the struggle, despite the great discrimination in the army and in the civilian agencies that served the army. The Negroes who remained at home were no less enthusiastic, both in support of the war and in flight from the South during the war. A severe recession in the South in 1914 and 1915 sent wages down to 75 cents a day or less. To those dependent on the cotton crop, damage done by the boll weevil in 1915 and 1916 was disastrous. Floods in the summer of 1915 left thousands of rural Negroes destitue. At the same time, Northern industry was expanding rapidly and foreign immigration was declining. The North came to be viewed as the land of promise by thousands of southern Negroes.

The talk of democracy during the war and the sudden relative prosperity had raised hopes of even the most militant Negroes that the postwar world might turn out to be a cheerier one. If Negroes were determined to secure democracy for themselves, there were many more others who were determined to prevent it. The Ku Klux Klan had been revived in the southern states as early as 1915, but its real growth began after the war. The semiofficial role it assumed, not alone in the South but also in New York, Indiana, Illinois, and Michigan, stimulated the lawlessness and violence that characterized the postwar period. More than seventy Negroes were lynched during the first year after the Great War, including ten soldiers, some still in their uniforms. It was the summer of 1919, called by James Weldon Johnson "The Red Summer," that ushered in the greatest period of interracial strife the nation had ever witnessed. From June to the end of the year there were some twenty-five race riots.

When the crash came in October of 1929, many Negroes were already suffering. Overrepresented in the lower echelons of American society, the Negro was also overrepresented in the suffering that came with the depression. Nevertheless the migration of large numbers of Negroes to northern urban centers and the ambitious and restless nature of many of them combined to produce a new power, which some of them were quick to understand. There developed a political resurgence that placed the Negro in the midst of American politics, although more often as the manipulated rather than the manipulator.

To appreciate the limitations under which Negro political thought developed, scan the names of the most outstanding Negro leaders from the Civil War to the present: Frederick Douglass, Booker T. Washington, W. E. B. Du Bois, Marcus Garvey, Martin Luther King, Malcolm X.

Each struggled with the problem of survival in a situation in which only unsatisfactory alternatives were available. The tactic each used is what aids the rest of us in classifying them as "radical" or "conservative." "Militant" or "radical" are words defined in terms of white society, that is, of how many demands the Negro makes on white society. As in our tradition in general, terms like "radical" or "conservative" are toned down and have a meaning quite different when used in a context of Latin American, Asian, or European affairs.

What makes Frederick Douglass a radical is that he demanded, immediately and completely, those rights for Negroes which other Americans had. He certainly had no wish to make any serious changes in American society, except that he wished his people to share in it. The program of Douglass' Equal Rights League states just this. It demanded integration into American society and the total elmina-

tion of segregation of any sort. The Negro Reconstruction convention movement in general, which was heavily influenced by Douglass,
stressed thrift, industry, frugality, morality, land-ownership, and
acquisition of wealth, combined with the elimination of distinctions
among Americans of different colors. The Colored National Labor
Convention, meeting in Washington in 1869, insisted upon the right
of Negro labor, as well as all labor, to organize, but constantly stressed
the theme that there was no conflict between capital and labor and
that every man should strive to be a capitalist. Like the white unions
of the day, these conventions exhibited a characteristic *petit bourgeois*
psychology. "The fact that they looked forward to a future of independent entrepreneurship for Negroes as well as whites simply shows
that they had absorbed well the regnant American economic myth."[28]

In a sense, Booker T. Washington was simply continuing this tradition, but in a period of great hostility and violence directed at the
Negro, and so his modifications tried to make their peace with the
changed mood. Is not Booker T. Washington the embodiment of the
American dream, with his concern for the yeoman farmer and his
stress upon self-sufficiency and the gospel of money, his deprecation
of protest and agitation, his acceptance of social Darwinism? He is,
indeed, the perfect *petit bourgeois*. It was Peter Kropotkin, the Russian
anarchist, who allegedly roared with amusement at the description of
Washington as a conservative Negro leader. "What does he have to
conserve?" he wanted to know.

The radicals who opposed Washington were radical in the Frederick
Douglass tradition: they were radical on the race question in that
they denied the status of inferiority assigned to the Negro. Thomas
Fortune's Radical League saw its role in a program to protest and
take legal action against disfranchisement, inequitable distribution
of school funds, exclusion from juries, barbarous prison conditions,
lynchings, segregation on public carriers; and to encourage migration
from "terror-ridden sections."[29] Similarly, the radical Niagara
program announced that Negroes should protest emphatically against
abridgement of political and civil rights and against inequality of
economic opportunity. It refused to allow the impression to remain
that "the Negro-American assents to inferiority, is submissive under
oppression and apologetic before insult." Above all, it stated, "We do

not hesitate to complain, and to complain loudly and insistently." A humane and praiseworthy program, but hardly a radical one.

In W. E. B. Du Bois we find a tormented man living out the dilemma. Too much has been made by his biographers of his wavering between integrationist aims and separatist aims; they were both efforts to solve the same problem. In 1903, for example, he at first said that William Jennings Bryan was as bad as William Howard Taft, and that the Socialist party was the only one to treat Negroes as men. He soon regarded Bryan's silence as better than the statement of Taft, the "Coward of Brownsville."[30] In 1912, Du Bois, after toying with the idea of working with the Progressives, withdrew from the Socialist party to support Wilson. He felt that Eugene V. Debs was the ideal candidate for President, but that Wilson was the only realistic choice. His erratic political course and the erratic political course of the leaders in the Negro community, from the effort to break with the Republican party to support Grover Cleveland and the Democrats to the present time, in which the alternatives are not appreciably better, demonstrates that Negroes have had no place to go.

Du Bois' bitter but honorable struggle encompassed all possibilities. It began with the hope of education: educate the talented tenth within the Negro community and they will serve both as respected example to the white world and teachers to the black masses. It included efforts to achieve unity with what he felt to be the similarly oppressed white masses. It reached out to Pan Africanism and international identification with blacks throughout the world. Ultimately it ended in total alienation from his homeland: association with the U.S. Communist party as a gesture of defiance, and a flight to die, respected and loved, in another country. Flight has been the final repudiation of many, among them Marcus Garvey and his followers, Robert Williams, a handful of Negro émigrés living in Europe. Comfort is sought too in psychic flight, as in the great increase in Negro homosexuality and the steady increase in "passing" as white.

The traditional Negro leader, however, has spoken with the optimistic rhetoric summed up by Louis Lomax, rather than echoed the bitterness of Du Bois.

Whatever else the Negro is, he is an American. Whatever he is to become—integrated, unintegrated, or disintegrated—he will become it in America. . . . It has just never occurred to us that the Negro Revolt will not, in the end, succeed. This fundamental optimism is, I submit, a resounding statement of faith in the American dream.[31]

Bayard Rustin, who is more profound, more astute and more sophisticated intellectually, in a recent issue of *Commentary* offered a much more subtle analysis but ended up in the same place as Lomax—with faith in a delusive dream. His discussion of Black Power and the reasons for his opposition to it[32] can be substantively divided. The sections of Black Power in which he deals with the history and present condition of the Negro in America are pessimistic, critical and unyielding. To read those paragraphs alone would give no one confidence in the future. The alternative Rustin then proposes to those advocates of Black Power is a "liberal-labor-civil rights coalition which would work to make the Democratic Party truly responsive to the aspirations of the poor, and which would develop support for programs (specifically those outlined in A. Philip Randolph's $100 billion Freedom Budget) aimed at the reconstruction of American society in the interests of greater social justice." This in the face of an impressive and persuasive analysis that indicates precisely why his program will not materialize.

Rustin is a bit shabby in his critique of what he calls the "historical myth" that the Irish and the Jews and the Italians, by each ethnic group sticking together and demanding their share, won enough power to overcome their initial disabilities. The truth is, says Rustin, that it was through alliances with other groups that they acquired their power. No group in American society has ever "pulled themselves up by their bootstraps," and therefore on tactical grounds alone the Black Power advocates are incorrect. Surely Rustin is aware that the alliance with other groups followed a substantial period during which the ethnic groups did for their members precisely what Black Power advocates are claiming for theirs. Negroes have been making alliances with political machines and individuals for decades, but so long as it is done from weakness, without the bargaining position of a power bloc that has historically been crucial in American politics, they will continue to be scorned after the votes are delivered.

Malcolm X is perhaps the only one who showed signs that he might some day have come to terms with the dilemma, as Du Bois did. He was able to communicate both its nature and its resolution to the Negro community, as Du Bois could not.

Someone had to rise and speak the fearful reality, to throw the light of reason into the hallucinatory world of the capitalist and biracial society that thinks itself egalitarian, that thinks itself humanitarian and pacific. But it was unexpected that the speaking should be done with such power and precision by a russet-haired field Negro translated from conventional thief to zealot and at the end nearly Marxist and humanist.[33]

He isolated and spoke to the self-hatred that afflicts the Negro community and placed responsibility for it. As the death he expected grew near, the grotesque distortions, which were also part of his appeal, the historical inaccuracies, the anti-Semitism, the religious dogma all waned, and his knowledge and judgments deepened. If his language was terrible, if it terrified white America, the reality he wished to present has been the more terrible.

He, too, was not immune from the contradiction inherent in the dilemma. "What kind of success did they get in Birmingham? A chance to sit at a lunch counter and drink some coffee with a cracker— that's success?"[34] Of a sort, yes. Total success, no, but then neither did his separatist path lead to that. Toward the end of his life, Malcolm was coming to deal with the total problem, the problem that is American and not simply black. If it is more oppressive to the black man than to the white, the white is not free from its degradation. As Malcolm was beginning to learn the relationship between racism and capitalism so he was beginning to understand that no moral man, white or black, "could be happy in the world of color TV and Metrecal and napalm."[35]

The student militants associated with the Student Nonviolent Coordinating Committee have much to learn from Malcolm. What they want is in the tradition of American-style radicalism, and they are therefore the heirs of Frederick Douglass. They have much to offer, but then they too get trapped in the old dilemma. They are the true descendants of the contributors to that landmark volume, *What the Negro Wants*, published twenty-three years ago. The preface by the editor, Rayford W. Logan, might appear without change today.

Race relations in the United States are more strained than they have been in many years. Negroes are disturbed by the continued denial of what they consider to be their legitimate aspirations and by the slow, grudging granting of a few concessions. White Americans express alarm at what they call the excessive insistence by Negroes upon a too rapid change in the *status quo*. Serious riots have broken out in both Northern and Southern cities. . . .

This tension urgently requires a definition of terms and a clarification of issues by competent Negroes representing various shades of opinion. . . . [What is so significant is the] surprising unanimity with respect to what the Negro wants. Conservatives, liberals and radicals alike want Negroes eventually to enjoy the same rights, opportunities and privileges that are vouchsafed to all other Americans. . . .

The titles of the individual contributions corroborate this statement: "The Negro Wants First-Class Citizenship"; "The Negro Wants Full Equality"; "The Negro Wants Full Participation in the American Democracy"; "Count Us In."[36]

The student militants are radical in this sense too: they demand full equality now. Their tactics not their ideology, separate them from Martin Luther King. Until now they have not only had no ideology, they have repudiated the idea of ideology. They are not by temperament or position unwilling to challenge any institutions in our society, and so their experience in the South and their genuine commitment and honesty have radicalized them, as it was beginning to radicalize Malcolm, as it has even begun to radicalize Martin Luther King. Notice has increasing ardent attacks on the war in Vietnam and his associating the war there with a reduced commitment to the Great Society at home. The hostile response from the liberal community, white and black, to the slogan, Black Power, corroborated for the students their radicalism and thereby strengthened it.

Still, one suspects that the rhetoric of the SNCC militants is more radical than their analysis, just as a few years ago they spoke so sincerely of their opposition to "the white power structure" until one pressed them for a closer definition.

Witness Stokely Carmichael's effort (*New York Review of Books*) to explain his position to the white intellectuals:[37]

> We should begin with the basic fact that black Americans have two problems: they are poor and they are black.... We had to begin with politics because ... with power the masses could make or participate in making the decisions which govern their destinies.... It means the creation of power bases from which black people can work to change statewide or nationwide patterns of oppression through pressure from strength—not weakness. Politically, black power means what it has always meant to SNCC: the coming-together of black people to elect representatives and to force those representatives to speak to their needs.

Into this old radical tradition, the tradition of the Frederick Douglasses, Carmichael introduced the ambiguous and imprecise concept of participatory democracy.

> We have no infallible master plan and we make no claim to exclusive knowledge of how to end racism; different groups will work in their different ways. SNCC cannot spell out the full logistics of self-determination but it can address itself to the problem of helping black communities define their needs, realize their strength, and go into action along a variety of lines which they must choose for themselves.

Then the new approach is introduced as if it were simply a continuation of the preceding, and not a departure.

> Ultimately, the economic foundations of this country must be shaken if black people are to control their lives. For a century this nation has been like an octopus of exploitation, its tentacles stretching from Mississippi and Harlem to South America, the Middle East, southern Africa, and Vietnam.... For racism to die, a totally different American must be born.

Carmichael continued: This society prefers to talk about integration, but integration talks not at all to the problem of poverty, only to the problem of blackness. The example of African black men ruling their own natives gives blacks everywhere a sense of the possibility of power. Carmichael proclaimed his aim to be, eventually, a coalition between poor blacks and poor whites. "We see such a coalition as the major internal instrument of change in American society," although it is "surely academic today to talk about bringing poor blacks and whites together."

But our vision is not merely of a society in which all black men have enough to buy the good things of life.... It is a society in which the spirit of community and humanistic love prevail.... We are going to work ... on goals we define, not for civil rights but for all human rights.

The black militants are accused of separatism, of isolating themselves, of supporting a concept which is not feasible in a society where the Negro represents 10 per cent of the whole. However, the specific program, while on the surface all of these things, is in reality based on a broader vision, in the long run a more feasible concept than the one that struggles for day-to-day improvement in integrated housing, schools, or restaurants. It is more feasible because it is truer. When Du-Bois reached this position he fled the country, an alienated and lonely man; as Malcolm X was nearing it, he was assassinated. Whatever success the young black radicals have in working out a program, only hints of which appear, and whatever minimal success they have in communicating that program to the Negro community, and to some sections of the white community, will help diminish the world of make-believe that imprisons the American Negro.

NOTES

1. E. Franklin Frazier, *Black Bourgeoisie: The Rise of a New Middle Class in the United States* (New York: The Free Press, 1957).

2. For a discussion of one of the important roots of such an attitude, the

tradition of accommodation, see "The Legacy of Slavery and the Roots of Black Nationalism," paper delivered by Eugene D. Genovese to the Second Annual Socialist Scholars Conference, September, 1966, published, together with the comments of Herbert Aptheker, Frank Kofsky, and C. Vann Woodward, and a rejoinder, in *Studies on the Left* (January, 1967).

3. For a discussion of this point see Elbert Lee Tatum, *The Changed Political Thought of the Negro, 1915–1940* (New York: Exposition Press, 1951), esp. chaps. 1 and 11.

4. W. E. B. Du Bois, *Black Reconstruction in America, 1860–1880* (New York: S. A. Russell Company, 1956), p. 703.

5. *The Negro American*, ed. Talcott Parsons and Kenneth B. Clark (The Daedalus Library, Vol. 7, Boston: Houghton Mifflin Company, 1966).

6. I. F. Stone, "People Without a Country," *The New York Review of Books* (August 18, 1966), p. 8.

7. Rashi Fein, "An Economic and Social Profile of the Negro American," pp. 102–34.

8. *Ibid.*, p. 115.

9. Philip M. Hauser, "Demographic Factors in the Integration of the Negro," *The Negro American*, p. 84.

10. Bayard Rustin, " 'Black Power' and Coalition Politics," *Commentary* (September, 1966), p. 37.

11. Rashi Fein, "Social Profile," *The Negro American*, p. 119.

12. Daniel Patrick Moynihan, "Employment, Income and the Ordeal of the Negro Family," *The Negro American*, p. 139.

13. Hauser, "Demographic Factors," *The Negro American*, p. 84.

14. This thesis is developed by Lee Rainwater, "Crucible of Identity: The Negro Lower-Class-Family," *The Negro American*, pp. 160–205.

15. See Gunnar Myrdal, *An American Dilemma: The Negro Problem and Modern Democracy* (New York: Harper and Row, 1944), chap. 1 for a fuller discussion.

16. See Paul A. Baran and Paul M. Sweezy, *Monopoly Capital: An Essay on the American Economic and Social Order* (New York: Monthly Review Press, 1966), chap. 9, "Monopoly Capitalism and Race Relations."

17. *Ibid.*, p. 2864.

18. *Ibid.*, pp. 265–66.

19. Everett C. Hughes, "Anomalies and Projections," *The Negro American,* p. 695.

20. Raymond S. Franklin and Michael D. Tanzer, "Disutility, Discrimination and the Negro's Relative Economic Status" (unpublished paper, my possession), p. 25.

21. See the preface to Rayford W. Logan, *The Betrayal of the Negro: From Rutherford B. Hayes to Woodrow Wilson,* originally published as *The Negro in American Life and Thought: The Nadir, 1877–1901* (New York: Collier Books, 1965).

22. A fascinating account of the entire episode is in William E. Bittle and Gilbert Geis, *The Longest Way Home: Chief Alfred C. Sam's Back-to-Africa Movement* (Detroit: Wayne State University Press, 1964).

23. Rustin, "Black Power," *Commentary,* p. 37.

24. John Hope Franklin, *From Slavery to Freedom: A History of American Negroes* (New York: Alfred A. Knopf, 1956), p. 328.

25. Quoted by C. Vann Woodward, *The Strange Career of Jim Crow* (New York: Oxford University Press, 1955), p. 45.

26. See Woodward, *Jim Crow,* especially chap. 11.

27. A reference to the unexpected editorial by Du Bois in the NAACP journal *Crisis,* which he edited, calling for all American Negroes to forget temporarily their grievances to support the war effort. *Crisis,* XVI (July, 1918), pp. 9–10.

28. August Meier, *Negro Thought in American 1880–1915: Racial Ideologies in the Age of Booker T. Washington* (Ann Arbor: The University of Michigan Press, 1963), p. 16.

29. *Ibid.,* p. 129.

30. In August, 1906, three companies of the Twenty-fifth Regiment, all-Negro troops, were allegedly involved in a riot in Brownsville, Texas. President Theodore Roosevelt dismissed the entire battalion without honor. The Negro community, almost without exception, was outraged. Taft, as Secretary of War, carried out Roosevelt's order, although he was hesitant about the harshness and speed of the punishment.

31. Louis E. Lomax, *The Negro Revolt* (New York: New American Library, 1962), p. 264.

32. Rustin, "Black Power," *Commentary,* pp. 35–41.

33. John Illo, "The Rhetoric of Malcolm X," *Columbia University Forum* (Spring, 1966), p. 6.

34. *The Negro Protest: James Baldwin, Malcolm X and Martin Luther King Talk With Kenneth B. Clark* (Boston: Beacon Press, 1963), p. 27.

35. Illo, "Malcolm X," *Columbia Forum*, p. 8.

36. *What the Negro Wants*, ed. Rayford W. Logan (Chapel Hill: The University of North Carolina Press, 1944).

37. Stokely Carmichael, "What We Want," *The New York Review of Books* (September 22, 1966), pp. 5–8.

5

Atlanta in the Progressive Era: A Dreyfus Affair in Georgia*

by LEONARD DINNERSTEIN

Frustration and disillusionment with the rapid social changes caused by the industrial transformation at the end of the nineteenth century set off racial attacks in the United States and Europe. Alfred Dreyfus, Mendell Beiliss, the Haymarket anarchists, and Sacco and Vanzetti were all aliens victimized by societies undergoing rapid conversion. Jews, Italians, Germans, immigrants, anyone, in fact who deviated from the ethnic norm easily served as a scapegoat for the turmoil accompanying industrialism. Barbara Tuchman attributed anti-Semitism in France to "building tensions between classes and among nations. Industrialization, imperialism, the growth of cities, the decline of the countryside, the power of money and the power of machines . . . churning like the bowels of a volcano about to erupt." To a considerable extent, many of these same forces—in greater or lesser degree—also applied in Kiev, Chicago, and Boston. In Russia, Maurice Samuel tells us, "the Beiliss case was mounted by men who hoped by means of it to strengthen the autocracy and to crush the liberal spirit that was reviving after the defeat of the 1905 revolution."

* I wish to thank Frederic C. Jaher for his valuable editorial criticism.

127

In Chicago, fear of foreigners, social revolution, and labor ascendency triggered the vigilante response to eight immigrant anarchists charged with the bomb-throwing incident in Haymarket Square. "A biased jury, a prejudiced judge, perjured evidence, extraordinary and indefensible theory of conspiracy, and the temper of Chicago led to the conviction. The evidence never proved the guilt." Sacco and Vanzetti, atheists, labor agitators, and "Reds" of Italian birth, were convicted of robbery and murder in Dedham, Massachusetts in 1920. The case made by the prosecution led many observers to believe in the innocence of the defendants, but the jury foreman allegedly concluded, "Damn them, they ought to hang anyway."[1]

Social bias played a crucial role in obtaining the convictions described above. The industrial transformation of society uprooted too many too quickly, and made those caught up in the whirlpool of change cling all the more tightly to their old ways. Situations that might have been tolerated or handled differently in more stable societies seemed like conspiratorial attempts to undermine civilization. Dreyfus, Beiliss, the Haymarket anarchists, and Saco and Vanzetti symbolized unwelcome innovations. So, too, did Leo Frank, a Jew upon whom Atlantans would vent their unveiled, nervous tensions in 1913.

1

Atlanta was not spared the problems that industrialism brought to other cities. Indeed the traditions of southern culture intensified the burden of social change. Typical of most American cities during the Progressive era, Atlanta's population practically doubled between 1900 and 1913 (89,870 to 173,713). The population in other urban areas in the United States also increased at an impressive rate during the first decade of the twentieth century. In the South, though, of cities with populations over 100,000, only Birmingham outpaced Atlanta's population spurt between 1900 and 1910.[2] Newly established industrial enterprises offered jobs to all comers. Although urban conditions were better than rural squalor, the city fell far short of the industrialists' promise of the good life. Large groups of recently displaced Georgia crackers mingled uneasily with each other and with the foreign immigrants who wore strange costumes and spoke unintelligible tongues. In the concrete jungle, the newcomers worked together in the most menial jobs and congregated in the least desirable housing. Although foreigners comprised less than 3 per cent of the city's residents,[3] the few Europeans loomed as a great menace to those many Southerners who retained strong feelings about racial purity and community homogeneity.

Working conditions in Atlanta compared unfavorably with those in other parts of the country.[4] Despite a periodic shortage of workers, factory wages were low and hours long. The normal work week lasted sixty-six hours, and, except for Saturday, the working day generally extended from 6 A.M. to 6 P.M. with only a half hour for lunch.[5] In 1902, the average wage-earner took home less than $300 a year. Atlanta's Commissioner of Public Works commented that the prevailing wages did not enable the men in his department to provide even the minimum necessities for their families.[6] By 1912, when average earnings rose to $464[7] living costs had increased correspondingly and Atlanta's relief warden reported a record number of public assistance applications. "Even where women and children worked," he observed, "the money they receive is not enough for their support." "There are too many people on the ragged edge of poverty and suffering," the warden concluded.[8] A year later, some children still earned 22 cents a week for their labor in the city.[9]

Atlanta's unplanned growth plagued officials and created problems similar to those in other cities at the time. Health hazards abounded, educational facilities were found wanting, and recreational outlets could not increase fast enough to service the burgeoning population. As late as 1912, for example, Atlanta provided no public swimming pools or parks for its Negro citizens. An overabundance of gambling dens, dope dives, and brothels, on the other hand, beckoned both whites and Negroes who sought to escape from factory drudgery and dingy tenements. On a number of occasions, in fact, the Mayor of Atlanta, James G. Woodward, "disgraced the city . . . by public drunkenness." His private conduct, however, proved no political liability. Woodward received a third renomination after being "found in a state of intoxication in the red light district of the city. . . ."[10]

Living conditions were no better than public facilities. In 1910, there were only 30,308 dwelling units for 35,813 families. Eighty-two miles, or more than half of the city's residential streets, existed without water mains and more than 50,000 people—over a third of the population—were forced to live in areas of the city not served by sewers. A continuous fog of soot and smoke irritated people's lungs and eyes, and an appalling number of urban dwellers suffered from ill health. Ninety per cent of the city's prisoners in 1902 were syphilitic.[11] Wherever records were kept, the statistics indicated that the problems grew worse during the next decade, rather than better. A comparison of the number of residents afflicted by disease in 1904 and 1911, when the city's population had increased by only 64 per cent, showed the following:

Table I[11]

	1904	1911	% Increase
Dyptheria	114	396	347
Typhoid Fever	85	315	307
Tuberculosis	37	223	602

Atlanta also suffered an above average death rate. A United States census report for 1905 noted that of 388 cities in this country, only twelve had more deaths per thousand persons than Georgia's capital. In 1911, Atlanta's figures still exceeded the national average by almost 40 per cent (13.9 to 18.75 per thousand). A year earlier, sixty-nine people had died from pellagra, a vitamin deficiency prevalent among the poor. This was more than triple the figure for any other city in the country. Birmingham and Charleston, S.C., the two cities that ranked second to the Georgian metropolis, reported only seventeen deaths from the illness in 1910. The situation did not improve much in succeeding years. In 1914 the United Textile Workers complained that far too many Atlanta children still fell victim to the disease. Although exact statistics for all ailments are difficult to obtain, industrialism provided its share of fatal illness. One Georgian official reported in 1912, "occupational diseases are much more common than is believed true. Lead, arsenic and phosphorous poisoning has caused much suffering and many deaths."[13]

The crime rate in Atlanta highlighted the stresses of the new urbanites. In 1905, Atlanta policemen arrested more children for disturbing the peace than did those in any other municipality in the United States. Two years later, only New York, Chicago, and Baltimore, cities with considerably larger populations, exceeded Atlanta's figure for children arrested. That very year, the police booked 17,000 persons out of a total population of 102,702. The Mayor found the statistic "appalling." "It places Atlanta," he said, "at or near the top of the list of cities of this country in criminal statistics."[14]

The police force, another city institution overwhelmed by the population spurt, proved unable to grapple with the new problems thrust upon it. The major reasons for its incapacity were inadequate staffing and facilities. In 1912, the Mayor acknowledged that two hundred men were unable to protect the city, "and, as a result, the residential sections cannot be effectively policed." Atlanta, alone among American cities whose area exceeded twenty-five square miles, existed with only one police station and no substations.[15]

Besides the pathological conditions that menaced the growing city, the southern heritage also conditioned the Crackers'[16] reaction to the enormous differences in urban living. Of all the sections in the country, none has been so tied to the past as has the South. W. J. Cash characterized this southern revulsion by change as "the savage ideal —the patriotic will to hold rigidly to the ancient pattern, to repudiate innovation, in thought and behavior, whatever came from outside and was felt as belonging to Yankeedom or alien parts."[17]

The race riot that erupted in Atlanta in 1906 was an example of the periodic explosions of violence that occurred when transplanted rural dwellers rebelled against the drudgery and disruptiveness of their new urban existence. Rampaging white mobs attacked Negroes with abandon. Before the National Guard successfully quelled the rioters several days later, twelve people had been killed (two white and ten Negro) and seventy had been injured (ten white and sixty Negro). The riot had been incited by sensational newspaper reports exaggerating Negro assaults upon white women. These incendiary statements were published a few weeks after Hoke Smith had whipped up popular passions in his racist campaign for the gubernatorial nomination. Subsequent explanations blamed the newspapers for the outburst, but the press could not be held responsible for the poverty and squalor of the new urban masses. One "educated negro" shrewdly noted that recently arrived rural whites resented the relative prosperity of Negro business people in the city. A national reporter spoke more bluntly in calling Atlanta "one of the very worst of American cities" filled with the "riff-raff that the mining towns of the West used to relieve us of."[18] In either case, the exacerbated race relations in Atlanta focused national attention upon the city. The upheaval was obviously an admission that discontent with city life had become unbearable for the erstwhile rural folk.[19]

The conservative nature of the dominant religious groups in the South compounded the difficulties of adjustment to urban life. No secular influence of any kind, C. Vann Woodward has attested, had the power to sway men's thoughts with as much vigor as did those who allegedly spoke with the authority of God.[20] Baptists and Methodists, the two largest denominations in the South since colonial times, have, for the most part, preached a Fundamentalist creed that opposed change, glorified the past, and uttered invectives against aliens of any stripe. During the nineteenth century, these sects "became centers of conservative political sentiment and of resistance both to the invasion of northern culture and to the doctrine of the New South." Their allegiance to the past and fundamental theological beliefs continued well into the twentieth century.[21]

The great bedrock of Fundamentalist support came from the rural population. When these people moved into the towns and cities, they brought their ministers along with them. Many of the Fundamentalist preachers, who had earlier railed against urban wickedness, "continued to regard the great city centers as 'jungle areas' no less pagan than the Congo, and looked upon themselves as life-saving missionaries."[22] Southern ministers also eyed the new industrialists with great suspicion. Among Methodists, both "pulpit and press inveighed against corporate wealth for denying labor a living wage,"[23] while Baptist objections "to industrialization arose from the fear that industry would lead to rapid urbanization which in turn would corrupt the morals of the people and hinder the spread of Christianity."[24]

The Fundamentalists stressed the godliness of maintaining the homely virtues and living a simple, agricultural life. They also believed in a literal obedience of God's word. In fact, they considered adherence to scriptural instruction as man's most sacred duty. Their preachers

continually railed against modern innovations and warned parish-
ioners that dancing, card-playing and theater-going undermined
Christian teaching. The Fundamentalists also abhorred the alteration
of woman's traditional role. She belonged in the home, they believed,
and any changes in her position must invariably lead to a loosening
of Christian morality.

The Fundamentalists hoped to stem the floodtide of progress by
condemning social change as blasphemy against God's revealed word.
This resistance, although unsuccessful, complicated and delayed
adjustments to modern times. Anyone and anything that violated
their own literal interpretation of the Bible became subject to assault.
Violence frequently accompanied accusations. The self-righteous
crusade to restore the simple, godly life often justified the use of
weapons against those who dissented.

Southern Baptists also considered the influx of immigrants one of
the great dangers of modern times. During the 1880s, southern Baptist periodicals expressed concern with the foreigners whom they regarded as "a threat to American customs and traditions." Many
Baptist editors attributed the moral corruption of the nation to the
newcomers and felt that national good demanded a cessation of our
traditional open-door policy. One spokesman enunciated his anxieties
at the Southern Baptist Convention in 1895.

> Foreigners are accumulating in our cities, and hence our cities are
> the storm centers of the nation. But the great misfortunes of all of
> this is that these foreigners bring along with them their anarchy,
> their Romanism, and their want of morals.[25]

In his analysis of southern mores, W. J. Cash perceptively summarized the Fundamentalists' demands. They wanted "absolute conformity to the ancient pattern under the pains and penalties of the most
rigid intolerance; the maintenance of the savage ideal, to the end of
vindicating the old Southern will to cling fast to its historical way."[26]

Despite the pervasive influence of the Fundamentalist creeds and
the inherent southern hostility toward innovation, the leaders of the
new South—the railroad magnates and the owners of cotton mills and
factories—endeavored to build an industrial community patterned

after the North. To a considerable extent they succeeded and "by 1900 the industrialization of the South had become largely a case of capital seeking labor supply." Atlanta's *Journal* succinctly expressed the prevailing need: "The Southern States have reached a point in their industrial progress where the work necessary . . . can not be done by the present force of workers. . . . The South needs more folks—folks for the farm, folks for the factory." In Georgia, for example, it was said that without immigrant labor, the development of the iron and cotton mills and the building of the railroads would have to be halted.[27]

The desperate plight of industry forced southern state governments to establish immigration bureaus in the hope of attracting suitable laborers. But most southerners were quite specific as to whom they would welcome. Senator Ben Tillman of South Carolina announced, "We do not want European paupers to come to the South." Tennessee's Governor Ben Hooper expressed his opposition to receiving the "motley mass of humanity that is being dumped upon our shores. . . ." And Georgia's Federation of Labor "objected to 'flooding' the South and Georgia with a population composed of the scum of Europe. . . ." Atlanta's two major newspapers stated their preferences clearly. The *Journal* desired persons of Teutonic, Celtic, and Scandinavian origins, "peoples near akin to [our] own by blood, and capable of full assimilation. . . . "And *The Constitution* editorialized, "The German makes a splendid citizen."[28]

Unfortunately for both the South and the arriving immigrants, most of the newcomers were from eastern and southern Europe. They were treated, for the most part, with conspicuous inhospitality. In some sections, Italians, or " 'dagoes' were regarded as about on a par with 'niggers', and the treatment of them corresponded."[29] In 1891, eleven Italians were lynched in New Orleans after three of them had been acquitted of murdering the police chief. Five years later, three Italians suspected of homicide were strung up in Hahnville, Louisiana. In 1899, five Italians were lynched in Tallulah, Lousisiana after injuring a doctor in a quarrel over a goat. The twentieth century had hardly begun when three more Italians were mysteriously shot in Erwin, Mississippi. Czechs and Slovaks established a colony south of Petersburg, Virginia, in the nineteenth century, yet forty years after their arrival, the "natives" still resented their presence.[30]

In Atlanta, the single largest influx of immigrants was 1,342 Russian Jews who comprised 25 per cent of the city's foreign-born in 1910.[31] Although this group made up less than 1 per cent of the population, it was well-known that they ran a large percentage of the saloons, pawnshops, and restaurants catering to Negro trade. The Jews were viewed contemptuously by other whites. One reporter wrote, "as to the white foreigners who cater to negro [sic] trade and negro [sic] vice . . . it is left to the judgment of the reader which is of the higher grade in the social scale, the proprietors or their customers." Sensual pictures of nude white women allegedly decorated the walls of the saloons, and some people even thought that the liquor bottle labels aroused the Negroes' worst passions. Many Atlantans thought that the beer parlors "served as the gathering and hatching place of criminal negroes." When the patrons got drunk and caused social disturbances, the nearby whites blamed the saloon owners for the mischief. One analyst of the 1906 riot, for example, observed, "It was the low dives where mean whiskey was sold to Negroes by whites that bred the criminality which furnished an excuse for the outbreak of the mob; and it was from the doors of the saloon that the ruffians of the mob poured forth to do their deadly work on the innocent."[32]

Although Jews had been in the South since colonial times, they had never been accepted by the dominant Protestant community. To be sure, opportunities to assimilate existed, but those who desired to retain their faith suffered restrictions upon their political and religious liberties. Denial of the trinity, for example, had subjected Jews to imprisonment in Virginia and Maryland in the colonial era. Therefore, Jews did not settle in Maryland until after the American Revolution. Virginia, on the other hand, did not permit Jews to enter the colony without express permission. Georgia granted Jews political and religious equality in 1798, but not until 1826 were Jews allowed to vote in Maryland. Although John Locke's original Constitution for the Carolinas provided for toleration, both North and South Carolina deprived Jews of their political rights. A South Carolina law of 1759 barred non-Protestants from holding office and the North Carolina Constitution of 1776 forbade them to vote. A Jew elected to the North Carolina Legislature in 1809 was challenged, upon taking his seat, but defended himself successfully. A Constitutional Convention, however, banned all Jews from holding office in the Tar Heel State in 1835, and the restriction remained in effect until 1868. In 1818, in a letter to the Jewish editor of a New York City newspaper, Thomas Jefferson acknowledged "the prejudice still scowling on your sect of our religion. . . ."[33]

Despite restrictions on office holding, concerted anti-Jewish prejudice did not occur in the South until the Civil War era. During this period, however, Jews did become scapegoats for Confederate frustrations. They were accused of being "merciless speculators, army slackers, and blockade-runners across the land frontiers to the North." One southern newspaper observed, "all that the Jew possesses is a plentiful lot of money together with the scorn of the world."[34]

Some Georgia towns specifically singled out the Jews as the cause of their woes. In 1862, 103 citizens of Thomasville resolved to banish all Jewish residents and a grand jury in Talbotton found the Jews guilty of " 'evil and unpatriotic conduct.' " Talbotton prejudices, in fact, forced the Lazarus Straus family—later to become famous for its development of Macy's department store in New York City—to leave Georgia during the Civil War.[35]

The next major anti-Semitic eruption occurred in the 1890s. The Populist crusade, the severe economic depression of 1893, and the squalid living conditions in urban slums all helped to intensify hostility toward those who loomed, on the one hand, as the seeming monopolizers of material possessions, and on the other, as the manipulators who unfeelingly deprived the people of their purchasing power. In Georgia, for example, it was "quite the fashion to characterize the Jew as exacting his interest down to the last drachma."[36]

Accusations of financial manipulation gave rise to suspicion of a vast Jewish international conspiracy. One writer, in fact, concluded that the "Rothschild combination has proceeded in the last twenty years with marvellous rapidity to enslave the human race." In North Carolina, Elias Carr, Governor from 1893 to 1897, frequently reiterated his point that "Our Negro brethren, too, are being held in bondage by Rothschild."[37]

When rural southerners flocked to the cities at the end of the nineteenth century, their impressions of the Jew combined traditional stereotypes of financial wiliness with the time-worn southern prejudices. In 1906, Horace M. Kallen, the Jewish philosopher, observed that "there is already a very pretty Jewish problem in our South. . . ." William Robertson, author of *The Changing South*, later noted, "It was enough for Jews to prosper right under [southern] noses, without affording the added insult of being the descendants of the murderers of Christ."[38]

A lack of scholarly studies makes it risky to generalize about anti-Semitism in the South or to suggest regional differences. The two most prominent historians who have investigated American attitudes towards Jews in the nineteenth and twentieth centuries—Oscar Handlin and John Higham—have found evidence supporting positive and negative judgments.[39] Both historians, however, dealt primarily with northern experiences and provided relatively few examples from southern states. Studies about alleged Populist anti-Semitism, moreover, have concentrated almost entirely on the expressions of northern and western agrarians.[40] There are no indications, for example, that Tom Watson, the Georgia leader, engaged in any anti-Semitic diatribes in his Populist heyday.

A significant clue to southern attitudes may be garnered, however, from Higham's findings. He noted that American anti-Semitism was deeply ingrained in the agrarian tradition—which was suspect of urban prosperity based upon the toil of others—and cropped up most frequently in times of crisis. "The prophets of anti-Semitism," Higham continued, "were alienated and often despairing critics of the power of money in American society," and frequently attributed their own woes to the "lords of finance and trade": banks, moneylenders, and bondholders. He discovered, moreover, that hostility toward Jews in this country was strongest in those sectors of the population where there were relatively few Jews and where "a particularly explosive combination of social discontent and nationalistic aggression prevailed."[41] Finally, he found nationalistic fervor "most widespread and in many ways most intense in the small town culture of the South and West."[42] The South was the least urbanized and most discontented region in the United States. Consequently, if Higham's conclusions are accurate, the South must figure as the most anti-Semitic area in the country.

Certain aspects of southern culture—aside from the squalor that existed in Atlanta and other fledgling urban areas—tended to make the natives react more violently to Jews than did residents of the North and West. Southerners were more inbred than were northerners and were, therefore, more concerned with the purity of their Anglo-Saxon heritage.[43] Religious fundamentalism, another force that encouraged anti-Semitism, was more widespread in the South than the North. According to William J. Robertson, most southern Methodists and Baptists were advised by their spiritual leaders that the Jews were "Christkillers."[44] Social instability accompanied by personal anxiety was the final factor that intensified regional hostility toward Jews. Throughout history, the position of the Jews has reflected the degree of security prevailing in a given society. They have frequently been blamed for defeats, depressions, and other disruptive crises.[45] Southerners, notoriously insecure and continually on the defensive, seized upon hatred for Jews as one outlet for the frustrations of their existence.

The above mentioned factors existed, to some extent, in different parts of the North as well, and anti-Semitism appeared among different northern groups. But despite temporary interludes of cataclysm and depression, most northerners expected progress to improve the conditions of life. Many southerners, however, clung to fantasies of past heroics to compensate for a forbidding contemporary life, and looked upon change as subverting cherished values.

It is against this complex background of social change and the resistance it engendered that the murder of a thirteen-year-old girl, in 1913, triggered a violent reaction of mass aggression, hysteria, and prejudice. Leo M. Frank, the Jewish superintendent and part owner of the National Pencil Factory where the dead girl, Mary Phagan, had been employed, became the prime suspect. It was to be Frank's misfortune that he symbolized the alien institutions about which the South had always had the greatest apprehensions.

2

Mary Phagan had been found dead and disfigured in the basement of the National Pencil Factory by a Negro nightwatchman at 3 A.M.

on April 27, 1913.[46] Near her body lay two notes, purportedly written by the girl while being slain. They read:

Mam that negro hire down here did this   i went to make water and he push me down that hole   a long tall negro black that hoo it wase   long tall negro   i wright while play with me.

he said he wood love me land down play like the night witch did it but that long tall black negro did but his slef.[47]

Georgia, and particularly Atlanta, newspapers milked every ounce of sensationalism that they could from the tragedy. One daily indicated that the "horrible mutilation of the body of Mary Phagan proves that the child was in the hands of a beast unspeakable,"[48] while the editors of another added: "Homicide is bad enough. Criminal assault upon a woman is worse. When a mere child, a little girl in knee dresses, is the victim of both, there are added elements of horror and degeneracy that defy the written word."[49]

An aroused public demanded vengeance. One of the victim's neighbors remarked to a reporter, "I wouldn't have liked to be held responsible for the fate of the murderer of little Mary Phagan if the men in this neighborhood got hold of him last night." The minister of Atlanta's Second Baptist Church thundered, "The very existence of God seems to demand that for the honor of the universe the murderer must be exposed."[50]

Atlanta's inadequate police force was under intense pressure to find the culprit. Aside from being understaffed, the force left much to be desired in terms of intelligent action. They had been accustomed to a slower pace and simpler life and their inability to handle the problems of an industrial metropolis made them rely increasingly on an irrational use of power. On one occasion, for example, when Atlanta had experienced a labor shortage, the police attempted to rectify the condition by arresting all able-bodied men found on one of the main streets. Employed and unemployed, black and white, were hauled into court, fined, and sentenced to the stockade without being given a chance to defend themselves. One man so punished had been in the city for only three days. Neither relatives nor employers were notified of the round-up or the sentencings.[51]

The police also had a poor record for solving crimes. A few years before Mary Phagan's death, a national periodical had revealed that only one murder in one hundred was ever punished in Georgia.[52] Atlanta policemen allegedly used brutality with those people who were picked up. In 1909, they were accused of beating one Negro to death and chaining a white girl to the wall until she frothed at the mouth. In 1910, a commission, investigating prison conditions in the city, uncovered "stories too horrible to be told in print."[53] During 1912–13, more than a dozen unsolved murders tried the public's patience.[54] Because these victims had been Negroes, there had been no great protestations over the constables' inefficiency. But Mary Phagan was, as a Georgian so characteristically put it, "our folks."[55] Failure this time would not be tolerated.

A great deal of action seemed to be taking place at the police station. Seven people were arrested, and although four were quickly released, three were still held on suspicion, including the Negro nightwatchman who had discovered the corpse. Of the trio, the one upon whom suspicion quickly fell was Leo Frank, the superintendent of the National Pencil Factory where Mary Phagan had been employed and where her body had been found.

When the police had first questioned Frank, he appeared quite nervous and overwrought. From him, they discovered that Mary Phagan had come to pick up her pay shortly after noon on April 26— Confederate Memorial Day. The superintendent admitted having been alone in his office, and having paid the girl her $1.20 in wages for the ten hours that she had worked that week. Mary had then left his office, and no one else ever admitted to having seen her alive again.[56]

The day after the corpse had been discovered, strands of hair "identified postively"[57] as Mary Phagan's, and blood stains, were found in a metal workroom opposite Frank's office. The night watchman had also told the police that Frank had asked him to come in early on the day of the girl's death, but dismissed him when he arrived and ordered him to return at the normal time. Frank's uneasy behavior before the police and the pressure from an hysterical public led to his arrest.[58]

Leo Max Frank was the Jewish superintendent and part owner of his uncle's pencil factory. Although born in Texas, in 1884, he had been reared in Brooklyn and educated at Cornell University. His first position had been with a firm in a Boston suburb, and he did not settle in the South until 1907. Once in Atlanta, however, he planned to stay. He married Lucile Selig, daughter of one of the more prominent Jewish families in the city, and was popular enough to be elected president of the local chapter of the B'nai B'rith in 1912.[59]

The arrest of the northern, Jewish industrialist won the approval of Atlanta's citizenry. Rumors spread that the prison might be stormed and the prisoners, Frank and the Negro nightwatchman, Newt Lee, lynched.[60] Street talk had it that one of the two must be guilty and killing both would avenge the murder. *The Atlanta Constitution* cautioned its readers to "Keep An Open Mind." "Nothing can be more unjust nor more repugnant to the popular sense of justice," its editorial read, "than to convict even by hearsay an innocent man."[61] The advice went unheeded.

The furor that erupted after the murder can largely be attributed to the deed having rekindled the residents' awareness of the harshness of their lives; having reawakened traditional southern resentment toward outsiders who violated southern mores; and having, once again, dramatized the inherent iniquities of industrial life. "What was uppermost in the minds of those who were indignant," The *Outlook* reflected in 1915, "was the fact that the accused represented the employing class, while the victim was an employee."[62] And the Jew, more than the Negro, provided a symbol for the grievances against industrial capitalism and its by-product, urbanism. The Baptist Minister of Mary Phagan's church made the conventional southern identification of Jewishness, evil, the stranger, and hated northern industrialism when he recalled:

[my] own feelings upon the arrest of the old Negro nightwatch-man, were to the effect that this one old Negro would be poor atonement for the life of this innocent girl. But, when on the next day, the police arrested a Jew, and a Yankee Jew at that, all of the inborn prejudice against Jews rose up in a feeling of satisfaction, that here would be a victim worthy to pay for the crime.[63]

The employment of minors in factories particularly aroused the ire of Atlanta's residents. A spokesman for those crusading to restrict child labor viewed Mary Phagan's death as the inevitable consequence of industrial perfidy: "If social conditions, if factory conditions in Atlanta, were what they should be here, if children of tender years were not forced to work in shops, this frightful tragedy could not have been enacted." The antagonism and venom harbored toward the entrepreneurs and their characteristically inhumane attitudes found expression in Atlanta's *Journal of Labor*:

> Mary Phagan is a martyr to the greed for gain which has grown up in our complex civilization, and which sees in the girls and children merely a source of exploitation in the shape of cheap labor. . . .

The Southern Ruralist, Atlanta's largest circulating periodical, also interpreted the slaying as the product of a heartless and cruel society. It branded "every Southern legislator" who thereafter refused to vote for laws prohibiting the employment of children in factories, "as a potential murderer."[64]

There were other reasons for resenting the factories. White females had always been placed on a pedestal, to be worshipped, exalted, and protected. To Southerners they embodied the purity and nobility of the South itself. Considered a "queen worthy of honor [and] deserving protection from the contamination of a man's world," the white woman had to be zealously guarded from the evils of society.[65]

Industrialism, however, had inaugurated factory work for women. Since tradition dictated that women belonged in the home, southern society regarded the change as subversive of regional honor and family ties. Few white men accepted the alteration without qualms. They may have felt unmanned because they could not maintain their families without an additional income—a feeling particularly disturbing in a society that had always emphasized virility. Guilt was also aroused in the traditionalist southern conscience because the factory system forced wives and daughters to come in contact with strange men. The Southern Baptists, it is said, had an "abnormal fear of the intimate association of the sexes."[66] An Atlanta judge later elaborating upon this argument claimed: "No girl ever leaves home to go to work in a factory, but that the parents feel an inward fear that one of her bosses will take advantage of his position to mistreat her, especially if she repels his advances."[67] A factory owner expressed similar southern sentiments:

> It was considered belittling—oh! very bad! It was considered that for a girl to go into a cotton factory was just a step toward the most vulgar things. They used to talk about the girls working in mills upcountry as if they were in places of grossest immorality. It was said to be the same as a bawdy house; to let a girl go into a cotton factory was to make a prostitute of her.[68]

Given the nature of southern prejudices, Atlantans were particularly receptive to the devastating indictments the authorities apparently unearthed against Leo Frank. One newspaper reported that pictures of Salome dancers "in scanty raiment" adorned the walls of the National Pencil Factory.[69] At the coroner's inquest, a thirteen-year-old friend of Mary Phagan's told his audience that the girl had confessed her fears of the superintendent's improper advances. Former factory employees recalled that Frank had flirted with the girls, that he had made indecent proposals, and that he had even put his hands on them.[70]

Regardless of the veracity of the accusations, other witnesses at the inquest corroborated Frank's statements as to his whereabouts on the day of the murder which, if true, made it almost impossible for him to have been the culprit.[71] Nevertheless the coroner's jury ordered Frank held on suspicion of murder.

Subsequent police disclosures incriminated the factory manager even more in the eyes of many Georgians. A park policeman swore that he had seen Frank and a young girl behaving improperly in a secluded section of the woods a year earlier, while the proprietress of a bordello confessed that the superintendent had phoned her repeatedly on the day of the murder in an effort to obtain a room for himself and a young girl. Both statements were eventually repudiated but not before an impact had been made upon the public. At the time of the madam's affidavit, newspaper readers were informed that her remarks constituted "one of the most important bits of evidence" that the state had against the factory superintendent.[72]

The numerous suggestions dropped by newspapers and police gave rise to the wildest rumors, most of them concerned with the "lasciviousness" of the "notorious" Leo Frank. The Jewish faith, it was widely asserted, forbade violations of Jewesses but condoned similar actions with Gentiles. Frank had allegedly killed another wife in Brooklyn, had illegitimate offspring too numerous to count, drank heavily, was about to be divorced by his wife, and finally, was a pervert. One man said he knew that Frank was a "moral pervert" because he looked like one.[73] These tales, lacking any foundation in fact, suggest how concerned Atlantans were with the religious and social background of Mary Phagan's suspected slayer. Gossip magnified fears. The people, it seemed, wanted Frank to have the characteristics attributed to him.

3

The trial of Leo Frank for the murder of Mary Phagan opened on July 28, 1913, amidst great hullabaloo. It lasted until August 26. During the entire period, the temper of the crowd indicated the antipathy Atlantans felt toward the defendant. "The fact that Frank is under indictment today," one reporter explained the day before the trial began, "means to many minds that he is therefore guilty...."[74]

The state's case rested primarily upon the testimony of Jim Conley, a Negro sweeper who had been employed in the National Pencil Factory. He charged Frank with having committed the murder and acknowledged that he had helped his employer remove the body to the factory basement.[75] There were no witnesses to corroborate any of the sweeper's statements.

The defense based its case primarily upon proving that Frank did not have the time to commit the murder. Witnesses were presented who corroborated the superintendent's account of his whereabouts on the fatal day. Frank maintained his innocence and characterized Conley's tale as "the vilest and most amazing pack of lies ever conceived in the perverted brain of a wicked human being."[76]

The jury needed less than four hours of deliberation before finding the defendant guilty. The judge sentenced Frank to hang. Atlantans were jubilant with the verdict. A crowd outside of the courthouse, estimated at between two and four thousand, screamed itself hoarse. As he stepped out of the courthouse, the prosecuting attorney was lifted to the shoulders of two husky men and carried to his office amidst huzzahs and cheers. After what was perhaps one of the wildest celebrations in Atlanta's history *The Marietta Journal and Courier* observed, "It seems to be the universal opinion that Frank was guilty and that he was the cause of the demonstration when the verdict was announced.[77]

Frank's lawyers appealed his case through the Georgia courts and ultimately to the United States Supreme Court. None of the tribunals ordered another trial. The Governor of Georgia re-evaluated the evidence in June, 1915, and commuted the death penalty to life imprisonment. Two months later, in August, 1915, a band of men stormed the prison, kidnapped Frank, and lynched him.[78]

4

The joyousness with which Frank's conviction was received revealed the people's desire for a scapegoat for their deeper resentments.[79] Georgia's Governor, John M. Slaton, explained the hostility toward Frank as "the prejudice of the employe [sic] against the employer. The fact that the head of a large factory is accused of attacking a girl, one of his employes, has been sufficient to give rise to this kind of prejudice."[80]

The anti-Semitism that erupted in Atlanta also suggested the need for a particular type of a villain. Manifestations of this sentiment are evident in the widespread acceptance of Negro Jim Conley's testimony; the numerous rumors that Frank's Jewish friends had collected a "fund of hundreds of thousands of dollars" to buy the jury; and tales to the effect that some defense witnesses had been bought with "jew money." In addition, Frank's lawyers had received anonymous phone calls with the cryptic message, "If they don't hang that Jew, we'll hang you." Crowds outside of the courtroom frequently hurled epithets like, "Lynch him!" and "Crack that Jew's neck!" The jury was also threatened with lynching if it did not "hang that 'damned sheeny!'"[81] This passionate hatred disclosed the Atlantans' intense yearning for some culprit upon whom they could fix blame for the frustrations of their barren lives. "People haunted by the purposelessness of their lives," Eric Hoffer has written, "try to find a new content not only by dedicating themselves to a holy cause but also by nursing a fanatical grievance."[82] This was especially true of the newly urbanized working classes in the South.[83]

Ignorant, frustrated, and frightened, the workers sought a devil to exorcise. Moreover, their severe tribulations and limited education made necessary a dogmatic oversimplification. In such a situation, Leo Frank could easily be visualized as the diabolical perpetrator of savage crimes against society.

Reinforcing these cultural and emotional sources of prejudice is the herd tendency in human nature. Widely shared personal opinions are difficult to sway. People tend to absorb the knowledge to which they are exposed through the refraction of their own emotional needs and experiences and through the evaluations prevalent among the groups with which they identify. Facts and opinions that differ from one's own or that are disturbing to convention are frequently not perceived. Psychologists have found a high correlation between belief and desire ($+.88$) but a negative one in regard to belief and evidence ($-.03$). In other words, factual information is insufficient to disturb established opinions.[84] Ellen Glasgow, the Virginia novelist, has noted that in the South for people "to think differently meant to be ostracized."[85]

Enthusiastic acceptance of Frank's conviction was further enhanced because people are conditioned to defer to those whom they have been trained to respect. Statements made by public officials are accepted as accurate unless there is some reason to suspect obfuscation. This was especially true in the South where the ruling classes "had extraordinary powers over the whole social body."[86] Hugh Dorsey, the Georgia-born prosecutor, had announced before the trial: "the possibility of a mistake having been made is very remote."[87] Southern Pinkerton and Burns detectives, who had conducted separate investigations, had also expressed their firm belief in the factory manager's guilt.[88] Why, then, should the masses have assumed that the alien Jew was telling the truth while their own leaders were not?

The members of the jury, a representative cross-section of Atlantans,[89] pleased their peers with the verdict. A spokesman for the jurors stated that they had all accepted the prosecution's arguments and conclusions.[90] To be sure, they may have been convinced of Frank's guilt on the basis of the evidence presented in court. But even if the material had been less persuasive, the opinion of the Atlanta crowds would certainly have influenced those who had to decide Frank's fate. What would have happened to their jobs, their social relationships, and the position of their families, for example, if the jurors had voted to acquit the man who most of Atlanta assumed had ravished the little girl? More than a year after the trial had ended, one juror confessed to a northern reporter that he was not sure of anything except that unless Frank was found guilty the jurors would never get home alive.[91]

5

A Boston newspaperman wrote in 1916 that had Frank been a native Georgian he would never have been convicted of Mary Phagan's death.[92] More likely, had he been a respected member of the gentile community, no southern prosecutor would have staked his case on a Negro's accusations. Moreover, had the people of Atlanta not found the cares of life so great a burden, there would have been less demand for a scapegoat to pay for their accumulated frustrations. The coming of industrialism was not solely responsible for Frank's fate. But the technological changes in society, which uprooted people and set them down in strange, urban areas, aggravated whatever intolerance and anxiety the southern culture had already nurtured.

The murder of Mary Phagan stood out as a symbol of industrial iniquity. She was continually referred to as "the little factory girl" long after the focus of the case had shifted to Leo Frank. A newspaperman observed during the trial: "The little factory girl will be remembered as long as law exists in Atlanta." A Confederate War veteran contributed "a dollar for the erection of a monument to Mary Phagan, the little factory girl who recently laid down her life for her honor." And Georgia's patrician historian, L. L. Knight, narrating the events of the murder and the solution arrived upon, years later wrote, "Espousing the cause of the little factory girl, [Tom] Watson in a most dramatic vein of appeal, summoned the true manhood of the

South to assert its chivalry in vindicating the child's honor."[93] The "little factory girl's" death, and the factory owner's responsibility for it, had at last provided an acceptable outlet for the discontented. Employment of minors, unconventional association of the sexes, and the evils of the factory system deeply disturbed a conservative society uneasily confronting the beginnings of industrialism. Most Atlantans, having uprooted themselves from rural origins, were alienated by their work in the factory and by life in the city. The murder of an innocent southern girl by a northern, Jewish factory superintendent evoked the hostility latent in their unsettled existence and directed this hostility to the symbol of their fears and grievances.

NOTES

1. Barbara Tuchman, *The Proud Tower* (New York: Macmillan, 1966), p. 182. Maurice Samuel, *Blood Accusation* (New York: Alfred A. Knopf, 1966), p. 7. Henry David, *The History of the Haymarket Affair* (New York: Russel & Russell, 1936), pp. 528, 535, 541. Louis Joughin and Edmund M. Morgan, *The Legacy of Sacco and Vanzetti* (Chicago: Quadrangle Books, 1964), pp. 201–203.

2. A partial listing of growing American cities, and their population figures for 1900 and 1910, follows:

| | | POPULATION | |
State	City	1900	1910
Alabama	Birmingham	38,415	132,685
California	Los Angeles	102,479	319,198
	San Francisco	342,782	416,912
Colorado	Denver	133,859	213,381
Florida	Tampa	15,839	37,782
	Miami	1,681	5,471
Georgia	Atlanta	89,872	154,839
Illinois	Chicago	1,689,575	2,185,283
Indiana	Indianapolis	169,164	233,650
Kansas	Kansas City	51,418	82,331
Louisiana	New Orleans	287,104	339,075
Massachusetts	Boston	560,892	670,585
Michigan	Detroit	285,704	465,766
Minnesota	Minneapolis	202,718	301,408
Mississippi	Jackson	7,816	21,262
Missouri	Kansas City	163,752	248,381
Nevada	Reno	4,500	10,867

State	City	POPULATION 1900	1910
New Jersey	Newark	246,070	347,469
New Mexico	Alburquerque	6,238	11,020
New York	Buffalo	352,387	423,715
	New York	3,437,202	4,766,883
North Carolina	Charlotte	18,091	34,014
Ohio	Cleveland	381,768	560,663
	Youngstown	44,885	79,066
Oklahoma	Oklahoma City	32,452	64,205
	Tulsa	7,298	18,182
Oregon	Portland	90,426	207,214
South Dakota	Aberdeen	4,087	10,753
Tennessee	Memphis	102,320	131,105
	Nashville	80,865	110,364
Texas	Dallas	42,638	92,104
	Fort Worth	26,688	73,312
	San Antonio	53,321	96,614
Utah	Salt Lake City	53,531	92,777
Virginia	Norfolk	46,624	67,452
	Richmond	85,050	127,628
Washington	Seattle	80,671	237,195
	Tacoma	37,714	83,743
West Virginia	Charleston	11,099	22,966

Abstract of the Thirteenth Census of the United States, 1910, pp. 65–75, passim.

3. *The Atlanta Constitution*, January 18, 1915, pp. 1, 2. Cited hereafter as AC.

4. The cost of living in 1913 was the second highest in the nation (Boston was first), and wages lagged behind those paid in northern cities. *The Atlanta Journal*, September 17, 1913, p. 1, hereafter cited as AJ. See also W. J. Cash, *The Mind of the South* (New York: Alfred A. Knopf, 1941), p. 247. C. Vann Woodward reported that in 1912 and 1913 hourly earnings in New England averaged 37 per cent above those in the South, *Origins of the New South* (Baton Rouge: Louisiana State University Press, 1951), pp. 420–21.

5. United States, *Report of the Industrial Commission*, 1901, VII, 56, 57. A few years later the U.S. Senate's *Report on Conditions of Woman and Child Wage-Earners in the United States*, 61st Cong., 2nd Sess., 1910, Senate Document #645, Serial #5685, I, 261, noted that the average work week in Georgia cotton mills in 1908 was 64 hours, which was longer than that in Virginia, North Carolina, South Carolina, Alabama, and Mississippi. Of the thirty-one establishments the Commission investigated, sixteen had a sixty-six hour week; forty minutes was the average lunch time.

6. *Annual Reports of the Committees of Council, Officers and Departments of the City of Atlanta*, 1902–1903, pp. 96, 192. During the period 1900–1914,

the average hourly wage in the United States was 20–21 cents an hour. For a sixty-hour week this would be about $12. The average annual earnings in manufacturing for the following years indicated: 1907: $522; 1908: $475; and two different estimates for 1909: $518 and $557. John R. Commons and Associates, *History of Labor in the United States, 1896–1932* (New York: The Macmillan Co., 1935), pp. 59–61.

7. Atlanta, *Comptroller's Report for 1913*, p. 57.

8. Quoted in *Journal of Labor*, November 7, 1913, p. 4.

9. "Dixie Conditions Stir Unionists—Description of Actual State of Atlanta Textile Workers Make Delegates Weep," *The Textile Worker*, III (December, 1914), 21.

10. AC, March 4, 1907, p. 3; June 4, 1913, p. 2. Franklin M. Garrett, *Atlanta and Environs* (3 vols.: New York, 1954), II, 574. "Decency As An Issue," *The Outlook*, 90 (December 19, 1908), 848. "An Advertising Campaign Against Segregated Vice," *The American City*, IX (July, 1913), 3, 4. *Annual Report of the Park Commissioner of the City of Atlanta for the Year Ending December 31, 1910*, p. 20. *Report... for the Year Ending December 31, 1913*, p. 32.

11. Atlanta Chamber of Commerce, *Annual Report for 1909*, p. 5. U.S. Bureau of the Census, *General Statistics of Cities: 1909*, pp. 88, 148. Atlanta, *Comptroller's Report for 1911*, p. 41. Atlanta, *Annual Reports, 1902–1903*, pp. 100–101. Herbert R. Sands, *Organization and Administration of the City Government of Atlanta, Georgia* (New York: New York Bureau of Municipal Research, November, 1912), p. 62.

12. AC, January 18, 1915, p. 1. U.S. Bureau of the Census, *Statistics of Cities Having a Population of Over 30,000: 1905*, p. 111. Atlanta's population in 1904 was 98,776; in 1911 it was 161,515. Atlanta, *Comptroller's Report, 911*, p. 19.

13. Ibid., p. 20; *Annual Report of the Atlanta Chamber of Commerce, 1909*, p. 5. U.S. Bureau of the Census, *Historical Statistics of the United States: Colonial Times to 1957*, p. 27. U.S. Bureau of the Census, Bulletin, #109, *Mortality Statistics, 1910*, p. 31. "Dixie Conditions Stir Unionists...," *The Textile Worker*, III, 21. *Preliminary Report of the Commissioner of Commerce and Labor, State of Georgia, for the Term Ending June 11, 1912*, p. 7.

14. U.S. Bureau of the Census, *Statistics of Cities Having a Population of Over, 30,000: 1905*, p. 111; U.S. Bureau of the Census, *Statistics of Cities Having a Population of Over 30,000: 1907*, pp. 102, 107, 410. Inaugural Address of Mayor James G. Woodward, *Annual Report of Atlanta for 1905*, p. 27.

15. *Comptroller's Report, 1911*, p. 43. *Annual Report, 1902–1903*, p. 302; Sands, *Organization and Administration*, p. 36.

16. The term "cracker" connoted isolated, ignorant, backward frontiersman. Bevode C. McCall, "Georgia Town and Cracker Culture" (Unpublished Ph.D. dissertation, Dept. of Sociology, University of Chicago, 1954), pp. 105–106.

17. Cash, Mind of the South, p. 327. See also Stewart G. Cole, The History of Fundamentalism (New York: R. R. Smith Inc., 1931), p. 26; Josephine Pinckney, "Bulwarks Against Change," in Culture in the South, ed. W. T. Couch (Chapel Hill: University of North Carolina Press, 1935), p. 41.

18. "Facts About the Atlanta Murders," The World's Work, XIII (November, 1906), 8147.

19. Glen Weddington Rainey, "The Race Riot of 1906 in Atlanta" (Unpublished Master's essay, Emory University, 1929), no pagination: Ray Stannard Baker, "Following the Color Line," The American Magazine, LXIII (April, 1907), 569. Anon., "The Atlanta Massacre," The Independent, 91 (October 4, 1906), 799–800.

20. Woodward, Origins, p. 448.

21. Joseph H. Fichter and George L. Maddox, "Religion in the South, Old and New," in The South in Continuity and Change, ed. John M. McKinney and Edgar T. Thompson (Durham: Duke University Press, 1965), pp. 360, 364.

22. Carroll Edwin Harrington, "The Fundamentalist Movement in America, 1870–1920" (Unpublished Ph.D. dissertation, University of California at Berkeley, 1959), p. 102.

23. Hunter Dickinson Farish, The Circuit Rider Dismounts (Richmond: The Dietz Press, 1938), pp. 333–34.

24. Rufus B. Spain, "Attitudes and Reactions of Southern Baptists to Certain Problems of Society, 1865–1900" (Unpublished Ph.D. dissertation, Vanderbilt University, 1961), p. 229.

25. Ibid., p. 230. Carl Dean English, "The Ethical Emphases of the Editors of Baptist Journals Published in the Southeastern Region of the United States, 1865–1915" (Unpublished Th.D. dissertation, Southern Baptist Theological Seminary, 1948), p. 187.

26. Cash, Mind of the South, p. 347. The major sources of my commentaries on fundamentalism have been Norman F. Furniss, The Fundamentalist Controversy, 1918–1931 (New Haven: Yale University Press, 1954), pp. 35–44; Harrington, Fundamentalist Movement, pp. vi-vii; Cash, Mind of the South, p. 341; Cole, Fundamentalism, pp. 53, 322; and H. Richard Niebuhr, "Fundamentalism" in the Encyclopaedia of the Social Sciences, ed. Edwin R. A. Seligman (15 vols.: New York: The Macmillan Co., 1931), VI, 526–27.

27. Rupert B. Vance, Human Geography of the South (Chapel Hill: University

of North Carolina Press, 1932), p. 279. AJ, December 23, 1906, as cited in *Congressional Record*, 59th Cong., 2nd Sess., p. 3018. Rowland T. Berthoff, "Southern Attitudes Toward Immigration," *The Journal of Southern History*, XVII (August, 1951), 329.

28. *Congressional Record*, December 15, 1907, p. 3031. Berthoff, "Attitudes," XVII, 329. "Amendment of Immigration Laws," Senate Document #251, 62nd Cong., 2nd Sess., 1912, Serial #6174, p. 5. AJ, December 23, 1906, December 30, 1906, as cited in *Congressional Record*, 59th Cong., 2nd Sess., pp. 3018–19; AC, March 13, 1914, p. 4.

29. "Southern Peonage and Immigration," *The Nation*, 85 (December 19, 1907), 557.

30. Berthoff, "Attitudes," XVII, 344.

31. Solomon Sutker, "The Jews of Atlanta: Their Social Structure and Leadership Patterns" (Unpublished Ph.D. dissertation, Dept. of Sociology, University of North Carolina, 1950), p. 74; AC, January 18, 1915, p. 1.

32. Thomas Gibson, "The Anti-Negro Riots in Atlanta," *Harper's Weekly*, L (October 13, 1906), 1457–58. "Results in Atlanta," *The Independent*, LXII (January 3, 1907), 52. Rainey, *Race Riot*, chap. 3; *The Baltimore Morning Sun*, November 23, 1914, p. 3.

33. Miriam Kotler Freund, "Jewish Merchants in Colonial America" (Unpublished Ph.D. dissertation, New York University, 1936), p. 96. Merle Curti, *The Growth of American Thought* (New York: Harper & Brothers, 1943), p. 51. Anson Phelps Stokes, *Church and State in the United States* (3 vols.: New York: Harper & Brothers, 1950), I, 854, 857. Jacob Rader Marcus, *Early American Jewry: The Jews of Pennsylvania and the South, 1655–1790* (Philadelphia: Jewish Publication Society of America, 1953), pp. 167, 228, 231, 333. Paul Masserman and Max Baker, *The Jews Come to America* (New York: Black Publishing Co., 1932), p. 88. Peter Wiernik, *History of the Jews in America* (New York: Jewish Publication Society of America, 1931), p. 127. Joseph L. Blau and Salo W. Baron, editors, *The Jews of the United States, 1790–1840* (3 vols.: New York: Columbia University Press, 1963), I, 17. Clement Eaton, *Freedom of Thought in the Old South* (New York: Peter Smith, 1951), p. 27. Thomas Jefferson to a New York Jewish editor, quoted in "Legislature of Maryland," *Niles' Register*, XV, Supplement (1819), 10. Although voting and office holding were generally restricted to Protestants in all of the American colonies, the restrictions upon Jews tended to last longer in some of the southern States. See, for example, Jacob Rader Marcus, *Early American Jewry: The Jews of New York, New England and Canada, 1649–1794* (Philadelphia: Jewish Publication Society of America, 1951), pp. 103, 116.

34. Eaton, *Old South*, p. 233. E. Merton Coulter, *The Confederate States of*

America (Baton Rouge: Louisiana State University Press, 1950), p. 226. Rudolpf Glanz, *The Jew in the Old American Folklore* (New York: Waldon Press, 1961), p. 54.

35. Rufus Learsi, *The Jews in America: A History* (Cleveland: The World Publishing Co., 1954), p. 103. Margaret Case Harriman, *And the Price is Right* (Cleveland: The World Publishing Co., 1958), p. 34.

36. Lucian Lamar Knight, *Reminiscences of Famous Georgians* (2 vols.: Atlanta: Franklin Turner Co., 1907), I, 512.

37. William M. Stewart, "The Great Slave Power," *The Arena*, XIX (May, 1890), 580. Carr quoted in Harry Golden, *A Little Girl is Dead* (Cleveland: The World Publishing Co., 1965), p. 226.

38. Horace M. Kallen, "The Ethics of Zionism," *The Maccabean*, XI (August, 1906), 69. William J. Robertson, *The Changing South* (New York: Boni and Liveright, 1927), p. 99.

39. John Higham, "Social Discrimination Against Jews in America, 1830–1930," *Publication of the American Jewish Historical Society*, 47 (1957), 1–33. Higham, "Anti-Semitism in the Gilded Age: A Reinterpretation," *Mississippi Valley Historical Review*, 43 (March, 1957), 559–78. Oscar Handlin, "American Views of the Jew at the Opening of the Twentieth Century," *Publications of the American Jewish Historical Society*, 40 (June, 1951), 323–44. John Higham, "American Anti-Semitism Historically Reconsidered," *Jews in the Mind of America*, ed. Charles Herbert Stember (New York: Basic Books, 1966).

40. No anti-Semitic remarks are attributed to any Southern Populists *during the Populist era* in any of the following works: Richard Hofstadter, *The Age of Reform* (New York: Alfred A. Knopf, 1955), V. C. Ferkiss, "Populist Influences on American Fascism," *Western Political Quarterly*, X (1957); Norman Pollack, *The Populist Response to Industrial America* (Cambridge: Harvard University Press, 1962); W. T. K. Nugent, *The Tolerant Populists* (Chicago: University of Chicago Press, 1963), C. Vann Woodward, "The Populist Heritage and the Intellectual," *The American Scholar*, XXI (Winter, 1959–60), Frederic Cople Jaher, *Doubters and Dissenters* (New York: The Free Press, 1964).

41. Higham, *Mississippi Valley Historical Review*, 43, 572.

42. Higham, *Mississippi Valley Historical Review*, 43, 559–78. Higham, *Publications of the American Jewish Historical Society*, 47, 22. Higham, *Jews in the Mind of America*, pp. 248–49. Although Atlanta was not a small town after 1900, in part, it did have a "small-town culture."

43. Benjamin Kendrick, "The Study of the New South," *The North Carolina Historical Review*, III (January, 1926), 10.

44. Robertson, *Changing South*, p. 99.

45. Elias Rivkin has written: "At every moment of economic or social crisis, especially since the 1890's, anti-Semitism has manifested itself [in the United States]. This anti-Semitism more and more linked the Jews with the sources of disintegration and decay and attempted to identify the Jews with the twin threat of international capitalism and international communism." Rivkin has also observed that "the position of the Jews in every society of the past has been as secure as the society itself. For every stress the Jews have been held essentially responsible; for every collapse they have been blamed." *Essays in American–Jewish History* (Cincinnati: American Jewish Archives, 1958), p. 60. In our own times, many southern Jews still feel defensive and hesitate to disrupt the status quo. Alfred O. Hero, Jr., a sociologist, has written that "small-town, Deep Southern Jews have feared especially that someone with a Jewish name would express controversial ideas and thus stimulate unfavorable reactions to Jews in general." *The Southerner and World Affairs* (Baton Rouge: Louisiana State University Press, 1965), p. 501. Hero's chapter, "Southern Jews," is the best historical discussion that I have seen on the subject.

46. AC, April 27, 1913, "extra," pp. 1, 2.

47. Henry A. Alexander, *Some Facts About the Murder Notes in the Phagan Case* (privately published pamphlet, 1914), pp. 5, 7.

48. *The Augusta (Georgia) Chronicle*, May 2, 1913), p. 1.

49. AC, April 29, 1913, p. 4.

50. AC, April 28, 1913, p. 3. *The Atlanta Georgian*, May 4, 1913, p. 2. Cited hereafter as AG.

51. Philip Waltner, "Municipal and Misdemeanor Offenders," in *The Call of the New South*, edited by James E. McCulloch (Nashville, Southern Sociological Congress, 1912), pp. 110–11.

52. Hugh C. Weir, "The Menace of the Police," *The World To-Day*, 18 (January, 1910), 52.

53. Weir, "The Menace of the Police," *The World To-Day*, 18 (March, 1910), 174.

54. In regard to the conduct and competency of its policemen, Atlanta was typical of other American cities. "There is probably not a city in the South where the police do not make needless arrests." Weltner, "Offenders," *New South*, p. 107. Crime existed in every major city in the United States and the failure of police forces to control the widespread lawlessness evoked extensive comment. The Conference for Good City Government discussed the lack of competent policemen in 1906, 1909, and 1910. Delegates to these con-

ventions argued that police reform could not be postponed. Better laws, better methods, and better men were essential to meet the needs of growing cities. In 1910, a national periodical ran a series of articles condemning police incompetence, inefficiency, and brutality. The author warned, "Gentlemen of the police, you are on trial." Edward M. Hartwell, "The Police Question," *Proceedings of the Atlantic City Conference for Good City Government*, 1906, p. 397. Augustus Raymond Hatton, "The Control of Police," *Proceedings of the Cincinnati Conference for Good City Government*, 1909, pp. 157–61. Leonhard Felix Field, "The Organization of Police Forces," *Proceedings*, 1910, p. 281. Weir, "Menace of the Police," 59.

55. Wytt E. Thompson, *A Short Review of the Frank Case* (Atlanta: n.n., 1914), p. 29.

56. AC, April 28, 1913, pp. 1, 2.

57. AG, April 28, 1913, p. 1. It was later made known that a microscopic test had not proven the hair to be Mary Phagan's.

58. AC, April 28, 1913, pp. 1, 2; April 29, 1913, pp. 1, 2; April 30, 1913, pp. 1, 2.

59. *The New York Times*, August 26, 1913, p. 18; February 18, 1914, p. 3; AC, June 1, 1915, p. 4; AG, May 13, 1913, p. 2. Interview with Alexander Brin, a Boston reporter who covered the later stages of the Frank case, in Boston, August 19, 1964. Mr. Brin now publishes *The Jewish Advocate*.

60. *The Savannah Morning News*, May 2, 1913, p. 1.

61. AC, May 2, 1913, p. 4.

62. "The Frank Case," *The Outlook*, 110 (May 26, 1915), p. 167.

63. L. O. Bricker, "A Great American Tragedy," *The Shane Quarterly*, IV (April, 1943), 90.

64. AG, April 30, 1913, p. 1. *The Journal of Labor*, XV (May 2, 1913), 4. "Accessory After the Fact," *Southern Ruralist*, XX (June 15, 1913), 13.

65. English, "Ethical Emphases," p. 219.

66. Spain, *Attitudes*, p. 299.

67. Arthur G. Powell, *I Can Go Home Again* (Chapel Hill: University of North Carolina Press, 1943), p. 287.

68. Broadus Mitchell, *The Rise of Cotton Mills in the South* (Baltimore: The Johns Hopkins Press, 1921), p. 195.

69. AG, April 29, 1913, p. 3.

70. AC, May 9, 1913, p. 2. AG, May 8, 1913, p. 2; May 9, 1913, pp. 1, 2. *The Savannah Morning News*, May 9, 1913, p. 1.

71. AJ, June 2, 1913, p. 9.

72. AC, May 11, 1913, p. 1; May 23, 1913, p. 1.

73. AG, May 11, 1913, p. 2. *The Augusta Chronicle*, May 5, 1919 p. 2. *The Baltimore Morning Sun*, November 19, 1914, p. 3. A. B. MacDonald, "Has Georgia Condemned an Innocent Man to Die?" *The Kansas City* (Mo.) *Star*, January 17, 1915, p. 1C. Thompson, *Short Reviews*, p. 25. C. P. Connolly, *The Truth About the Frank Case* (New York, 1915), p. 14. Abraham Cahan, *Blätter Von Mein Leben* (5 vols.: New York: Forward Publishing Co., 1931), V, 494.

74. AG, July 27, 1913, p. 2.

75. Frank vs. State, *Brief of the Evidence*, pp. 54–57.

76. Quoted in AJ, August 4, 1913, p. 1.

77. AG, August 25, 1913, p. 1; August 26, 1913, p. 1. AC, August 26, 1913, p. 4. *The Herald-Journal* (Greensboro, Ga.), August 29, 1913, p. 4. *The Marietta Journal and Courier*, August 29, 1913, p. 2.

78. AC, June 22, 1915, pp. 1, 2, 9. *The New York Times*, August 18, 1915, pp. 13; August 19, 1915, pp. 1, 3; August 23, 1915, p. 5.

79. Daniel Bell has written: "Social groups that are dispossessed invariably seek targets on whom they can vent their resentments, targets whose power can serve to explain their dispossession." "The Dispossessed," in *The Radical Right*, edited by Daniel Bell (Garden City, N.Y.: Doubleday & Company, 1963), pp. 2–3.

80. *The New York Times*, November 28, 1914, p. 5.

81. *The Greensboro, Georgia Herald-Journal*, August 29, 1913. Thompson, *Short Review*, p. 9. Connolly, *The Truth*, p. 11. "Frank's Prophesy of Vindication Comes True 10 Years After Georgia Mob Hangs Him as Slayer." *The Jewish Avocate*, 42 (October 18, 1923), 20. *Minutes* of the executive committee of the American Jewish Committee, November 8, 1913 (located in the American Jewish Committee Archives, New York City).

82. Eric Hoffer, *The True Believer* (New York: New American Library, 1958), p. 92.

83. Alfred O. Hero, Jr. has written: "the newly urbanized Southern working class . . . seemed especially open to leadership by charismatic and authoritarian figures who would appeal to their anxieties and insecurities, with dogmatic, oversimplified 'solutions,'" *The Southerner and World Affairs*, p. 354.

84. Frederick Hansen Lund, "The Psychology of Belief," *The Journal of*

Abnormal and Social Psychology, XX (1925), 194–95. Gordon W. Allport and Leo Postman, *The Psychology of Rumor* (New York: Henry Holt & Co., 1947), p. 191. Melvin M. Tumin, *An Inventory and Appraisal of Research on American Anti-Semitism* (New York: Freedom Books, 1961), p. 115. Eunice Cooper and Marie Jahoda, "The Evasion of Propaganda: How Prejudiced People Respond to Anti-Prejudice Propaganda," *The Journal of Psychology*, XXIII (1947), p. 15. Mahlon Brewster Smith, "Functional and Descriptive Analysis of Public Opinion" (Unpublished Ph.D. dissertation, Dept. of Social Psychology, Harvard University, 1947), pp. 500, 507. George Cornewall Lewis, *An Essay on the Influence of Authority in Matters of Opinion* (London: Longmans, Green & Co., 1875), p. 10.

85. Quoted in William H. Nicholls, *Southern Tradition and Regional Progress* (Chapel Hill: University of North Carolina Press, 1960), p. 135.

86. Cash, *Mind of the South*, p. 310.

87. Quoted in AG, July 27, 1913, p. 2.

88. AC, May 25, 1913, p. 1; May 27, 1913, pp. 1, 2.

89. One bank teller, one bookkeeper, one real estate agent, one manufacturer, one contractor, one optician, one railroad claim agent, one mailing clerk, two salesmen, and two machinists. Garrett, *Atlanta*, II, 622.

90. AJ, August 26, 1913, p. 1.

91. *The New York Times*, February 23, 1915, p. 9.

92. Clipping from the morgue of the Boston *Herald-Traveller*, August 17, 1916.

93. AG, August 5, 1913, p. 4. *The North Georgia Citizen* (Dalton, Ga.), August 28, 1913, p. 4. Lucian Lamar Knight, *A Standard History of Georgia and Georgians* (6 vols.: Chicago: The Lewis Publishing Co., 1917), II, 1190.

6

Metropolism and Urban Elites in the Far West

by GUNTHER BARTH

Although urban life in the United States dates back to the early phases of colonization, the period of significant urban development belongs to the years after 1850, which encompass the rise of the industrial city.[1] These same years coincide with the growth of San Francisco and Denver typifying the emerging forms of settlement in the Far West. Both communities experienced similar stages of development although they represent two different types of cities: San Francisco was a seaport linked to the harbors of the world, and Denver, a landlocked town confined to direct contact only with certain metropolitan centers. In both areas the coming of the railroad spurred the growth of urban society, and four decades later, the advent of the automobile presaged its disintegration. A discussion of some aspects of the impact of industrialism on the elites in these emergent urban societies will throw light on stages of social development in San Francisco and Denver.

One reaction of San Francisco's elites to the impact of industrialism on their city is exemplified in the Second Street cut through Rincon Hill. The grading of the hill affected in various ways the interests of the entire elite community. Examining their reactions to the particular situation of the Second Street cut brings out the diverse elements within the elites. The different responses to the crisis situation point out the men and women active in a specific elite. Such diversity is characteristic of a pluralistic society and amplifies the contours of the commonly envisioned stratified society, which identifies persons eminent in various fields by the general descriptive term "elite". Probing the crisis situation expands the relatively stable world of a stratified society, which is influenced primarily by the ups and downs of an accelerated urban growth. This analysis adds to the economic, political, cultural, and social influences on the stratified society the dimensions of a dynamic and pluralistic society with its fluctuating and changing composition.

The response of the elites in the Rincon Hill affair is of dual significance for the conceptual framework of the present study. An investigation of the crisis situation provides a set of analytic categories for San Francisco elites, and when used in conjunction with a concept of metropolism, delineates a phase in the growth of urban societies in the Far West. This concept of metropolism designates the tendency of certain citizens in emergent urban societies to inaugurate and maintain a style and tone of life characteristic of great cities and to foster a quality of urban behavior symptomatic of large centers. The many characteristics of urban societies that the studies of cities identify direct attention to this trend, which marks various phases of city growth in history. Both the extension of the *polis* into the Hellenistic world and the growing towns accompanying the migration of European people to America, Australia, and Asia show the role of metropolism in a broad framework.[2] In a specific locality, the use of the concept of metropolism makes it possible to indicate growth and changes in particular urban societies by measuring the degree to which some citizens attained and sustained a way of life approximating that of great cities.

Metropolism in early San Francisco and Denver, in settings but a few steps removed from the wilderness, describes the tendency of men and women to retain an urban outlook and to aspire to a style of city life undeterred by the vast expanse of nature separating their new homes from their old ones in Boston, New York, Philadelphia, Charleston, and Savannah as well as Chicago, St. Louis, and New Orleans.

Evoking their former life in cities on the Atlantic seaboard and in the Mississippi Valley, metropolism was more than a sequence of delightful evening entertainments or a series of ostentatious receptions. It found its outward expression in substantial residences, a sturdy four-square mansion or a solid row house facing a square or a street, in a western version of Beacon Hill, Rittenhouse Square, Meeting Street, or even London's Berkeley Square. Based on a man's origin, creed, education, and profession, the common outlook of some men and women reinforced loyalties by their identification with a familiar way of urban life in their new cities.

This style of life, consciously transplanted from distant eastern cities to western towns, contrasted sharply with that of rich families who preferred to live in fashionable hotels because it did not commit them to the locale and promised an easy drift to the next bonanza. Metropolism furthered a ready identification of the untamed new world with the familiar sites of the East by the transfer of architectural styles; interior decoration; landscape gardening; etiquette; patronage of arts and letters; concepts of charity; civic consciousness; social organizations; and a mode of life. As a "thoroughly Eastern city," Richard Harding Davis regarded Denver, "a smaller New York in an encircling of white-capped mountains," which earlier had already enchanted another devotee of Gotham, Walt Whitman.[3]

By identifying San Francisco's Rincon Hill and Denver's Fourteenth Street with their counterparts in other cities, some westerners could create the illusion that they were not in fact in the midst of a wilderness and had not in fact endured an arduous overland journey or a long sea voyage to reach their new homes. The trend was reaffirmed by the presence of large numbers of federal office-holders. With their contacts to Washington they served as a channel through which San Francisco and Denver life moved more rapidly into the currents of national affairs.

Although wealth was appreciated as an ingredient of the settled, urban way of life, these men and women did not allow it to dominate their values and to define the extent of their world. One of the most prominent men in San Francisco society in the 1850s, and its best dancer, was William Stone Botts. Homely and impoverished, he had a sinecure in the "Virginia Poor House," as the San Francisco Custom

House was known during that decade, because so many Virginia gentlemen were employed there as clerks. No ball or party was a success without the dimunitive man, with his bald head, huge red mustache, and peculiar hoarse voice. Billy Botts social graces were his chief and, as one socialite remembered, his only distinction.[4] Mrs. Margaret Evans's guest list of her annual "At Home" reception in 1881, "one of the most notable in Denver social events," gives not only the names of the political and financial associates of Colorado's former governor, John Evans, but also of a wide range of people who belonged to the party merely because their background, or their role in the Methodist Church, or their participation in cultural or charitable work qualified them for her Fourteenth Street world.[5]

Rincon Hill, because of the topographical peculiarities of the San Francisco peninsula, became the center of metropolism in the 1850s and 1860s. An examination of this specific setting permits us to view metropolism, at this stage, as an attribute of a social elite committed to maintaining a particular style of life characteristic of large cities. While pursued most strictly by the social elite, this way of life attracted many followers in the general elite community. However, the struggle of conflicting interests accompanying the leveling of Rincon Hill brought out the primary loyalties of these men, and indicates that they were actually committed to values other than those sustaining this phase of metropolism on Rincon Hill. In other words, they responded to the destruction of the Rincon Hill world by the forces of industrialism in ways suggesting that they were not reacting as members of the social elite, but as representatives of financial, political, and cultural elites. Their primary concern with economic, political, and cultural activities kept them in touch with the changing forms of eastern urban life as the older cities were transformed from commercial to industrial centers. Through their ties with railroad and mining enterprises and other foci of industrial activities in the Far West, these men saw an additional significance in the new eastern models of city life, which sanctioned the rejection of the dated metropolism of Rincon Hill modeled after the urbane values of the fading commercial city.

Rincon Hill, extending from Folsom Street to Bryant, and from Spear Street to Third, was the most significant urban site in San Francisco before the coming of the railroad. Wooded with oaks and underbrush, the locality had formed a striking contrast to the peninsula's barren hills when the Argonaut's fleet sailed into Yerba Buena Cove, and it soon caught the fancy of the newcomers. In 1852 George Gordon laid out South Park on the hill's southern slope to be modeled after Berkeley Square, a residential square of his native London. On the one end of the city's first Omnibus Railroad Company line, at a convenient distance from the business section of the burgeoning metropolis, South Park furnished the most elegant residential sites in San Francisco.[6] Its very compactness, with houses crowded together on twenty-five-foot frontages, gave the residents a physical metropolism amid the sprawling sand dunes that obscured the rest of the city.[7]

Rincon Hill was soon studded with homes and gardens overlooking South Beach and Bay. Their magnitude thoroughly impressed Mark Twain's friend Ralph Keeler, who taught languages in a fashionable school on the hill. He repeatedly referred to the "aristocratic mansion[s] on Rincon Hill" and the "elegant house[s] on Folsom Street" in his San Francisco novel of 1869.[8] The "rows of houses were the proudest achievements of Western masonry," another novelist wrote, "and had a somewhat haughty air, as if conscious of the importance they sheltered," tempered only by "that atmosphere of happy informality peculiar to the brief honeymoon of a great city."[9] Rincon Hill became the social center of the city, the editor of San Francisco's first *Elite Directory* recalled in 1879, and "little" was "stylish or correct . . . except in its vicinity."[10] Gertrude Atherton, who was born there in 1857, remained certain throughout her long life that Rincon Hill was one of the few places "in those days where one could be born respectably."[11]

The background of the leaders of the Rincon Hill world imparted a markedly southern influence to the area. Some of its principal residents had come from the South. Others had spent their formative years there as federal office-holders. Along with their loyalty to the Democratic party, the party of federal appointees during the 1850s, they showed an affection for the South as one of the safeguards of Democratic control in Washington. Others had obtained a military bearing at West Point that blended well with the proverbial hauteur of the southern aristocrat. Southern niceties, chivalry, and folkways persisted in the activities and thoughts of the social elite. Unlike the reproduction of eastern metropolitan styles of life, however, there was little conscious transplanting of the southern social system. Since most Californians objected to slavery, the economic foundation of the southern world, and many were opposed to any Negroes, slave or free, entering the state, there was little possibility for a western Charleston or New Orleans.[12] Elements of southern culture, however, contributed to an aristocratic vision that even drifters from New England found compelling. Two-penny clerks back home, they had witnessed the grandeur of merchant princes and, after making good in commercial and social ventures in Latin America, realized boyhood dreams by adopting a style of life that enabled them to claim similar distinctions.[13]

In its early years, San Francisco society appeared less rigid than society in the older centers of the East, because newcomers easily gained access to the general elite community. Entry was affected by this apparent egalitarianism, and membership in the elite was more a matter of acceptance on one's merits than the result of formal selection. The process evaluated men's backgrounds and their present positions and, while recognizing the possibility that all men were created equal, it reflected the certainty that some were more equal than others. Explicit statements were studiously avoided, but the system operated efficiently in practice. It would not serve any purpose, one insider felt, to tell men why they did not belong, while those who did, knew the reason anyway.[14] However, since even certain immigrants were accepted into the social elite, it is clear that entrance requirements functioned not only to guarantee exclusiveness but also to recruit new blood.

Other indexes of Rincon Hill's metropolism ranged from the names of residents to the reflection of their world in the works of artists. At one time or another, most of San Francisco's citizens who achieved high status in the 1860s lived there, among them industrialists (Peter Donahue and Irving M. Scott), politicians (William M. Gwin and Milton S. Latham), and bankers (Pedar Sather and William C. Ralston). A cattle king (Henry Miller), a grain king (Isaac Friedlander), and a poet (Bret Harte) shared this enclave with the "Monarch of Second Street Hill" (Bishop William I. Kip).[15] Probably no one on the hill was more citified than Matthew Hall McAllister's family, whose second son identified New York's "Four Hundred" and created the caricature of a social elite in the East in later years.[16] Bret Harte, Samuel Clemens, Charles Warren Stoddard, Ambrose Bierce, Robert Louis Stevenson, and Gertrude Atherton explored some of the facets of this world.[17] Harte's epitaph on George Gordon furnished insights that bring to life again the many faces of Rincon Hill, the essential metropolism of which is vividly epitomized in Fortunato Arriola's painting of the 1860s, *Howard Street by Night*.[18]

The Rincon Hill version of metropolism was destroyed by the forces of industrialism led by John Middleton. A real-estate operator, Middleton got himself elected as a Democrat to the seventeenth session of the California Legislature in 1867, the year in which his party returned to power after the Civil War.[19] Near the end of his only term at Sacramento he introduced Assembly Bill 444, modifying the grade of Second Street running over Rincon Hill.[20] He had secured the approval of the city's delegation and now waited confidently until the final day of the session, when the Democratic House and the Senate passed his act without debate and the Democratic governor signed it within hours.[21] The San Francisco Board of Supervisors, acting apparently at the behest of alarmed residents of Rincon Hill, ignored the new law.[22] Middleton, not to be thwarted, applied to the California Supreme Court for a peremptory writ of mandate and the court responded by ordering the supervisors to proceed with the grading without delay.[23] Five hundred men and two hundred and fifty teams excavated in seven months a seventy-five-foot-deep canyon through the one-hundred-foot-high hill.[24] The winter rains of 1869 added their effect and the erosion of soil that began in December of that year spelled the ultimate destruction of much of the hill. What now serves as abutment for the western anchorages of the Bay Bridge is a far cry from the impressive site of San Francisco's essential metropolism of nearly a century ago. Why did the social elite and men of power, wealth, and culture sharing the metropolism of Rincon Hill fail to prevent the destructive cut?

During his lifetime John Middleton was hardly ever criticized.[25] What appeared in later years as the epitome of villainy went unchecked by a generation that had more hills than level space suitable for industry and housing. These men did not consider a seemingly ubiquitous wilderness attractive enough to include some version of it in their precocious urban world, nor were they driven to appreciate the stark qualities of deserts as the only part of nature not yet spoiled by their countrymen. They superimposed upon their unpromising hills a gridiron of streets that facilitated the sale and resale of lots in advance of actual settlement and thus assured their community the promotional benefits of real-estate speculation. Their singlemindedness baffled apostles of organic urban growth whose country-like city streets would have followed the contours of the forty-two elevations that came to make up what Robert Louis Stevenson called San Francisco's "cition hills."[26] Middleton's generation could see nothing objectionable in a project that decisively tackled another obstacle in the way of progress, which it defined by the number of industries and people attracted to their community. In their determination to live up to and profit from their exalted dreams about the future of their city, these San Franciscans embraced the rationality and efficiency of an industrial technology as welcome allies in their struggle with an environment hostile to their vision. Their choice hastened their clash with the sanctioned concepts of beauty and urbaneness embodied in the commercial city and expressed through the metropolism of Rincon Hill.

Middleton's design appealed to many San Franciscans because it offered a partial solution to problems they had wrestled with for years. In the long view, the Second Street cut would prove to be of advantage to all except the social elite. Its far-reaching implications limited the opposition to the cut to isolated efforts of the social elite defending its way of life. Aided by only a few sympathizers among the other groups, these men alone were unable to block the cut. A review of the various factors bearing on the significance of the grading of Rincon Hill for the development of San Francisco will indicate their intimate connection with the interests of the elites.

The scheme's real importance lay in its solution to the city's critical space problem. As early as 1796, Don Pedro de Alberni had labeled the "hilly and barren waste" the "worst place for settlement" in California.[27] The lack of irrigable lands, pasturage, forests, and water was compounded by the desolate hills. These hills, a mixture of sand and mud, decomposed gradually on exposure and offered little in the way of building stones and minerals.[28] Some Americans who arrived during the Mexican War were convinced that a future metropolis, the "New York of the Pacific," was to be located on the continental side of the bay.[29] Insiders from Mariano G. Vallejo to Thomas O. Larkin promoted town sites further up the bay to remedy the illogical location of California's major city.[30] However, all vessels bound for San Francisco Bay with cargo for the interior continued to follow the practice of the hide-traders and anchored in Yerba Buena Cove. If the city had emerged in the 1860s after the introduction of railroads into the area, its future in a location where ship and train could meet only with difficulty would have been in doubt.[31] But in this decade, when Frederick Law Olmsted was still unable to discover a single "full grown tree of beautiful proportions near San Francisco," the harbor's position as the center of commercial redistribution to and from a vast hinterland was so firmly established that even the impact of the railroad could not shatter its hegemony and repeat the experience of St. Louis and the lesson of Chicago.[32]

These factors explain to a considerable degree the response of San Francisco elites to the forces of industrialism in the railroad age. Hand in hand with the projection of rail schemes went the intensified search for industrial sites and housing in expectation of future economic booms and incoming multitudes. The impact of these speculations was sensed not merely by the financial elite. Politicians showed a growing concern when they considered the advantages inherent in the control of the anticipated hordes of newcomers.[33] Even the members of the cultural elite felt the influence of the railroad which not only would end intellectual isolation but also would provide temptation to depart to the eastern centers of art and culture.[34] Within three years after its completion, the Transcontinental Railroad actually was to carry east Bret Harte and Ambrose Bierce, as well as Fortunato Arriola and William Keith, although Bierce and Keith returned to California.[35]

On the eve of the industrial era, the promises of the novel situation thoroughly occupied San Francisco's financial, political, and cultural elites. In the 1850s the commercial city, flourishing on maritime trade and apprehensive that it might not be a suitable railroad terminus, may have been unaware of the closeness of its own railroad age.

During these years the daily need for level space was supplied by filling the cove between Telegraph Hill and Rincon Point, building "half of the city in front of Montgomery Street."[36] Speculators saw in the extension of the waterfront a great opportunity to make a fortune. Some tried to get control of the development through the lawmakers, but their Bulkhead bill was vetoed. Whatever the details of the case, the state assumed control of San Francisco's waterfront and blocked further significant encroachment on the bay.[37]

Denied access to reclaimed tidelands and convinced that the Pacific Railroad would be reality within a few years, the land speculators turned to the Mission Creek area and the Potrero Nuevo, then a section of inlets and swamps south of Rincon Hill.[38] Here, by fills and drainage, could be created the level land suitable for railroad yards, machine shops, passenger stations, transfer points, and housing. Projected train ferries would connect the new sites with Alameda and Oakland.[39] The area provided the only entry for railroad tracks into the city, because the mountains recede at Point San Bruno and the strip of level ground widens to the south and joins the Santa Clara Valley. After the San Francisco and San Jose Railroad managed to enter the town at the Mission District via the San Bruno Pass in 1864, the entrepreneurs pressed for the development of this newly recognized space·for industries.[40]

Auspicious omens heightened the preoccupation of the financial elite and the political elite with the land. They reaffirmed their judgment about the industrial potential of the area. At its western edge, on Harrison and Eighth streets, was the San Francisco and Pacific Sugar Company, the largest building in the state except for some forts.[41] The Mission Woolen Mill on Folsom and Sixteenth streets employed four hundred men.[42] Dow's Distillery on Mission Creek produced three thousand gallons of whisky daily.[43] Cornelius Vanderbilt's Pacific Mail Steamship Company located its new wharf for the Hong Kong steamers at Townsend and First, at the northern gateway to the new expansion, while the southern one at Hunters Point was occupied by the installations of the California Dry Dock Company.[44] The twelve homestead associations that had been incorporated in 1861 in response to the national homestead movement now found themselves in business. Between 1867 and 1869 they multiplied to one hundred and fifteen.[45] The gridiron pattern for streets was projected on promotional maps over tidelands and swamps as though the land was already reclaimed.[46] Sales and resales of lots resulted in nearly hopeless legal tangles.[47] The Central Pacific Railroad recognized the future of the South Bay as a site for the western terminus of the line that would be in working order from Omaha to San Jose by September, 1869. Although the Railroad Tideland Act of 1867 reduced its grant for 6,620 acres between Mission Rock and Point San Bruno to a mere sixty acres, the Central Pacific found it could make do with the land for its transportation needs and located its transcontinental terminus south of Rincon Hill in San Francisco.[48]

In other vital areas Middleton's project also touched on the basic interests of San Francisco elites. After William C. Ralston had failed to complete New Montgomery Street by purchasing lots and opening up a new thoroughfare, the grading of Rincon Hill promised the only direct connection between the city's commercial center and the new and projected industrial sites, railroad yards, and housing developments south of the hill.[49] It would also furnish the fill to convert portions of Mission Bay and the swamps of the Potrero Nuevo into real estate.[50] The fundamental problem of their city, intensified by the industrialism of the railroad age, determined the outlook of most members of the financial and political elites living on Rincon Hill. They considered it more profitable to suffer temporary losses and inconveniences than to pass up participation in shaping the city's growth in their favor. They hoped to recoup their immediate losses on Rincon Hill by the anticipated industrial boom in the new area, by the control of the expected electorate, and, most directly, through manipulation of contracts, assessments, and franchises.[51] The graft and corruption accompanying the Second Street cut in form of political schemes operated by "Democratic Commissions" was castigated in a broadside, "Let Us Prey," which probed some of these dimensions of the Rincon Hill affair.[52] Members of the cultural elite viewed favorably any scheme that would lead to an advantageous railroad connection with the East and its centers of culture. Some of them considered an acceptance of the changes that the Second Street cut was bound to bring as the only sensible adjustment to the forces of industrialism already penetrating the fringes of the Rincon Hill world in the form of factories and boardinghouses.[53]

Their support or their acquiescence in the Rincon Hill project divided men of finance and politics and culture from the members of the social elite, who were committed to a static version of metropolism. Although outwardly sharing the forms of metropolism of Rincon Hill, the financial, political, and cultural elites responded in this specific situation to other stimuli than the defense of this way of life. For each resident of Rincon Hill who, like Thomas Selby, called the cut an "act of vandalism," fifty others felt that their response to the forces of industrialism marked them as advocates of progress.[54] They saw their course outlined and sanctioned by the elites of older cities in the East who, in analogous conflicts between the urban tradition of the commercial city and the promises of industrialism, were taking similar steps in their attempts to capitalize on the new opportunities.[55] By turning against the Rincon Hill world, these members of the financial, political, and cultural elites updated San Francisco's metropolism. While they succeeded immediately in this limited area of urban life, their vision of expanding industries and new residents materialized only slowly. Henry George's nostalgia for what was passing and his accurate prophecies of a forthcoming severe depression not only announced a new phase in the life of San Francisco, but also offered a fitting epitaph for the metropolism of Rincon Hill.[56]

The varying reactions of the members of San Francisco's elites to the impact of industrialism in the grading of Rincon Hill depicts the outlines of a pluralistic society. By combining this picture of a pluralistic society with the general diagram of a stratified society, the present analysis arrives at an overall image of a composite society. Analyzing the Second Street cut has pinpointed the objectives of the elites, has separated form-serving members of the social elite from committed members, and has defined the social elite as those Rincon Hill residents who opposed the grading because it endangered a way of life they considered as crucial to the city as to themselves. The investigation has focused on the social elite's commitment to a form of metropolism linked to the commercial city at a time when this way of life collided with the demands of industrialism. The study has thus outlined one stage in the growth of urban societies in the Far West. The distinct characteristic of San Francisco's social elite at the time of the Second Street cut made it possible to isolate one phase of a complex development.

The investigation of the grading of Rincon Hill suggests that the active members of one type of elite will likely prove to be active members in another type of elite when, under different conditions, a different interest calls for and produces a different response. In 1869, Irving M. Scott, the thirty-two-year-old General Manager of the Union Iron Works, in search of a broader base for his enterprise which eventually led to the Potrero works and shipyard, supported the Second Street cut. Forty-nine-year-old industrialist Thomas Selby raged at the destruction of Rincon Hill's physical and intangible cultural assets. Unlike Selby, Scott acted like the overwhelming number of entrepreneurs, promoters, and financiers and shared their active membership in the financial elite. However, thirteen years later, during the critical months of launching the second *Overland Monthly*, Scott gave generous financial aid to the magazine, while other industrialists like Leland Stanford and Charles Crocker were not yet willing to do so. During that decisive year in San Francisco's literary life, Scott also presided, on December 22, 1882, at the *Overland* Dinner celebrating the new venture. Amidst writers, bohemians, poets, Berkeley professors, San Francisco ministers, and publishers, the industrialist was flanked by Milicent Shinn, the editor of the new *Overland*, and Ina Coolbrith, poetess and living link to Bret Harte's old *Overland Monthly*.[57]

The circumstances accompanying the grouping and regrouping of elites provide vantage points for probing the dynamics of emergent urban societies. The investigation of the Rincon Hill affair indicates that "elites" can be employed in two ways. In a general descriptive sense, the term "elites" designates groups of people eminent in various areas of life. John Middleton, Thomas Selby, William I. Kip, Bret Harte, Isaac Friendlander, William C. Ralston, Pedar Sather, William M. Gwin, and Henry Miller, different perhaps in all aspects but eminence in their respective fields, are linked together as members of these elites. In an analytical sense, however, "elite" refers to a theoretically developed membership of a specific group at the specific time as established by the examination of a specific historical event. The leveling of Rincon Hill is a case in point, and the investigation of this specific event reveals the divisions of interest that separated John Middleton from Thomas Selby and placed the former in a specific financial elite and the latter in a specific social elite.

In the purely descriptive context, the records of the elites disclose a complex situation in which men of divergent ethnic and social origins adapted to a new environment that not only telescoped the process of American growth from wilderness to city into a single generation, but also endured the strains of a maturing industrial society along with the rest of the country. The individuals' intertwined and overlapping activities reveal a collective experience of internal migration and immigration, ethnic and racial struggle, and economic opportunity and social mobility, as well as the adjustment of an agrarian democracy to the city, the development of mass culture, and the incorporation of an intensified technology into the fabric of life.

However, when the collective behavior of the elite community in a general, descriptive sense is investigated in a critical situation affecting their interests, they can be separated according to their primary commitments in that crisis. Under these specific circumstances, their individual actions place them in distinct analytical elites. The analytically conceived groups constitute a theoretical device that isolates and freezes stages of the fluid social situation and allows us to perceive individual phases of the broad development.

An examination of the behavior of the elite community in a particular episode also reveals its merely passive members. The bankers Pedar Sather and Joseph A. Donohoe possessed name and wealth; Francisco Herrera held public office as consul of Colombia and Nicaragua; and the painter Juan B. Wandesforde was to become the first president of the San Francisco Art Association in 1871. They all lived on Rincon Hill at the time of the Second Street cut, and while these attributes gave them an entree into a financial, political, cultural, or social elite, or into all of them, their temperament or interests kept them from using their credentials to shape the affairs of their city.[58]

The responses of the San Francisco elites in the Rincon Hill cut helped to isolate one stage of the development of emergent urban societies in the Far West. A change in the attitude of all elites towards metropolism, noticeable in the aftermath of the affair, outlines another. Uprooted physically by the Second Street cut, the men and women who had constituted Rincon Hill's social elite scattered over the city. Increasingly their concern for an urban way of life was adopted by representatives of the financial, political, and cultural elites. However, a different outlook replaced the rationale that had sustained Rincon Hill's style of metropolism. While the old social elite had considered the attainment and the maintenance of a patrician way of life resembling that in large cities an end in itself, the newly emerging group subordinated this view of metropolism to other considerations. The major attempt to replace the Rincon Hill world came from men and women connected with those forces of industrialism that in the larger context had contributed to its demise: the Nob Hill world of the railroad barons and silver kings. One essential distinction between the old social elite of Rincon Hill and the *arriviste* social elite of Nob Hill involved the new meaning of metropolism. No longer primarily an end in itself, metropolism now became more a means to an end in the hands of members of all elites. Increasingly dominated in its outlook by the capitalists' motivations of profit, rationality, and efficiency, the general elite community was acting like their counterparts in the eastern cities. In the updating of metropolism in the Far West, the traditional notions of an urban life of gentility and *noblesse*, as embodied in San Francisco's old social elite, fell before the impact of industrialism and disappeared with the destruction of the Rincon Hill world.

In Denver the rush of the *nouveaux riches* to Capitol Hill in the late 1870s and early 1880s reflected this new phase of city life even while the established social elite continued to cling to its Fourteenth Street world, epitomized by the house of John Evans on the corner of Arapahoe Street.[59] No single event like the Rincon Hill cut helps to bring the outlines of Denver's old social elite into sharp analytical focus, but a series of real estate transactions in response to the impact of industrialism on the community can be utilized to mark the transition between the two stages of metropolism. The topography of Denver offered more possibilities than that of San Francisco for the development of industrial areas as well as exclusive residential areas. The old Fourteenth Street elite at various intervals saw the rise and decline of potential foci of social life in other parts of the city. An abundance of level space invited the establishment of railroad yards, smelters, and factories. However, preoccupied with its trading function and commercial role, the community largely ignored these opportunities. The many possibilities primarily taxed the perceptivity of speculators who tried unsuccessfully to promote specific areas, such as the Highlands in the northwest of Denver, or failed to attract factories and workers to their projected industrial parks.[60]

In the life of the Denver elites the impact of industrialism initiating the new phase of metropolism was felt first through such men as John L. Routt and H. A. W. Tabor who had amassed fortunes in the silver industry at Leadville. In their search for respectable residences some of these newly rich purchased houses on Fourteenth Street, and the former owners, established members of the social elite, moved to Capitol Hill. The growing interest in Capitol Hill by certain members of the social elite attracted other newcomers who had failed to gain admittance in the Fourteenth Street world but who literally found room in the yet open spaces of the Hill. Thus the social focus of the city was divided. While the old center remained on Fourteenth, the new one was located in an area which in the mid-1870s had but one outstanding house, that of William N. Byers on Sherman and Colfax.[61] When the banker Charles B. Kountze sold his home on Fourteenth to Routt in 1879 and built a new residence on his Capitol Hill block bounded by Sixteenth and Seventeenth avenues, Sherman and Grant streets, for which he had paid $3,000 in 1872, he "figuratively threw a bombshell into Fourteenth," the Denver *Rocky Mountain Daily News* recalled, and the "mad rush for the hill began."[62]

The impact of the mining magnates on Denver was not restricted to forming the nucleus of a new social elite. Nor was Leadville the only camp that sent its wealth to Denver. Bullion and ore poured in from many mining districts. They soon assumed a dominant role in the business affairs of the community, initiating the "Great Boom" in Denver history.[63] Tabor's heavy investments in real estate represented one extreme to which the new money went. He followed up the erection of his first office building with the construction of the Tabor Block. He leased the nearby Windsor Hotel, which had just been completed by an English corporation, and by June, 1880, he turned it into a showcase replica of eastern splendor. After outdoing Denver's established millionaires privately by purchasing the magnificent Henry C. Brown residence, he publicly proclaimed his elevated position on September 5, 1881, with the opening of the Tabor Grand Opera House, thus superbly exploiting the new phase of metropolism to enhance his own glory. While Eugene Field editorialized in the

Denver *Tribune* on Tabor's craving for recognition, eulogists heralding the new phase in the life of the community felt that Tabor alone, through the lavish use of part of his vast fortune, had "changed Denver from a town to a city."[64]

With the concentration of the *nouveaux riches* in Denver, some of their industries also gravitated to the city. In 1881 a fire destroyed the entire plant and office of the Grant smelter, one of the largest reduction works in Leadville. In the following year the consolidated Omaha and Grant Smelting Company erected its new plant in Denver. The relocation of the Grant Smelter, "one of the greatest industrial institutions that has yet been founded at any point between the Missouri River and San Francisco," had been foreshadowed by the transfer of the Black Hawk plant of the Boston and Colorado Smelting Company to Denver. The new Boston and Colorado Smelter began operating in January, 1879, on a tract of land two miles northeast of the city. These moves shortened the expensive long haul of coal and coke into the mountains and, coming just before and after the first great miners' strike in Colorado history, located both smelters close to a large source of laborers.[65]

The relocation of the smelting works introduced new blood into Denver's political elite. It brought to the city James B. Grant, who became the first Democratic governor of Colorado, in 1882. Nathaniel P. Hill of Black Hawk moved to Denver and served as a Republican in the United States senate from 1879 to 1885. The position of senator "came to him not as a politician," Hill emphasized for posterity through the words of Hubert Howe Bancroft's amanuensis, "but as one who had contributed very largely to the growth and the prosperity of the state."[66] Tabor achieved less lasting but more spectacular political success since his ingenuity for exploiting elements of metropolism for his personal ends was not restricted to the Tabor Grand Opera House and the Tabor Hose Company. He was lieutenant governor of Colorado from 1878 until 1884. This tempted him, in his role as the embodiment of the coming industrial age, to arrange also for his election as a Republican to the United States Senate. Outmaneuvered for the long term of six years by another mining magnate, Thomas M. Bowen, he was given the short term and served only during the lame duck session of Congress from January 27 to

March 3, 1883. Two days before the end of his brief stay in Washington he married Elizabeth McCourt Doe in the parlors of Willard's Hotel, with the President of the United States among his guests.[67]

The growing influence of the newly arrived men, their capital, factories, politics, and style of life signified for Denver the beginning of the transition from a commercial to an industrial city. In contrast to San Francisco, in Denver the railroads had done little to initiate this change. The coming of the rails, which had reached the town roughly ten years before the smelters, climaxed the center's commercial phase rather than inaugurating its industrial era. The railroad established Denver as the commercial hub and distributing center at the foot of the central Rocky Mountain mining district. The rails arrived, again unlike San Francisco, without the exalted promises of and grave misgivings about industrialism.[68] In 1870 the town rejoiced to see its greatest handicap, lack of cheap transportation, overcome and looked forward to realizing the Jacksonian dream of a commercial empire in the heart of the continent. It had gained control of the three prerequisites for greatness and wealth set forth by Thomas Hart Benton, the West's most eloquent spokesman of Jacksonian hopes: control of trade routes, flourishing commerce, and gold.[69]

Denver's established elites were wedded to that commercial dream. Their leading men, represented by John Evans, Walter S. Cheesman, and David H. Moffat, had built the tracks of the Denver Pacific to the Union Pacific at Cheyenne and managed to bring the first train into the city on June 22, 1870. Their dealings with the Kansas Pacific ensured the arrival of the second company on August 15, 1870. The Colorado and Central Railroad connected Denver and Golden on December 13, 1870. The completion of these three lines realized the town's basic commercial ambition and closed Denver's first era of railroading. Although the total length of roads built in Colorado Territory during this stage of railroad construction was just under three hundred miles, Denver had accomplished its goal: access to both coasts.[70]

With trade links to a growing hinterland of mining camps, Denver managed to weather the ups and downs of the early gold excitements in Colorado. New bonanzas reaffirmed the town's commercial future by substituting new markets for the vanishing ones. In a different geological setting than California, and without the guidance that the Mother Lode had furnished in the hunt for gold, Colorado represented a field of unlimited possibilities and failures for the ordinary prospectors and miners. Having little knowledge of geology, metallurgy, and chemistry, they continued to see placers of gold beyond the next divide and to work bodies of rich ore inefficiently.[71] The hope and tenacity of these men in the gullies and gulches kept Denver's trade alive. Not until extracting gold and silver from the refractory ores of the Colorado mountains became so difficult that it demanded complex smelting and reduction processes, and not until scientific solutions to the problems of extraction had been developed in Colorado did Denver grasp the promises of and opportunities for industrialism. Until then the familiar techniques of achieving progress, perfected in the course of the westward migration of the American people, had sufficed to exploit the easily accessible natural resources and to sustain the commercial town.

The prolonged crises in Colorado mining, the hectic laying of tracks, the intense struggle between rival railroad companies, and the shifting alliances of promoters that characterized most of the 1870s began to divert Denver elites from their predominantly commercial orientation. John Evans, S. H. Elbert, William N. Byers, A. B. Daniels, Walter S. Cheesman, Henry C. Brown, Charles B. Kountze, and a host of others formed an industrial association in 1873.[72] The altered outlook, however, did not gain acceptance in the established elites until the spectacular success and the self-promotion of the young industrialists began to leave their mark on the city, at the start of the 1880s.

When the new men eagerly attempted to demonstrate the importance of the change for the community, the superiority of their ways, and their young eminence to the general public, they were well prepared to utilize the current forms of metropolism to achieve their end. They selected the Tabor Grand Opera House as a meeting place for the National Industrial Convention under the leadership of Senator Hill, and hastily arranged the National Mining and Industrial Exposition in August and September, 1882. They officially added to the city's preoccupation with commerce a growing concern for industrial growth, agricultural technology, scientific mining, promotion of immigration, and the fostering of a cultural life expressive of the tenets of the emerging industrial society.[73]

Some of the aspirations of the entrepreneurs were cast into a physical mold by Willoughby J. Edbrooke, the architect of the imposing exposition building. The magnificent structure on a forty-acre tract again reflected the concern for self-promotion that Edbrooke had already expressed in his design of the Tabor Block and the Tabor Grand Opera House. But the three-story, five-hundred-foot-long and three-hundred-foot-wide hall, with its four corner towers and north and south wings, also revealed contact with similar promotions of industrialism in the older urban centers of the nation, as well as the fact that Edbrooke had gained his experience as an architect in Chicago. An impressive western example of the exposition architecture of the Gilded Age, inspired by the designs of the Centennial Exposition in Philadelphia, the building, even more than the quickly assembled technological exhibits, transmitted to Denver some of the spirit of the Machine Age and sanctioned the novel position of the industrialists in the community.[74]

The changed role of metropolism in San Francisco and Denver delineates a phase in the development of emergent urban societies in the Far West. The new stage marks the rise of industrial society in the Far West, as measured by the shifting attitude of the elites toward metropolism. The updating of metropolism gains additional significance because it also represented a response of the elites to certain characteristics of a rapidly emerging urban democracy. In both cities the concentration of newcomers intensified the potential for popular political action. This egalitarian trend was stimulated by the blocked social mobility of the vast majority of the people. For each Crocker, Stanford, Hopkins, and Flood who literally made it to the top of Nob Hill, for each Mackay, Fair, O'Brien, and Huntington who figuratively shared the height, there were thousands of San Franciscans who found only the rooming houses and tenements that had taken over the Rincon Hill district after the Second Street cut. The rhetoric of the sandlot rioters, the Kearneyites, and the Workingman's Party of California indicated, by the end of the 1870s, that some of these men realized they had been bypassed by the new age.[75]

Although not plagued with the material deprivation of Kearney's followers, or of those who joined the Workingman's Party, the newly rich, in the sensitive and explosive context of the young urban democracy, saw themselves limited in their search for status symbols.

High political offices were in their reach, but most of them considered the burdens of the positions and the exposure to the public too demanding to justify direct involvement in politics. The increasing concentration of people in a small area made it difficult to utilize land ownership as a symbol of eminence. The newness of urban society in the Far West and the multitude's recollections of the low origins of the *nouveaux riches*, as well as the difficulties of applying to the industrial city the marks of distinction that had differentiated residents of the earlier commercial city increased the dilemma of the parvenu.

Some of the manifestations of metropolism played a considerable role in resolving the impasse. Bland politeness, elegance of manners, ostentation, and civic consciousness came to affect the relationship between elites and the majority of people because they were now employed to set apart members of the elites in a democratic society, which scorned traditional devices to differentiate men. The elites' residences, their styles of life, their patronage of arts and letters, and their participation in the affairs of the community went beyond the fulfillment of immediate needs and aimed at the erection of lines of distinction in a professedly egalitarian world.

The process affected elite individuals and the *arriviste* groups as a whole. The gaudy innocent from the Far West who covered herself with jewelry even at breakfast, in William Black's *Green Pastures and Piccadilly*, ultimately possessed the sensitivity to defer to refined conventions.[76] She outlived the unsympathetic reflections applied to the newly rich and received the acclaim reserved for gentility and refinement. Groups of elites, too, found various ways to demonstrate their prominence in the urban community through their new use of metropolism. Collecting books and paintings, establishing libraries and art galleries, or supporting theaters and opera houses took on new meaning as people sought to buy instant prestige and to establish themselves among the chosen few. The acquisition and importation of old masters, precious manuscripts, and volumes of fashionable authors influenced the development of an artistic and literary life in an area of the country that looked east for the legitimate expressions of its culture. In 1893 the San Francisco elites captured a segment of the Chicago World's Fair, brought it west as a capsulated display of the cultural norm, and in the following year placed it and themselves on exhibit in the Midwinter Fair to demonstrate to the country their accomplishment and to the city their elevated position.[77] In Denver, fourteen years earlier, H. A. W. Tabor had shown a similar but more candid spirit when, so the stories go, he substituted his likeness for that of Shakespeare just before the opening of his opera house.[78] The desire for public recognition of the newly rich residents of Denver's Capitol Hill was finally answered by Mrs. Crawford Hill when she codified her "Sacred Thirty-six" in the "social guidebook" of 1908.[79]

These stages of metropolism in San Francisco and Denver found expression in the values of their elites. Their world contrasted with the life of most of the other people who faced the transition from the commercial to the industrial city without achieving sudden riches and political success, or struggled to adapt to a novel setting conflicting sets of values, which farmers and immigrants among them derived from different social and ethnic origins. McTeague, the miner-dentist; the Sieppes, immigrants in search of their farm; Marcus Schouler, ward heeler and cowboy; Maria Macapa, the charwoman; and Zerkow, the junk dealer, all "The People of [San Francisco's] Polk Street," characters in Frank Norris' *McTeague*, reflect the stresses and strains of life in the industrial city.[80] The role of metropolism in accentuating as well as adjusting some of the differences between elites and the rest of the people throws light on urban growth in the West up to the moment when the coming automobile brought physical and social mobility and, through the rise of suburbia, opened a new era in the life of the city.

The various functions of metropolism obtain significance through the country's political creed and the cities' recent origins within such a potentially leveling phenomenon as the westward migration. In imposing modes of class distinction and norms of cultural excellence standardized in the East, the young western elites continued to transplant stereotypes of American society. Adapting eastern conventions to gain prestige, they curtailed indigenous growth. The elites' role in San Francisco and Denver, as well as the cities' positions as metropolitan centers on the coast and in the mountains, clarify the part played by the urban environment in extending recognized status symbols to the West. The investigation into the emergent societies of these far western cities thus delineates the extent to which their growth took unique forms and the degree to which it manifested a phase of nation-wide and world-wide development of urbanization and industrialization, in a distinct setting.

NOTES

1. I am indebted to the Institute of Social Sciences and the Department of History, University of California, Berkeley, for several grants that made the research possible. Dr. Albert Shumate, Mr. Robert L. Perkin, Mr. Grant T. Skelley, and Mr. Judd L. Kahn shared with me their knowledge of San Francisco and Denver society. I am grateful to Mrs. Alys Freeze who patiently initiated me into the rich holdings of the Western History Department, Denver Public Library. Mrs. Dolores Renze, Colorado State Archivist, placed some of her research notes at my disposal. Mrs. Enid T. Thompson assisted me in the library of the State Historical Society of Colorado, Dr. Liston E. Leyendecker as Colorado State Historian, and Mr. H. William Axford, University of Denver Librarian, made possible the reproduction of rare materials. Mr. Robert Becker and the staff of the Bancroft Library, Mrs. Gladys Hansen of the San Francisco Public Library, Mr. Allan R. Ottley of the California State Library at Sacramento, Mr. Richard Dillon of the Sutro Library at San Francisco, Mr. John Brennan of the Western Historical Collection, University of Colorado, the members of the Western History Department, Denver Public Library, and the staff of the library of the State Historical Society of Colorado never tired of making available their resources. Mrs. Janet Purcell, Administrative Assistant of the Berkeley History Department, and her clerical staff helped with the typing of the manuscript. My search for directions profited from discussions with my colleagues at Berkeley, particularly Professor James R. W. Leiby and Professor Woodrow W. Borah, who generously contributed knowledge and encouragement. Professor Richard M. Abrams and Professor A. Hunter Dupree, University of California, Berkeley, Professor Earl Pomeroy, University of Oregon, Professor Richard T. Ruetten, San Diego State College, Professor Moses Rischin, San Francisco State College, Professor Charles Glaab, University of Wisconsin at Milwaukee, Professor Bayrd Still, New York University, and Professor Frederic C. Jaher, University of Chicago, commented on an earlier draft of the paper. As on previous occasions the unfailing interest and the learning of Dr. John Barr Tompkins of the Bancroft Library saved me from errors in style and fact.

2. For evidence of the role of metropolism in the urban growth of the United States turn to Carl Bridenbaugh, *Cities in the Wilderness; The First Century of Urban Life in America, 1625–1742* (New York: The Ronald Press Co., 1938). *Cities in Revolt; Urban Life in America, 1743–1776* (New York: Alfred Knopf,

1955). Richard C. Wade, *The Urban Frontier; The Rise of Western Cities, 1790–1830* (Cambridge: Harvard University Press, 1959).

3. Richard Harding Davis, *The West from a Car-Window* (New York: Harper & Brothers, 1892), p. 215. Rollo G. Silver (ed.), "Whitman Interviews Himself," *American Literature* (Durham), X (March, 1938), 86.

4. San Francisco *News Letter and California Advertiser*, July 14, 1888, p. 17.

5. Denver *Tribune*, February 4, 1881.

6. Albert Shumate, *A Visit to Rincon Hill and South Park* (San Francisco: privately printed, 1963), pp. 2–7.

7. *San Francisco Block Book*, 100 Vara Blocks, 317–420, 1868–1869 (Bancroft Library, University of California, Berkeley), p. 359.

8. Ralph Keeler, *Gloverson and His Silent Partners* (Boston: Lee and Shepard, 1869), pp. 16, 43–44, 169, 176.

9. Gertrude Atherton, *A Daughter of the Vine* (London: J. Lane, 1899), p. 59.

10. Argonaut Publishing Company, *The Elite Directory for San Francisco and Oakland* (San Francisco: Argonaut Publishing Co., 1879), p. 17.

11. Gertrude Atherton, *Adventures of a Novelist* (New York: Liveright, Inc., 1932), p. 4.

12. San Francisco *Californian*, March 15, 1848. San Francisco *Herald*, December 29, 1851. San Francisco *Daily Alta California*, February 18, 1853.

13. "William M. Gwin," DAB, VIII, 64–65. "Milton S. Latham," DAB, XI, 13. Floride Green (ed.), *Some Personal Recollections of Lillie Hitchcock Coit* (San Francisco: Grabhorn Press, 1935), p. 2. Doyce B. Nunis, Jr. (ed.), *The California Diary of Faxon Dean Atherton, 1836–1839* (San Francisco: California Historical Society, 1964), pp. xiv–xxxii.

14. *News Letter*, February 16, 1889, p. 6.

15. A roster of residents can be found most conveniently in Dr. Shumate's detailed survey, *A Visit to Rincon Hill*.

16. Douglas I. Watson, "The San Francisco McAllisters," *California Historical Society Quarterly* (San Francisco), XI (June, 1932), pp. 124–28. Allen L. Chickering (ed.), "Hall McAllister to 'Minnie,'" *ibid.*, XXIV (September, 1955), pp. 231–37. Ward McAllister, *Society as I Have Found It* (New York: Cassell Publishing Co., 1890).

17. F. Bret Harte, "Neighborhoods I Have Moved From. By a Hypochondriac. Number Three," San Francisco *Californian*, June 11, 1864, p. 1. Samuel Clemens, "New Year's Day," San Francisco *Golden Era*, January 14, 1866, p. 3. Charles

Warren Stoddart, "Social San Francisco," *In the Footprints of the Padres* (San Francisco: A. M. Robertson, new ed., 1912), pp. 82–93. Ambrose Bierce, "Town Crier," *News Letter*, June 18, 1870, p. 8. Robert Louis Stevenson, "A Modern Cosmopolis," *Magazine of Art* (London), VI (May, 1883), 276. Stevenson, *The Wrecker* (New York: C. Scribner's Sons, 1923), pp. 159–61. Gertrude Atherton, "The Randolphs of Redwoods. A Romance," San Francisco *Argonaut*, March 31, pp. 1–2; April 7, pp. 1–2; April 14, pp. 1–4; April 28, pp. 1–2; May 5, 1883, pp. 1–2.

18. F. Bret Harte, "San Francisco, by the Poets. Number Two. South Park—After Gray," *Californian*, September 24, 1864, p. 9. Fortunato Arriola's painting is in the possession of Dr. Albert Shumate; a reproduction can be found in Lucius Beebe and Charles Clegg, *San Francisco's Golden Era; A Picture Story of San Francisco Before the Fire* (Berkeley: Howell-North, 1960), p. 121.

19. *Call*, August 10, 17, September 5, 6, 7, 8, 1867.

20. *News Letter*, February 8, 1868, p. 8. San Francisco *Times*, February 18, 19, 1868. *California Assembly Journal*, 17th Sess., p. 491.

21. *Ibid.*, pp. 748, 953, 972, 977, 986, 991–92, 1001–1002. *Statutes of California*, 17th Sess., pp. 594–99.

22. *Call*, May 5, 1869. *News Letter*, May 15, 1869, p. 2.

23. The People of the State of California, *ex rel.* John Ferguson, v. the Board of Supervisors of the City and County of San Francisco, J. E. Hale (comp.), *Reports of Cases Determined in the Supreme Court of the State of California at the October Term 1868 and January Term 1869* (San Francisco: Sumner Whitney, 1869), pp. 595–606.

24. *Call*, 1869: April 30; May 6, 12, 18; July 16, 17, 24; August 3, 12, 15, 27; September 14; November, 11, 18, 30; December 8, 10, 11, 26.

25. None of John Middleton's obituaries that I have seen mentioned the Second Street cut. San Francisco *Abendpost*, January 9, 1874; San Francisco *Alta California*, January 9, 10, 1874; *Bulletin*, January 9, 1874; San Francisco *Chronicle*, January 10, 1874; San Francisco *Examiner*, January 9, 1874; *News Letter*, January 10, 1874, p. 8; Sacramento *Union*, January 10, 1874.

26. Frederick Law Olmsted, *Preliminary Report in Regard to a Plan of Public Pleasure Grounds for the City of San Francisco* (New York: W. C. Bryant, 1866), pp. 30–31. Lewis Mumford, "The Sky Line; Not Yet Too Late," *New Yorker*, XXXIX (December 7, 1963), 147. San Francisco *Chronicle, Hills of San Francisco* (San Francisco: Chronicle Publishing Company, 1959), pp. 2–3.

27. "Report of Don Pedro de Alberni, July 1, 1796," John W. Dwinelle, *Colonial History of the City of San Francisco* (San Francisco: Towne & Bacon, 1863), Addenda No. IX, p. 18.

28. Josiah Dwight Whitney, *Geological Survey of California* (2 vols., Philadelphia: Caxton Press of Sherman & Co., 1865–1882), I, 77–79.

29. William T. Sherman, *Memoirs* (2 vols., New York: D. Appleton & Co., 2nd rev. ed., 1889), I, 61.

30. See the correspondence published in the *Larkin Papers*, VIII, particularly Robert Baylor Semple to Thomas Oliver Larkin, January 24, 1849, George P. Hammond (ed.), *The Larkin Papers*, 10 vols. (Berkeley: University of California Press, 1951–1964), VIII, 111–12.

31. Werner Hegemann, "The Great City on the East Side of the Bay," *Report on a City Plan for the Municipalities of Oakland and Berkeley* (Oakland: Kelly-Davis Co., 1915), pp. 3–17.

32. Olmsted, *Preliminary Report*, 17. James H. Lemly, "The Mississippi River: St. Louis' Friend or Foe?" *Business History Review* (Boston), XXXIX (Spring, 1965), 7–15.

33. *News Letter*, 1867: March 23, p. 9; April 6, p. 4; April 13, p. 4; May 18, p. 4; 1868: January 11, p. 8; February 8, p. 8; March 7, p. 8; April 4, p. 8; April 18, p. 8. *San Francisco Real Estate Circular* (San Francisco), I (October, 1867), 4; II (February, 1868), 3; (May, 1868), 1; (June, 1868), 4; (July, 1868), 1; (October, 1868), 1; III (November, 1868), 3; (May, 1869), 4.

34. F. Bret Harte, "Etc.," *Overland Monthly* (San Francisco), I (July, 1868), 99–100.

35. "An Allegorical Picture," San Francisco *Call*, January 2, 1870. George R. Stewart, *Bret Harte, Argonaut and Exile* (Boston: Houghton Mifflin Co., 1931), p. 185. Paul Fatout, *Ambrose Bierce, The Devil's Lexicographer* (Norman: University of Oklahoma Press, 1951), p. 94. Brother Fidelis Cornelius, *Keith, Old Master of California* (New York: Putnam's, 1942), pp. 30–32.

36. Sherman, *Memoirs*, I, 84. Frank Soulé, John H. Gihon, and James Nisbet, *Annals of San Francisco* (New York: D. Appleton & Co., 1855), pp. 158, 163, 195.

37. Lamerta Margarette Voget, "The Waterfront of San Francisco: 1863–1930; A History of Its Administration by the State of California" (Ph.D. thesis, University of California, Berkeley, 1943), pp. 10–21.

38. "Table Showing the Total Sales of Real Estate Made in all Sections of the City and County during the year 1870; also the Total Sales made during the years 1869, 1868, 1867, and 1866," *San Francisco Real Estate Circular*, V (December, 1870), 2.

39. *News Letter*, September 11, 1869, p. 4.

40. Louis Richard Miller, "The History of the San Francisco and San Jose

Railroad" (M.A. thesis, University of California, Berkeley, 1947), p. 68. *San Francisco Real Estate Circular*, I (December, 1866), 4.

41. San Francisco City Directory, 1863, pp. 35–36.

42. Ibid., 1867, pp. 43–44.

43. Ibid., 1865, p. 678.

44. Ibid., 1867, p. 521; 1868, pp. 16–17. For a brief summary turn to "Business on the Potrero and at Bay View," *San Francisco Real Estate Circular*, II (May, 1868), 3.

45. San Francisco City Directory, 1863, pp. 28–29; 1867, pp. 39, 678; 1868, pp. 39–40, 780–81; 1869, pp. 46, 707; 1871, p. 747.

46. Map of the San Francisco and San Jose Railroad, San Francisco 1862; Plan of the O'Neil and Haley Tracts, San Francisco, 1867; Property of the Willows Real Estate Association Comprising the Whole of Mission Block No. 68, and one-half of Mission Block No. 69, San Francisco, 1870 (All maps in Bancroft Library).

47. *San Francisco Real Estate Circular*, I (February, 1867), 2–3, 4; (June, 1867), 3; (September, 1867), 3; (October, 1867), 4; II (November, 1867), 2; (January, 1868), 2; (March, 1868), 3, 4; (May, 1868), 1; (August, 1868), 1; III (November, 1868), 3; (April, 1869), 3.

48. Stuart Daggett, *Chapters on the History of the Southern Pacific* (New York: Ronald Press, 1922), pp. 94–100.

49. Call, February 3, June 27, 1869. *News Letter*, September 11, 1869, p. 4. *San Francisco Real Estate Circular*, III (May, 1869), 3.

50. Call, August 22, 1869.

51. "The New City: A Dream of the Future," *News Letter*, August 7, 1869, p. 18.

52. "Let Us Prey," unidentified broadside in the Bancroft Library. I am indebted to Mr. Neil Shumsky who brought the cartoon to my attention.

53. F. Bret Harte, "Etc.," *Overland Monthly*, I (October, 1868), 385; III (September, 1869), 290–91. *News Letter*, February 8, 1868, p. 8.

54. Call, May 5, 23; June 7; December 7, 1869.

55. *News Letter*, 1867: March 23, p. 9; April 6, p. 4; July 27, p. 4; December 7, p. 6; 1868: February 8, p. 8; March 7, p. 8; August 15, p. 16; October 31, p. 9; 1869: January 16, p. 8; August 7, p. 2.

56. Henry George, "What the Railroad Will Bring Us," *Overland Month*, I

(October, 1868), 297–306. Charles Albro Barker, *Henry George* (New York: Oxford University Press, 1955), pp. 102–104.

57. Milicent Shinn to Robert Underwood Johnson, November 7, 1890 (*Century Collection*, New York Public Library). *News Letter*, 1869: June 26, p. 20, September 18, p. 4, December 4, p. 3. Ambrose Bierce, "Literary Notes," *Wasp* (San Francisco), X (February 3, 1883), 3. "The *Overland* Dinner" Supplement to *Overland Monthly*, I (n.s., February, 1883), 1. Charles S. Greene, "Memories of an Editor," *Overland Monthly*, XL (n.s., September, 1902), 266. Hubert Howe Bancroft, *Chronicles of the Builders of the Commonwealth* (7 vols., San Francisco: The History Company, 1892), I, 463–69.

58. San Francisco *City Directory*, 1869, pp. 202, 305, 543, 623.

59. Denver *Rocky Mountain Daily News*, February 2, 1881, September 8, 1906, August 1, 1926. Denver *Tribune*, February 4, 1881. Denver *Times*, August 31, 1899, November 5, 1900. Denver *City Directory*, 1873, p. 104; 1890, p. 420.

60. *News*, May 24, 28, 1874; May 28, 1875; January 6, April 28, May 23, October 8, 1882; February 2, 1883; January 1, 1885; July 11, 1890. *Tribune*, May 28, 1874; December 29, 1875; November 30, 1881. Denver *Republican*, January 1, 1884; May 4, July 12, 1890; June 1, 1891; March 12, 13, 1894. *Times*, June 12, 1893, March 14, 1894. Denver *Post*, November 1, 11, 13, 14, 15, 1904.

61. *Times*, September 4, 1879. *News*, September 5, 1879. *Post*, June 15, 1919. Denver *City Directory*, 1875, p. 89. Rezin H. Constant, "Colorado as Seen by a Visitor of 1880," *Colorado Magazine* (Denver), XII (May, 1935), 109-11.

62. *News*, June 15, November 18, 1911; October 28, 1920; March 1, 1923. *Times*, October 28, 1920. *Post*, October, 28, 1920.

63. Jerome C. Smiley, *History of Denver* (Denver: Times-Sun Publishing Co., 1901), p. 480. Robert L. Perkin, *The First Hundred Years; An Informal History of Denver and the Rocky Mountain News* (Garden City: Doubleday, 1959), pp. 358–59.

64. Elmer S. Crowley, "The Opening of the Tabor Grand Opera House, 1881," *Colorado Magazine*, XVIII (March, 1941), 41–48. Lewis Cass Gandy, *The Tabors; A Footnote of Western History* (New York: The Press of the Pioneers, Inc., 1934), pp. 215–16. Some of Eugene Field's "Taborisms" were collected by Willard S. Morse, *Clippings from Denver Tribune, Written by Eugene Field, 1881–1883* (New York: privately printed, 1909).

65. *News*, February 1, 12, 16, 1878. Frank Hall, *History of the State of Colorado*, 4 vols. (Chicago: The Blakely Printing Co., 1889–95), II, 449–51. Smiley, *History of Denver*, 551–54. C. D. Wright, *A Report on Labor Disturbances in the State of Colorado, from 1880–1904* (Washington: Government Printing

Office, 1905), pp. 73–74. Frank E. Shepard, "Industrial Development in Colorado," James H. Barker (ed.), *History of Colorado* (5 vols., Denver: Linderman Co., 1927), II, 701–704. Jesse D. Hale, "The First Successful Smelter in Colorado," *Colorado Monthly*, XIII (September, 1936), 161–67. Don L. and Jean Harvey Griswold, *The Carbonate Camp Called Leadville* (Denver: University of Denver Press, 1951), pp. 63–66, 79, 178–99, 240.

66. Bancroft, *Builders of the Commonwealth*, IV, 387. Jerome C. Smiley, *Semi-Centennial History of the State of Colorado* (2 vols., Chicago: The Lewis Publishing Co., 1913), II, 43–44.

67. Bancroft, *Builders of the Commonwealth*, IV, 319–25. Gandy, *Tabors*, 239–40.

68. Denver *Rocky Mountain Herald*, April 22, June 18, 1869. Edgar Carlisle McMechen, *Life of Governor Evans* (Denver: Wahlgreen Publishing Co., 1924), pp. 163–74. E. O. Davis, *The First Five Years of the Railroad Era in Colorado* (Denver: Sage Books, 1948), p. 89. A. J. Flynn, "The Moffat Tunnel," *Colorado Magazine*, I (November, 1923), p. 40. Robert G. Athearn, *Rebel of the Rockies; A History of the Denver and Rio Grande Western Railroad* (New Haven: Yale University Press, 1962), pp. 5, 251–52.

69. Howard Roberts Lamar, *The Far Southwest, 1846–1912; A Territorial History* (New Haven: Yale University Press, 1966), pp. 252, 301.

70. S. D. Mock, "The Financing of Early Colorado Railroads," *Colorado Magazine*, XVIII (November, 1941), 201–209. Harry Edwards Kelsey, Jr., "John Evans" (Ph.D. thesis, University of Denver, 1965), pp. 325–32. Richard Overton, *Gulf to Rockies; The Heritage of the Fort Worth and Denver–Colorado and Southern Railways, 1861–1898* (Austin: University of Texas Press, 1953), p. 14.

71. Rodman Wilson Paul, "Colorado as a Pioneer of Science in the Mining West," *Mississippi Valley Historical Review*, XLVII (June, 1960), 38–41.

72. *Times*, March 24, 1873.

73. *News*, 1881: October 2, December 31; 1882: February 1, 2, 11, March 1, 2, April 3, 20, 27, June 24, 28. *Denver Journal of Commerce*, II (September 16, 1882), 1, 4. *Programme for the First Annual Exhibition of the National Mining and Industrial Exposition at Denver* (Denver: Tribune Publishing Co., 1882).

74. *Republican*, March 26, 1896. *Inter-Ocean* (Denver), V (August 19, 1882), 590, 599; (September 16, 1882), 574–75. *Exposition Guide Book* (Denver: Shield Brothers, 1882), pp. 11–13. W. B. Ewer, *Report on the National Mining and Industrial Exposition* (Sacramento: California State Printing Office, 1883), p. 15. W. H. Jackson and Co., *The National Mining and Industrial Exposition, Denver* (Denver: W. H. Jackson & Co., 1882), contains sixteen photographs of the exposition.

75. *Bulletin*, July 24, 1877. *Chronicle*, 1877: August 19, 23, September 24. *Call*, 1877: August 23, 31, September 2, 13, 17, 23, October 6. Henry George, "The Kearney Agitation in California," *Popular Science Monthly*, XVII (August, 1880), 434–35, 440, 449, 451–52.

76. William Black, *Green Pastures and Piccadilly* (3 vols., London: Macmillan and Co., 1877), II, 177–78.

77. Michael H. de Young, "The Columbia World's Fair," *Cosmopolitan*, XII (March, 1892), 599–611. De Young, "Benefits of the Midwinter Exposition," *Californian Illustrated Magazine*, V (March, 1894), 393–95. "Our World's Fair," *News Letter*, June 3, 1893, p. 3.

78. Edgar Carlisle McMechen, "Literature and the Arts," Barker (ed.), *History of Colorado*, III, p. 1258. Perkin, *First Hundred Years*, p. 357. "Tabor and the Painting of Shakespeare's Profile," an appendix in Elmer S. Crowley, "The History of the Tabor Grand Opera House, Denver, Colorado, 1881–1891" (M.A. thesis, University of Denver, 1940), pp. 244–45, explodes the fallacious stories.

79. W. H. Kistler Stationary Co., *Who's Who in Denver Society, 1908* (Denver: W. H. Kistler Stationary Co., 1908).

80. Frank Norris to William Dean Howells, December 31, 1898, Franklin Walker (ed.), *The Letters of Frank Norris* (San Francisco: The Book Club of California, 1956), p. 23. James Childs, "The First Draft of McTeague: 1893," *American Notes and Queries*, III (November, 1964), 37–38.

7

The Boston Brahmins in
the Age of Industrial Capitalism

by FREDERIC COPLE JAHER

Approximately forty families dominated the economic, political, and social affairs of Boston for a century after the Revolution and remain prominent in the life of the city. Most eminent in this group were the Lees, Higginsons, and Cabots, who achieved ascendancy through success in foreign trade during and immediately after the Revolution; the Lowells, a family established by representing

A grant from the Social Science Research Council enabled the author to pursue the research necessary for this paper at the Massachusetts Historical Society, Houghton Library at Harvard University, and Baker Library at the Havard Business School. In connection with another essay, Professor Oscar Handlin raised important questions about Brahmin commercial endeavors. My wife, Susan Jaher, and Professors David Greenstone, Peter Stearns, and Paul Goodman have read this essay incisively and made valuable comments for its improvement. In addition I profited greatly from reading Professor Goodman's unpublished manuscript, "Social Sources of Business Enterprise: Studies in the Longevity of Boston Financial Institutions." The Massachusetts Historical Society, The Harvard College Library, and Baker Library at the Harvard Business School have generously given me permission to quote from manuscript collections in their possession.

mercantile princes and Tory landowners in litigation; and the Lawrences, whose position stems from successful entrepreneurship in the early nineteenth-century textile industry. The preeminence of the Higginsons, Lawrences and Lowells, founded on commerical wealth, was expanded and perpetuated through literary, educational and religious activities by essayist Thomas Wentworth Higginson, William Lawrence, Episcopal Bishop of Massachusetts, and A. Lawrence Lowell, President of Harvard University. The Cabots, on the other hand, maintained power and reputation by repeated triumphs in business. One constellation of prominent Bostom families, the Wigglesworths, Quincys, Saltonstalls, Endicotts, Winthrops, and Otises were able to preserve their pre-Revolution status by retaining political influence and wealth. Later arrivals, the Adamses, Danas, Holmses, Channings, Warrens, Minots, Bigelows, Eliots, Morses, and Prescotts embellished family stature through accomplishments in the professions, in literature, or in society; the Derbys, Amorys, Lymans, Perkinses, Sturgises, Russells, Storrows, Searses, Philipses, Forbeses, and Coolidges were noted for entrepreneurial achievements in foreign trade, cotton manufacturing, railroads and investment banking; the Parkmans, Lodges, Peabodys, and Wendells buttressed their status by outstanding attainments in more than one sphere of life. These groupings never settled into rigid familial specializations because recurrent intermarriage among Boston's first families intimately connected upper class personnel in economic, political, and cultural activities.

Families of the first magnitude did not always preserve their preeminence within the group even though they remained Brahmins. The Perkinses and Russells, early Boston's greatest mercantile families, and the Appletons, unsurpassed in Boston cotton manufacturing, lost ascendancy because later generations lacked the acumen and energy of their forebears. Conversely the Lees, Higginsons, Cabots, and Lawrences retained their importance because the heirs of the family founders repeated their success in new areas of business or in political, professional, or intellectual endeavors. Family reputations were sometimes resurrected when successful sons followed faltering fathers. The business triumphs of John Murray Forbes' rejuvenated a family whose position had been seriously compromised by the elder Forbes' bankruptcy and early death. Similarly, the fame of Charles William Eliot as President of Harvard refurbished a name somewhat tarnished by his father's failure in 1857. If social position could be retained despite reverses, some formidable figures like Oliver Wendell Holmes, Jr., whose influence in the community was enormous, were unable to transmit their prestige for want of male issue.

At first there was flexibility in permitting entry as well as in maintaining membership. Although becoming ever more exclusive as positions in business and society increasingly were bequeathed through inheritance, the Brahmins were not a completely closed class until the 1860s. In the first quarter of the nineteenth century, it was possible for bright country lads like Amos and Abbott Lawrence and Nathan Appleton eventually to gain admittance to the inner sanctum of the Boston business establishment. The family firm and diminishing drive in staking out new areas of commercial conquest, however, lessened the desire for recruitment of new blood. By the 1830s, commercial success had been virtually closed as an avenue to class membership. Entry through political and cultural activities, on the other hand, remained relatively open until the late nineteenth century. As the Bostonians broadened themselves from an economic elite into an urban upper class, skills in civic, social, and cultural functions became highly valued. Consolidation of commercial ascendancy and class cohesion were perceived as dependent upon exercising leadership over variegated phases of city life. Thus Edward Everett established a place for himself by representing the interests of the textile magnates in the state and federal government, Henry Wadsworth Longfellow and Alexander Agassiz became cultural ornaments of the class, and John Torrey Morse was in considerable demand as a clubman and institutional trustee.

The Boston Brahmins' response to industrialism ranged from eager acceptance of mechanization and social change to flight into a utopianized past of homogeneous communities bound by ancestral ties to well-worn traditions. A few bluebloods struggled to the top in the competitive and mobile world of post-bellum America. The majority, however, made limited gains, barely sustained their bequeathed status, or could not preserve ascendancy when confronted by new men and new forces.[1] The ability of upper class individuals to establish or retain a place during this period shaped patterns of adjustment in elite Boston. Their response also was influenced by class structure and values, personal traits, and extent of allegiance to the national creed or to the culture of genteel Boston. The full impact of industrialism upon this elite cannot be understood unless analysis proceeds from theories and attitudes to policies and results. The blend of mood and concept with practice and outcome provides a clearer view of proper Boston in industrial America.

Boston bluebloods had to face, in varying degrees depending upon personal experiences and adjustments, the disruption of traditional patterns of behavior and status by the triumph of the factory and the machine. Many gentlemen feared that changes in production had reverberated into challenges to social position. Their apprehensions were accurate. Long-established ascendancy was threatened by new-comers and the demands of ancestral continuity clashed with the pressures to adjust to new times. The parvenu challenge for com-munity leadership might be overcome through timely adaptation to contemporary conditions, but the vitality of the old upper class could also be sapped by renouncing the claims of the past. The tragic dil-emma presented by conflicting commitments to the necessities of maintaining power and preserving precious class values makes Boston Brahmin behavior fascinating to investigate. Members of the class, however, rarely contemplated their fate in the spirit of academic in-quiry. For them it was a passionate issue of triumph or disaster.

1. Proper Bostonians and Ante-Bellum Industrialism

Brahmin Boston began to take shape when merchant princes Thomas Handysyd Perkins, Samuel Cabot, Henry Lee, and others made fortunes pioneering overseas trade with the Far East and founded the dynasties that determined the destiny of the city in the nineteenth century.[2] When Thomas Jefferson's embargo and the War of 1812 temporarily destroyed this lucrative trade, many enterprising Bostonians shifted their interests to cotton manufacturing. Scions of mercantile families, such as Francis Cabot Lowell and Patrick Tracy Jackson, united with newcomers Nathan Appleton and Amos and Abbott Lawrence to establish textile manufacture as the new base for Brahmin economic hegemony in Massachusetts. This group of families, often called the Boston Associates, core of the Boston Brahmins, belonged to the same clubs, patronized the same charities, lived in the same neighborhoods, educated their children at the same schools and intermarried so frequently that they were blood relations of one another.[3] Constituting the richest and most powerful commercial group in the Bay State, these families were preeminent in politics until Massachusetts Whigs split over slavery. Conjugal links with the ancient Quincy, Otis, and Winthrop clans or with rising politicians like Edward Everett facilitated the acquisition of political power. In some cases, notably those of Nathan Appleton and Abbott Lawrence, the Associates themselves held office. For the most part, however, they allowed professional politicians like Robert C. Winthrop and Daniel Webster to represent their interests.

Involved in consolidating economic and political power was the assumption of upper-class social and cultural functions. The organization and direction of museums, schools, clubs, libraries, hospitals, and charities brought mercantile and political figures into close relationship with families such as the Holmeses and Bigelows, and after the Civil War, with the sons of Charles Francis Adams, Sr., who possessed distinguished social, cultural, and intellectual credentials.

By establishing themselves in cotton manufacturing during the mercantile crisis of the early 1800's, the Brahmins mastered the first challenge to their community leadership and ensured their ascendant position for the next two generations. At Waltham, in 1814, the Boston Manufacturing Company, organized by Patrick Tracy Jackson and Francis Cabot Lowell and financed by mercantile capital, introduced the first modern factory to America. All cloth-making operations took place in one mill, labor was specialized and departmentalized, output was standardized, cost accounting was used, and the processes of production was performed by water-power-driven machinery. In order to meet the growing demand for cotton cloth, the Boston Associates built other factories along the Merrimac River and in Maine and New Hampshire. By 1833, Lowell, Massachusetts was the largest manufacturing center in the country, and the Brahmins dominated the first great industry in America.[4]

Textile interests involved the Hub elite in other ante-bellum technological and industrial developments. In the 1830s and 1840s the Associates financed and organized the first long lines in New England to transport goods from textile towns to Boston.[5] Railroad and textile activities led the group to incorporate the Lowell Machine Shop, which made cotton-manufacturing machinery, steam boilers, paper-making machinery, and machine tools, and which became, before the Civil War, the largest domestic producer of locomotives.[6]

Achievement in trade, textiles, and railroads was in part due to capital resources available to the Bostonians. The first public commercial bank in Boston, The Massachusetts First National Bank of Boston, was organized by Brahmin merchants in 1784. Until 1827, the Massachusetts Bank was the largest financial institution in the city. Although it had declined because of conservative banking and investment policy, the bank was still third largest in Boston in 1863.[7] The Massachusetts Bank lost ground to other Brahmin financial institutions, reflecting in its decline the shift of Brahmin interests from trade to industry. The old organization was displaced in preeminence by the Massachusetts Hospital Life Insurance Company, designed to be an investment vehicle for the textile manufacturers. Massachusetts Life became the repository of the great Brahmin industrial fortunes in the form of family trusts.[8] In addition to controlling these institutions, elite businessmen were directors and their familes prominent stock-holders in five of the seven largest banks in Boston.[9] The Associates, when they deemed it necessary, exercised their financial dominion over the region. Fearing the instability of inflation they imposed the Suffolk System, which forced rural banks to redeem their own banknotes with specie, thus restraining the circulation of these notes.[10]

Accumulation of wealth and consolidation of economic power reached heroic proportions by 1850. The Boston Associates controlled 20 per cent of the national cotton spindleage, 30 per cent of Massachusetts railroad mileage, 39 per cent of Massachusetts insurance capital, and 40 per cent of Boston banking resources.[11] A survey of wealthy Bostonians made in 1846 listed twenty-five inhabitants as being worth at least $500,000. Twenty-one owed their fortunes to Brahmin birth, marriage, or business association. Typically, men either inherited mercantile wealth earned in the 1780s and 1790s, were self-made entrepreneurs who wrought fortunes from Canton silks or Lowell cottons, or were scions of colonial families who had intermarried with the offspring of successful parvenus.[12]

Supremely confident in the fullness of their prosperity and power, the Boston Brahmins lauded the mechanical and organizational accomplishments of their class. Encomiums were heaped upon Patrick Tracy Jackson and Francis Cabot Lowell, whose talents had been largely responsible for establishing the first large-scale, mechanized factory in America.[13] Praise for specific aspects of commercial life—technological innovation or administrative skill—was a facet of the homage given to business. Textile magnate Nathan Appleton knew "of no purer morality in any department of life than that of the counting room. In no other class of men" had he found "more harmony, mutual respect and liberality of sentiments."[14] Amos A. Lawrence, another Associate, expressed similar opinions in telling Freeman Hunt, editor of *Hunt's Merchant's Magazine*, that "You will accomplish good work in collecting the biographies of the merchants." He expected Hunt's project to show businessmen as "examples of honour and public spirit."[15]

Sincere attachment to business is manifest in the desire of Boston businessmen to pass on the vocation to their sons. Overseas trader Thomas Handysyd Perkins considered "my life upon the whole more happy from having been actively employed in business" and sent his boy on a mercantile voyage to Canton "in hopes his ambition will have a spring and he will take to business."[16] Textile titan Amos Lawrence was "truly rejoiced to see" Amos Adams Lawrence "engaged in the same business as your uncle Abbott and I was [sic] engaged in twenty years ago."[17]

Commendation of entrepreneurship is to be expected from self-made merchants and manufacturers, but plaudits were forthcoming from other, unexpected quarters. The older, mercantile wing of the class, for the most part easily adapting to industrialism, accepted those entrepreneurs who did not stem from established mercantile families. Merchant prince Thomas Handysyd Perkins originally snubbed one of the parvenu textile titans, but in 1852 he was calling Nathan Appleton "my friend" and extolling his value "in the councils of the nation."[18] Cordiality toward self-made manufacturers may have increased with a shift in commercial interests after foreign trade declined. Perkins' investments in 1835 included large holdings in railroad stocks and cotton mills.[19] By 1834, seven eighths of the Boston merchants were identified with New England cotton mills as stockholders, selling agents, or directors.[20]

Businessmen were not alone among proper Bostonians who praised commerce. Despite traditional friction between Americans who followed the life of the countinghouse and those who embraced the life of the mind, ante-bellum Brahmin intellectuals usually respected the calling. Historian William Hickling Prescott referred to "the noble post of head of a cotton factory." Although regarding this vocation as unsuited to his reflective personality, it nonetheless encouraged "an active development of the powers ... better suited, perhaps, to the circumstances of the country, where so much is to be created, than the intellectual civilization...."[21] Cultural celebrities like Prescott and Robert C. Winthrop frequently memorialized dead merchants. Intellectuals evinced their sincerity by lauding entrepreneurs in private. When William Lawrence published an edition of the diary and correspondence of his father, Amos, congratulatory letters from class luminaries in literature, politics, religion, and science recalled the saintliness of the departed magnate.[22] Numerous marriages between the offspring of those devoted to commerce and those devoted to culture was the surest indication of the esteem given businessmen. The daughters of parvenu millionaires Nathan Appleton, Abbott Lawrence and Peter Chardon Brooks married respectively Henry Wadsworth Longfellow, a son of William Prescott, and Charles Francis Adams.

Business achievements, values, and personalities dominated upperclass Boston until the Civil War. Patricians who dissented from the entrepreneurial life felt guilty about their misgivings and uncomfortable in their surroundings. Nathan Appleton's son Thomas, gentleman artist, gourmet, traveler, essayist, and conversationalist, felt himself viewed in Boston as "the pitiful, idle creature who does nothing." The younger Appleton was tormented by the conviction that he had failed his father and earned the displeasure of his community.[23] Brahmins who decades later would be culture heroes of the group tried to escape community reprobation by initially seeking careers in more socially accepted vocations. Oliver Wendell Holmes,

James Russell Lowell, and Francis Parkman repressed literary inclinations for fear that professional success might be compromised or because of parental opposition. Charles Eliot Norton, later a noted literary and art critic, set out to be a merchant; Prescott turned to history when failing eyesight made a law career impossible; and Lowell tried both business and law.[24] Norton regarded early publication of Lowell's poetry as "scarcely a judicious venture for a young man ... to whom the repute of being devoted to his profession was important."[25] The low place held by those who devoted themselves to the muses was also affirmed in Edward Everett Hale's recollection of Boston in this period. "It is pathetic now," recalled the Brahmin biographer, "to see how little welcome there was then for a young poet, or how little temptation for a literary career."[26]

Power in Boston society resided in the entrepreneurial elite. Thomas Handysyd Perkins, considered "the great merchant of Boston" and a model for the Hub gentlemen of his day, was colonel of the Governor's Guard and president of the Boston Branch of the United States Bank. He served in both state houses and refused nomination to Congress and secretaryship of the Navy.[27] "No two citizens of Boston then [1840s] stood higher in public estimation than Abbott Lawrence and Nathan Appleton" wrote Charles Francis Adams in 1900.[28] The two textile titans, in addition to amassing fortunes in cotton manufacturing, served in Congress, and Lawrence was Minister to England. Although Everett, Webster, and Winthrop also achieved positions of community and national prominence without being directly involved in business, they represented industrial interests, and Everett married into the group. Late nineteenth-century Brahmin investment banker Thomas Jefferson Coolidge accurately remembered Boston in these years as a place where "Everybody was at work trying to make money and money was becoming the only real avenue to power and success both socially and in the regard of your fellow men."[29]

2. Proper Bostonians in the Era of Industrial Capitalism: 1870–1950

Pre-Civil War Brahmins were, for the most part, a group of self-assured entrepreneurs secure in their social status and proud of their role in the community. In the closing decades of the nineteenth century, the emergence of new forces and problems undermined the confidence of the class. A group of capitalists chiefly centered in New York deposed the Bostonians from industrial preeminence and even challenged their hegemony in New England. In politics, similar defeats were suffered. Brahmin paladins Charles Sumner and John Lothrop Motley were humiliated in the Grant administration. Richard Henry Dana, scion of a colonial family, was overwhelmingly defeated in the congressional election of 1868 by Benjamin F. Butler, personification of machine politics and champion of the immigrant masses. Dana and his peers endured another reverse when Congress refused to confirm his appointment as minister to Great Britain. These initial indignities were merely a prelude to events in the 1880s and 1890s. Massachusetts mugwumpery, embodiment of political Brahminism, proved inadequate in defending the interests and values of genteel Boston against the onslaught of the urban machine. In the 1870s candidates appealing to newly arrived ethnic groups began to challenge scions from old New England families. By the next decade, the first son of Erin had been elected mayor, as Irish Democrats wrested power from native Yankees. Upper-class Bostonians responded to political and economic decline with movements for civil service reform and immigration restriction designed to curb the growth, or at least to control the development, of immigrants, industrialists, and ward bosses—threats to the established elite.[30]

Although the Brahmin reaction to ethnic and political issues has been closely examined, their response to industrialism needs further analysis. Indeed it is difficult to speak of a single Boston upper-class response to industrialism. There were gentlemen who condemned industrial capitalism as a dangerous enemy encroaching upon their position and threatening the future of America. Other patricians, swept up in the burgeoning national power and prosperity of the late nineteenth century, praised the production of unprecedented wealth and strength. Even these major distinctions, however, are too broad to grasp the variegated reaction: The most enthusiastic did not approve the system in all its particulars. Several severe critics, on the other hand, saw a residue of promise that might be realized if modern productive and financial forces were purified.

Structural changes occurring within the elite influenced proper

Boston's response to post-Civil War industrialism. Ante-bellum Brahmins made mercantile success a crucial criterion for community respect. In the late nineteenth century, when fewer bluebloods engaged in commerce, the course of honor no longer led exclusively through the countinghouse. Although some members of prominent families pursued business, other community leaders preferred religion, education, or letters to the calling of their fathers. William A. Lawrence, the enormously influential Episcopal Bishop of Massachusetts, Endicott Peabody, keeper of the community conscience as headmaster of Gorton Academy, and Harvard presidents Charles W. Eliot and A. Lawrence Lowell were sons of bankers and textile magnates. Lowell, whose brothers Guy and Percival were respectively renowned as an astronomer and architect, once remarked to another patrician, "I'm getting rather worried about the Lowell Family, George. There's nobody in it making money anymore."[31] The ante-bellum situation was now reversed, for Brahmin figures in education, literature, and politics achieved higher national reputations and received more community prestige than did blue-blood businessmen.

Even those who remained in commerce no longer pursued vocational ends with the avidity of their mercantile ancestors. The earlier generation also had sat on boards of directors at elite charitable and educational institutions, but had derived primary satisfaction from commercial careers, and had single-mindedly devoted themselves to business until fortunes had been amassed and corporate position consolidated.[32] The Brahmins buttressed ascendancy in Boston by assuming a variety of civic and social functions that broadened this entrepreneurial elite into an urban upper class. Later blueblood businessmen continued this trend. Godfrey L. Cabot, Henry Lee Jr., Henry Lee Higginson, James Jackson Storrow, Ralph Lowell, and Charles Francis Adams, III, in addition to tending business affairs served on governing boards at Harvard, the Boston Symphony Orchestra, the Boston Atheneum, the Boston Parks Commission, the Humane Society, and the Massachusetts General Hospital and frequently entered politics as reformers or candidates.

Older entrepreneurs proclaimed the honor and significance of their calling; successors sometimes deprecated their own roles, doubted their own abilities, and questioned their own life goals. "Money, Money, success in material pursuits," warned Higginson, "is injuring our generation ..."[33] The banker felt that innate incapacity for financial matters had been aggravated by making "too much of duties and wishes outside and too little of the firm."[34] Vocational frustration accompanied uncertainty of ability. In 1878, Higginson confided to cousin Thomas Wentworth Higginson that "I wanted to do something decent, to leave a little relic of my own behind me, or at least to lead a life full of something to satisfy one's soul—a little—I tried, but failed—partly by accident, chiefly however, from want of brains —and so with the really bright interlude of the war I have become and am a money-getter with struggles for better things."[35]

Brahmin businessmen's ambivalence toward their own calling reflected the negativism displayed by other members of the class. No longer was it the rule for patrician writers to celebrate the accomplishment of their compeers in business. Gentlemen intellectuals Brooks and Henry Adams, Barrett Wendell, Charles Eliot Norton, James Russell Lowell, Francis Parkman, Richard Henry Dana, II, and William Minot condemned commerce. During the Civil War Francis Parkman warned that "the spirit of trade, in the excess of its predominance has done us a wide-spread and deadly mischief."[36] James Russell Lowell also feared "the increasing power of wealth and its combinations as one of the chief dangers with which the institutions of the United States are threatened in the not distant future."[37] Brooks Adams voiced similar sentiments in declaring that "I can't disguise from myself that the victory of capital ... will lead to anything but disaster to us."[38] Distaste for business motivated William Minot to advise young Henry Cabot Lodge that "If you go into business for ten years you will have prostituted the best ten years of your life to trade."[39]

Brahmin attacks on businessmen excluded class associates and ancestors. Reflecting the transformation of the group from an entrepreneurial into a hereditary upper class, contempt focused on the *nouveaux riches*: they were corruptors of American life, vulgarizers of culture, dangers to national existence, and displacers of established elites. For Brooks and Henry Adams these attributes were embodied in Jewish bankers whose parasitic mania for gold would eventually destroy Western civilization. Although not as cataclysmic in their condemnation, James Russell Lowell, Francis Parkman, Richard Henry Dana, Jr., Henry Cabot Lodge, and Charles Francis Adams, Jr. characterized "the self made man," or "parvenu" as "vulgar," "irresponsible," "shifty," "unattractive," holding a "thorough disregard of all the courtesies and amenities of civilized life," lacking "tradition," and having only "one standard, money or money's worth."[40]

Disgust expressed by Brahmin intellectuals was shared by businessmen from the class. Blue-blood entrepreneurs, reflecting their more immediate commercial concerns, emphasized selfishness and duplicity rather than vulgarity and ignorance as negative traits of the robber barons. John Murray Forbes, the Boston railroad magnate, criticized the stock manipulations of Vanderbilt and Gould which turned his self-alleged patrician rectitude into a disadvantage in western railroad competition.[41] Banker brothers Henry and Francis Lee Higginson characterized self-made businessmen as lacking the restraint of personal honor or public responsibility. "He is a self made man without the backing of a family to keep him straight," wrote Francis to his brother about one of their associates. "I have never met one such yet in my business life who has not sooner or later lied to me, or at least tried to cheat me."[42]

Brahmins who condemned industrial capitalism for breeding corruption through materialism, and ugliness through technology expressed sentiments traditionally associated with aristocrats and intellectuals. Self-conscious attachment both to a mental and a social elite reinforced resistance to commerce and mechanization. Charles Eliot Norton, descendant of a mercantile family and professor of fine arts at Harvard, expressed the ideal of this group in asserting that "The love of beauty, the service of it, the production of beautiful things are the best and measure the true worth of the individual and of the nation. They are the final measure of civilization."[43] Norton found this ideal impossible to attain in the materialistic democracy of post-Civil War America. "The rise of the democracy in America," he declared, "is the rise of the uncivilized, whom no scholarly education can suffice to provide with intelligence and reason. . . . I fear that America is beginning a long course of error and of wrong, and is likely to become more and more a power for disturbance and for barbarism."[44] Francis Parkman also conceived an intellectual elite to be a counterforce against a parvenu democracy. A "class of strong thinkers is the palladium of democracy" claimed Parkman. "They are the natural enemies of ignorant, ostentatious, and aggressive wealth. . . ."[45] The antidote of intellectuality was not, however, coping very effectively with the poison of materialism. Parkman was disappointed in "the present condition and prospect of American literature." In great part the nation's lack of cultural accomplishment could be attributed to "speculation . . . that race for wealth" producing a "morbid stimulus . . . applied to trade and industry" that has "created an atmosphere where the scholar and thinker find it hard to breathe."[46] James Russell Lowell joined this chorus of criticism against the self-made businessman. "Hereditary wealth," for Lowell, became "the security of refinement, the feeder of all those arts that ennoble and beautify life." Generations of "accumulated culture" and accumulated wealth were "a prophylactic" against the vulgarity of democratically spawned "new gold."[47]

Industrialism was condemned not only for its effusions of materialism and mindlessness but in its essence as a technological process. Even as a youth, Francis Parkman had dissented from the praise accorded mechanization by Brahmin intellectuals of the 1840s. While traveling through Canada he came upon a mill town, "a despicable manufacturing place."[48] Parkman's lifelong disenchantment with factories and railroads left him somewhat alienated from national culture. "I am a bad American," he wrote in 1892, "inasmuch as I do not pin my faith on railroads and steam engines."[49] Richard Henry Dana also rued the advent of technology. The "steam engine, *wheezing* along with a cloud of smoke, and a train behind," looked to him "like a demon broke loose, and *dragging his spoils behind him*" (Dana's italics).[50] Charles Eliot Norton and James Russell Lowell expressed the same negative attitude toward the technology of industrialism when they regretfully ruminated about innocent old Cambridge being violated by modern apparatuses.[51] The philosophically inclined Henry Adams was able to articulate the feelings of his class in a more general manner than that of Parkman, Norton, Dana, or Lowell. In his vision the ugliness of a particular mill town or railroad, or the destruction of homogeneous Cambridge became general principles of the violation of the past by the present—diversity destroying order. Adams had once been "the confident child of Darwin and Lyell," secure in the "thought of science as a force for unity and progress." By 1900, however, science and technology had become incomprehensible and dictatorial. "The new American," overwhelmed by "complexity," had become the "child of steam and the brother of the dynamo." He was a standardized "product of some such mechanic power" who now served "the powerhouse."[52] These critics of the commercial, productive, and esthetic aspects of modern mechanization were spokesmen for both an intellectual and a community elite. As an established class they feared to confront new wealth, new relationships, and innovations in technological techniques or social structure. As intellectuals they expressed dismay over emphasis on things instead of ideas, over glorification of undifferentiated quantity rather than selectivity according to beauty, and over the mania for money that destroyed the delicacy vital for literary and artistic attainment. The Lowells, Nortons, and Adamses were horrified at the violation of the abstract by the concrete, of contemplation by action, and of culture by power.

The revulsion of Brahmin intellectuals can be traced to the types of existences chosen by or forced upon them. Lowell, Norton, Holmes, Parkman, Wendell, and the Adamses had either forsaken or never embarked on mundane careers. Norton and Lowell left law and trade for literature and academia. Holmes was a teaching rather than practicing physician, and later in life largely gave up medicine to devote himself to writing. Charles Francis Adams, Jr., after being deposed as president of the Union Pacific, turned from business to familial and antiquarian concerns. The personal anguish caused by this aloofness can be read in the response of these figures to their isolation from more worldly activities. Francis Parkman studied law and had a propensity for involvement in wordly affairs, but his illness dictated an inactive life. Contemplating "the future which now opens before me," Parkman foresaw " a weary death in life, with the remembrance of worthy purposes unfulfilled, the consciousness of strong energies paralyzed, high hopes crushed to the dust—a blanket of passive endurance where courage and determination avail nothing."[53] A consciousness of denied achievement and suppressed promise also haunted Henry and Brooks Adams. Years of public irrelevance and personal tragedy turned Henry into an elegant but savage critic of the country from which he had once expected so much.[54] His brother Brooks also made America a macrocosm of his personal situation. In 1902 Brooks confessed to Henry: "Ten years ago, I admit I should have liked to hold office, but a man cannot be young forever, nor can he be Jack of all trades. I have turned toward writing not from chance but from necessity."[55] When his friend Theodore Roosevelt became President, Adams was sure that at last he would be rescued from obscurity. Years of self-pity and ominous prognostication regarding the country's future gave way to the belief "that we have the world at our feet." Brooks was "for the new world . . . electric cars, mobiles, plutocracy and all." How the tune changed when success was the piper! "I don't live but once, and when one is dead it's for a long time and a nation is only great once. One might as well try to cut off a hunk of fat, even if you don't like a particular kind."[56] Less than a year later, frustrated in his expectation of finally wielding power and obtaining recognition, Brooks Adams reverted to self-pity and predictions of national disaster.[57]

Class membership, vocational role, and self-image formed the consciousness of these patrician intellectuals and determined their response to industrialism. Earlier Brahmins, except in moments of Jeffersonian or Jacksonian triumph, had accepted democracy with equanimity, if not enthusiasm, and had certainly not consistently conceived cataclysmic situations in which cities and immigrants became agents of disaster. The negativism of their descendants, however, was not limited to condemnations of technology, business organization, and commercial values. The full range of late nineteenth-century blue-blood criticism encompassed immigration, labor unions, industrial conflict, socialism, political corruption, democracy, and the city. These phenomena were seen as interrelated facets of the potentially fatal malaise of modern times. According to the aristocratic commentators, the catastrophic combination of these evils would crush refinement, tradition, community, excellence, beauty, restraint, learning, altruism and decency—qualities necessary to the continued existence of the republic; characteristics possessed by the Boston elite, and ultimately (it was feared) the noble attributes that would cause the group's downfall. "Men in cities and towns," warned Charles Eliot Norton, "feel much less relation with their neighbors than of old." Urban centers produced "less civic patriotism; less sense of a spiritual and moral community." For Norton, the city, by atomizing society, was responsible for the "selfishness of individualism" characteristic "in a well-to-do democracy."[58] Francis Parkman fixed on the same constellation of evils. "Universal suffrage becomes a questionable blessing," argued the historian, in "a populous city, with its factories and workshops, its acres of tenement-houses, and thousands and ten thousands of restless workmen, foreigners for the most part, to whom liberty means licence and politics means plunder, to whom the public good is nothing and their own most trivial interests everything, who love the country for what they can get out of it, and whose ears are open to the promptings of every rascally agitator...."[59] James Russell Lowell, though not possessed of such a dramatic vision, expressed apprehension about immigrants "untamed" because of unlimited suffrage and untutored in "American habits" flooding the nation's cities.[60]

To these Brahmin observers materialism, corruption, immigration, mob rule, and urban blight were mutually merging aspects of industrialism, a mixture of elements with explosive content of class conflict. Barrett Wendell feared that industrial capitalism created implacable classes, the precursor of anarchism and socialism. "The discontent now rising about us," warned the Brahmin literary critic, might result in "radical revolution" that would "be the end of our ancestral democracy."[61] Francis Parkman regarded the railroad strikes of 1877 as a harbinger of revolution. "The bloody riot" made "the friends of order" look to "lead and steel" in "the last resort."[62]

Gigantic industrial growth created foreign problems as well as domestic difficulties. America's economic power and search for markets as outlets for a mammoth productive system involved the nation in world affairs. Apart from seeking to secure markets, the United States engaged in expansionist activities in order to obtain an international status commensurate with great wealth and power. The drive for territorial acquisition culminated in the Spanish-American War. Many Brahmins, opposing the course of empire, enlisted with Thomas Wentworth Higginson, Charles Eliot Norton, Charles William Eliot, and Charles Francis Adams, Jr., in the anti-Imperialist crusade, a movement dedicated to prevent international adventurism from undermining traditional values. Norton thought imperialism to be another phase of the materialism and barbarism jeopardizing the future of the country.[63] Moorfield Storey, a prominent Boston lawyer, even went so far as to link the Rockefeller-dominated National City Bank, "the very citadel of the 'interests' which have so long sought to influence the government of the United States for their private gain," with financing the quest for empire.[64] Brahmins who were not horrified by America's desire for possessions also feared the outcome of world events. Henry Adams flatly predicted an international debacle.[65] Brooks Adams, one of the hawks of his day, perceived an unfolding pattern of competition between the great industrial powers for the world's remaining markets. This contest made inevitable "a war to the death." A revivified martial spirit would bring victory in the coming conflict, and America, enfeebled by the commercial ethos, would suffer defeat and death.[66]

Through the aristocratic perspective of Brahmin criticism, inherent value was discerned in tradition, family, community, authority, order, excellence, leadership, beauty, and heredity. Conversely materialism, mechanization, mobility, equality, individuality, democracy, and innovation were condemned as enemies of these Burkean principles. By elevating its preferences into moral absolutes, the Boston elite sought to discredit parvenu encroachment upon upper-class status. Canons of classical conservatism thus shaped specific criticisms of materialism, democracy, and the self-made man. For Norton "the steady growth of disrespect for rightful authority" resulted in vulgarity and disorder.[67] Parkman subjected the American creed of Lockean liberalism to the unsympathetic scrutiny of the skeptical conservative. "No political right is absolute and of universal application," he declared, speaking of universal suffrage. "Each has its conditions, qualifications, and limitations.... It is in the concrete, not in the abstract, that rights prevail in every sound and wholesome society. They are applied where they are applicable. A government of glittering generality quickly destroys itself."[68]

Burkean echoes in Boston reverberated patrician anguish over threats to class ascendancy. Henry Adams forecast "total ruin to be now only a question of time for all of us survivals of a misty past, who know not the tricks of money making."[69] Brooks Adams indulged in a sentimental requiem for their class with his nostalgic older brother. The "blood is exhausted," he observed to Henry, "we have come to the end. Apparently our generation was all right. We seemed to have ability, energy and opportunity, and yet we all have tried and have not suited ourselves or anybody else."[70]

Many blue-bloods, feeling bypassed in modern times, hungered for the lost community of their youth. Self-asserted relics of the past, they dreamed of ante-bellum Boston, Quincy, or Cambridge; with ancestral homes lining quiet streets; where everyone belonged and neighborliness prevailed. In the old days, the best days for Norton, "the very pleasantest little oasis of space and time was ... New England from about the beginning of the century to about 1825."[71] America's future looked bleak to this aging aristocrat who found himself a misfit in the modern era. The past seemed so much happier, especially when colored by the nostalgia of an old man's memories and the poignance of an old man's loneliness. The Cambridge of his youth, when "the intermixture of foreign elements was so small as not to affect the character of the town," provided an idyllic existence in which "everybody knew everybody else in person but also much of everybodies traditions, connections, and mode of life." Norton recollected an age when everyone had a place and when having a place still meant something. Now those years merely served to make more painful Norton's awareness that "it has been a pathetic experience for me to live all my life in one community and to find myself gradually becoming a stranger to it."[72] James Russell Lowell described the Cambridge of "Thirty Years Ago" in much the same terms. Before the war "the town had indeed a character. Railways and omnibuses had not rolled flat all the little social prominences and peculiarities, making every man as much a citizen everywhere as at home." During those days when tradition, homogenity, and community reigned supreme, life was warmer, richer, and more meaningful. "Everybody knew everybody, and all about everybody." Intimacy was possible in a community not disrupted by change. "Things were established then ... and men did not run through all figures on the dial of society so swiftly as now, when hurry and competition seem to have quite unhung the modulating pendulum of steady thrift and competent training. Some slow minded persons even followed their father's trade" in the past where "Life flowed in recognized channels, narrower perhaps, but with all the more individuality and force."[73] Indeed the new Cambridge where Thomas Wentworth Higginson was defeated as a congressional candidate in 1888 and Godfrey Lowell lost the mayoralty election in 1923 bore little resemblance to the homogeneous Yankee community so fondly remembered by Norton and Lowell. Quincy "up to 1850" meant as much to Charles Francis Adams Jr. as had old Cambridge to Norton and Lowell. At that time "Quincy was practically what it had always been—a quiet, steady-going, rural Massachusetts community ... peopled by those of the original stock; for the foreign and more particularly the Irish element had not yet reached the self-asserting point." In this traditional society "The factory and the machine-made shoe were as yet unknown or in their earliest stages of development." But now "the place I as a child loved so well no longer exists." Mechanization made Adams a stranger in the town his family had called home for generations. "No one knows me now as I walk the once familiar streets," mused the lonely old aristocrat, "and I recall no faces." With local feeling gone traditions had vanished. "As I pass to-and-fro in Quincy I now seem to wander with ghosts."[74]

The quest for community did not always lead back to the home town of yesteryear. Henry Adams sought shelter from the bewildering modern world by fleeing to the twelfth and thirteenth centuries, when all social forces united in one faith and everyone moved in the same direction. The vitality, unity, nobility, and even the tragic irrelevance of the Middle Ages were symbolized, for Henry Adams, in the Virgin. The Virgin, antithesis of the technological thrust of the Dynamo, was warm, eternal, protective, and traditional. Mary rejected *arrivistes*, Jews, and money-lenders, and imposed order on the anarchy of science and the meaningless of modern times. For the reality of modern science, "a raft to which limpets stuck for life in the surge of a supersensual chaos," she substituted "an ordered universe which she knew to be unity...."[75] The Virgin reversed those disintegrative tendencies in contemporary society that mirrored Adams' own sense of impotence and decline. She was the comforter of the alienated, the emancipator of those enslaved by the dynamo. Brooks Adams' exit from modern times was vicarious immersion in the community of his illustrious ancestors. He spent summers in the

"Old House" at Quincy and turned it into a memorial. Adams collected the family memorabilia and wrote a biography of his presidential grandfather. In his later years, disgust for democratic, scientific, and materialistic individualism led him to make a confession of faith at the First Parish Church in Quincy (an adherence to an old Puritan custom.) "No society which we or our ancestors have known, can cohere without a faith in revealed religion," was the principle of his confession.[76] "Perfection," to the new saint, presupposed "a code of moral standards" that would provide barriers against selfish irresponsibility. Sensual desire offered one challenge, but the real task lay in overcoming the sin of pride. Adams, who had once used the perspective of science and reason to criticize Puritan ancestors,[77] echoed his stern-visaged forefathers by declaring that man's "greatest enemy is always his own vanity and self esteem," his refusal "to admit his own intellectual impotence in the face of the infinite, and endure with resignation his destiny. He is always aspiring to dominate nature and is always suffering defeat." In the same manner as John Winthrop had rejected "Natural Liberty," Adams condemned "Democracy," which reveled in "personal liberty," encouraging rebellion against proper restraint and enabling lust and pride to master men.[78]

Inseparable from the longing for lost community was regret over the snapping of family ties. Sentimental attachment to ancestral homes revealed the poignancy with which Brahmins regarded the passing of old families. James Russell Lowell "never saw a house which I thought old enough to be torn down." A permanent domicile was vital because the formation of "character is cumulative ... the influence of the same climate, scenery, and associations for several generations is necessary to its gathering headway, and ... the process is disturbed by continual change of place." The present-day "American is nomadic in ideas, in morals, and leaves his faith and opinions with as much indifference as the house in which he was born."[79] Norton, in an essay entitled "The Lack of Old Homes in America," also bewailed the rootlessness reflected by the casual destruction of family residences. Similar sentiments were expressed by Oliver Wendell Holmes, Sr., who mourned the destruction of his birthplace "as a part of my life gone from me." The person "to be envied" most in this world, according to the poet, "is the one who is born to an ancient estate, with a long line of family traditions...."[80]

Brahmin critics confronted industrial capitalism with fundamental opposition to its values and structure. The modern hero was the achieving individual. Free from ties to the past, the community, or the family, he could move anywhere and adjust to almost anything. Stripped of long-standing attachments or traditions, the emancipated individual could more easily meet the needs of a rationalized, bureaucratically structured, dynamic social system. Against the modern demands for efficiency, mobility, adaptability, innovation, objectivity, achievement, and coordination, the genteel objectors raised the claims of loyalty, steadfastness, sentiment, inheritance, tradition, and community. But these challengers, fighting with weapons from another era, were doomed to defeat in a society oriented to the present and the future.

Although blue-blood critics agreed in their diagnosis of the forces plaguing the nation, prognoses differed. Most upper-class Bostonians expected the country to recover from the diseases attacking the body politic, but they disagreed in locating the sources of America's fundamental vitality. Some patricians felt that the persistence of old American homogeneity and moral fiber could contain the ravages of industrialism. Francis Parkman was among those reassured by the continued vigor of the old ways. "There are prophets of evil," he asserted, "who see in the disorders that involve us the precursors of speedy ruin." He did not share this gloom because "complete disruption and anarchy are, we may hope, still far off, thanks to an immense vitality and an inherited conservative strength."[81] Other observers, while aware of the danger of the new forces, derived hope from discovering promise in recent developments rather than from the resiliency of the past. James Russell Lowell's early zest for reform, democracy, and the brightness of the future waned somewhat after the 1860s, but recent social changes still inspired in him hope for a revivified America. In an era "in which wealth has [never] been more sensible of its duties," violent upheaval was unlikely.[82] The fact that "most of our rich men have risen from the ranks" convinced Lowell of "the benign influence of democracy rightly understood."[83] The rise of responsible wealth was but one indication of the promise of modern America. Such benevolence could redeem even the immigrant: "we have taken from Europe the poorest, the most ignorant, the most turbulent of her people, and have made them over into good citizens who have added to our wealth, and who are ready to die in defense of a country and of institutions which they know to be worth dying for."[84]

Charles Eliot Norton and Barrett Wendell were more pessimistic than Lowell or Parkman. Norton had mixed feelings about America's future. In the midst of growing disenchantment with democratic capitalism, the Cambridge aristocrat maintained that some progress had been made in recent years. No doubt "a commercial aristocracy" diminished "respect for intellectual and spiritual things; . . . yet we may be content in reflecting that . . . the multitudes of the lower class . . . are rising from degradation into comparative civilization and comfort."[85] This hopeful note, however, was a small counterpoint to the dirge he sang on other occasions. Populism, imperialism, and materialism were undermining "the vitality of the republic." Appalled by these developments, Norton wondered "whether our civilization can maintain itself, and make advance, against the pressure of ignorant and barbaric multitudes; whether the civilized part of the community is eventually to master the barbaric, or whether it is to be overcome in the struggle."[86] Barrett Wendell was another offspring of an old mercantile family who felt that the country's future trembled in the balance. Unrestrained democracy and unrefined wealth were the Scylla and Charybdis of the nation. "If American democracy turned tyrant," Wendell warned, by "implacably favoring either the many or the few in the tyranny which both seem attempting to exert, that faith [American democracy] must perish in the whirlwind, or the morass of such catastrophe we have never known—the full reality of American Revolution." Failure to check rampant finance capitalism, the class-conscious conservative claimed, ironically repeating an argument of progressive reformers, might mean "the end of our ancestral democracy—the abandonment of all that our conservative revolution won us with our independence while we are struggling amid the confusion and the violence of the radical revolution conceivably to come."[87]

There were patricians even more pessimistic than Norton or Wendell. A minority of prominent Bostonians had become convinced of imminent disaster. John Torrey Morse, William Sturgis Bigelow, and Henry and Brooks Adams, sharers of a cataclysmic vision, expressed deep feelings of self-revulsion and futility. Other Brahmins regretted the advent of new forces that challenged the position of their class, but they did not identify their souls with the threatened demise of their social order. The more optimistic Brahmin critics possessed professional commitments, and, with the exception of Parkman, institutional affiliations. Richard Henry Dana, Jr. was an outstanding member of the Massachusetts bar; James Russell Lowell had been an editor, Harvard professor, and ambassador to Spain and England, as well as a world-famous poet and essayist; Oliver Wendell Holmes was a noted physician and professor at the Harvard Medical School, as well as a famous man of letters. Even pessimistic commentators like Norton and Wendell had been Harvard professors. The cataclysmists, on the other hand, withdrew from professional activities for the larger part of their mature lives. John T. Morse retired as a practicing lawyer at age forty and became a minor biographer of Brahmin figures and a Boston clubman.[88] William S. Bigelow, while still in his thirties, gave up medicine to study Japanese art and Buddhism.[89] Henry Adams, although an editor, historian, and member of the Harvard history department for nine years, regarded editing and teaching with distaste and refused reappointment to the faculty.[90] Brooks Adams, after a short law career, joined his brother as an observer of (but never an active participant in) American life. Unable to draw support and satisfaction from institutional attachments and vocational accomplishments, the Cassandras were left to confront life alone. No alternatives were available to divert or mitigate the intertwining consciousness of class prospects with personal frustrations. John T. Morse claimed to be one of those "who stands aside and makes no effort" to undertake " 'public business.' " He felt "an utter personal incapacity (to say nothing of distaste) that I could never tackle it with any efficiency."[91] Late in life, Morse described himself as "an obscure and powerless old man."[92] William S. Bigelow was a self proclaimed "decrepit Mayfly on a straw" who watched "with interest" the disintegration of the republic.[93] The same attitude of personal irrelevance and weakness permeated the outlook of Henry Adams. A pathetic account of his lost life was conveyed in a letter to brother Charles in which "look[ing] back on our sixty years of conscious life," he had "to search hard for a word of warm satisfaction." Life had left him "dying alone, without a twig to fall from," leaving "no followers, no school, no tradition."[94] Brooks Adams possessed a similar negative self-image. He was "but one lonely man against whom all society is banded ... to crush me, to ridicule and suppress me."[95] The younger Adams felt that he "approach[ed] pretty nearly being utterly without a use in the world I live in."[96]

Morse, Bigelow, and the Adams brothers expected revolution or foreign war to bring American civilization to a catastrophic end. This simplistic prophecy was perhaps a reflection of their own feeble, frustrated, and confused self-images. In a final, all-consuming chaos would be swept away feelings of irrelevance, anguish, failure, and the forces in whose triumph these pessimists read class defeat. Morse, frightened and disgusted by the specter of mass rule, sensed imminent upheaval. He would meet force with the counterforce of a large standing army; he dreamed of making the revolutionaries "a target for the firing squad." Only by "reestablish[ing] a despotic class rule" could the proletarian-immigrant uprising be beaten back.[97] Bigelow, who feared similar events, also felt the necessity of a "military dictatorship."[98] But the most resolute resistance could no longer reverse the disastrous trend. "In short, as I have so frequently had occasion to remark to you," he told Henry Cabot Lodge, who was trying to hold the line in the Senate, "the country is going straight to the devil. No, that statement is erroneous. It has already gone."[99] Despair drew Bigelow into agreement with the speculations of Henry Adams. "What has happened in Russia will happen everywhere," forecast Bigelow echoing Adams. "It will be the French Revolution on a world scale. It will end in ... corruption, disintegration and putrefaction—just what Henry predicted."[100]

Henry and Brooks Adams, while sharing with Bigelow and Morse the expectation of catastrophic conflict, added a less dramatic, but just as solemn philosophical dimension to the vision. By applying a version of the second law of thermodynamics to modern capitalism, the brothers conceived a theory that the United States was suffering an irreparable loss of energy that would eventuate in doom. Evidence of the decline of vital energy abounded in the triumph of the commercial ethic over martial spirit, in diversity displacing unity, and in atrophy of esthetic values and intellectual imagination. Institutions of administration and coordination could no longer cope with the growth of business and the accumulation of wealth, and these uncontrolled social forces had brought the republic to the verge of chaos.[101]

The Adamses predicted that deterioration of energy would result in national destruction through class conflict or in defeat in foreign war. Domestic politics, Henry Adams forecast, would end in the domination of commercial interests, the chaos of a Bryan victory, or the tyranny of the trade union.[102] International troubles would culminate in global holocaust putting an end to the republic.[103] The "only question" remaining was whether society "will break down suddenly, or subside slowly, after a long lapse of time into motionless decay."[104] At first the disgruntled patrician was relatively optimistic foreseeing "more than two hundred years of futile and stupid stagnation."[105] But misgivings about self and society made the estimate continually shorter until only a few decades separated civilization from chaos.[106] Brooks Adams agreed with brother Henry in predicting business domination through the rule of McKinley and Morgan or violent revolution via Bryan.[107] International prospects were equally gloomy. Defeat loomed in the forthcoming death battle for world supremacy. Since luxury and commerce had eroded America's military power beyond repair, victory in the impending war of the races awaited the East. At best the younger Adams gave Europe three generations and the rest of the "system" until the twenty-first century before total disintegration.[108] Depressed at the apparent mastery displayed by the magnates, disappointed over political reverses, and watching his contemporaries succumb to old age, Adams foreshortened his ominous anticipations. "1925" became the dire date, but subsequently the belligerent Brahmin doubted whether disaster could hold off that long.[109] Imminent defeat by Asia, disorganized administration, and the triumph of desire over discipline indicated total collapse swiftly approaching. "Democracy in America has conspicuously and decisively failed," declared the morose aristocrat, "capitalistic civilization . . . is nearing an end."[110]

Most proper Bostonians conceived of post-Civil War industrialism as a threat to high status or the country's survival, and vociferously criticized forces and groups that allegedly threatened the prerogatives of the establishment. A few prominent bluebloods, however, involved in various facets of the productive system or having committed themselves to the new era, enthusiastically worked to modernize America. Brahmin businessmen, with occasional reservations about their calling or their associates, celebrated trusts, titans, and technology. Railroad entrepreneur John Murray Forbes, nephew of Thomas Handysyd Perkins, engaged in "ventures ... to give his partners and perhaps his older grandsons occupations and industries."[111] His son-in-law successor as president of the Chicago, Burlington & Quincy Railroad, Charles Elliot Perkins, doubtlessly agreed with Forbes about preparing descendants for business careers. According to Perkins, captains of industry were "public benefactors" who "lessen the cost of living" through "successful improvement and organization of the means of production and distribution."[112] Henry Lee Higginson, despite reservations about the rectitude of many businessmen, found them on the whole as honest and public spirited "as anybody in our country."[113] Business organization as well as businessmen pleased the banker. "Incorporation," asserted Higginson, "is the most brilliant invention of our past century...."[114]

Several Brahmins not engaged in commerce praised entrepreneurship. William Lawrence, the leading blue-blood churchman of his generation, wrote a laudatory life of his father, cotton manufacturer Amos A. Lawrence.[115] Thomas Wentworth Higginson, the well known patrician reformer and writer, found "merit" in businessmen because they were "doing something in the present," rather than living on the memory of "something which has long gone by." The active life that had produced "the aristocracy of the millionaires" was, for him, a necessary "prelude to the aristocracy of the millions." Unlike other aristocratic intellectuals he discerned among capitalists "a secret reverence for science, for history, and even for literature...." The vulgar materialism of the age was, therefore, a passing symptom of its immaturity. Higginson expected "all the proprieties of life" to be eventually reestablished on a much broader scale.[116] Justice Oliver Wendell Holmes also praised "the great masters of combinations." Magnates James J. Hill and Edward H. Harriman were men of "very superior timber" who embodied "one of the greatest forms of human power, an immense mastery of economic details, an equal grasp of general principles, and ability and courage to put ... conclusions into practice with brilliant success....[117] Unlike alienated Brahmin intellectuals, Holmes did not castigate or cringe before the seizure and exercise of power, nor did he feel that great thoughts precluded great commercial deeds. Just as he refused to polarize intellectual and economic accomplishment, so he denied that commercial gains primarily resulted from exploitation and corruption. The "talk of 'exploitation,' as a hostile characterization of modern commercial life" was "drivelling cant...."[118] The presidents of Harvard in the period from 1869 to 1932 also affirmed business activity. Charles William Eliot, in an article written in the depths of the 1890s depression, cited corporate service as one reason "Why the American Republic May Endure." "If we direct our attention to the banks, trust companies, manufacturing corporations," asserted Eliot, "we shall realize that the quality of corporate service is really good, and that the great majority of corporate servants exhibit, in high degree, the admirable virtues of fidelity and loyalty."[119] Abbott Lawrence Lowell shared his predecessor's respect for businessmen. Lowell, who regretted that no one of his own family remained in business, was a firm supporter of the Harvard Business School.[120]

The sincerest belief in industrial capitalism was demonstrated when these figures applied its methods to their chosen fields. Eliot specifically criticized aristocratic esthetes and traditionalists who rejected modern society. "One of the most discouraging phenomena of the last twenty years," he wrote in 1896, was "the reaction in the New England community towards ritualism and aestheticism...."[121] Embracing new departures, he sought to apply commercial and technological values and techniques of rationality, efficiency, practicality, and order in his primary concerns of educational and political reform. "The people see that every complicated business into which applied science enters largely as a factor needs the services of men selected for fitness and merit," he wrote concerning civil-service reform. "They perceive that the business of the government is extremely complicated in its higher departments, hard to learn completely, and needing the same faithful and continuous service which private enterprises profit by and reward."[122] Given such a political situation, "the merit system is the only practical business-like method of selecting, developing, and promoting officials of any government which has modern business to do."[123] Eliot subjected the citadel of Brahmin education to these same principles. He transformed Harvard from a provincial, traditional, upper-class college into a great cosmopolitan university. The iconoclast president improved graduate schools, extended the elective system, encouraged science at the expense of the old classical curriculum, and introduced a course in civil engineering.[124] These innovations were implemented despite opposition from blue-blood conservatives. "Any outsider who heard the conversation of Boston clubs in those days," commented Samuel Eliot Morison in *Three Centuries of Harvard*, "might well have concluded that President Eliot was 'Public Enemy No. 1.' "[125] Eliot was not alone in his determination to modernize Harvard. Brahmin businessmen Charles Francis Adams, Jr., John Murray Forbes, and entrepreneur-scientist Alexander Agassiz supported Eliot's heresy. Forbes preferred "a graduate from the Technological school to one from Harvard" because the college did not prepare men "to get a living" in the world.[126] Adams expressed the same conviction in answering Norton's plea for classical studies. "I think we have had all we want of 'elegant scholars' and 'gentlemen of refined classical tastes'," he retorted, adopting a man-of-affairs stance. "I want to see more university men trained up to take a hand in the rather rough game of American twentieth century life."[127]

Holmes tried to modify the law in accord with the same principles that guided Eliot's actions at Harvard. He argued for a flexible legal system responsive to concrete social needs and changing circumstances, to replace absolute canons enshrined in tradition and defended by deductive logic and precedent.[128] Law must be made empirical and adaptable. It must become scientific because "science" alone can correctly "determine ... the relative worth of our different social ends." Scientific determinism, never to be fully realized, was nonetheless the "ideal" to which all efforts should be aimed.[129]

Brahmins who accepted the techniques and values of industrial capitalism tended to be less pessimistic in their attitudes about newcomers, class relations, and democracy. Xenophobia, a mania among those who felt dispossessed was not as marked among patricians who felt at home in contemporary surroundings. The Chinese and the

Irish, two of the most despised immigrant groups, found defenders in Forbes and Thomas Wentworth Higginson, while Eliot considered America's assimilation of foreigners to be "a demonstration that people belonging to a great variety of races or nations are, under favorable circumstances, fit for political freedom."[130]

Prospects of violent conflict between labor and capital haunted the vision of many blueblood alarmists but was absent from the calculations of Thomas Wentworth Higginson, Eliot, and A. Lawrence Lowell. Higginson could see "no omens of any fierce upheaval."[131] Eliot concluded that "Within the last fifteen years" workers and management had grown closer together because employers were more concerned with employee welfare and correspondingly employees were less inclined to violence.[132] Lowell discerned "an advance in wisdom ... in industrial relations in this country." He, too, found capitalists "more frequently solicitous for the welfare of their work-people, more inclined to regard them as participants in a common enterprise, than when I was young." Conversely "labor leaders" in recent times "take longer views of the true interest of their followers."[133]

Capitalist democracy, thought pessimistic Bostonians, intensified disintegrative social forces. Brahmins at peace with their age praised egalitarian, industrial society. Thomas Wentworth Higginson "affirm[ed] that democratic society, the society of the future, enriches and does not impoverish human life, and gives more, not less, material for literary art."[134] Eliot, who refused to raise tuition at Harvard and who took pride in the scholarship fund, "wanted to have the College open equally to men with much money, little money, or no money, provided they all have brains."[135] World War I, which evoked condemnations of the national government from Brooks Adams and Barrett Wendell, brought forth a reaffirmation of faith by Eliot. Democracy, he believed, would emerge victorious, because "liberty is the vital air of strong human character."[136] Eliot's successor worked in a similar fashion to democratize Harvard. Lowell introduced the house system, designed to end the class and wealth distinctions between students who lived on the luxurious "Gold Coast" and those quartered in plebian Harvard Yard.[137] Students placed together in disregard of social or economic preferences, predicted Harvard's president, would prevent formation of "cliques based upon similarity of origin and upon wealth" and "make Harvard a more democratic college."[138] Henry Cabot Lodge, aristocratic senator from Massachusetts, expressed his support for the American political system in rejecting the misgivings of friends John T. Morse and Brooks Adams. Despite democracy's weaknesses, he once answered Morse, no other system "has worked as well on the whole."[139]

Contained in Eliot's defense of democracy was a touch of egalitarianism that made men of his persuasion impatient with social and intellectual snobs like Barrett Wendell. Eliot criticized Wendell's *A Literary History of America* for "The way he dwells on the birth or family of literary people. . . ." Wendell's emphasis "shows that he has not observed how quickly American men and women acquire not only the manners and customs but the mode of thought and speech, and the sentiments which prevail among 'ladies and gentlemen.' The sons and daughters of mechanics, farmers, and shopkeepers," concluded Eliot, "have not only the bodily characteristics of 'gentle birth' but their best mental and spiritual qualities."[140] T. W. Higginson shared this faith in the people. The "strength of society," he asserted, "lies more, after all, in the many than in the few."[141] Higginson disputed the intellectual elitism of Norton and Parkman. The man of learning, declared the reformer, should have "no advantage [i.e., weighted vote] over the man who cannot read or write."[142] Genteel aloofness also annoyed Oliver Wendell Holmes, Jr., who while not a defender of democracy, rejected the pose of patrician disengagement. "Charles Eliot Norton was a flat," charged the justice. "Did you ever hear of his beginning a lecture to one of his classes: 'Probably none of you has ever seen a gentleman?' "[143]

Faith in democracy and distaste for aristocratic alienation marked those Brahmins who achieved fame through their own efforts in their own era. Holmes in law, Higginson in letters, Eliot and Lowell in education, and Lodge in politics gained power and prestige through their accomplishments. These national figures, transcending genteel Boston's orbit, did not depend on membership in an exclusive enclave for support or satisfaction. The same held true for magnates Higginson and Forbes who, while not specifically praising democracy or condemning Brahmin esthetes, obviously accepted the conditions of modern times. These men, concerned with career and national reputation, adopted contemporary values. In the case of Lodge and Eliot, this meant straining class ties by violating the sacred canons of mugwumpery or classical education. Having derived psychic strength from triumphs in careers whose scope passed beyond the community of their origins, these figures firmly rooted themselves in the age of industrial capitalism.

Commitment to their careers and concern for the concrete reality of the workaday world gave a tough-minded, pragmatic texture to the outlooks of these men. Vocational success demanded energetic, practical, and disciplined types whose drive for achievement would not be diminished or deflected by self-doubt, noncomformity, uncompromising idealism, or pessimism. T. W. Higginson's distinction between himself and those who sought refuge in the past reveals the significance of social role in determining perspectives on self and society: "It must be borne in mind that one who has habitually occupied the attitude of a reformer must inevitably have some satisfactions, at the latter end of life, which those who are conservative by temperament can hardly share." Traditionalists tend to look with disfavor upon social change. The profession of reformer, however, would lose all meaning if social change brought disintegration. Higginson thus contrasted himself with the conservative pessimist, "a dreary companion as the years advance. The reformer, on the other hand, sees so much already accomplished, in the direction of his desires, that he can await in some security the fulfillment of the rest."[144] Henry Cabot Lodge appealed to the values of activistic accomplishment through realistic accommodation in order to justify breaking with the Brahmin community by choosing regular Republicanism over mugwump purity. Lodge claimed to prefer concrete gains over aloof righteousness.[145] When Brooks Adams, with the idealism of despair charged that democracy was doomed, Lodge rebutted in the spirit of the man of affairs concerned only with what is workable and contingent: "I have to deal with things as they are and not as I want them to be or as they ought to be." The realistic office-holder had "to accept the proposition that Democracy is able to defeat Autocracy ... whether as an abstract proposition I believe it or not, ... because if I did not I should be crying in the wilderness and what little I am able to do for the cause which I have most at heart would be sacrificed." The Brahmin politician advised the alienated aristocrat that "If you are to accomplish anything, you must confine yourself to the practicable and the possible."[146] Ambition, the work ethic, lust for life, and practicality shaped Oliver Wendell Holmes, Jr.'s attitude toward the world and himself. In letters to friends Holmes constantly complained of his compulsion to keep busy.[147] But the lawyer enjoyed his work and was gratified by the esteem it brought. Law fascinated him and once appointed to the Supreme Court, he was "even more absorbed, interested and impressed than ever I had dreamed I might be."[148] Professional recognition enhanced interest. On receiving an LL.D. from Yale, Holmes candidly included himself in the admission that honor rather than altruism motivated most men. The degree would "fan the spark in me" and inspire attempts "to maintain the honor you have bestowed."[149] Vocational involvement and personal achievement created an affirmative outlook. "I still enjoy life and am very willing for it to keep on," wrote the nonagenarian in 1932.[150] This positive attitude extended from personal matters to the destiny of the nation. Dire forecasts of associates Bigelow, and Brooks and Henry Adams were regarded as cranky, "pitiable drool."[151] "As I grow older I grow calm," remarked the justice. Beyond "the vision of battling races and an impoverished earth I catch a dreaming glimpse of peace."[152] Holmes dedicated himself to making the law a flexible instrument responsive to concrete demands of social change. The same preoccupation with practical fulfillment of contemporary social needs guided the educational reforms of Eliot and Lowell. The Harvard presidents also shared the jurist's emphasis on labor in a chosen calling. On his ninetieth birthday, Eliot advised Harvard students to select "in what calling, in what profession, in what occupation am I going to find the work which will give me joy all my days." He told the audience that "a large part of the happiness in life for me ... has come out of the joy in work." Vocational dedication unhindered by excessive "introspection" was Eliot's "last exhortation" to the undergraduates.[153] Pragmatic engagement defined Eliot's perspective. Unlike those patricians overcome with despair "the only question" for him "when a good cause has been defeated ... is when do we fight again."[154] "Looking back" at the age of eighty, the great educator had stated that he had "lived in the work of the passing day, neither regretting the past nor fearing the future, but trying in the passing moment to gain good ends which were often immediate but sometimes far distant."[155] Eliot, like Higginson and Holmes, found that the passing years brought his share of accomplishments. Accumulation of attainments made possible "a sense of growth and of increased capacity for useful service." Unlike the pessimistic patricians, the unfolding of whose lives was accompanied with a deepening consciousness of defeat and futility, Eliot's existence was "enriched and amplified from year to year."[156] A secure sense of personal growth grounded a firm faith in national progress. The spread of education, religious tolerance, corporate service, and the gradual substitution of community responsibility for class conflict ensured "the American Republic long life."[157] Eliot's successor continued to preach the gospel of hard work and useful public service. In a baccalaureate speech, Lowell emphasized "the necessity, in every career, of intense, continuous, accurate labor...."[158] "True success" yoked personal effort to moral purpose by being achieved in "something worth doing."[159] Character could be built through public service because there was "much virtue and public spirit" in the United States. "The observation of a lifetime" convinced Lowell "that these qualities have not diminished, but on the whole have gained in strength."[160] Faith that men would ultimately labor for community welfare survived the shocks of depression and world war. Throughout this troubled period Lowell was an "incurable optimist" certain "that mankind will recover the principles necessary for its moral preservation."[161]

Brahmin optimists viewed life in concrete, practical terms, accepted the dominant values of their era, attained vocational success, and believed in America's future. Their despairing peers remained aloof from practical affairs, disappointed in, or indifferent to vocational accomplishments, immersed in self-doubt, attached to the past, and haunted by visions of impending disaster. These categories, though true, are subject to the oversimplification and abstraction inevitable with general types. A brief investigation of the changing career and convictions of Charles Francis Adams, Jr. conveys more graphically the intensely emotional impact of industrial capitalism.

Like his younger brothers, Adams' attitudes toward himself and society varied with success or failure in public roles. After courageous service in the Civil War, Adams headed the Massachusetts Railroad Commission and then succeeded Jay Gould as president of the Union Pacific Railroad. During this period he expressed the conventional wisdom held by men of achievement in commercial affairs. Adams pursued wealth as an avid speculator in real estate and in industrial and railroad securities because riches enabled him to be "received with deference and listened to with acceptance...." Fortune was "the spring-board to influence, consideration, power and enjoyment," and Adams meant to have his share of these prerogatives.[162] For him, in common with other captains of industry, money not only gratified material needs but brought power. As an investor and railroad administrator, Adams hoped to exercise this power to bring order to the nation's transportation system. At first, the future railroad president criticized industrial combinations and the monopolists who constructed them.[163] Arguments that concentration created dangerous centers of irresponsible power, however, gave way to the assumption that size meant stability and efficiency. Adams had once criticized the machinations of Drew and others involved in manipulating the affairs of the Erie Railroad; now he contended "that with each new railroad the Vanderbilt or the Jay Gould or the Huntingdon [sic] interest acquires, the more cautious they become. They realize the responsibilities and dangers of their position...."[164] A "general combination among all railroad corporations" would impose a rational structure in this as in other areas of business activity. Concentration leading to a more rational organization would thus create a more efficient and financially sounder railroad system.[165] During these years of corporate service, ends of power and wealth were primary, and their realization depended upon rational administration to achieve organizational efficiency and commercial stability. Adams, preoccupied with these issues, looked with amused contempt upon Brahmin associations irrationally steeped in tradition and sentiment. The venerable Massachusetts Historical Society was "a cross of the genealogical tree with the female prig."[166] Similar propensities in Boston evoked castigation for living in the past instead of adapting to changing conditions.[167] "It is useless to cast back regretful glances at the old quiet days of other years and another order of things" wrote the young Adams. "We had best go on cheerfully and hopefully, for we are enlisted for the war. We must follow out the era on which we have entered to its logical and ultimate conclusions, for it is useless for men to stand in the way of steam engines."[168] Buoyant in the incoming wave of industrialism, he had not yet assumed the family role of being the embittered conscience of the republic. Like brother Brooks, waiting expectantly early in Theodore Roosevelt's administration, Charles Francis was willing to live and let live if he could get his slice of life. "After all, men and systems can best develop themselves in their own way and it is hardly worthwhile either to continually prognosticate evil, or to pass one's life in fighting shadows."[169]

Adams was deposed by Jay Gould after failing to rectify financial weakness or reverse the decline of the Union Pacific. The dispossessed captain of industry attributed his defeat to his "weak[ness] of will."[170] Adams, conquered by a commercial corsair and threatened with bankruptcy in the Panic of 1893, turned on former associates and ideas. Now he belonged to "the producing and debtor class . . . ground down" by "the Rothschilds and Morgan."[171] Adversity made him feel peripheral to the main developments of his time. "I can influence no one," he cried, echoing the alienation of his brothers. "Everyone I could influence thinks as . . . I do, while those who think otherwise regard me as belonging essentially to the 'classes,' and as, therefore, not even entitled to a hearing, much less to any degree of confidence. . . ."[172] Thoughts of personal failure had created an oracle of doom. "Disastrous consequences" awaited a nation in which surrender to Morgan and the Rothschilds could only be avoided by capitulating to the radicalism of Bryan.[173]

Loss of eminence meant retirement to the Boston upper-class community. Existence among proper Bostonians became a refuge from personal defeat and the chaos already engulfing the country. The path of retreat led from America to Boston, from the present to the past, from the corporation to the family, from self-confidence to alienation. The deposed executive became an historian of ancient Brahmins, a biographer of his father and of Richard Henry Dana, Jr., and a president of the Massachusetts Historical Society. The Society, formerly lightly regarded as an ancestral relic, became valued for its "social side."[174] The once ambitious entrepreneur, eager to get a toehold in the contemporary world, now castigated young relatives for ignoring family traditions, criticized former business associates in the mausoleum of his autobiography, and spent his later life immersed in self pity for his own feebleness.[175] Adams' submergence in family and group rituals could not compensate for his defeats, any more than it could for Brooks Adams or John Morse. Living in the past merely placed Adams in the shadow of his great forebears. The only relief offered by comparison with illustrious ancestors was the cavil that although having "accomplished nothing considerable, compared with what my three immediate ancestors accomplished," I "got more enjoyment out of" life than they and "In this respect I would not change with any of them."[176]

The Brahmin response to industrialism cannot be fully ascertained without analyzing the relationship of personal and class attitudes to actions, circumstances, and conditions. A discussion of what genteel Boston thought, no matter how extended or ingenious, must be combined with an account of what the group did. Feelings, impressions, and ideas cannot themselves explain behavior because consciousness and action do not inevitably correlate. This lack of complete correspondence necessitates a move from the explanation of blueblood opinions to an investigation of policies, methods, and results. Regional resources and views toward commerce were the factors that determined the scope of blueblood business activity. The crucial issues were whether patrician values compelled adherence to a code of behavior less businesslike than the practices of parvenu associates or competitors, and whether traditional leadership could maintain itself when confronted with new products and processes and when challenged by self-made men and other regions' advantages of better location, higher growth rate, better transportation, and greater physical resources.

The Brahmins entered the post-Civil War era with a reputation for commercial rectitude and community responsibility. For several generations, business relationships had been chiefly confined to the cohesive Boston upper-class society. Interrelated dynasties controlled the mills, railroads, and financial institutions upon which rested the power and wealth of the Boston elite. Commercial endogamy undoubtedly contributed to ethical behavior. Faltering merchants recouped their losses through opportunities made available by more successful relatives; cut-throat competition was restrained by ties of blood and by group association; and speculation and financial manipulation were curbed through desires to preserve familial fortune and class status for future generations. The broadening of commercial leadership into social and political ascendancy engendered an attitude of *noblesse oblige* that made even the entrepreneurial family founders like Nathan Appleton and Amos and Abbott Lawrence famous for monetary and organizational contributions to charitable, educational, and artistic associations.[177] A similar spirit of community responsibility combined with business interests led many prominent Bostonians to campaign for political office.

Notions that wealth should play a constructive social role persisted in the twentieth century. Banker James Jackson Storrow served on the Boston City Council and ran for mayor, industrialist Godfrey Lowell Cabot campaigned as a reform candidate for Mayor of Cambridge, and corporation director Charles Frances Adams, III served as secretary of the Navy. The coffers of select Boston charitable, educational, and artistic institutions continued to be filled by Brahmin contributions and directed by descendants of old families. The Boston Museum of Fine Arts and the Boston Symphony Orchestra, salient among the city's cultural organizations, were founded after the Civil War. Henry Lee Higginson, the most beloved Boston gentleman of his generation, was celebrated for his gifts and services to Harvard and to the orchestra. "We earn our money sometimes hardly and sometimes otherwise," declared this community leader expressing the aristocracy's commitment to stewardship of wealth, "but it is to be used for the good of the public in a great measure and not alone for the good of our families."[178]

Patrician businessmen conceived of corporate honor and service in a manner that matched their belief in personal rectitude and responsibility. The fundamental concerns of Lee Higginson & Co., according to senior partner Henry Lee Higginson, were to sell "only reliable goods," pay back loans promptly, and assume responsibility for poor investments—these qualities he called "character."[179] James Jackson Storrow, Higginson's successor, also attested to the altruistic aims of the firm. Although banking "is sometimes called making a living or making money," Storrow thought "of it as being of some use to the world."[180]

By condemning self-made entrepreneurs, as much as by professions of personal honor and corporate responsibility, blueblood businessmen claimed to perpetuate the high principles established by ante-bellum Boston merchants. Brahmin magnates freely criticized robber barons for being vulgar, irresponsible, and dishonest, but I have uncovered only two instances in which corporate reverses were blamed on commercial corsairs like Gould or Vanderbilt. C. F. Adams, Jr., as indicated above, was removed from the Union Pacific presidency by Jay Gould and thereafter reproved the titans of finance and industry. John Murray Forbes, president of the Chicago, Burlington & Quincy Railroad, attributed problems in attracting investment capital to "Vanderbilt and Gould hav[ing] a great advantage over us in these stock operations—they can buy or sell millions of company stock as though it were their own." The Brahmin owned and managed Chicago, Burlington & Quincy "never" engaged in such manipulation because Forbes "fear[ed] the effect of it, especially as I know how such operations have always been looked upon in Boston."[181]

The actions of proper Bostonian industrialists and bankers provides more accurate evidence of honorable standards than does criticism against parvenu capitalists or expressions of commercial idealism. Isolated instances of fine gestures can be cited: Forbes discharged C. B. & Q. executives who had interests in construction companies working for the road; Storrow refused to channel business toward a cotton mill in which he had invested.[182] No pattern of exalted business dealing, however, can emerge from these few examples. In fact, the small number of losses and defeats attributed to the allegedly more supple tactics of those without Bostonian scruples indicates that patricians regarded contemporary mores and practices as inoffensive or necessary, and hints at involvement in similar methods.

Ascertaining Brahmin business morality is crucial in discovering the impact of industrial capitalism upon the Boston upper class. Standards of permissible conduct reveal the degree of will and ability to adjust to the contemporary business world. Patrician entrepreneurs whose aristocratic inhibitions regarding vulgarity and irresponsibility prevented them from adopting the aggressive, speculative tactics of competitors would be severely handicapped, as Forbes indicated in his remarks about Gould and Vanderbilt, in obtaining capital, pushing innovation, achieving efficient organization, and expanding operations. Under these conditions, eminence won before the Civil War would be difficult to maintain.

If analysis is restricted to proper Bostonian evaluation of self and other businessmen, to the upper-class social structure, and to the composition of elite enterprises, the nobility of the group's commercial behavior can be plausibly argued. By the late nineteenth century, the Brahmins had become an urban upper class. No longer exclusively a commercial elite, they had acquired status as community leaders in ethics and esthetics. Vulgarity and corruption had become, at least to some figures, more horrendous than missed opportunities, surrender of economic hegemony, or even bankruptcy. Businessmen like Higginson, Henry Lee, and Storrow were almost as heavily involved as arbiters of culture or consultants in charity as they were with Lee, Higginson and Co. The Brahmins, having established ascendancy in social as well as economic affairs, manifested traits of a hereditary aristocracy. Unlike family founding merchants in early nineteenth century Boston, they were responsible for a legacy of values and customs. Brahmin businessmen could no longer evaluate new methods or new products solely in terms of countinghouse rationality. Involved in their business operations were memories or notions of ancestral activities, the reputation and traditions of their family and class, and conceptions of *noblesse oblige* community responsibility.

Considerations of morality and style, vital to group cohesion and runction, could be obstacles to objective assessments about investment opportunities, corporate tactics, and the uses of capital. The consanguine nature of Brahmin enterprises reinforced the role of tradition, family, and class in commercial undertakings. Intermarriage, the basis of Brahmin unity and creator of business advantages such as trust and stability, potentially threatened innovation. Entrepreneurially inspired corporations of the early nineteenth century became family firms as business leadership was now inherited. Commercial status, was, therefore, ascribed through family connections rather than achieved by vocational merit. After the Civil War, the upper-class

Boston community manifested aristocratic attributes that hindered entrepreneurship, for inventive and speculative skills are difficult to pass on. Inheritance enhances acceptance of traditional practices and blunts desire for material achievement, thus making men less competitive, and it constricts the social mobility necessary for adequate supply of talent. America worships competition and rewards those who expand economic opportunities. The Boston elite, through the family firm, was committed to an institution that might stress security at the expense of innovation and expansion, that tended to limit investment to relatives, and that lent itself to making blood rather than merit the test for advancement.

Similar to problems regarding expansion and efficiency presented by the family firm were obstacles to the accumulation and investment of capital offered by the numerous Brahmin fortunes tied up in family trusts. The family trust was a device designed to protect status continuity over the generations by prohibiting heirs from touching the principal of their legacy. The management of family fortunes was given to trusted, blue-blood lawyers and bankers who would preserve the bequest from depredations by impulsive or spendthrift descendants. These considerations of security and continuity were clearly uppermost for family founder Abbott Lawrence, who instructed the trustees of his estate to keep "at all times carefully in view, in every transaction, the trust's purposes and intents herein expressed, and the two great objects of safety and productiveness."[183] The wishes of family founders were safe with men like William H. Forbes, son of John Murray Forbes, and administrator of many Bostonian fortunes. Over the objections of a member of the family, he refused to invest Perkins money in Calumet & Hecla copper mines. "I see by looking at the trust deed that Article One binds us to keep the funds safely invested in such securities as we may deem judicious. I know it is likely that the purchase of Calumet & Hecla stock at the present prices may be a good business operation," reported the prudent counselor, "but if I should buy into it and it should go wrong I should be directly responsible, because no one can claim that copper stocks are safe and judicious investments for trustees."[184] Forbes chose conservative holdings rather than potentially more profitable but riskier investments. Failure to buy Calumet & Hecla, however, deprived the Perkins family of a share in one of the most successful ventures of the period. The inhibitions of Forbes and other watchdogs of family fortunes kept a substantial amount of blueblood capital in the low-yield securities of textile companies and railroads. Since older and well-known companies were not necessarily safer, conservative tactics did not always lead to security. "The people who have done worst this last year to two in our town are the conservative trustees who have had a lot of non-taxable stocks," remarked banker Higginson in the recession of 1914–15. "Think of the amount of New Haven, Boston & Albany, Boston & Providence, Old Colony and Boston & Maine which the trustees held."[185]

Economically inhibiting tendencies of family firms and trust funds curbed the growth of two famous Boston financial institutions, The First National Bank of Massachusetts and the Massachusetts Hospital Life Insurance Company. The former, organized as a commercial bank in 1784 to finance the business ventures of the great Boston merchants, drew capital and executives from Brahmin mercantile families. Until 1812, the bank occupied a preeminent position in Boston financial circles. When foreign trade declined, however, the institution did not explore emerging possibilities in manufacturing. The directors were steeped in the tradition of mercantile dealings and reluctant to commit the deposits of old families to what they considered as risky and undignified manufacturing enterprises. Conservative leadership rejected investment opportunities and ignored new techniques in banking. Refusal to service industrial growth created an investment vacuum into which moved more energetic and modern bankers. By 1860, the bank was last among the national banks of Boston in bills of circulation, deposits, bills held on other banks, and total resources. Not until 1900, under midwestern leadership, did the bank recover from its long decline.[186]

The Massachusetts Hospital Life Insurance Company had a similar history. Founded in 1818 mainly as an investment and trust-fund house, Massachusetts Life became the chief repository of fortunes made in cotton manufacturing and the primary source of capital for blueblood textile magnates. As the vehicle of finance for the industrial sector of Boston's upper class, the company shared in the burgeoning prosperity of textiles at a time when the ebbing financial strength of the First National Bank reflected the decline of the older mercantile enclave. Eventually, however, Massachusetts Life shared the fate of the older institution. Diminished productivity and profit in textiles undermined its financial base. Conservative Brahmin leadership refused to seek new funds, adopt new techniques, acquire additional investors, or broaden investment policies. On the contrary, directors committed themselves to guarding Brahmin trusts from speculative risks and to preserving the exclusiveness of the firm's clientele. In the 1830s the company had been the largest single institutional source of funds in New England. After this decade, its importance relative to other Boston financial organizations declined. Between 1900 and 1937 the resources of Massachusetts Life increased only 41 per cent while other Boston banks, insurance companies, and trust funds multiplied their capital several times over.[187]

Setbacks in proper Bostonian economic activities were not restricted to the deterioration of the First National Massachusetts Bank and the Massachusetts Hospital Life Insurance Company. After the Civil War, cotton manufacturing ceased to be the largest American industry; textile profits diminished due to increasing costs of production. Many of the old Brahmin companies closed their mills, although a few saved themselves by moving south to take advantage of cheaper labor costs and easier access to raw materials. Between 1860 and 1910, dividends in textile manufacturing averaged an unspectacular 7 per cent. In the 1920s, with the industry struggling under depressed conditions, dividends averaged less than 4 per cent.[188]

The sectional disadvantages of relatively poor natural resources, high labor costs, low regional growth rate, conservative business practices, and low profits in cotton manufacturing were obstacles to the accumulation of capital, a condition severely handicapping proper Bostonians who ventured into new business endeavors. In 1879 Brahmin entrepreneurs led by William Forbes and Henry Lee Higginson assumed control of the American Bell Telephone Company. Until 1900 the corporation was directed and financed by bluebloods William Forbes, the president; J. J. Storrow, the corporation counsel; and by the patrician house of Lee, Higginson & Co., the primary financier. The Bostonians, however, failed to sustain their initiative because the group could not supply funds necessary for Bell Telephone's growth.

By 1904 Bell's bonds were exclusively financed by J. P. Morgan & Co. The New York banking firm had dispossessed Lee, Higginson as Bell's primary source of capital and had replaced many of the old patrician executives with its own representatives.[189] "We used to sell all the Telephone bonds," commented Higginson to his brother in 1910, "but now the company has outgrown us and passed into other hands."[190] Inability to provide sufficient capital to underwrite expansion also destroyed Brahmin ascendancy in the electrical industry. In 1887 banker aristocrats Higginson, Thomas Jefferson Coolidge, S. Endicott Peabody, and George P. Gardner took over the Thomson-Houston Electric Company. When this organization joined the General Electric Co., Higginson and Coolidge were appointed to the parent corporation's board of directors. The Bostonians, however, were again displaced by J. P. Morgan and other New York bankers. Higginson clearly spoke from a subordinate position when he told C. A. Coffin, president of General Electric, "that we can not without disrespect to Messrs. Morgan, make any definite propositions to you" about underwriting General Electric debentures "until after you have talked with those gentlemen,—and those gentlemen means Jack Morgan."[191]

Inability to sustain commercial position by consolidating initiatives occurred even in copper mining and railroads, where bluebloods had secured a more substantial foothold than in public utilities. In 1866, brothers-in-law Quincy A. Shaw, son of an old Boston mercantile family, and Alexander Agassiz, whose mother was a Perkins and who had married a sister of Henry Higginson, purchased control of the Calumet copper mine in Michigan and organized the Hecla Mining Company. Agassiz managed technical matters at the mine while Shaw arranged financing in Boston. Higginson and H. S. Russell, another Brahmin brother-in-law, were the major backers. When sons of Shaw and Agassiz succeeded their fathers as company executives, Calumet & Hecla, organized, financed, and managed by proper Bostonians, assumed the family structure typical of upper-class firms. During the 1870s the mining operation produced over one-half of the total American copper output and earned phenomenal profits.[192] Since Brahmins were the chief investors such success buttressed or began many patrician fortunes. "In the matter of money," remarked Henry Higginson to Quincy Shaw, "the Company has been the making of my father's children and lots of other families."[193] Unfortunately promising beginnings in copper, as in electricity and the telephone, were not developed. When Michigan veins showed signs of exhaustion, Calumet & Hecla delayed expansion to the far west until the late 1890s, when the best mining territories had already been preempted. "We have ground enough for this generation and one or two more," said one executive in 1892, "and we therefore are not looking for further fields for our energy." Two years later Alexander Agassiz rejected an offer to buy western property because "Mr. Shaw was getting old and hard to move to anything and . . . I was always away and could not run anything new."[194] Conservative management and scattered energy destroyed entrepreneurship at Calumet & Hecla, as was the case with many Brahmin firms. Failure to expand cut output and after 1918 Kennecott, Anaconda, and Phelps-Dodge became the new giants of the copper industry. With passing years conditions worsened. The industry was devastated by the depression of 1929, and during World War II Michigan produced only 4 per cent of domestic copper.[195]

Blueblood enterprise was more firmly established in railroads than in copper. New England railroad building in the 1830s led to Brahmin initiatives in organizing and financing lines in the west during the 1840s. During this period Boston was the primary source of railroad capital in the nation.[196] John Murray Forbes, nephew of T. H. Perkins, was the outstanding Boston enterpriser in these early ventures Forbes, returning home after having made his first fortune as Canton agent for J. & T. Perkins, looked for lucrative investment possibilities. Although professing to abhor speculation, the former merchant became a self-proclaimed plunger. "A certain amount of boldness is true prudence" remarked the former overseas trader as he put money into railroads, western lands, coal mines on the Ohio River, Ericsson's steamship, and Pennsylvania coal fields and iron works.[197] In 1846 the entrepreneur embarked on a great career as a railroad magnate by purchasing the Michigan Central. In this and other ventures Forbes received aid from connections with New York and Boston capitalists and with Baring Brothers. To enable the Michigan Central to enter Chicago, Forbes, assisted by William Amory and other patrician financiers, bought the Chicago, Burlington & Quincy Railroad.

Eventually the Burlington system, the first Brahmin venture in western railroad activities, expanded from Illinois and Michigan into Iowa, Missouri, Wyoming, Nebraska, and Colorado. Forbes became the first president, later to be succeeded by son-in-law Charles Elliot Perkins. Brahmin banking houses Lee, Higginson & Co., The Old Colony Trust, and Kidder, Peabody & Co. provided a major share of the capital for the system while proper Bostonians Charles J. Paine, Henry Lee Higginson, Stephen E. Perkins, Thomas Jefferson Coolidge, Edward W. Hooper, Henry S. Russell, John Lowell Gardner, and William Endicott Jr. sat on the board of directors.[198]

Forbes claimed to be guided by an honorable business code. The C.B. & Q. president acted according to principle by discharging executives who had interests in corporations that did business with the road, an in occasionally denying himself the advantages that Vanderbilt and Gould, unrestrained by Brahmin consciences, obtained through stock manipulations. The Burlington system, however, competed with robber baron run railroads, and Forbes frequently adopted the prevailing practices of the era. He charged discriminatory rates, watered stock, granted passes, broke pools by cutting rates, tried to influence the election of public officials, and defended the Union Pacific in the Credit Mobilier scandal. This offspring of an old family committed himself to the demands of commercial role rather than to class values.[199]

Despite connections with eastern and European capital, the advantages of early entry, and the willingness to adopt contemporary business methods, Forbes never equalled the entrepreneurial scope of a Hill or a Harriman. He restricted the C.B. & Q. to remaining a large regional line, while other magnates put together transnational organizations. Forbes conceded that acquisition of other roads might have been "a success; but, oh, the work it would be to manage them with such a population for ground-work, and such complications of ship owning, and controlling or coaxing the legislatures." Forbes' refusal to direct his will and energies to the consolidation of a railroad empire was another case of faltering Brahmin entrepreneurship. "Thank Heaven the cup passed from our lips however tempting. I hope the Adam's apple [Union Pacific] and other Paradise fruits may not tempt us into the dream of universal empire."[200] In the face of this impotent response to the vision of a transcontinental system, little wonder that the more youthful and ambitious Perkins sought "to get young blood into the concern," which would provide "the zeal and spirit so essential to economy and efficiency."[201] Despite Perkins' efforts, the C.B. & Q. never rose to the challenge of continental grandeur and in 1901 James J. Hill absorbed the line into his Great Northern system.

Charles Francis Adams also involved himself in railroad affairs. Adams, like Forbes, was a speculator who abhorred adventurism in others but practiced it himself.[202] During his six years in office (1884–90) the patrician president, as had Forbes, adopted the conventional methods of railroad magnates. This double standard assumed in Union Pacific operations enabled Adams to apply the methods of his competitors while loathing them. Lobbyists were hired for political dirty work, senators were bribed to procure favorable legislation even though Adams conceded the affair to be a "most extraordinary discreditable negotiations." These practices notwithstanding, Adams' tenure in office was a failure. Union Pacific earnings stagnated, Congress remained hostile, and the corporation debt mounted. In 1890 Gould regained control of the road and forced Adams' resignation.[203] Once again a Brahmin businessman was bested by a robber baron.

Adams' deposition and the arrested growth of the C.B. & Q. were symptomatic of the general course of events in Brahmin railroad enterprise. Patrician financial institutions, Lee, Higginson & Co., Kidder, Peabody, & Co., and The Old Colony Trust Co. had been leading investors in New England and western railroads. In addition to C.B. & Q., these houses had large holdings in Union Pacific and the Atchison, Topeka & Sante Fe, where T. J. Coolidge served as president. During the 1880s New York investment capital syndicates assumed major roles in financing and directing these lines and even wrested control of New England roads from Boston bankers and entrepreneurs.[204] In railroads, as in the case of the utilities, insufficient capital resources to meet the demands of expansion was the chief factor in the decline of upper class enterprise. Kidder, Peabody had been the leading American financier for the Santa Fe Railroad but when the line went bankrupt in 1894 it was reorganized by other interests.[205] Higginson revealed the incapacity of Boston bankers when he wrote Howard Elliot, president of the New York, New Haven and Hartford Railroad, that Lee, Higginson could not sell the road's bonds because "we are not strong enough to find money in all kinds of weather."[206]

Although defeats inflicted by New York capitalists and parvenu entrepreneurs in mining and railroads diminished the national power of Boston's upper class, such reverses did not necessarily destroy local hegemony. Corporate bankruptcies, which would have aborted Brahmin investment and thus collapsed its position, were not involved in these contests for control of healthy companies in growing industries. But withdrawal from promising enterprises curtailed opportunity to acquire an abundance of capital indispensable in commercial competition. After the 1880s no more Calumet & Hecla windfalls awaited upper-class Boston. Regional leadership, however, was threatened by the rise in Boston of men and enterprises outside the sphere of influence of the old elite. An example of this new departure was the United Fruit Co., organized and financed by New Englanders of obscure origin.[207] Higginson, a leader of the blue-blood financial community, indicated the aristocracy's remoteness from the new venture when he regretted not having bought the company's stock before it soared.[208] Trade in exotic products with distant lands had been responsible for the formation of Boston's upper class. When United Fruit applied this ancient technique to importation of bananas from South America the descendants of the old Far East merchants ignored the company. Like the tycoons of United Fruit, Jordan Marsh, founder of the Hub's largest department store, and Harvey Parker, owner of the city's largest hotel were born too late to gain acceptance by genteel Boston. Earlier self-made merchants who came to Boston and made their fortunes were frequently incorporated into the upper class, but ante-bellum flexibility gave way to the rigidity of inherited status. Immoveable genealogical barriers prevented entrepreneurs Elias M. Loew and Howard Johnson who respectively made millions in movie theaters and restaurants from entering the elite. Similarly rejected were New England railroad titans C. P. Clark, Onslow Stearns, and F. L. Ames.[209]

In the first half of the nineteenth century, the Brahmins admitted new men who initiated new commercial ventures. During these decades proper Bostonians monopolized positions of wealth in Boston (see p. 193). Twenty-one of twenty-five Bostonians worth at least half a million dollars were connected by birth, marriage, or business association to the Hub aristocracy. Broad acceptance revivified the entrepreneurial spirit of the class, afforded a fresh supply of talent, and enabled the group to accumulate capital necessary to expand commercial holdings and acquire power. As the decades passed, however, the Brahmins developed aristocratic traits—notions about birth, education, and style—which raised barriers for those who had not undergone a multigenerational transformation from businessman to gentleman. Exclusion resulted in blue bloods no longer preempting positions of wealth in Boston. Between 1870 and 1915 over 60 per cent of the Hub's millionaires were not included in the listings of old Boston families published by the Boston Transcript (the favorite newspaper of the elite).[210] Business ability ceased to be the primary prerequisite for access when the commercial elite broadened into an urban upper class, which established ascendancy over many areas of city life. While group cohesion was enhanced by exclusion, aloofness brought the penalty of diminishing sources of capital and of entrepreneurial talent and encouraged the formation of counter elites who challenged Brahmin leadership.

Post-Civil War Brahmin entrepreneurship was not an unrelieved dismal situation of missed opportunity, diminished stature, or brilliant beginnings terminated by inevitable defeat. In 1882 Godfrey Lowell Cabot built his first carbon black plant in Buffalo, New York. Carbon black proved highly useful to the automobile and rubber industries. Cabot's factories multiplied and made him reputedly the richest man in Boston. The corporation, moving with the spirit of the times, organized its own engineering firm and research and development plant. Yet Cabot carbon was a traditional family enterprise: the founder became chairman of the board, succeeded in the presidency by his son, with a grandson next in line occupying the positions of vice president and treasurer. The success of Godfrey L. Cabot, Inc. indicated that a patrician family firm need not invariably fail under modern business conditions.[211] James Jackson Storrow was another Boston gentleman whose career ran counter to the prevailing commercial decline of his class. Storrow's adoption of new techniques in selling securities rejuvenated Lee, Higginson & Co. The banker also reorganized General Motors in 1910 after the company went bankrupt, and founded with Charles W. Nash the highly prosperous (until 1929) Nash Motor Co.[212] The achievements of Charles Francis Adams, III, who served on fifty-six boards of directors including Raytheon Manufacturing Company, also reveals a residue of business triumph amidst attenuation of entrepreneurial spirit in old upper-class Boston.[213] The accomplishments of Cabot, Storrow, and Adams could not, however, reverse the deteriorating trend factually registered in the 1880s when the New York Stock Exchange passed the Boston exchange as the nation's greatest trader in industrial securities.[214]

Despite the decline of the Massachusetts First National Bank and the Massachusetts Hospital Life Insurance Co., Brahmins were better able to maintain stature in investment banking than in industry. Blueblood businessmen who opposed New York bankers for control of G.E. and A.T. & T. were dispossessed, but these same Brahmin financiers proved useful in assisting the New York bankers in marketing and underwriting securities. J. P. Morgan and his associates contended against Lee, Higginson and other proper Boston bankers for control of the utilities, but mutual investment banking interests led to cooperative relationships which sustained patrician preeminence in Boston and prominence in national financial circles long after industrial hegemony had been lost. Upper-class Boston's position in finance was also buttressed by windfalls like Calumet & Hecla profits, connections with London banking houses, the growth of blueblood firms Kidder, Peabody, Lee, Higginson and the Old Colony Trust, and the reservoir of capital created through accumulations, connections, and institutions built up over decades. Control over Boston capital, however, was not as complete as in the heyday of the Massachusetts Bank, Massachusetts Life, and the Suffolk System. Several of the city's largest banks were owned and directed by outside interests.[215]

Encroachments by new financiers like James Beal or Abraham T. Lowe or new institutions like the Second National Bank or the National Shawmut Bank did not seriously disturb the position of upper-class Bostonians in banking. The ancient First National Bank and Massachusetts Life lost ground to newer Brahmin houses rather than to other groups. Lee, Higginson, Kidder, Peabody, and the Old

Colony Trust dominated Boston banking during the period between the Civil War and the depression of 1929. These organizations were directed by proper Bostonians, and a major share of their resources consisted of old family funds deposited for investment. Kidder, Peabody and Lee, Higginson organized the great mergers of 1898–1912, which consolidated investment banking in the city and controlled the institutions that emerged.[216] The ascendancy of these firms indicated that some Brahmin financiers were willing to accept contemporary values and methods in investment banking.

The three leading Boston investment firms eagerly embraced turn of the century industrial capitalism. They were heavily committed to new and sometimes speculative securities. Between 1900 and 1913 Lee, Higginson, under the leadership of younger partners Storrow and Gardiner M. Lane, transferred the bulk of its holdings from conservative low-yield railroad bonds to riskier but more profitable industrials. The house specialized in the securities of General Electric, Calumet & Hecla, Westinghouse, U.S. Smelting and Refining, United Shoe Machinery, and U.S. Rubber.[217] In the 1890s Kidder, Peabody made a similar switch from railroads to become the leading distributor of new industrial issues. The firm was most active in handling issues of the Sugar and Tobacco Trusts, and of A.T. & T. and U.S. Steel.[218] The Old Colony Trust, concentrating chiefly in industrials, had an investment portfolio similar to that of Kidder, Peabody, and Lee, Higginson.[219]

Earlier upper-class investment institutions limited themselves to supplying funds for Brahmin ventures, but Lee, Higginson, Kidder, Peabody, and Old Colony invested on an international scale. Provincial operations, primarily consisting of financing activities of friends or relatives, strengthened the commercial code of the upper-class community. Conservatism, honesty, responsibility, and security guided the capital disbursements of the Massachusetts First National Bank and Massachusetts Life. The newer blue blood financial institutions, on the other hand, operating in a national market, involved themselves with companies and capitalists whose rectitude and stability they could neither vouch for nor control. Moreover, customers of Lee, Higginson, Kidder, Peabody, and Old Colony now came primarily from outside the Boston upper class. Thus ties of blood and friendship no longer reinforced abstract principles of honor and responsibility. The demands of the national market and the impersonality of the new clientele weakened the resistance of traditional group mores to contemporary financial practices.[220]

By the 1880s the spirit of speculation already influenced the policies of Lee, Higginson & Co. Several partners considered to be stock "gamblers" were forced out of the firm. Higginson himself had a reputation for recklessness. His successor Storrow and Barrett Wendell, the historian of the house, discerned in him a great "love of adventure as applied to business."[221] Higginson referred to his role in Bell Telephone and the Submarine Signal Co. as risks taken in the hope of handsome profits.[222] Surveying the company in 1915 he admitted to New York partner Frederic W. Allen that "I do think that in the last ten years we have hurried in certain ways, and tumbled over our toes. That is really gambling."[223]

Speculation was but one phase of the modernization of Lee, Higginson. Although Brahmin leadership continued to direct overall strategy from Boston, new branches were established in London, New York, and Chicago, and dynamic young men of undistinguished families were promoted to partnerships. Policy innovations accompanied changes in personnel. Under Storrow, customer orientation shifted to tap a new market for securities. Before 1900, Lee, Higginson sold stocks and bonds to a few wealthy investors from old Boston families. Storrow, however, adopted sales techniques designed to appeal to a national clientele of many smaller investors. He opened a school to train salesmen and hired a publicity director to improve business.[224] In the 1920s, when sales temporarily slumped, Storrow gave Babbitt-like talks to employees. "The need of the hour is more thought," declared the senior partner, "more imagination, more enterprise, more pep and more team play throughout the organization in getting new business."[225]

Similar changes in Kidder, Peabody's organization and investment policies also yielded results of increased clientele and sales, high profits, and growing irresponsibility. The house transcended its originally provincial market by opening branches in Providence and Hartford, by acquiring new lines of securities, and by using modern salesmanship. "We deal directly with thousands of customers and our correspondents deal with many more" said an officer of the company in the 1920s. "This nation-wide system of branches has been a large factor in making the name of Kidder, Peabody & Co. well known and respected throughout the country."[226]

The Old Colony Trust, founded in 1890, was another Brahmin banking firm that accepted contemporary financial strategy. Under the direction of Thomas Jefferson Coolidge, descendant of an old Boston seafaring and textile family, the Trust company invested in promising but somewhat risky ventures such as General Electric and A.T. & T. Old Colony also speculated in Chinese and Costa Rican railroads, western real estate, West Indies chemical works, and the Submarine Signal Co.[227]

Despite the prodigious capital accumulation and sales of Lee, Higginson, The Old Colony, and Kidder, Peabody, Boston never regained her lost preeminence as a source of railroad and industrial capital. Boston bankers, ceasing to originate corporate issues, moved in the shadow of New York financiers. Kidder, Peabody partner, Robert Winsor, was the House of Morgan's New England representative.[228] Lee, Higginson established a New York branch and cooperated so closely with Gotham's capitalists that there were suggestions to move Storrow to this branch.[229] The largest Boston financiers, conscious of their own limitations, displayed a deep respect for the power of New York capitalists. Coolidge told Charles Elliot Perkins that he would serve on the executive board of the C.B. & Q. only if a New York banker was also appointed because "New York . . . is the center of all finance."[230] Higginson put a ceiling of "ten million" on loans that Lee, Higginson could float alone.[231] This limit was obviously too small for independent operations in the mammoth market of twentieth-century industrial capitalism. Although he was Boston's most eminent banker, Higginson's relations with the House of Morgan were humble. He refused to underwrite the sale of General Electric debentures until receiving Morgan's approval. "As you know," he informed G.E.'s president, "our relations with Messrs. Morgan & Co. are entirely friendly, and we wish to do as they wish." Higginson's "abundant caution least we should offend Morgan & Co." reflected the dependence of Boston financiers who now underwrote rather than originated corporate issues.[232]

Neither impressive profits and sales volume nor association with New York capital saved Lee, Higginson and Kidder, Peabody from disaster in 1929. Lee Higginson became the American financial agents for stock manipulator and industrial financier Ivan Kreuger. The house, with its own partners sinking their savings in the match king's empire, underwrote and marketed his securities. The firm became so deeply involved that it went bankrupt in the debacle that destroyed Krueger's holdings.[233] The promise of speculative windfall also concluded abortively for Kidder, Peabody. In the early 1900s the house undertook the formation of the New England Cotton Yarn Corporation, an attempt to consolidate the domestic production of cotton yarn. This venture turned into an albatross as corporate profits and stock prices never rose.[234] Kidder, Peabody's funding of the expansion of the Winchester Repeating Arms Co. was another unfortunate involvement. After World War I, the arms market contracted and notwithstanding Kidder, Peabody loans the company failed and toppled its creditor.[235]

Blue blood influence on Boston banking waned after the depression but the failures of Lee, Higginson and Kidder, Peabody did not completely obliterate the Brahmin presence on State Street. In 1937 the Massachusetts Hospital Life Insurance Company was reorganized by directors descended from the original stockholders and officers. Application of modern investment policies and administrative procedures increased Massachusetts Life's profits and assets.[236] The State Street Trust Co., and the Boston Safe Deposit and Trust Co., New England's largest independent trust organizations, are also directed by proper Bostonians who administer old family fortunes.[237]

These Brahmin strongholds survive in spite of the declining patrician role in Boston banking. In 1956 a transplanted westerner who became president of a prominent Boston financial institution noted that "For some reason most of our Boston banks have gone far afield for their Presidents: Maine, Missouri, Nebraska, New York, and Iowa are some of the States which can claim our Boston bank presidents."[238] The vanishing of aristocratic figures on State Street was accompanied by a deterioration of the Hub's prominence in national and New England financial activities. In 1959, the Federal Reserve Bank of Boston reported that the post-World War II growth rate of New England commer-

cial bank deposits was slower than the national rate, that Boston's
share of the region's deposits had decreased 28 per cent between 1941
and 1958, and that between 1945 and 1958, the city's share of inter-
bank deposits fell 8 per cent.[239]

The success of scattered elite businessmen and firms cannot be read
as a class triumph for Boston Brahmins in post-Civil War industrial
capitalism. Failure to retain ante-bellum economic leadership was due
in part to disadvantages in natural resources and geographical
location. Aristocratic traits, values, and functions assumed in developing from a business elite into an urban upper class also contributed
to the eclipse of Brahmin entrepreneurship. Older industries dominated by proper Bostonians declined in importance, while emerging
opportunities usually were not exploited fully because of conservatism
or lack of capital. Ascendancy and even independence were lost in
turn of the century business dealings. Deterioration of national
position affected community status because bluebloods no longer
exclusively determined advancement in business, or incorporated
successful entrepreneurs and their commercial achievements. Traditional economic leadership was outflanked by businessmen who
rose in new industries and by newcomers who challenged the establishment in old areas of endeavor. The Boston aristocracy did not
disappear as a formidable commercial entity nor was it without important accomplishments in modern capitalism. Proper Bostonians, however, suffered irreparable losses of commercial and class position in
competition with capitalists from other regions and origins.

The transformation of the Boston Brahmins from an entrepreneurial
elite into an urban upper class entailed a diversion of thought and
energy from business into the social and cultural functions assumed
by those who successfully aspire to community leadership. This broadening of activity, accompanied by an increasing commitment to
inherited social status, bred class values inimical to the pursuit of
wealth and economic power. The evidence indicates that this shift
in consciousness took place at the same time that the group found its
commercial position being undermined. In some cases, notably that
of Charles Francis Adams, Jr., changes in attitude toward business
rationalized commercial defeats. Others, such as Brook Adams or John
T. Morse, never embarked on business careers because of their negative

feelings. Even those who triumphed in the commercial world, Alexander Agassiz or John Murray Forbes, for example, were inhibited by class values and activities. There was a reciprocal relationship between consciousness and practice. Class values rationalized class failures in commerce and Brahmin defeats strengthened resistance to the demands of competitive commercial life. As a result, many potential magnates practiced their entrepreneurial skills in other fields. The monumental achievements of brilliant fund raisers and organizers William Lawrence and Endicott Peabody occurred in religion and education. Scattered energies, diverted talent, and curtailed commitment grievously disadvantaged the Boston Brahmins in the rationalized and competitive world of American business.

NOTES

1. For a different view of upper class Boston's role in industrialism see Gabriel Kolko, "Brahmins and Business, 1870–1914: A Hypothesis on the Social Basis of Success in American History," Kurt H. Wolff and Barrington Moore, Jr. (eds.), *The Critical Spirit, Essays In Honor of Herbert Marcuse* (Boston: Beacon Press, 1967), pp. 343–63.

2. For the Boston mercantile establishment see Samuel Eliot Morison, *Maritime History of Massachusetts, 1783–1860* (Boston: Houghton Mifflin Co., 1930), pp. 44–49, 76, 129, 165–70; Foster Rea Dulles, *The Old China Trade* (Boston: Houghton Mifflin Co., 1930); Robert E. Peabody, *Merchant Venturers of Old Salem* (Boston: Houghton Mifflin Co., 1912).

3. The most convenient place to trace interrelationships among Boston families is Mary Caroline Crawford, *Famous Families of Massachusetts*, 2 vols. (Boston: Little, Brown & Co., 1930). Genealogical information in the Jackson and Lee families can be found in Kenneth Wiggins Porter, *The Jacksons and the Lees* (Cambridge: Harvard University Press, 1937), pp. 6–34; on the Cabots in L. Vernon Briggs, *Historical Genealogy of the Cabot Family*, 2 vols. (Boston: Charles E. Goodspeed & Co., 1927); on the Lowells in Ferris Greenslet, *The Lowells and Their Seven Worlds* (Boston: Houghton Mifflin Co., 1946), pp. 423–24. There is much information on marriages among bluebloods in memoirs of Brahmins, in family histories, and in *The New England Historical and Genealogical Register*.

4. Hannah Josephson, *The Golden Threads* (New York: Duell, Sloan, and Pearce, 1949), pp. 31–32, 100, 103, 111–13. Caroline Ware, *The Early New England Cotton Manufacture* (Boston: Houghton Mifflin Co., 1931), pp. 66–70,

78, 145, 146; Ovra L. Stone, *History of Massachusetts Industries*, I (Boston: The S. J. Clarke Publishing Co., 1930), pp. 91–92, 734. Malcolm Keir, *Industries of American Manufacturing* (New York: The Ronald Press, 1928), pp. 295–97. Victor S. Clark, *History of Manufacturing in the United States*, I (New York: Peter Smith, 1949), p. 450.

5. Edward Chase Kirkland, *Men, Cities and Transportation: A Study in New England History, 1820–1900*, I (Cambridge: Harvard University Press, 1953), pp. 99–252. Thomas C. Cochran, *Railroad Leaders, 1845–1900* (Cambridge: Harvard University Press, 1953), pp. 34–36. Thelma M. Kestler, *The Rise of Railroads in the Connecticut River Valley*, Smith College Studies, 23 (Northampton: Smith College Press, 1938), pp. 47–51, 84, 93–94, 152–65, 220–37. Francis B. C. Bradlee, *The Boston and Lowell Railroad, The Nashua and Lowell Railroad, and The Salem and Lowell Railroad* (Salem: The Essex Institute, 1918), *passim*. Boston upper class overseas merchants also played a large role in providing capital and personnel for railroad development. See Arthur M. Johnson and Barry Supple, *Boston Capitalists and Western Railroads* (Cambridge: Harvard University Press, 1967), *passim*.

6. Stone, *Massachusetts Industries*, I, 734.

7. N. S. B. Gras, *The Massachusetts First National Bank of Boston* (Cambridge: Harvard University Press, 1937), pp. 15–16, 54–132, 710–18.

8. Gerald T. White, *A History of The Massachusetts Hospital Life Insurance Co.* (Cambridge: Harvard University Press, 1955), pp. 5, 12, 12n–13n, 31–32, 34, 81–82, 89–90.

9. N.a., *A List of Stockholders in the National Banks of Boston, May 1, 1866* (Boston: Alfred Mudge & Son, 1866), pp. 43–54, 242–51, 264–99, 401–50, 484–98. Gras, *Massachusetts Bank*, pp. 19, 55, 70, 127, 142. N.a., *The National Union Bank of Boston* (Boston: n.p., 1904), p. 12.

10. Gras, *Massachusetts Bank*, pp. 100–102. D, R. Whitney, *The Suffolk Bank* (Cambridge: Riverside Press, 1878), pp. 8–15.

11. Vera Shlakman, *Economic History of a Factory Town*, Smith College Studies in History, 20 (Northampton: Smith College Press, 1934–35), pp. 37–40, 44. M. T. Copeland, *The Cotton Manufacturing Industry of the United States* (Cambridge: Harvard University Press, 1912), p. 6.

12. N.a., *Our First Men: A Calendar of Wealth, Fashion and Gentility* (Boston: n.p., 1846), pp. 19–20, 25, 32, 34, 37, 39, 41–42, 48.

13. Nathan Appleton, *The Introduction of the Power Loom and the Origin of Lowell* (Boston: B. H. Penhallow, 1858), pp. 8–15. John Amory Lowell, "Memoir of Patrick Tracy Jackson," *Hunt's Merchants' Magazine*, New York, 1848, *passim*. For Charles Russell Lowell's satisfaction in his work as an iron-

monger after graduating from Harvard and for his aspiration to own a bronze foundry see Edward W. Emerson (ed.), *Life and Letters of Charles Russell Lowell* (Boston: Houghton Mifflin Co., 1907), pp. 13, 87–89, 180, 185.

14. Nathan Appleton to E. S. Gannett, January 24, 1828, Appleton Papers, Massachusetts Historical Society. Cf. Nathan Appleton, "Memoir of Hon. Abbott Lawrence," *Massachusetts Historical Society Proceedings*, 3 (1856), 69–70.

15. Amos A. Lawrence to Freeman Hunt, June 9, 1855, Amos A. Lawrence Papers, Massachusetts Historical Society.

16. Thomas Handysyd Perkins to John P. Cushing, September 18, 1826; cf. Perkins to Cushing, July 12, 1821, Perkins Papers, Massachusetts Historical Society.

17. Amos Lawrence to Amos A. Lawrence, December 5, 1836; cf. A. Lawrence to A. A. Lawrence, July 26, 1835; December 4, 1836; A. Lawrence to Abbott Lawrence, September ?, 1832, Lawrence Family Papers, Massachusetts Historical Society.

18. Cleveland Amory, *The Proper Bostonians* (New York: E. P. Dutton & Co., 1947), pp. 54–55. Thomas Handysyd Perkins to Elizabeth Perkins, May 1, 1852, Perkins Papers, Massachusetts Historical Society.

19. Perkins to Samuel Cabot and Thomas G. Cary, January?, 1835, Perkins Papers, Massachusetts Historical Society. For a similar change of heart by Henry Lee see Porter, *Jacksons and Lees*, I, 123. Robert K. Lamb, "Entrepreneur and Community" in William Miller ed., *Man in Business* (Cambridge: Harvard University Press, 1952), pp. 110–11.

20. Keir, *Industries*, p. 299.

21. William Hickling Prescott to Francis Lieber, December 31, 1840, in C. Harvey Gardiner (ed.), *The Papers of William Hickling Prescott* (Urbana: University of Illinois Press, 1964), p. 171.

22. See William H. Prescott, *Memoir of Abbott Lawrence* (Boston: privately printed, 1856); Robert C. Winthrop, *Memoir of Hon. Nathan Appleton* (Cambridge: John Wilson and Son, 1862). For congratulatory messages to William Lawrence from Brahmin intellectuals see the following letters to Lawrence in the Lawrence Family Papers, Massachusetts Historical Society: William H. Prescott, May 15, 1855; A. P. Peabody, August 11, 1855; Jacob Bigelow, October 4, 1855; R. C. Winthrop, May 17, 1855; Edward Everett, September 18, 1855; George Ticknor, May 19, 1855; J. C. Warren, May 22, 1855; Charles Lowell, September 2, 1855.

23. Thomas Gold Appleton to Nathan Appleton, June 12, 1844, Nathan Appleton Papers, Massachusetts Historical Society. Cf. T. G. Appleton to N. Appleton, December 26, 1844, from same collection. For a fuller treatment

of the Appleton father and son relationship and the place of culture in ante-
bellum genteel Boston see my "Businessman and Gentleman: Nathan and
Thomas Gold Appleton—An Exploration in Intergenerational History,"
Explorations in Entrepreneurial History, second series, 4 (Fall, 1966), 17–40.

24. Oliver Wendell Holmes to John T. Holmes, June 12, 1833, in John T. Morse,
The Life and Letters of Oliver Wendell Holmes (Cambridge: Riverside Press,
1896), p. 101. H. D. Sedgwick, *Francis Parkman* (Boston: Houghton Mifflin
Co., 1904), pp. 135–36. Edward Everett Hale, *James Russell Lowell and His
Friends* (Boston: Houghton Mifflin Co., 1901), p. 54. Bliss Perry (ed.), *Life and
Letters of Henry Lee Higginson* (Boston: Atlantic Monthly Press, 1921), pp.
37, 43, 45, 64–65, 107–10, 121. George Ticknor, *The Life of William Hickling
Prescott* (Philadelphia: J. B. Lippincott Co., 1863), p. 55. For Lowell's resolve
to embark on a business career see James Russell Lowell to Loring Elmwood,
October ?, 1838, in Charles Eliot Norton (ed.), *Letters of James Russell Lowell*,
I (New York: Harper & Row,1894), pp. 32–33.

25. Norton, *Lowell*, I, 53.

26. Hale, *Lowell and Friends*, pp. 81–82.

27. Thomas G. Cary, *Memoir of Thomas Handysyd Perkins* (Boston: Little,
Brown & Co., 1856), p. 264. Amory, *Proper Bostonians*, pp. 49–50.

28. Charles Francis Adams, *Charles Francis Adams Jr.* (Boston: Houghton
Mifflin Co., 1900), p. 74.

29. Thomas Jefferson Coolidge, *An Autobiography* (Boston: Massachusetts
Historical Society, 1923), p. 32.

30. For studies of the Brahmin response to these late nineteenth-century
developments see my *Doubters and Dissenters: Cataclysmic Thought in
America, 1885–1918* (New York: The Free Press, 1964), pp. 141–87; John
Higham, *Strangers in the Land* (New Brunswick: Rutgers University Press,
1955), pp. 22, 32, 75, 96, 109–109, 134–35, 152; Barbara Miller Solomon, *Ancestors
and Immigrants* (Cambridge: Harvard University Press, 1956); Ari Hoogenboom, *Outlawing the Spoils: A History of the Civil Service Reform Movement,
1865–1883* (Urbana: Universty of Illinois Press, 1961), pp. 11, 15–19, 29–46,
73, 115, 149, 200; Geoffrey Blodgett, *The Gentle Reformers: Massachusetts
Democrats in the Cleveland Era* (Cambridge: Harvard University Press, 1966).

31. A. Lawrence Lowell quoted in Amory, *Proper Bostonians*, 44.

32. See the remarks of Amos Lawrence in Freeman Hunt, "The Lives of
American Merchants, II," *Hunt's Merchants' Magazine*, New York, 1856,
p. 250. Cf. the remarks of Peter Chardon Brooks in *ibid.*, I, 86; statements
of William Appleton in Susan Loring (ed.), *Selections from the Diaries of
William Appleton, 1786–1862* (Boston: privately printed, 1922).

33. Higginson quoted in Perry, *Higginson*, 275.

34. Higginson to Sir Hugh Levick, August 2, 1918, *ibid.*, pp. 520–21. Cf. Higginson to Mrs. George R. Agassiz, July ?, 1918, *ibid.*, p. 507.

35. Higginson to Thomas Wentworth Higginson, January 14, 1879, Higginson Letters, Houghton Library, Harvard University.

36. Francis Parkman to The *Boston Daily Advertiser*, June 30, 1863, in Wilbur Jacobs (ed.), *Letters of Francis Parkman*, I (Norman: University of Oklahoma Press, 1960), p. 160. Cf. Parkman, "Review of H. H. Bancroft, *The Native Races of the Pacific States*, *North American Review*, 120 (January, 1875), 34.

37. James Russell Lowell, *The Works of James Russell Lowell*, VI (Boston: Houghton Mifflin Co., 1890), p. 6.

38. Brooks Adams to Henry Adams, April 22, 1896, Brooks Adams Letters, Houghton Library, Harvard University. For Henry Adams' reciprocal sentiments see H. Adams to Mrs. Elizabeth Cameron, September 15, 1893, in Worthington Chauncy Ford (ed.), *The Letters of Henry Adams*, II (Boston: Houghton Mifflin Co., 1938), 33.

39. William Minot Jr. to Henry Cabot Lodge, March 18, 1880, Henry Cabot Lodge Papers, Massachusetts Historical Society.

40. Brooks Adams, *The Law of Civilization and Decay*, Second edition (New York: Alfred A. Knopf, 1943) pp. 303–305. Henry Adams to Mrs. Cameron, June 10,'1888, in Ford, *Letters*, I, 388. H. Adams to Mrs. Cameron, September 15, 1893, in *ibid.*, II, 33. H. Adams to Charles Milnes Gaskell, November 26, 1893, in *ibid.*, II, 34. H. Adams to Gaskell, January 23, 1894, in *ibid.*, II, 35. Henry Cabot Lodge, *Early Memories* (New York: Charles H. Scribner's Sons, 1913), 209. Charles Francis Adams, *An Autobiography 1835–1915* (Boston: Houghton Mifflin Co., 1916), p. 190. Francis Parkman to The *Boston Daily Advertiser*, September 4, 1861. Jacobs, *Parkman Letters*, I, 143. Parkman, "The Failure of Universal Suffrage," *North American Review*, 263 (July–August, 1878), 16–17. James Russell Lowell, *Works*, VI, 26–27. Lowell, *The Complete Writings of James Russell Lowell*, I, (Boston: Houghton Mifflin Co., 1904), p. 327. Richard Henry Dana Jr. quoted in Samuel Shapiro, *Richard Henry Dana Jr. 1815–1882* (East Lansing: Michigan State University Press, 1961), p. 184.

41. John Murray Forbes to John N. A. Griswold, May 12, 1880, in Cochran, *Railroad Leaders*, 338.

42. Francis Lee Higginson to Henry Lee Higginson, June 20, 1888, Henry Lee Higginson Papers, Baker Library, Harvard Business School. For a similar characterization by Henry Lee Higginson see H. L. Higginson to Barrett

Wendell, November 14, 1919, Higginson Papers, Massachusetts Historical Society.

43. Norton, *Address Read at the Opening of the Slater Memorial Museum* (Norwich: n.p., 1888), p. 22.

44. Norton to Leslie Stephen, January 8, 1896, in Sara Norton and M. A. DeWolfe Howe (eds.), *Letters of Charles Eliot Norton*, II (Boston: Houghton Mifflin Co., 1913), pp. 236–37. Cf. Norton to Sir Mountstuart, E. Grant-Duff, November 8, 1895, in *ibid.*, II, 235. Norton to E. L. Godkin, July ?, 1900, in *ibid.*, II, 293–94. Norton, *Tercentenary Festival of Emmanual College* (Cambridge: C. J. Clay and Son, 1884), p. 29.

45. Parkman, "The Tale of the Ripe Scholar," *The Nation*, 95 (December 23, 1869), 559.

46. Parkman, "Bancroft," p. 130.

47. J. R. Lowell, *Works*, VI, 27. Lowell to William Dean Howells, November 2, 1865, Howells Letters, Houghton Library, Harvard University, Cf. Lowell, *Writings*, I, 327.

48. Mason Wade (ed.), *The Journals of Francis Parkman* (New York: Harper & Row, 1947), p. 60. Cf. *ibid.*, p. 43.

49. Parkman to H. R. Casgrain, September 30, 1892, in Mason Wade, *Francis Parkman, Heroic Historian* (New York: Viking Press, 1942), p. 438.

50. Dana quoted in Shapiro, *Dana*, p. 23.

51. Lowell, *Writings*, I, 20–21. Cf. Norton to Samuel G. Ward, April 14, 1901, in Norton and Howe (eds.), *Norton Letters*, II, 304–305; Norton to Ward, September 19, 1900, in II, 300.

52. H. Adams, *The Education of Henry Adams* (Boston: Houghton Mifflin Co., 1918), pp. 343–44, 346. For similar views see Brooks Adams, "Introductory Note," H. Adams, *The Degradation of the Democratic Dogma* (New York: The Macmillan Co., 1919), pp. v–viii.

53. Francis Parkman to Mary Dwight Parkman, April 15, 1853, in Jacobs, *Letters of Parkman*, I, 103–104.

54. H. Adams to Gaskell, September 25, 1868, in Ford (ed.), *Letters*, I, 145. Adams to Gaskell, November 25, 1877, in Ford (ed.), *Letters*, I, 302. Ford (ed.), *Letters*, II, *passim*. Jaher, *Doubters and Dissenters*, pp. 149–58.

55. B. Adams to H. Adams, April 28, 1902, B. Adams Letters, Houghton Library, Harvard University.

56. B. Adams to H. Adams, October 13, 1901, B. Adams Letters, Houghton

Library, Harvard University. Cf. B. Adams to Henry Cabot Lodge, March 27, 1901, from the same collection. For a study of these moods in B. Adams see Jaher, *Doubters and Dissenters*, pp. 158–88.

57. B. Adams to H. Adams, April 10, 1906; April 28, 1902; February 3, 1902; October 6, 1904; July 2, 1905; January 9, 1906; April 15, 1908; March 2, 1910. All in the B. Adams Letters, Houghton Library, Harvard University.

58. Norton to J. B. Harrison, July 23, 1882, Norton and Howe (eds.), *Norton Letters*, II, 135. Norton, "Some Aspects of Civilization," *Forum*, XX (February, 1896), 650, 666.

59. Parkman, "Failure," p. 6. Cf. Parkman, "The Woman Question," *North American Review*, 265 (October, 1879), 312, 318, 320. Parkman to H. R. Casgrain, May 9, 1875, in Jacobs, *Letters of Parkman*, II. 82.

60. Lowell, *Works*, VI, 10–11. Cf. *ibid.*, 205. For other blueblood anxieties about cities, immigrants, and democracy see C. F. Adams, "The Protection of the Ballot in National Elections," *Journal of Social Science*, I (June, 1869), 107, 110–11; Lodge, "The Census and Immigration," *Century Magazine*, XLVI (September, 1893), 737; Higham, *Strangers*, 102–103; Solomon, *Ancestors*, passim: Barrett Wendall, *Privileged Classes* (New York: Charles Scribner's Sons, 1908), p. 114; John T. Morse to Henry Cabot Lodge, April 21, 1920, Lodge Papers, Massachusetts Historical Society; William Sturgis Bigelow to Lodge, February 20, 1913; May 21, 1913, from the same collection.

61. Wendell, *Privileged Classes*, p. 122.

62. Parkman, "Woman Question," p. 319.

63. Norton to Leslie Stephen, June 25, 1898, Norton and Howe, *Letters of Norton*, II, 270–71. Norton, Memorials of Two Friends (New York: n.p., 1902), pp. 101–102.

64. Moorfield Storey, *The Democratic Party and Philippine Independence* (Boston: George H. Ellis, 1913), p. 7.

65. H. Adams to B. Adams, June 11, 1897, in Ford (ed.), *Letters*, II, 120–21. H. Adams to B. Adams, September ?, 1895, in *ibid.*, II, 82–83. H. Adams to B. Adams, November 1, 1910, in *ibid.*, II, 551. H. Adams to Mrs. Cameron, January 25, 1903, in *ibid.*, II, 393. H. Adams to Mrs. Cameron, August 20, 1905, in *ibid.*, II, 460. H. Adams to Mrs. Cameron, February 7, 1904, in *ibid.*, II, 424. H. Adams to Mrs. Cameron, June 22, 1911, in *ibid.*, II, 570.

66. B. Adams, "The New Industrial Revolution," Atlantic Monthly, LXXVII (February, 1901), 164. B. Adams to H. Adams, March 7, 1896, B. Adams Letters, Houghton Library, Harvard University. B. Adams, "War as the Ultimate Form of Economic Competition," *Scribner's Magazine*, XXXI (March, 1902),

35². B. Adams, *America's Economic Supremacy* (New York: The Macmillan Co., 1900).

67. Norton, "Some Aspects," p. 650.

68. Parkman, "Woman Question," p. 312. Parkman, "Failure of Suffrage," 20.

69. H. Adams to Gaskell, November 26, 1893, in Ford (ed.), *Letters*, II, 34. Cf. H. Adams to Gaskell, January 23, 1894, *ibid.*, II, 35.

70. B. Adams to H. Adams, July 5, 1901, B. Adams Letters, Houghton Library, Harvard University. Cf. B. Adams to H. Adams, January 1, 1908; May 21, 1905; January 9, 1906, from the same collection.

71. Norton to Ward, April 26, 1896, in Norton and Howe (eds.), *Norton Letters*, II, 244.

72. Norton, "Reminiscences of Old Cambridge," *Cambridge Historial Society Proceedings*, I (1905), 13. Cf. Norton, "The Lack of Old Homes in America," *Scribner's Magazine*, V (May, 1889), 636–40.

73. Lowell, *Writings*, I, 20–21. Cf. Lowell to Miss Jane Norton, September 9, 1856, in Norton (ed.), *Lowell's Letters*, I, 270–71. For the same response in John Holmes, brother of Oliver Wendell Holmes, Sr., see John Holmes to Waldo Higginson, March ?, 1891, in William Roscoe Thayer (ed.), *Letters of John Holmes to James Russell Lowell and Others* (Boston: Houghton Mifflin Co., 1916), pp. 249–50.

74. C. F. Adams, *Autobiography*, pp. 7–8. Cf. Adams to Norton, January 26, 1907, Charles Francis Adams Letters, Houghton Library, Harvard University. For Brahmin nostalgia over old Boston see Henry Lee quoted in Perry, *Higginson*, p. 83.

75. H. Adams, *Education*, pp. 260, 384–85, 388, 434–35, 459. Cf. Adams, *Mont-St. Michel and Chartres* (Boston: Houghton Mifflin Co., 1905), pp. 45, 276. H. Adams to Alan Stanburrough Cook, August 6, 1910, in Ford, *Letters*, II, 546–47. Adams to John Hay, November 7, 1900, in *ibid.*, II, 301. Adams to Hay, September 7, 1895, in Cater, *Adams and Friends*, p. 347. Adams to B. Adams, May 6, 1899, in *ibid.*, p. 463. Adams, *Mont-St. Michel*, 45. H. Adams, "Prayer to the Virgin of Chartres," in Mabel LaFarge (ed.), *Henry Adams: Letters to a Niece* (Boston: Houghton Mifflin Co., 1920), p. 131.

76. B. Adams quoted in M. DeWolfe Howe, *Who Lived Here* (Boston: Little, Brown & Co., 1952), p. 12.

77. B. Adams, *The Emancipation of Massachusetts* (Boston: Houghton Mifflin Co., 1887), *passim*.

78. B. Adams, "Can War Be Done Away With?" *Publications: American*

Sociological Society, X (December, 1915), 106, 115.

79. Lowell, *Writings,* I, 76–77.

80. Norton, "Lack of Old Homes," pp. 636–40. Cf. Norton, "Reminiscences of Cambridge," pp. 11–23. Oliver Wendell Holmes, *A Moral Antipathy* (Boston: Houghton Mifflin Co., 1913), p. 31. For the similar sentiments of Charles William Eliot see C. W. Eliot to Mrs. William James, February 6, 1900, in Henry James, *Charles W. Eliot* (Boston: Houghton Mifflin Co., 1930), II, 100.

81. Parkman, "Failure of Universal Suffrage," p. 13.

82. Lowell, *Works,* VI, 36.

83. *Ibid.,* VI, 96.

84. *Ibid.,* VI, 25.

85. Norton to W. L. Mackenzie King, January 26, 1903, in Norton and Howe (eds.), *Norton Letters,* II, 333. Cf. Norton to Edward Lee-Childs, June 26, 1898, in *ibid.,* II, 272–73

86. Morton, "Some Aspects," p. 654. Cf. Norton, "Memorials," pp. 101–102. Norton, "The Public Life and Services of William Eustis Russell," *Harvard Graduates Magazine,* V (December, 1896), 191. Norton to Stephen, June 24, 1898, in Norton and Howe (eds.), *Norton Letters,* II, 270–71. Norton to Ward, October 10, 1898, in *ibid.,* II, 276. Norton to Godkin, July 7, 1900, in *ibid.,* II, 293–94.

87. Wendell, *Privileged Classes,* pp. 112, 114.

88. Harold Clark Durell, "John Torrey Morse," *New England Historical and Genealogical Register,* XCI (October, 1937), 307–12.

89. Frederick C. Shattuck, "William Sturgis Bigelow," *Proceedings: Massachusetts Historical Society,* 60 (November, 1926), 15–19.

90. H. Adams, *Education,* pp. 103, 301–308, 327, 382.

91. John T. Morse to Henry Cabot Lodge, March 20, 1892, Lodge Papers, Massachusetts Historical Society.

92. Morse to Lodge, May 14, 1918, same collection.

93. William S. Bigelow to Lodge, April 3, 1912, same collection. Cf. Frederick C. Shattuck to Lodge, April 28, 1921, same collection.

94. H. Adams to C. F. Adams, November 10, 1911, in *ibid.,* II, 576. In Ford, *Letters,* II, 576. Cf. Adams to Mrs. Chanler, August 11, 1905, *ibid.,* II, 547. Adams to Mrs. Cameron, February 8, 1904, in *ibid.,* II, 423–24. January 13,

1910, in *ibid.*, II, 529. Adams to Gaskell, January 4, 1897, in *ibid.*, II, 120. H. Adams to Mrs. Cameron, February 7, 1904, in *ibid.*, II, 423.

95. B. Adams to H. Adams, June 24, 1895, Brooks Adams Letters, Houghton Library, Harvard University. Cf. B. Adams to H. Adams: September 21 1893; October 13, 1895; August 17, 1896; October 6, 1904; March 20, 1915, same collection.

96. B. Adams to H. Adams, July 5, 1901. Cf. B. Adams to H. Adams, December 21, 1899, same collection. B. Adams to Mark DeWolfe Howe, June 22, 1921, same collection.

97. Morse to Lodge, March 20, 1892; May 14, 1898. Cf. Morse to Lodge: November 14, 1892; January 3, 1912; May 14, 1920, Lodge Papers, Massachusetts Historical Society.

98. Bigelow to Lodge, April 3, 1912, Lodge Papers, Massachusetts Historical Society.

99. Bigelow to Lodge, May 21, 1913. Cf. February 20, 1913; May 30, 1912, same collection.

100. Bigelow to Lodge, June 3, 1918, same collection.

101. For the Adamses despair see: H. Adams, *Degradation*; H. Adams to Edward H. Davis, February 3, 1911; January 12, 1912, in *Yale Review*, p. 220; Adams to Mrs. Chanler, April 11, 1909, in Ford, *Letters*, II, 517; Adams to Gaskell, December 17, 1908, in Cater, *Adams and Friends*, p. 514; Adams, *Education*, pp. 384–85, 388, 343–44, 396. B. Adams, *Civilization and Decay; The Theory of Social Revolutions* (New York: The Macmillan Co., 1913). *Emancipation*, 1919 edition, pp. 152–67. "The Heritage of Henry Adams," "Introductory Note," in *Degradation*. "The American Democratic Idea," *Yale Review*, V (January, 1916), 225–33. "Can War Be Done Away With," pp. 103–24. B. Adams to H. Adams, February 10, 1910, B. Adams Letters, Houghton Library, Harvard University.

102. H. Adams to B. Adams, September ?, 1895, in Ford, *Letters*, II, 82–83. H. Adams to Mrs. Cameron, August 4, 1896, in *ibid.*, II, 114–15. H. Adams to B. Adams, June 11, 1898, in *ibid.*, II, 184n.

103. H. Adams to B. Adams, June 11, 1897, in *ibid.*, II, 20–30. H. Adams to Mrs. Cameron, February 7, 1904, in *ibid.*, II, 424, H. Adams to Mrs. Cameron, June 22, 1911, in *ibid.*, II, 570.

104. H. Adams to B. Adams, September 20, 1910, in *ibid.*, II, 549.

105. H. Adams to B. Adams, September ?, 1895, in *ibid.*, II, 82–83.

106. H. Adams to Mrs. Cameron, June 25, 1903, in *ibid.*, II, 393. Adams to

Mrs. Cameron, August 20, 1905, in *ibid.*, II, 460. H. Adams to B. Adams, November 11, 1910, in *ibid.*, II, 551.

107. B. Adams to H. Adams, April 22, 1896; July 12, 1896; April 10, 1906, B. Adams Letters, Houghton Library, Harvard University.

108. B. Adams to H. Adams, March 7, 1896; cf. July 2, 1905, same collection.

109. B. Adams to H. Adams, January 9, 1906; April 15, 1908; March 2, 1910, same collection.

110. B. Adams, *Emancipation*, 1919 edition, pp. 166–67. Cf. B. Adams, "Collective Thinking in America," *Yale Review*, VIII (April, 1919), 623–40.

111. John Murray Forbes, paper written possibly in 1895, *Letters (Supplementary)*, III (Boston: George H. Ellis Co., 1905), 296–97.

112. Charles Eliot Perkins to H. L. Higginson, March 8, 1900, in Perry, *Higginson*, pp. 433–34.

113. H. L. Higginson to H. C. Lodge, October 19, 1907, Lodge Papers, Massachusetts Historical Society. Cf. Higginson to C. W. Eliot, December 15, 1914, in Perry, *Higginson*, pp. 442–43.

114. H. L. Higginson to Lodge, February 19, 1908, Lodge Papers, Massachusetts Historical Society.

115. William Lawrence, *Life of Amos Lawrence* (Boston: Houghton Mifflin Co., 1899).

116. Thomas Wentworth Higginson, *Part of a Man's Life* (Boston: Houghton Mifflin, Co., 1905), pp. 103–104, 110.

117. Oliver Wendell Holmes to Sir Frederick Pollack, December 31, 1911, M. DeWolfe Howe Jr. (ed.), *Holmes–Pollack Letters* (Cambridge: Harvard University Press, 1941), I, 187. Holmes to Pollack, September 1, 1910, *ibid.*, I, 167. Cf. Holmes to Pollack, August 10, 1908, *ibid.*, I, 141.

118. Holmes to Dr. John C. H. Wu, June 21, 1908, *Justice Holmes to Dr. Wu* (New York: Central Book Co., n.d.), p. 48. Cf. Holmes to Pollack, August 10, 1908, in Howe, *Holmes–Pollack Letters*, I, 141.

119. Charles William Eliot, "Why the American Republic May Endure," *Forum Magazine*, 18 (October, 1894), 58.

120. Henry A. Yeomans, *Abbott Lawrence Lowell* (Cambridge: Harvard University Press, 1948), pp. 233–35.

121. C. W. Eliot to H. L. Higginson, March 31, 1896, Letters of Charles William Eliot, Houghton Library, Harvard University.

122. Eliot, *The Merit System and the New Democratic Party* (New York: National Civil Service Reform League, 1913), p. 6.

123. Eliot, *Merit System*, 10. Cf. Eliot to ?, November 7, 1910, in James, *Eliot*, II, 207.

124. James, *Eliot*, I, 244–94. Morison, *Three Centuries of Harvard* (Cambridge: Harvard University Press, 1936), pp. 334–89. Morison, *The Development of Harvard University* (Cambridge: Harvard University Press, 1930), pp. 36, 42–44, 259–77, 454–62, 557–58.

125. For some samples of the opposition see Parkman to William Watson Goodwin, December 25, 1891, in Jacobs, *Parkman Letters*, II, 251; Norton to Ward, September 19, 1900, in Norton and Howe, *Norton Letters*, II, 300; Kermit Vanderbilt, *Charles Eliot Norton; Apostle of Culture in a Democracy* (Cambridge: Harvard University Press, 1959), pp. 181, 200. For Morison's remark, see Morison, *Three Centuries*, p. 358.

126. Forbes to J. D. Washburn, September 11, 1879, *Letters (Supplementary)*, III, pp. 150–51. John Murray Forbes, *Reminiscences* (Boston: George H. Ellis, 1902), I, 90-91.

127. C. F. Adams to Norton, November 30, 1883, Charles Francis Adams Letters, Houghton Library, Harvard University. For a similar view see Alexander Agassiz to Lodge, April 18, 1885, Lodge Papers, Massachusetts Historical Society.

128. Holmes, *Collected Legal Papers* (New York: Harcourt, Brace & World, 1920), pp. 167–202, 210–43, 310–16. Holmes, *The Common Law* (Cambridge: Harvard University Press, 1963), *passim*.

129. Holmes, *Legal Papers*, p. 242.

130. On the defense of the Chinese see Forbes to George F. Hoar, April 2, 1882, *Letters (Supplementary)*, III, 174. For praise of the Irish see T. W. Higginson, *Cheerful Yesterdays* (Boston: Houghton Mifflin Co., 1899), pp. 345–46. Eliot, *America's Contributions to Civilization* (New York: The Century Co., 1897), pp. 130–31. Cf. Eliot to ?, November 21, 1892, in James, *Eliot*, II, 52–54.

131. T. W. Higginson, *Atlantic Essays* (Boston: James R. Osgood and Co., 1871), p. 25.

132. C. W. Eliot, *The Fortunate or Happy Conditions for a Life of Labor* (Electrical Manufacturers Club, 1913), pp. 23–24.

133. A. Lawrence Lowell, *Facts and Visions* (Cambridge: Harvard University Press, 1944), pp. 154–55.

134. T. W. Higginson, *Atlantic Essays*, p. 65.

135. C. W. Eliot to C. F. Adams, June 9, 1904, in James, *Eliot*, II, 150-51. Cf. Eliot, "Inaugural Address," in Morison, *Development of Harvard*, 68–69.

136. C. W. Eliot to James Bryce, March 6, 1918, in James, *Eliot*, II, 279. Cf. Eliot to Bryce, November 13, 1916, in *ibid.*, II, 271. For Wendell's view of World War I and democracy see Wendell, "Conflict of Idolatries," *Harvard Graduates Magazine*, XXVII (September, 1918), 4, 15–16.

137. Morison, *Three Centuries*, pp. 417–18, 477–79. Yeomans, *Lowell*, pp. 169–70.

138. A. L. Lowell quoted in Yeomans, *Lowell*, pp. 166, 174. Cf. *ibid.*, 169, 183.

139. Lodge to Morse, April 7, 1921, Lodge Papers, Massachusetts Historical Society. Cf. Lodge to B. Adams, February 5, 1918, same collection.

140. Eliot to L. B. R. Briggs, March 13, 1901, in James, *Eliot*, II, 134–35.

141. T. W. Higginson, *Part of a Man*, p. 302.

142. *Ibid.*, pp. 300–301.

143. Holmes to Pollack, January 28, 1914, in *Holmes–Pollack*, I, 211.

144. T. W. Higginson, *Cheerful Yesterdays*, pp. 362–63.

145. H. C. Lodge, "Journal," January 19, 1887; December 20, 1890, Lodge Papers, Massachusetts Historical Society.

146. Lodge to B. Adams, February 5, 1918, Lodge Papers, same collection. For a more positive and idealistic appraisal of American democracy see Lodge to Mrs. Winthrop Chanler, September 9, 1921, same collection.

147. See Mark DeWolfe Howe, *Holmes–Pollack Letters*, 2 vols., *passim*; Mark DeWolfe Howe (ed.), *Holmes–Laski Letters* (Cambridge: Harvard University Press, 1953), 2 vols., *passim*.

148. Holmes to Pollack, December 28, 1902, in Howe, *Holmes–Pollack*, I, 102.

149. O. W. Holmes, *Speeches by Oliver Wendell Holmes* (Boston: Little, Brown & Co., 1934), p. 27.

150. Holmes to Pollack, March 17, 1932, in Howe, *Holmes–Pollack*, II, 305. Cf. Holmes to Pollack, January 17, 1887, in *ibid.*, I, 30. Holmes to Pollack, March 22, 1891, in *ibid.*, I, 37. Holmes to Pollack, July 31, 1902, in *ibid.*, I, 102. Holmes to Pollack, December 11, 1928, in *ibid.*, II, 234. Holmes to Pollack, April 5, 1932, in *ibid.*, II, 307.

151. Holmes to Pollack, August 9, 1897, in *ibid.*, I, 75–77. Holmes to Pollack, December 31, 1911, in *ibid.*, I, 187. Holmes to Pollack, March 24, 195, in *ibid.*, I, 235.

152. Holmes, *Speeches*, p. 103.

153. C. W. Eliot, *The Ninetieth Birthday of Charles William Eliot* (Cambridge: Harvard University Press, 1925), pp. 29–30.

154. Eliot quoted in James, *Eliot*, II, 289. Cf. Eliot to Bryce, January 6, 1920, in *ibid.*, II, 281.

155. Eliot to James Ford Rhodes, March 25, 1914, in *Ibid.*, II, 237.

156. Eliot to William James, January 20, 1895, in *ibid.*, II, 86–87. Cf. Eliot to Charles Francis Adams, Jr., April 26, 1914, in *ibid.*, II, 238–39.

157. Eliot, "Some Reasons," p. 145. Cf. Eliot to Bryce, September 20, 1921, in James, *Eliot*, II, 286.

158. A. L. Lowell, *Facts*, p. 10; cf. pp. 37, 120–30.

159. *Ibid.*, pp. 37, 41.

160. *Ibid.*, pp. 154–55.

161. A. L. Lowell quoted in Yeomans, *Lowell*, p. 398.

162. C. F. Adams, Jr. quoted in Edward Chase Kirkland, *Charles Francis Adams Jr. 1835–1915: The Patrician at Bay* (Cambridge: Harvard University Press, 1965), pp. 79–80.

163. C. F. Adams, *Chapters of Erie* (Ithaca: Great Seal Books, 1946), pp. 95–98, 135–38. C. F. Adams, "The Railroad System," *North American Review*, CIV (April, 1867), 492–93, 502.

164. C. F. Adams, *Railroads Their Origin and Purpose* (New York: G. P. Putnam's Sons, 1888), p. 213.

165. *Ibid.*, p. 78ff.

166. C. F. Adams to T. W. Higginson, May 9, 1882, Charles Francis Adams, Jr. Letters, Houghton Library, Harvard University.

167. C. F. Adams, "Boston," *North American Review*, CVI (January, April, 1868), 1–25, 557–91.

168. C. F. Adams, "Railroad System," NAR, p. 49.

169. C. F. Adams, *Railroads*, p. 213.

170. C. F. Adams quoted in Kirkland, *C. F. Adams Jr.*, 127. Cf. C. F. Adams, *Autobiography*, pp. 191, 193–95, 198.

171. C. F. Adams quoted in Kirkland, *C. F. Adams Jr.*, pp. 178–79.

172. C. F. Adams quoted in *ibid.*, p. 185.

173. *Ibid.*, pp. 178–84.

174. *Ibid.*, p. 219.

175. C. F. Adams, *Autobiography*, pp. 190–92, 202.

176. *Ibid.*, pp. 210–11.

177. For Brahmin pre-Civil War attitudes on commerce and community see: Robert Bennet Forbes, *Personal Reminiscences* (Boston: Little, Brown & Co., 1878), pp. 138–39, 164–65; Porter, *Jacksons and Lees*, II, p. 1532; H. L. Higginson to Barrett Wendell, November 14, 1919, Massachusetts Historical Society; Anna Eliot Ticknor, *Samuel Eliot, 1739–1820* (Boston: n.p., 1869), p. 172; Nathan Appleton to Thomas Gold Appleton, February 18, 1827, Appleton Papers, Massachusetts Historical Society; N. Appleton to E. S. Gannett, January 24, 1828, same collection; Jaher, "Nathan and Thomas Gold Appleton," pp. 17–39; Loring, *William Appleton*, pp. 107–108; William Lawrence, *Amos A. Lawrence*, pp. 23–24, 52–54; Prescott, *Abbott Lawrence*, pp. 41–50; Amos Lawrence to Amos A. Lawrence, October 5, 1828, Lawrence family papers, Massachusetts Historical Society; Amos Lawrence to Amos A. Lawrence, November 1, 1836, same collection; Amos Lawrence to Giles Richard, December 20, 1836, same collection; Amos Lawrence to Robert Lawrence, May 30, 1836; July 17, 1836, same collection; Amos A. Lawrence to Bishop Potter, January 4, 1864, same collection; Amos A. Lawrence to W. J. Barney, December 8, 1865, same collection; Amos Lawrence, "Will of Amos Lawrence," 1841, same collection; Abbott Lawrence to J. C. Brigham, May 5, 1849, same collection; Hamilton Andrews Hill, *Memoir of Abbott Lawrence* (Boston: Little, Brown & Co., 1885), pp. 4, 47–50, 92, 115–23, 139; N. Appleton, "Abbott Lawrence," pp. 69–71; Abbott Lawrence, *Will of Abbot Lawrence* (Boston: John Wilson and Son, 1857), pp. 21–26; William R. Lawrence, *Extracts from the Diary and Correspondence of Amos A. Lawrence* (Boston: Gould and Lincoln, 1855), pp. 82, 221–33, 264, 311; Hunt, *Lives*, I, 151, 159, 434–35, II, 288–93, 306–309, 360–61; Paul Goodman, "Ethics and Enterprise: The Values of the Boston Elite, 1800–1860," *American Quarterly* (Fall, 1966), pp. 437-51.

178. H. L. Higginson to H. C. Lodge, December 24, 1906, Lodge Papers, Massachusetts Historical Society. Cf. Higginson to Wendell, November 14, 1919, Massachusetts Historical Society. Higginson to William Cameron Forbes, November 22, 1910, H. L. Higginson Letters, Houghton Library, Harvard University. Higginson, "The Soldiers' Field Address," in Perry, *Higginson*, p. 535.

179. Higginson quoted in Perry, *Higginson*, p. 449.

180. James Jackson Storrow quoted in Henry Greenleaf Pearson, *Son of New*

England: James Jackson Storrow 1864–1926 (Boston: Thomas Todd Co., 1932), p. 122.

181. J. M. Forbes to N. A. Griswold, May 12, 1880, in Cochran, *Railroad Leaders*, p. 338.

182. Forbes, *Reminiscences*, III, 128–45. Cochran, *Railroad Leaders*, pp. 114–15. Pearson, *Storrow*, p. 167.

183. Abbott Lawrence, *Will*, p. 45. For same sentiments see Nathan Appleton, "Will of Nathan Appleton," May 23, 1855, Appleton Papers, Massachusetts Historical Society; Amos Lawrence "Wills of Amos Lawrence," Lawrence Papers, Massachusetts Historical Society. For discussions of trust funds as inhibiting entrepreneurship in the elite community see n.a., "City of Boston," *Fortune Magazine*, VII (February, 1933), 26–37, 98, 100, 102, 104, 106; Donald Holbrook, *The Boston Trustee* (Boston: Marshall Jones Co., 1937).

184. William H. Forbes quoted in Arthur S. Pier, *Forbes: Telephone Pioneer* (New York: Dodd, Mead & Co., 1953), p. 99.

185. H. L. Higginson to F. S. Grand d'Hauteville, August 6, 1915, Higginson Letterbooks, Baker Library, Harvard University.

186. Gras, *First National*, pp. 34–55, 74–80, 87–90, 126–27, 132–52, 305–307, 335, 338, 380–81, 538–44, 706–43.

187. White, *Massachusetts Hospital Life*, pp. 5–13, 16–21, 54–70, 72–73, 77, 116–21, 129, 134–38, 150.

188. For dividends in cotton manufacture see Copeland, *Cotton Manufacturing*, pp. 264–65, 395–97; Clark, *Industries*, III, 340–41. For other accounts of the condition of the textile industry see Clark, *Industries*, II, 105, 394, 404–12; *Ibid.*, III, 171–74, 183, 339–43; J. Herbert Burgy, *The New England Cotton Textile Industry* (Baltimore: The Waverley Press, 1932), pp. 175, 178–206; George F. Kenngott, *The Record of a City: A Social Survey of Lowell, Massachusetts* (New York: The Macmillan Co., 1912), pp. 160–61; Thomas R. Navin and Marian V. Sears, "The Rise of a Market for Industrial Securities 1887–1902," *The Business History Review*, 29 (June, 1955), 110; Morton Pepper, "The Development of Cotton Manufacturing in New England and in the South 1900–1923," in Edwin F. Gay and Allyn A. Young (eds.), *The New England Economic Situation* (Chicago: A. W. Shaw Co., 1927), pp. 101–76.

189. N. R. Danielian, *A.T. & T.: The Story of Industrial Conquest* (New York: The Vanguard Press, 1939), pp. 40–65. Horace Coon, *American Tel & Tel* (New York: Longmans Green and Co., 1939), pp. 31–94. Pier, *Forbes*, pp. 116–17, 132–33, 153–56.

190. H. L. Higginson to Francis Lee Higginson, September 29, 1910, H. L. Higginson Letterbooks, Baker Library, Harvard University.

191. Jon Winthrop Hammond, *Men and Volts: The Story of General Electric* (Philadelphia: J. B. Lippincott Co., 1941), pp. 147, 193, 195, 223–24. H. L. Higginson to C. A. Coffin, July 11, 1913, H. L. Higginson Letterbooks, Baker Library, Harvard University.

192. William B. Gates, Jr., *Michigan Copper and Boston Dollars* (Cambridge: Harvard University Press, 1951), pp. 12–45. G. R. Agassiz (ed.), *Letters and Recollections of Alexander Agassiz* (Boston: Houghton Mifflin & Co., 1913), pp. 56–85. Barrett Wendell, "History of Lee, Higginson & Co." (unpublished typescript, Massachusetts Historical Society, 1919), pp. 5–6.

193. H. L. Higginson to Quincy A. Shaw, March 27, 1911, H. L. Higginson Letterbooks, Baker Library, Harvard University.

194. Gates, *Michigan Copper*, p. 91; Agassiz quoted in *ibid.*, p. 91.

195. *Ibid.*, pp. 121–22, 143–48, 161–79.

196. Johnson and Supple, *Boston Capitalists*, p. 81.

197. Forbes quoted in Cochran, *Railroad Leaders*, p. 217. For Forbes's speculations see Forbes, *Reminiscences*, I, 255–58; J. M. Forbes to Paul S. Forbes, April 30, 1847; May 10, 1848; December 2, 1855; January 28, 1856; February 20, 1857; August 12, 1863, Forbes Letters, Baker Library, Harvard University.

198. For Forbes's capitalist connections see Forbes, *Reminiscences*, II, pp. 8–9, 37, 40. For further information on Forbes's connections with British and New York financiers see Cochran, *Railroad Leaders*, pp. 11–40; Henry Greenleaf Pearson, *American Railroad Builder—John Murray Forbes* (Boston: Houghton Mifflin Co., 1911), pp. 30–42. For the formation of Forbes's railroad empire see Cochran, *Railroad Leaders*, pp. 41–90, 95–97; Pearson, *Forbes*, pp. 41–89; Wendell, "Lee, Higginson," pp. 7–8; H. L. Higginson Letters, *passim*; H. L. Higginson Letterbooks, *passim*; "Lee, Higginson Accounts and Investments"; Letters, Letterbooks, and "Accounts and Investments" in H. L. Higginson Papers, Baker Library, Harvard University; Thomas Jefferson Coolidge Letterbook I–IV; "Trust Account Ledger," Old Colony Trust Company, 1901–1908; Letterbooks and "Ledger" in Thomas Jefferson Coolidge Papers, Baker Library, Harvard University; Ralph Budd, *The Burlington Railroad's Boston Background* (New York: American Newcomen Society, 1959); Richard C. Overton, *Burlington West* (Cambridge: Harvard University Press, 1941), pp. 26–44; Overton, *The First Ninety Years, A Historical Sketch of the Burlington Railroad 1850–1940* (Chicago: n.p., 1940); Overton, *Milepost* (Chicago: n.p., 1949); Ernest E. Calkins, "Genesis of a Railroad," *Illinois State Historical Society Proceedings* (1935), pp. 39–72; W. W. Baldwin, *The Making of the Burlington* (no city: n.p., 1920); Alvin F. Harlow, *The Road of the Century* (New York: Creative Age Press, 1947), p. 219; Johnson and Supple, *Boston Capitalists*, pp. 92ff.

199. Cochran, *Railroad Leaders*, pp. 121–22, 161–72, 188, 193. Forbes to Thomas S. Howland, October 19, 1885, in *ibid.*, p. 341. Forbes to William Endicott, Jr., May 12, 1885, in *ibid.*, p. 441. Forbes to J. Sterling Merton, January 20, 1886, in *ibid.*, pp. 443–44. Forbes to J. B. Sanborn, June 10, 1878, in *ibid.*, p. 336. C. F. Adams, Jr., "Railroad Inflation," *North American Review*, CVIII (July, 1869), 141.

200. Forbes quoted in Cochran, *Railroad Leaders*, pp. 138–39. For other examples of his resistance to expansion see Forbes to C. E. Perkins, May 8, 1879, in *ibid.*, p. 336; Forbes, *Reminiscences*, II, 3–4; Forbes to William C. Endicott, October 3, 1883, in Budd, *Burlington*, p. 12.

201. C. E. Perkins to Forbes, July 17, 1878, in Cochran, *Railroad Leaders*, p. 431.

202. Kirkland, *C. F. Adams Jr.*, pp. 66–79.

203. *Ibid.*, pp. 92–128. Nelson Trottman, *History of the Union Pacific* (New York: The Ronald Press Co., 1923), pp. 200–240.

204. Kirkland, *Men, Cities and Transportation*, II, 60–62. L. L. Waters, *Steel Trails to Santa Fe* (Lawrence: University of Kansas Press, 1950), pp. 195–207. Gurensey Cam, Jr., "The Influence of New England Capital in America's Railroad Development," in Gay and Young (eds.), *New England Economic Situation*, pp. 39–68. Wendell, "Lee, Higginson," pp. 7–8. Edward W. Weeks, *Men, Money and Responsibility: A History of the Lee, Higginson Corporation* (Boston: privately printed, 1962), p. 12. Kirkland, *C. F. Adams Jr.*, pp. 90–91. Johnson and Supple, *Boston Capitalists*, pp. 287, 299, 303, 307–309, 319–28. H. L. Higginson Papers, *passim*. H. L. Higginson Letterbooks, *passim*. "Lee, Higginson Accounts and Investments." Thomas Jefferson Coolidge Papers, Letterbook I–IV. "Trust Account Ledger," Old Colony Trust Company, 1901–1908.

205. Waters, *Steel Trails*, pp. 195–207.

206. H. L. Higginson to Howard Elliot, October 6, 1913, H. L. Higginson Letterbooks, Baker Library, Harvard University.

207. Frederick Upham Adams, *Conquest of the Tropics* (New York: Doubleday & Co., 1914), pp. 39–85. Charles Morrow Wilson, *Empire in Green and Gold* (New York: Holt Rinehart & Winston, 1947), pp. 69, 71, 107–109, 206–207.

208. H. L. Higginson to Francis Lee Higginson, Jr., September 29, 1910, H. L. Higginson Letterbooks, Baker Library, Harvard University.

209. Amory, *Proper Bostonians*, pp. 54, 343–44. Kirkland, *Men, Cities and Transportation*, II, 435.

210. Norton Mezvinsky, "The Social Aristocracy of Boston and New York 1870–1915," unpublished MS., p. 6.

211. N.a., *The Flame*, X (October, 1957), 27–33. *The Flame* is the company magazine of Godfrey L. Cabot, Inc. This seventy-fifth anniversary issue was devoted to the history of the company. Amory, *Proper Bostonians*, p. 348.

212. Alfred D. Chandler, Jr., *Strategy and Structure* (Cambridge: M.I.T. Press, 1962), p. 120. Lawrence H. Seltzer, *A Financial History of the American Auto Industry* (Boston: Houghton Mifflin Co., 1938), pp. 164, 252–55. Pearson, *Storrow*, pp. 123–24.

213. Amory, *Proper Bostonians*, p. 346.

214. Navin and Sears, "Market for Industrial Securities," p. 115.

215. Thomas P. Beal, *The Second National Bank of Boston* (New York: The American Newcomen Society, 1958), pp. 1–2, 7–8, 19. Edwin A. Stone, *A Century of Boston Banking* (Boston: Rockwell and Churchill, 1894), pp. 16–17. N.a., *A List of Stockholders in the National Banks of Boston* (Boston: n.p., 1866), pp. 378–88, 390–400. N.a., *The Book of the Shawmut Bank* (Boston: The National Shawmut Bank of Boston, 1923). Frederick H. Curtiss, *Fifty Years of Boston Finance 1880–1890* (Boston: n.p., 1930), p. 7. Gras, *Massachusetts National Bank*, pp. 161, 166–67.

216. Fritz Redlich, *The Molding of American Banking*, vol. 2, part II (New York: Hafner Publishing Company, 1951), pp. 189–90, 379, 394. Curtiss *Fifty Years*, pp. 2, 7. Gras, *Massachusetts Bank*, pp. 180–84. Navin and Sears, "Market for Industrial Securities," pp. 124–26. N.a., *Old Colony Trust Company* (Boston: n.p., 1915).

217. Navin and Sears, "Market for Industrial Securities," pp. 124–26. Redlich, *American Banking*, vol. 2, part II, p. 288. Pearson, *Storrow*, pp. 190–92. H. L. Higginson Papers, *passim*. "Lee, Higginson Accounts and Investments," H. L. Higginson Letterbooks, *passim*.

218. Arthur S. Dewing, *Corporate Promotions and Reorganizations* (Cambridge: Harvard University Press, 1914); pp. 171 183. Navin and Sears, "Market for Industrial Securities," pp. 122, 124–26. Paul Goodman, "Success and Failure in Investment Banking," "Social Sources of Business Enterprise: Studies in the Longevity of Boston Financial Institutions," unpublished MS., p. 12. *Record of Dividends, Kidder, Peabody & Co.*, Baker Library, Harvard University.

219. T. J. Coolidge Papers, *Trust Account Ledger—Old Colony Trust Co.*, Baker Library, Harvard University.

220. For a discussion of this point see Goodman, "Success and Failure," pp. 7–27.

221. For the removal of speculating partners see H. L. Higginson to James J. Higginson, March 27, 1885; Higginson to Frederic W. Allen, April 20, 1915,

Higginson Letterbooks, Baker Library. Also, Higginson to Wendell, November 14, 1919, Massachusetts Historical Society; Wendell, "Lee, Higginson," pp. 5, 8. For Higginson's own propensity to plunge, see Storrow quoted in Pearson, Storrow, p. 90; Wendell, "Lee, Higginson," p. 5.

222. Higginson to Robert H. Fuller, December 23, 1908, Higginson Letterbooks, Baker Library.

223. Higginson to Allen, April 20, 1915, same collection.

224. Pearson, Storrow, pp. 100–103, 172–73, 193–95, 238–39. Wendell, "Lee Higginson," pp. 10–13, 15. Weeks, Fifty Years, pp. 19–20. Redlich, Molding, vol. 2, part II, pp. 288, 387–88.

225. Storrow quoted in Pearson, Storrow, p. 239.

226. Kidder, Peabody executive quoted in Goodman, "Success and Failure," p. 24.

227. Curtiss, Fifty Years, p. 7. N.a., Old Colony. Gras, Massachusetts National Bank, pp. 180–84. Redlich, Molding, vol. 2, part II, p. 190.

228. Redlich, Molding, vol. 2, part II, p. 388.

229. Pearson, Storrow, p. 196. Weeks, Men, Money and Responsibility, p. 17.

230. T. J. Coolidge to C. E. Perkins, January 2, 1899, T. J. Coolidge Papers, Baker Library, Harvard University.

231. Higginson to Howard Elliot, October 6, 1913, H. L. Higginson Letterbooks, Baker Library.

232. Higginson to C. A. Coffin, July 11, 1913, same collection.

233. Robert Shaplen, Kreuger, Genius and Swindler, (New York: Alfred A. Knopf, 1960, pp. 6–7, 77–78, 94, 181, 207, 209, 222, 226–27, 231, 234, 242–43, 250.

234. Dawing, Corporate Promotions, pp. 305–22.

235. Harold F. Williamson, Winchester, The Gun that Won the West (Washington: Combat Forces Press, 1952), pp. 260–62, 271, 320, 360–63.

236. White, Massachusetts Life, pp. 153–65.

237. Allan Forbes, Forty Years in Boston Banking (New York: The American Newcomen Society, 1948), pp. 9, 17. N.a., The Log of the State Street Trust Co. (Boston: privately printed, 1926). William W. Wolbach, The Boston Safe Deposit and Trust Co. (New York: The American Newcomen Society, 1962), pp. 8–11, 20, 23, 25–26.

238. Richard P. Chapman, 125 Years on State Street (New York: The American Newcomen Society, 1956), p. 5.

239. The Federal Reserve Bank of Boston, Commercial Banking in New England 1784–1958 (Boston: n.p., 1959), pp. 38, 41, 43, 45.

8

Class, Status, and Community Power in Nineteenth-Century American Industrial Cities —Paterson, New Jersey: A Case Study

by **HERBERT G. GUTMAN**

Much is known about the early history of New England textile towns, but too much is inferred from this single source about the nineteenth-century American industrial city. Although little is known about the development of the industrial city, urban historians as well as labor and business historians have generalized much about it. Unwarranted assumptions about the social and economic structure of the early industrial city, however, have distorted significant patterns in its early development. Paterson, New Jersey, an industrial city that attracted the attention of men as diverse as Alexander

A version of this paper was read at the December, 1964 meetings of the American Historical Association, Washington, D.C., and appeared in an abbreviated form as "Industrial Invasion of the Village Green," *Trans-action*, III (May/June, 1966), 19–24. The author expresses his gratitude to the Social Science Research Council and the State University of New York at Buffalo for research grants that made possible the gathering of much source material presented herein.

263

Hamilton, William Haywood, and William Carlos Williams and that had as its official motto *Spe et Labore* (With Hope and Labor), serves as a case study to test some of the generalizations and assumptions.

I

Little is known of the inner history of the nineteenth-century American industrial city. Historians have detoured around Paterson and other nineteenth-century industrial cities for many reasons. Perhaps the landscape seemed unattractive. Perhaps the roadways into and out of the city seemed simple and one-dimensional. Whatever the cause, specialists have built roadblocks that deny access to a rich and hitherto untapped social history. The urban historian apparently finds the large, complex metropolis a greater challenge and a more accessible source for information than the simpler, intensely specialized, and grim factory town. The labor historian learns quickly that industrial cities lacked permanent labor organizations, and since he is by tradition little more than the chronicler of trade union history he just ignores the factory town. And the business historian, anxious to trace the detailed internal development of a particular firm or industry, all too often takes for granted its external relationships to the larger community. These attitudes, among others, have focused attention away from the industrial city as a legitimate subject for detailed and careful inquiry.[1]

Only two events in Paterson's history, for example, have attracted detailed attention: Alexander Hamilton's ill-fated effort to start "the Society for establishing useful Manufactures" in the 1790s and William Haywood's equally troubled effort to organize the immigrant silk workers into the Industrial Workers of the World, in 1913. No less than 120 years separates these two incidents—a period of time that sheds light on the transition from Hamilton to Haywood. But historians have not filled in the void between these two men in ways that make the transition meaningful. Instead, they have too often relied on crude and utterly misleading generalizations about the industrial city, its social order, and its power structure. Here one of these misleading generalizations, perhaps the most important, is subjected to close and critical examination: the widely held view that from the start, industrialists had the social and political power and prestige to match their economic force, and that they controlled the towns. This generalization has several corollaries: industrialists faced ineffective opposition; town politics reflected their interests; other property owners—particularly small businessmen and professionals—identified with industrialists and applauded their innovations and pecuniary successes. Factory-workers enter this version of history only as passive, ineffective, and alienated victims, practically helpless before their all-powerful employers. Stated in another fashion, it is the proposition that from the beginning, there existed a close relationship between economic class, social status, and power and that control over "things" —especially industrial property and machinery—was quickly and easily transformed into authority and legitimized so that industrialists could do little wrong and, better still, quoting Max Weber, "realize their own will in communal action even against the resistance of others who are participating in the action."[2] In place of this common view, another is argued. Through its early years, for at least a generation, the factory and its disciplines, the large impersonal corporation, and the propertyless wage-earners remained unusual and even alien elements in the industrial town. They disrupted tradition, competed against an established social structure and status hierarchy, and challenged traditional modes of thought. In these years, therefore, the factory-owner symbolized innovation and a radical departure from an older way of life. His power was not yet legitimized and "taken for granted." Surely powerful because of his control over "things," the factory-owner nevertheless found it difficult to enforce noneconomic decisions essential to his economic welfare. He met with unexpected opposition from nonindustrial property-owners, did not dominate the local political structure, and learned that the middle and professional classes did not automatically accept his leadership and idolize his achievements. Moreover, the new working class, not entirely detached from the larger community, had significant ties to that community which strengthened its power at critical moments and allowed it, despite the absence of strong permanent labor organizations, often to influence events at the expense of the factory-owner.

Men hold authority in particular setting, Robert M. MacIver has observed, when they possess "the established right to determine policies, to pronounce judgments on relevant issues, or, more broadly, to act as the leaders or guide to other men."[3] The industrial town was too new at the start for the industrialist to command this kind of prestige and to hold this kind of authority. Class position and social status were closely related. But as a new class, the industrialists had not yet achieved high social status. In fact, the absence of the kind of authority described by MacIver shaped much of dramatic early history of the industrial city. The owners of disruptive and radical innovations—power-driven machinery, the factory, and the large corporation—sought to legitimize their economic power in these years. And Paterson is a good illustration of the frustrating search by the industrialist for status and unchallenged authority.

II

By the early 1870s, Paterson ranked as a major American industrial city. Located fourteen miles from New York City, its factories manufactured mainly locomotives, machinery, iron goods of all kinds, and silks and other textiles. Its three locomotive firms contained 25 per cent of the nation's locomotive capacity, and the products of its large ironworks helped construct the Philadelphia Centennial Exposition buildings; many eastern bridges; and New York's Metropolitan Museum of Art, its Lenox Library, and its first elevated railroad. Paterson also stood as America's preeminent silk manufacturing center, and its separate jute, flax, and mosquito net mills were each the largest of their kind in the nation. With a few exceptions, most of the mills came to Paterson after 1850 so that their owners ranked as relative newcomers to the city twenty years later. Older Patersonians saw their small city change radically betwen 1850 and 1870.[4]

Before 1850 Paterson had grown fitfully. Early in the nineteenth century, small cotton factories started there to take advantage of available water power and the New York market and port nearby. Although the city had twenty cotton mills in 1832, inability to compete with more efficient New England firms caused them to stagnate in the 1840s and 1850s. According to its official industrial historian, as late as 1838 most New Yorkers regarded Paterson as "an upcountry hamlet, chiefly noted for its fine waterfall and valuable waterpower."[5]

But the cotton mills attracted machinists to repair and build textile machinery, and the start of the railroad era in the 1830s led one of them, aided by New York capital, to begin locomotive manufacturing in 1836. His pioneer factory grew slowly before 1850, as did a number of smaller machine and iron shops. The great increase in the demand for railroad equipment, iron, and machinery after 1850 stimulated the rapid growth of these industries. Two more locomotive factories opened, and between 1850 and 1873 the three together produced 4,437 locomotives and sold them over the entire nation. In 1873, 3,000 men worked in the locomotive shops. Other iron works grew as quickly. Two Lancashire millwrights, for example, started a machine works in 1845 with ten hands and employed 1,100 in 1873.[6]

The silk industry grew even more quickly and spectacularly than the iron and locomotive industries. The pattern was quite simple. A declining cotton industry made available water power, cheap mills, and a resident labor force. These first attracted English silk manufacturer John Ryle to Paterson in 1839, after a successful start as a New York silk importer. Small spinning and weaving shops began in the 1840s and 1850s. But the great stimulus came from outside the city in the 1860s, when New York and Boston silk and textile manufacturers and importers moved their mills to Paterson or built new ones there. A few examples suffice. A Coventry Englishman brought his silk mill from New York in 1860. In the next two years, the nation's leading importer of tailor trimmings left Boston for Paterson, as did another Bostonian, a pioneer American silk manufacturer. In 1868, one of New York's great silk importers became a Paterson manufacturer. From the start, these men of wealth constructed large mills and introduced power machinery, and other innovations. One imported a whole English factory. These men transformed the industry. In 1860 four silk mills employed 590 workers. In 1876, eight silk ribbon and six broad silk factories gave work to 8,000 persons, two thirds of them women. One of every four silk workers was under sixteen years of age. Outside capital also financed other large textile mills in these years. A mosquito net factory came from New York, and Scottish money built the nation's largest jute mill. Eighty-one years after its founding in Northern Ireland, in 1865, Barbour Brothers opened a linen factory that quickly became one of Paterson's great mills.

Smaller workshops continued, but by the 1870s the large mills dominated the local economy.[7]

Older Paterson residents in 1873 lived in a different city than they had known in 1850. The coming of the large mills, particularly from outside the city, transformed Paterson in many ways. The mill-owners, a new industrial leadership mostly alien to the older city, represented a power unknown in earlier years. More than this, their factories drew in increasing numbers of immigrant and native workers and the city boomed. In 1846 Paterson had only 11,000 inhabitants. In the next twenty-four years, its population increased to 33,000. Immigrants made up more than a third of its residents. French and German skilled silk workers, but especially English skilled hands and an increasing number of unskilled Irish laborers, found work in the rapidly expanding factories. Built on two major industries, iron and textiles, the Paterson economy offered employment to whole families: the iron factories hired only men and textile mills relied mainly on female and child labor. Rapid growth in the 1850s and 1860s illustrated in Paterson all the severe social dislocations incident to quick industrialization and urbanization everywhere, but it also opened new opportunities for small retail businesses. Between 1859 and 1870, for example, the number of grocers rose from 105 to 230 and the number of saloonkeepers from 46 to 270. Paterson's industrial leaders in the early 1870s, mostly new to the city, had innovated boldly and caused a city to change radically in less than twenty years from one characterized by small workshops to one typified by large factories. Between 1873 and 1878 a severe depression halted temporarily this process.[8]

III

It is sufficient to report briefly that this first of modern industrial crises, 1873–1878, crippled the Paterson economy and strained the city's total resources and all its citizens. "Among all classes," it was noted as early as October 31, 1873, "there is a feeling of gloom and intense anxiety in regard to the future." Nearly three years later, a silk worker reported with good reason that "Paterson is in a deplorable condition." The unemployed regularly overtaxed limited public and private charities and occasionally paraded the streets demanding public works. The locomotive workers especially felt the diminished demand for labor. From 1871 to 1873 the three locomotive factories produced 1,185 engines; in 1875, 1876 and 1877 the figure totalled only 195. The 1873 wage bill for 3,172 locomotive workers came to $1,850,000; four years later (1877) the same firms paid 325 workers only $165,000. The silk and other textile workers apparently suffered less unemployment, but recurrent wage cuts between 1873 and 1877 ranged from 10 to 30 per cent and meant exceedingly hard times for nearly 10,000 textile workers. Sporadic silk strikes, particularly in 1876, illustrated the workers' reactions to these deplorable conditions. Despair permeated the city. Its population fell almost 10 per cent between 1875 and 1878. With good reason, a *New York Sun* reporter in September 1876 called Paterson an industrial ghost town comparable to a southern city after Lee's surrender.[9]

In analyzing the consequences of the 1873–1878 depression, historians have argued that the hardship resulting from extensive unemployment and lowered wages shattered labor organizations and immeasurably strengthened employers. But this exclusively economic interpretation ignores the fact that the same cyclical crisis, coming after two decades of radical economic and social change, also tested the status and power of Paterson's new industrialists and workers within the community. The depression created grave economic difficulties for the entire population, and, in trying to solve certain of their problems, the Paterson industrialists sought support and sanction at critical moments from the local community and its leaders. Their successes, but more importantly their failures, revealed much about their status and power in the city, measured the stability and legitimacy of the new industrial order, and gauged the attitudes of shopkeepers and merchants, professionals, politicians, and other prestigious persons in the precorporate city toward the new order and its leaders.

Four incidents between 1877 and 1880 involving Paterson's "public" —two textile strikes and two libel suits against a socialist newspaper editor—will be examined briefly in order to explore the early relationship between economic class, social status, and power.

IV

The first incident illustrated the inability of the new large manufacturers to commit the city government to their interests. It occurred between June and August, 1877 and was an unprecedented general strike of ribbon-weavers, mostly English, French, and German immigrants, against the biggest silk manufacturers. They protested a 20 per cent wage cut and an irksome labor contract and demanded a 10 per cent wage increase and a board of arbitration modeled on English and French precedent. At its peak, the strike—the greatest in Paterson to that time—idled 2,000 workers and closed the mills. After ten weeks, a compromise including restoration of the wage cut took place. What allowed the workers to effect this compromise in the absence of permanent labor organization and after forty-four months of depression? Why did the silk manufacturers fail? In part, the staying power of the weavers frustrated the manufacturers, but even more serious obstacles denied them success.[10]

Important and powerful groups in the community refused to sanction and support the mill-owners. Nonstrikers and elected city officials either supported the strikers or, more significantly, rejected pressure and commands from the mill owners. Small shopkeepers extended credit and subscribed relief funds to the strikers. A weekly, German-language newspaper also supported them. Although critical of the strikers, the two daily newspapers did not cheer the manufacturers and they even lectured the mill owners to "put conscience as well as capital" into their enterprises. The local courts displayed their independence of the manufacturers and on several occasions weavers charged with disorderly conduct went free or suffered, at best, nominal fines. After manufacturer William Strange successfully prosecuted two weavers for violating written contracts, pressure from city officials, including the mayor, convinced a local judge to postpone indefinitely forty additional trials.[11]

The Republican mayor, Benjamin Buckley, and the Democratic-controlled Board of Aldermen gave the manufacturers their greatest trouble. The aldermen were mostly self-made men : skilled workmen of independent means and retail shopkeepers. Their number included neither factory workers nor manufacturers. Mayor Buckley personified the precorporate American dream. Born in England in 1808, he had come to Paterson as a young man, worked first in a cotton factory, and then achieved wealth and high status. By 1877, he owned a small spindle factory, headed a local bank, and looked back on a successful career in Republican politics including several terms in the state legislature and the presidency of the state senate. He started the first of his several terms as Paterson's Republican mayor in 1875. Because he viewed his role as maintaining the public peace and little more, Buckley infuriated the silk manufacturers. During the dispute, he used his powers, especially the small police force, with great skill and tact to suppress overt disorders only. This angered the mill-owners. They insisted that inadequate civic authority allowed a few agitators to intimidate hundreds of loyal workers. In the strike's seventh week, therefore, the Paterson Board of Trade, dominated by the largest silk and iron manufacturers, called a special meeting to pressure the city authorities to enlarge the police force and also to declare a state of emergency limiting the strikers' use of the streets and their freedom of action. The Board publicly charged that "the laws of the land are treated with contempt and trampled upon by a despotic mob" led by immigrant radicals and "communists." A silk manufacturer warned that unless the authorities put down these troublemakers Paterson soon would be "a city without manufactories . . . with nothing . . . but the insignificant industries of an unimportant town." Other manufacturers expressed even graver anxieties: one urged that strike leaders be "taken out and shot" and another offered to finance a private militia. Iron manufacturer Watts Cooke admitted their deepest fear—the absence of sufficient status and respect in the city. "All the classes of the community," Cooke lamented, "are coming to lean to-wards and sympathize with the men rather than the employers." He and the others demanded the protection of the city authorities.[12] But Mayor Buckley and the Board of Aldermen turned a deaf ear toward the complaints and demands of the large manufacturers. Buckley did not issue a proclamation, defended his use of civic authority, and advised the aldermen that the Board of Trade did "great injury to the credit of the city." He especially commended "the good sense of the working people." The Democratic Board of Aldermen upheld the Republican mayor. It unanimously passed three resolutions: the first tabled without discussion the request for a larger police force; the second applauded Buckley's "wise and judicious course"; and the third, as if to reiterate the independence of the city government from the manufacturers, urged immediate prosecution of mill owners who violated local fire-escape ordinances. The manufacturers were unable to alter public policies during the strike. City officials—all property-owners—maintained an independence of judgment and explicitly rejected iron manufacturer Watts Cooke's insistence that the Board of Trade was "best able to judge what the city needed to protect it."[13]

After the strike, although the *Paterson Guardian* advised the Board of Trade to get into local politics and "pay the proper attention to the men ... elected to the city council," the large manufacturers turned away from politics and to the private militia. The Board listened approvingly to a member who found "more virtue in one well drilled soldier than in ten policemen or in one bullet than in ten clubs in putting down a riot." Silk manufacturer Strange led the group that subscribed the first $4,500 for arms and equipment. And of the 120 militiamen signed up by January, 1880, at least 50 per cent were manufacturers, merchants, clerks, salespeople, and professionals. It proved easier to subscribe funds for a militia than to "reform" the city government. The manufacturers had more than enough wealth to finance a private militia but inadequate prestige and power to dominate the city government. In 1877, Paterson had one police officer for every 1,666 residents; ten years later, it had a militia company but the ratio of police to population remained the same. The manufacturers' use of private power indicated weakness, not strength *vis a vis* the body politic and the city government.[14]

V

A year after the ribbon-weavers' strike, a second dispute involving textile workers again illustrated the limited power of the Paterson manufacturers. A third wage cut in less than a year convinced 550 unorganized workers, mostly women and children, to quit the textile mills owned by two brothers, Robert and Henry Adams. One of the East's great textile mills, R & H Adams and Company symbolized the rapid rise of the new industrialism in Paterson. It had moved a small factory there from New York City in 1857 and had thrived in the next twenty years, adding several large and efficient mills to its original plant. By far the largest of its kind in the country and perhaps in the world, the firm exported huge quantities of mosquito netting overseas, especially to Africa and Asia. Two more unequal adversaries than the unorganized Adams strikers and their employer hardly could be found. Yet, after a strike lasting nine months, the company conceded defeat in March 1879, and its senior partner, Robert Adams, who vigorously and publicly combatted the strikers, quit the firm and left Paterson.[15]

Once again, community attitudes toward the dispute shaped its outcome, and Robert Adams, not the striking women, had no allies in this battle. The Board of Trade kept silent. No one publicly protested Adams' recurrent threat to move the mills. The press remained neutral. With one exception noted below, Adams got no overt encouragement from other manufacturers, retail businessmen, or politicians. He even had trouble with his foremen and had to fire a few who defended the strikers. Unlike Adams, the strikers found strength in the community. Many took jobs in other local textile mills. Strike funds gathered mainly from local workers, shopkeepers, and merchants fed the others. Concerts and picnics buoyed their spirits and added to their funds. At least one of every eight Patersonians signed a petition attacking Adams. Frequent street demonstrations indicated additional support. Soon after the trouble began, an outspoken Irish socialist, Joseph P. McDonnell, came to Paterson from nearby New York to encourage the strikers. He organized them into the International Labor Union, an industrial union for unskilled factory workers led by immigrant socialists and Yankee eight-hour reformers. McDonnell stayed on and soon started a socialist weekly newspaper, the Paterson *Labor Standard*. Although its masthead quoted Karl Marx and its columns heaped abuse on local mill-owners and called Adams "Lucifer" and his mills "a penitentiary," its back pages contained numerous local business advertisements. Forty-five retail enterprises, mostly saloons, groceries, and clothing, drygoods, and boot and shoe shops sustained the paper as it railed against manufacturer Adams.[16]

Adams' power against the workers was limited to his firm's income. He sent special agents to Fall River and other New England towns to recruit new workers. Adams hired many new hands but retained few because the strikers made full use of the streets. The strikers and their sympathizers, at one time as many as 2,000 persons, met the new workers at the rail depot or in the streets, urged them to quit Adams, and even financed their way home. This tactic worked: the first time jeers, taunts, and ordinary discourse convinced twenty-two of twenty-five Fall River workers to leave immediately. Although the city authorities arrested a few workers when tempers flared, they quickly released them and made no effort to restrain strikers using the streets peacefully. By carefully separating "peaceful coercion" from "violence," the authorities effectively if unintentionally strengthened the strikers and Adams' wealth gained him no advantage. The freedom to use the streets to persuade outsiders from taking their jobs together with support from shopkeepers allowed the otherwise weak strikers to check Adams' power, thereby revealing his impotence and finally forcing him to surrender and to leave the city.[17]

VI

The third and fourth events centered on Joseph McDonnell and his socialist newspaper, the *Labor Standard*. Dublin-born McDonnell had crowded much radical experience into his thirty-two years before coming to Paterson in 1878 to aid the Adams strikers. He had edited several Dublin and London Irish nationalist journals, engaged in Fenian "conspiracies," represented Ireland at the 1872 Hague Congress of the First International and sided with the Marxists, organized several huge London labor free-speech demonstrations, and served four prison terms before coming to the United States in January, 1873. Soon after his arrival, McDonnell exposed steerage conditions in indignant letters, edited a New York socialist weekly, and traveled all over the East condemning capitalism, advocating socialism, and organizing weak socialist trade unions. According to traditional historical stereotypes, McDonnell should have been a pariah to all but a few Patersonians and therefore easy game for his opponents. But even though the Irish socialist had serious legal troubles and went to prison, he and his newspaper soon won acceptance as legitimate and useful critics of the new industrial order.[18]

McDonnell's difficulties began in October 1878, before the ink had dried on the *Labor Standard*'s first issue, and continued unabated for eighteen months. The formal complaint of a few loyal Adams workers whom the *Labor Standard* attacked as "scabs" convinced the County Grand Jury to indict McDonnell for libel. A petit jury found him guilty and a judge fined him $500 and court costs. A few months later, McDonnell apparently averted a second libel indictment. But in the fall of 1879, a second Grand Jury indictment did come, for McDonnell had printed a bitter letter by a young worker, Michael Menton, exposing inadequate working and living conditions in a Passaic River brickyard, where Menton had labored and become severely ill. In February, 1880 a jury found McDonnell and Menton guilty of libel and a judge sent them to the Passaic County Jail for three months. Viewed only in these narrow terms, McDonnell's difficulties prove to traditional labor historians only the repressive power of "capital" and the pliancy of the judiciary. Actually, McDonnell's difficulties strengthened him. If these legal troubles were intended to drive him from Paterson, the opposite resulted. Support from workers, mostly nonsocialists, and from other persons prominent in the community assured his survival.[19]

Although new to Paterson, McDonnell was not a complete outcast during his first trial. His lawyer, an old Patersonian, had grown wealthy as a real-estate speculator, fathered the state's first ten-hour law and important banking reforms, organized the city's waterworks, and been a prominent Republican for twenty years before becoming Greenback candidate for New Jersey governor. Despite the county prosecutor's plea to convict McDonnell as a "woman libeler," a "threat" to established order and a "foreign emissary" sent by English manufacturers to "breed discontent" in America, the jury, composed mostly of storekeepers and skilled workmen, remained deadlocked for three days and three nights. Only unusual pressure by the presiding judge finally brought conviction. The $500 fine, substantially less than the maximum $2,000 fine and two-year prison term, told much. A second judge, in the case, himself originally a Lancashire worker and then the owner of a small bobbin pin factory, convinced the presiding judge to go easy on McDonnell. After the conviction, storekeepers and merchants contributed handsomely to McDonnell's "defense fund."[20]

McDonnell's lower-class supporters made known their displeasure with the trial and used the threat of their potential political power. They crowded the courtroom to cheer McDonnell and after the conviction, raised the fine and court costs quickly and carried their hero through the streets. More important, the trial occurred during the bitter 1878 congressional election, and they humiliated the county prosecutor, a Democratic politician. Workers joined by sympathetic storekeepers crowded the annual Democratic election meeting and in a raucous demonstration refused to let it start until the prosecutor left the hall. The meeting ended quickly. McDonnell's supporters then jammed a second meeting and hundreds silently walked out when the prosecutor rose to speak. Politicians competing for labor votes got the point. A Republican argued that only free speech and a free press could preserve American liberty. Fearing the loss of labor votes, the Democrats publicly defended the right to strike and one Democrat declaimed: "Away with the government of the aristocracy! Away with legislators only from the wealthy classes! We have had enough of them!" A nearby newspaper sympathetic to McDonnell concluded: "In Paterson, he [McDonnell] is stronger than his accusers. Today he has the sympathy of the people, and his paper from this time forth is deeply rooted in Paterson."[21]

The second trial and subsequent imprisonment of McDonnell attracted national attention but only its local significance concerns us. The support McDonnell received this time revealed his growing local prestige and power. Except for the litigants, no one publicly attacked him. His competitor, the Democratic *Paterson Guardian*, found the verdict "to say the least, a great surprise to those who heard or read the testimony." The judge justified sending McDonnell to prison only because he feared that others again would pay a fine. This time, McDonnell's lawyers were the son of a former Democratic mayor and Socrates Tuttle, Paterson's most respected attorney, who had been Republican mayor some years before. Ably defending his client, Tuttle warned that a conviction would endanger the free press and mean that the working classes would "henceforth never be allowed to complain." Three northern New Jersey nonlabor weeklies emphasized the same point. McDonnell's sympathizers were led by two former silk factory foremen, one German and the other English, and both now successful entrepreneurs. Two clergymen, one a Baptist and the other a Methodist (both active in Republican politics and Paterson's most popular clergymen) condemned McDonnell's treatment and counseled the socialist. Several aldermen, former aldermen, and county freeholders visited him in prison. Garrett A. Hobart, a Paterson corporation lawyer, President of the State Senate and that year elected chairman of the Republican State Committee, sent McDonnell ten dollars for his defense, offered "to do his best" and sought to amend the state libel law. Even the son of Henry Adams and nephew of Robert Adams, McDonnell's 1878 adversary, gave the socialist twenty dollars and visited him in jail.[22]

McDonnell's jail experience, surely one of the most unusual in American penal history, depended upon John Buckley, the former mayor's son. He had been a locomotive worker as a young man, a prominent Republican, and warden of the county prison. Apparently distressed over the conviction, Warden Buckley did his best to assure McDonnell's comfort and his freedom while in prison. McDonnell kept a prison diary, and its entries record many surprising amenities. The warden let him edit his newspaper and organize a national and local protest campaign against his imprisonment. McDonnell's supporters visited him daily and often brought their children along. Buckley allowed them to meet in his office. One day as many as twenty-one persons called on McDonnell. Every day his meals arrived from outside, and saloon- and boardinghouse-keepers kept him overstocked with cigars, wines, and liquors. Others brought fresh fruits, cakes, and puddings. On St. Patrick's Day shamrocks came, and on his birthday, two fancy dinners. The day of his release, Warden Buckley publicly commended the good behavior of prisoner Joseph P. McDonnell.[23]

Let out ten days early, McDonnell benefited from a demonstration of popular support unprecedented in Paterson's history. Organized by a committee of seventy-five that was dominated by workers but included twelve saloon- and inn-keepers and five grocers, the demonstration counted between fifteen and twenty thousand persons. After that, few Patersonians doubted the labor agitator's place and power in their city. McDonnell's *Labor Standard* survived until his death in 1908. He founded the New Jersey Federation of Trades and Labor Unions and pioneered in pushing protective labor legislation. Several clues indicate his rapid acceptance as a radical critic. Soon after his imprisonment, the Democratic prosecutor who had called him a "woman libeler" and a "foreign emissary" sent by British manufacturers began advertising his legal services in the *Labor*

Standard. The city government regularly bought space to print legal public notices. In 1884, less than six years after he had come to Paterson and four years after his release from jail, socialist McDonnell was appointed New Jersey's first deputy inspector of factories and workshops.[24]

McDonnell never lost feeling for those who helped in the early days. In 1896, although the *Labor Standard* still carried Karl Marx's words on its masthead, McDonnell printed kind words about Garrett Hobart, then running with William McKinley against William Jennings Bryan. He called Hobart "a rare specimen of manhood in the class in which he moves" and, remembering Hobart's aid in 1880, concluded that "to know him is to like him whether you agree with his opinions or not."[25]

VII

What general meaning can be inferred from these Paterson events? If they are unique to that city, then only the local historian profits from them. In fact, they typified obstacles encountered by industrialists in other post-Civil War industrial towns and cities during crises similar to the 1877 and 1878 Paterson textile disputes. Time and again, the industrialist found his freedom of action confined by particular local "circumstances." Several examples illustrate his difficulties. A western Pennsylvania jury convicted a mine operator when violence resulted after he brought Italians there. The merchant mayor of an Illinois mining town disarmed Chicago Pinkerton police sent to guard an operator's properties. A sheriff raised a posse to chase special New York police sent to protect railroad repair shops in eastern Pennsylvania. Ohio Valley newspapers condemned iron manufacturers for arming strikebreakers. Northern Pennsylvania merchants housed striking evicted coal miners. A pronounced pattern emerges from these and similar events.[26] Unorganized or poorly organized workers displayed surprising strength and staying power and found sympathy from other groups in the community. Local political officials often rejected or modified the pressures of industrialists. Nonindustrial capitalists—persons with power and prestige locally and persons committed to competitive private enterprise and the acquisitive spirit in their own dealings—responded equivocally or critically to the practices of the new industrialists. Such behavior is quite different from that usually characterized as typical of early industrial America. And yet it occurred frequently in the first decades of the industrial city. How can this pattern of behavior be explained?

Unless two misleading and erroneous conceptions are disregarded, this pattern of response seems anomalous and even meaningless. The first is the idea that the industrialist achieved status and legitimized his power quickly and easily in his local community. The second is the belief that urban property owners as a group shared a common ideology in responding to the severe dislocations resulting from rapid industrialization and in reacting to the frequent disputes between workers and factory-owners. Because Congress gave huge land grants to railroads, and state governors frequently supplied militia to "settle" industrial disputes, it does not follow that the industrialists in Paterson and other cities so dominated the local political and social structure that their freedom of action remained unchecked. Because a grocer owned his business and a mayor presided over a bank, it does not mean they sympathized with the social policies of a large factory-owner. Because Andrew Carnegie applauded Herbert Spencer, it does not mean that jungle ethics reigned supreme in the industrial city. If we are free of these distorting generalizations, it is possible to look afresh at social behavior and conflict in Gilded Age America. Take the example of the use of state troops in industrial disputes. Such action may have resulted from the low status and power the industrialist had in his local community. Unable to gain support from locally elected officials and law-enforcement groups and unable to exercise coercive power in the community, he reached upward to the state level, where direct local pressures were felt less strongly. If, as E. D. Baltzell writes, "power which is not legitimized tends to be either coercive or manipulative," much is explained by the low status of the new industrialists. Careful examination of particular local industrial conflicts that involved the use of state as opposed to local police might help explain the widespread violence and corruption so often condemned by Gilded Age historians and yet so little understood.

In nineteenth-century America, power and status had meaning on several levels of society. Here the focus is a particular community.

If the industrialist is viewed as an innovator in a local context, the Paterson events take on broader meaning. The new industrialist—especially if he came from elsewhere—was a disruptive outsider. He did not create an entirely new social structure, but he confronted an existing one. He found a more-or-less static city, which thrived on small and personal workshops and an intimate and personal way of life. It was hardly ideal, but it was settled and familiar. Making goods and employing people differently, the industrialist abruptly disrupted this "traditional" way of work and life and, as a person, symbolized severe local dislocations. The older residents and the newer workers responded to these changes in many ways. But if the industrialist, in cutting costs and rationalizing production, violated traditional community norms or made unusually new demands upon the citizenry —such as the special use of a police force or the suppression of a newspaper—his decision often provoked opposition.

The size of the industrial city and the particular composition of its population made the industrialist's innovations more visible and his power more vulnerable there than in the larger complex metropolis. Residents of the early factory town had a more direct relationship with one another and with the innovations. Even persons indirectly affected by industrialism could hardly avoid close contact with the large factory, the corporation, and the propertyless wage-earners. The closeness of the middle class and the old resident population to the new industrialism gave such persons the opportunity to judge the industrial city's social dislocations and social conflicts by personal experience, and not simply through the opaque filter of ideologies such as laissez-faire liberalism and Darwinism. In addition, the worker had more power as a consumer and as a voter and could express particular needs more effectively in the factory town than in the metropolis. Street demonstrations had a greater impact in Paterson than in New York or Chicago. In the industrial city, the retail merchant depended heavily on a narrow class of consumers (mostly workers) and the politicians appealed to more homogeneous voting groups. All of these considerations contributed to the industrialist's difficulties. So, too, did the rapid growth of the mill-town itself weaken their chances for civic and police control. A number of studies of the mobility patterns of Paterson men (three thousand fathers and sons between

1870 and 1890) show that the more ambitious and able workers found expanding opportunities outside the factories in small retail business, politics, and city employment (including the police force)—the very areas in which the industrialists demanded cooperation or control.[27] Conservative in many ways, these men had a stake in the new society. Some identified entirely with their new class and repressed their origins. But others—a large number in the early years—still had memories, roots, and relatives among the workers. Some had even suffered from the same employers they were now called on to protect. In crisis situations such as those that occurred in the 1870s, their social origins and older community ties may have created a conflict between their fellow-feeling and even family sentiment and their material achievements. The evidence does not make explicit such conflict, but it makes clear that during strikes and other crises the industrialists could not expect and did not get unswerving loyalty or approval from them.

VIII

Historians have not emphasized sufficiently the subtle and complex patterns of response to social change in nineteenth-century America—particularly to the coming of industrial capitalism. Much has been omitted in these pages : No judgement is passed on working conditions or standards of comfort in the industrial city; nothing is said of the important but little studied working class sub culture that thrived in the industrial city, and no attempt is made to precisely measure the strength of the opposing forces of workers and industrialists. The conclusions stated here are that economic power was not easily translated into social and political power, and that the changes resulting from rapid industrialization stimulated sufficient opposition to the industrialist to deprive him of the status and the authority he sought and needed. The theme of this chapter illustrates Dorothy George's (*England in Transition*, 1953) view that "social history is local history" but local history in a larger context that permits the careful examination of grand and sweeping hypotheses. It is finally suggested, indirectly, that knowledge of the early history of American industrialization and urban growth tells much about modern society and the contemporary city: its social structure, its power relationships, and its decision-making process. The nineteenth-century city differed from its twentieth-century counterpart; so much of what "makes" a city has changed in the past seventy years. In *Victorian Cities* (1963), Asa Briggs wisely argued for historical specificity and interdisciplinary approaches to the study of nineteenth-century cities. Free of the nostalgia of those historians who compare the "city" only to the "country" but sensitive to the acute social disorganization that accompanied rapid industrialization and urban development, Briggs showed that different British cities each had a distinct history (shaped by particular inner social patterns) and also that their histories should not be confused with the later city so powerfully affected by radical innovations such as the automobile, the national corporation, and the revolution in communications. All too often, however, social scientists and even historians view the contemporary city in exceedingly ahistorical terms or only study its past by projecting present "trends" backward. For them, as Barrington Moore notes, the past becomes "merely a storehouse of samples," and "facts" are "drawn upon as if they were colored balls from an urn." Stephan Thernstrom's pioneering study of nineteenth-century Newburyport, Massachusetts, *Poverty Progress* (1964), splendidly illustrates the grave pitfalls of an ahistorical view of urban social mobility. It further shows that however carefully the present is studied and however refined the techniques of analysis, the present is not fully comprehended if the past is ignored or distorted.

Class and status altered as the industrial city matured. The industrialist's power became legitimized. The factories and their owners dug deeper into the lives of the mill towns and became more accepted and powerful. The old middle class, and those who revered the old, precorporate town, lost influence and disappeared. They were replaced by others who identified more fully with the corporate community. The city government became more bureaucratic and less responsive to popular pressures. Why and how these changes occurred remain important subjects for study. But in order to grasp the magnitude of these changes it is necessary to discard the notion that the nineteenth-century factory-owners moved into control of the industrial town overnight. This myth masks reality and prevents us from focusing on the differences between the nineteenth-century city and the contemporary city. If these differences are located and analyzed, "trends" no longer seem timeless, and the "modern condition"—so often tied to the "urban condition"—assumes a meaningful historical dimension because it is rooted in an understandable past.

NOTES

1. A pioneer study on this subject is Robert K. Lamb, "The Entrepreneur and the Community," in William Miller (ed.), *Men in Business* (New York: Harper & Row, 1952), pp. 91–117. The examples drawn upon in Blake McKelvey's study *The Urbanisation of America* (New Brunswick, N.J.: Rutgers University Press, 1963) show how little attention historians have given to the industrial city. Vera Shlakman's *An Economic History of a Factory Town* (Northampton, Mass.: Smith College, 1936) is the classic in the field but devotes little attention to the factory and the community at large. Any of the numerous labor histories can be consulted for any period of time to notice quickly how little attention labor historians have given to the industrial city.

2. Max Weber, *Max Weber: Essays in Sociology*, trans. and ed. by H. H. Gerth and C. Wright Mills (New York: Oxford University Press, 1946). 180.

3. Robert M. MacIver, *The Web of Government* (New York: The Macmillan Co., 1947), p. 83.

4. Data on the growth of Paterson's manufacturing industries comes from the 1850, 1860, and 1870 unpublished schedules for manufactures of the U.S. Census deposited in the New Jersey State Library, Trenton, New Jersey, and the following works: L. R. Trumbull, *A History of Industrial Paterson* (Paterson: C. M. Harrick, printer, 1882); Charles Shriner, *Paterson, New Jersey: Its Advantages for Manufacturing and Residences* (Paterson: The Press Printing and Publishing Co., 1892).

5. Details on the Paterson cotton industry are found in Trumbull, *History*, pp. 50–69.

6. The locomotive, machinery, and tool and iron industries of Paterson are described in detail in Trumbull, *History*, pp. 72–148. But see also the *Annual Reports* of the Paterson Board of Trade (Paterson: n.p.) that started to appear in 1873. A good early detailed survey on all Paterson industries is found in *Scientific America* 1 (October 29, November 5, 12, 19, 1859).

7. Especially useful information on the early development of the Paterson silk industry is in Trumbull, *History*, pp. 149–57, 176–253; Shriner, *Paterson*, pp. 196–206; William Wycoff, "Report on the Silk Manufacturing Industry."

Tenth Census of the United States, 1880. Statistics of Manufacture (Washington: U.S. Govt, Printing Office, 1883), 905–35; Victor S. Clark, *History of Manufactures in the United States, 1860–1893,* II (New York: McGraw Hill Book Co., Inc., 1929), 449–58. The reports of the New Jersey Bureau of Labor Statistics also are filled with much useful but scattered information on the silk manufacture. The 1878–1880 reports have been especially useful in this study.

8. Population data is found in *Tenth Census, 1880, Statistics of the Population* (Washington: U.S. Govt. Printing Office, 1883), 452, 671, 855–59. Information on retail enterprise comes from the 1859 and 1870 *Paterson City Directory* (Paterson: n.p.).

9. The severity of the depression in Paterson is described in *Chicago Times,* October 31, 1873; *New York Sun,* September 3, 1876; *The Socialist* (New York), April 29, 1876; *Chicago Tribune,* August 4, 1877; *New York World,* February 23, 1877; Paterson Board of Trade, *Annual Report, 1877* (Paterson, 1878), 13–17 and *Annual Report, 1880* (Paterson, 1881), 18–19; L. R. Trumbull, *History,* 147–48.

10. Background information on the 1877 ribbon weavers' strike is found in *Labor Standard* (New York), January 20–June 16, 1877; *New York Times,* May 15, June 20–23, 1877; *Paterson Guardian,* June 11, 19, 21, 25, July 10, 14, 1877; *Paterson Weekly Press,* June 21, 1877; Silk Association of America, *Sixth Annual Report, 1878* (New York: n.p., 1878), 15–17.

11. Pertinent editorial comment is in *Paterson Guardian,* June 21, 25, July 10, 14, 25, 30, 1877, and *Paterson Press,* July 5, 11, 12, 21, 1877. Full details on court action against the strikers and the postponement of trials is in *Paterson Guardian,* July 14, 17, 21, 25, 26, 27, 28, 31, 1877; *Paterson Press,* July 14, 16, 20, 1877; *Chicago Tribune,* August 4, 1877.

12. Biographical information on Benjamin Buckley is in E. H. Haines (ed.), *Paterson, New Jersey, 1792–1892. Centennial Edition of the Evening News* (Paterson: Evening News, 1892), 63; the composition of the Paterson Board of Trade is detailed in its *Third Annual Report, 1876* (Paterson, 1877), 88–90; the role of the Board of Trade is described in *Paterson Guardian,* July 31, August 1, 2, 3, 4, 1877; *Paterson Press,* July 31, August 1, 2, 1877.

13. Buckley's response to the Board of Trade is in *Paterson Guardian,* July 28, August 2, 3, 4, 5, 1877; *Paterson Press,* August 7, 8, 15, 1877. The action of the aldermen is in *Paterson Guardian,* August 7, 8, 1877, and *Paterson Press,* August 7, 8, 1877. Biographical information about the aldermen is in the *Paterson City Directory,* 1871–1872, 1877–1878, 1880-1881, 1887–1888.

14. Editorial comment on failure of the Board of Trade is in *Paterson Guardian,* August 16, 1877. Manufacturer talk about a city militia is found in *Paterson*

Press, August 15, 1877, and the early history of the Paterson militia is detailed in John Hilton, "Paterson's Militia," in Shriner, *Paterson*, 89–97. Failure by the manufacturers to enlarge the police force can be traced in the *Annual Reports of the City Government for* 1877, 1878, 1879, 1880, and 1886 (Paterson: n.p.).

15. A detailed history of the R. & H. Adams firm is found in Trumbull, *History*, 208–12, and an obituary of Henry Adams appears in *American Silk Journal* (June, 1890), 137–38.

16. Much information on the strike and community attitudes toward it are found in *Labor Standard* (New York), July 7, 14, 21, 28, August 4, 11, 18, 25, September 7, 14, 1878; *Paterson Guardian*, July 23, August 22, September 3, 5, 9, 14, 1878; *Paterson Press*, August 16, 17, 21, 22, 1878; *Irish World* (New York), September 21, 1878. Early issues of the *Paterson Labor Standard* that illustrate support for McDonnell from retail storekeepers are dated November 23, December 7, 1878.

17. The failure of the effort to bring in Fall River workers is found in *Paterson Guardian*, September 9, 10, 11, 12, 1878; *Paterson Press*, September 13, 1878; *New York Sun*, n.d., reprinted in *Labor Standard*, September 14, 21, 1878. The role of city officials and courts is in *Paterson Guardian*, August 14, September 9, 24, October 1, 1878; *Paterson Press*, October 1, 2, 3, 1878; *Labor Standard*, August 18, October 5, 1878. The end of the strike and the defeat of Adams can be traced in *Irish World* (New York), September 28, October 5, 19, 1878; *Paterson Labor Standard*, November 23, December 7, 1878; *Fall River Labor Standard*, October 30, December 14, 1878; *Paterson Press*, October 27, November 22, 1878.

18. Details on McDonnell's career are found in obituaries reprinted in *Paterson Labor Standard*, January 20, 1906, and "Interview with Mrs. J. P. McDonnell, 1908," McDonnell Mss., Wisconsin State Historical Society. Useful background material on the London milieux from which McDonnell came to the United States is found in Royden Harrison, *Before the Socialists. Studies in Labour and Politics, 1861 to 1881* (London: Routledge & Kegan Paul, 1965), 210–45. The Wisconsin Historical Society holds two manuscript lectures that McDonnell delivered in 1873–1875 and other useful information about his career before coming to Paterson is found in *New York Times*, February 17, 1874, and August 8, 1877; *National Labor Tribune*, May 8, August 7, September 28, October 16, 23, 1875, and March 4, 1876; *The Socialist*, April 15, June 19, 1876; *Labor Standard*, August 12, November 11, 1876, January 27, August 4, 1877; *New York Commercial Advertiser*, n.d., reprinted in *Labor Standard*, August 19, 1876; *Utica Observer*, n.d., reprinted in *Labor Standard*, March 3, 1877.

19. The author possesses a microfilm copy of McDonnell's 1878 Grand Jury

indictment; the original is in the Passaic County Courthouse, Paterson, New Jersey. Detailed reports on his first trial appear in *Paterson Guardian*, *Paterson Press*, and *Paterson Labor Standard*, October 20–November 10, 1878. The same newspapers contain materials on the 1880 trial in issues published between January 1 and April 5, 1880.

20. A biographical sketch of McDonnell's lawyer, Thomas Hoxsey, appears in Shriner, *Paterson*, 312. See also *Irish World*, November 3, 1877. Occupational information on the jury is found in *Paterson City Directory*, 1877–1878 and 1880–1881. John Daggers, the manufacturer and lay judge, who urged leniency in sentencing McDonnell, had the details of his life recorded in Shriner, *Paterson*, 209–10, and McDonnell later wrote warmly about him in *Paterson Labor Standard*, November 27, 1897, and November 3, 1898. Details on the payment of McDonnell's fine are found in Henry Rose to the editor, *Indianapolis Times*, November 2, 1878; *Paterson Labor Standard*, n.d., reprinted in *The Socialist* (Chicago), November 23, 1878; *Paterson Guardian*, October 26, 1878; *Paterson Press*, October 26, 1878.

21. The political tumult that followed McDonnell's trial is fully described (but in a partisan fashion) in *Paterson Guardian*, October 27, 28, 29, 30, November 1, 4, 5, 1878; *Paterson Press*, October 27, November 2, 4, 5, 1878; *Paterson Labor Standard*, November 23, December 7, 1878; *Passaic City Herald*, n.d., reprinted in *The Socialist* (Chicago), November 23, 1878.

22. McDonnell's prison diary is the most useful source for judging his support while in prison, and the manuscript copy is deposited in the Wisconsin State Historical Society. The names of his visitors have been checked to the *City Directory* for 1880–1881. Much additional information is found in *Paterson Labor Standard*, January 3, 24, 31, March 13, 20, 27, 1880; *Paterson Guardian*, January 30, 31, February 2, 3, 1880; *Paterson Press*, January 30, 31, February 2, 3, 1880; *Fall River Labor Standard*, February 28, 1880; *Irish World*, March 6, 13, 1880; *The Trades* (Philadelphia), March 13, 1880. Details on McDonnell's lawyer, former Republican Mayor Socrates Tuttle, appear in Shriner, *Paterson*, 319–20.

23. Here, again, McDonnell's prison diary offers the most evidence on his jail experiences. But see also the biographical sketch of Warden John Buckley in Haines (ed.), *Centennial Paterson*, 146.

24. McDonnell's release from prison and the celebration that followed are detailed in his manuscript diary, *Irish World*, April 17, 1880, *Paterson Press*, April 2, 1880, and *Fall River Labor Standard*, April 10, 1880. McDonnell's role in the New Jersey Federation of Trades and Labor Unions is detailed in its annual reports, and his work as Deputy Factory Inspector is noted in the *Annual Reports* of the Factory Inspector that appeared between 1884 and 1886.

25. *Paterson Labor Standard*, October 31, 1896.

26. Herbert G. Gutman, "The Buena Vista Affair," *The Pennsylvania Magazine of History and Biography*, 88 (July, 1964), 251–93. "The Workers' Search for Power," in H. Wayne Morgan (ed.), *The Gilded Age; A Reappraisal* (Syracuse: Syracuse University Press, 1963), pp. 38–68. "The Braidwood Lockout of 1874," Illinois State Historical Society, *Journal*, 53 (1960), 5–28. "An Iron Workers' Strike in the Ohio Valley," *The Ohio Historical Quarterly*, 58 (1959), 353–70. "Trouble on the Railroads in 1873–1874," *Labor History*, 2 (1961), 215–35.

27. Drawing from all fathers and sons in three wards as listed in the unpublished 1870 manuscript census, this study traces occupational mobility over a twenty-year period. Males listed in the 1870 census are searched for in the *Paterson City Directory 1887–1888*. Comparisons in the occupation of the father over this period as well as between the fathers and the sons are made. More than thirty per cent of the males listed in 1870 census have been traced and located in the later directory. Careful comparison of the *Paterson City Directory* between 1865 and 1885 makes it possible to trace the social origins of Paterson policemen, politicians, and small businessmen. In 1877–78, for example, the city had twenty patrolmen. Eight had been policemen in 1870. Six others had been workers in 1870. In 1877–78, at least five policemen, all different from the six who had been workers in 1870, had close female and male relatives who worked in the Paterson factories. Similar patterns occur for small retail businessmen.

9

Career Leadership and American Trade Unionism

by DAVID BRODY

In an essay in 1928, the labor writer J. B. S. Hardman imagined a conversation between a union president (XYZ) and His Younger Self (HYS).

HYS: ...Look what you have become. Is that what I meant to grow into?

XYZ: Why, a leader of labor, that was your dream.

HYS: No, old man, you are not a leader of labor, you are a labor leader.

XYZ: What is the difference?

HYS: All the difference in the world. One is a fighter, the other a professional.[1]

The hypothetical Younger Self was drawing a distinction vital in the history of American organized labor. Its leaders became professionals: they were paid, they worked full time, their offices became careers. Peculiarly an attribute of pure-and-simple unionism, professionalism helped shape the conservative movement.

American trade unionism took permanent form in the last decades of the nineteenth century. As pure-and-simple doctrine prevailed over

288

reformism, as the organizational structure crystallized and the trade unions stabilized, the career leaders emerged. The International Association of Machinists, for instance, began in the South in 1888 as a fraternal-benevolent order plus some reform notions derived from the Knights of Labor. Inside of half a dozen years the Machinists became, as their historian Mark Perlman put it, "a job-oriented trade union." The IAM simultaneously developed a career officialdom. When he took office in 1893, president James O'Connell assumed that men should be paid, and paid adequately, to do the union's work. The lack of an expense account bothered him. "This is certainly an injustice to your executive officer," he complained at the 1895 convention. "You should not ask him to expend the greater portion of his salary for hotel bills. . . ." O'Connell also urged the IAM to hire organizers. The first were appointed the next year to cover Chicago, New York, Cleveland, and Lynn, Massachusetts. The International Association of Machinists completed the professionalization of its leadership when full-time officers replaced the lay members of the executive board in 1925.[2]

The same process occurred at the local level. The early butchers' unions, for example, suffered from the rapid turnover of officers. They resigned to enter business or, as one unionist complained in 1902, refused "to keep their old offices, for they were tired of the hard work they had done for our local." The answer was to pay for leadership. "It is going to cost us a great deal at first," another member reasoned, "but in my opinion it is the only way that we can make a success of the union. . . . We will have a man in the field all the time, and he is a hustler. . . ." One by one, the surviving butchers' unions arrived at that conclusion. In the 1920s, the powerful Chicago local employed "high class fellows . . . who could go out and do business." The secretary received one hundred and fifty dollars a week, the business agents, one hundred dollars. "The local's business representatives," an admiring visitor from the West Coast reported in 1926, "were recognized as men of affairs and . . . all of them make their rounds in modern cars."[3] Such career men had long since become familiar figures in the labor circles of American cities.

Professionalization normally proceeded unremarkably from cumulative administrative decisions, and thus rarely became an explicit issue in the conflict between trade and reform unionism. The United

Brotherhood of Carpenters and Joiners provided the important exception. Peter J. McGuire, who founded the national union in 1881 and organized many of the local bodies, was a labor reformer. He saw trade unions not as ends in themselves, but as a means "to educate our class, to prepare it for the changes to come, to establish a system of co-operative industry in place of the wage system. . . ." Meanwhile, the carpenters' locals and district bodies in the 1880s began to employ business agents, a notoriously hard headed crew whose vision ended with wages, hours, and working conditions. McGuire and the business agents clashed over fundamental differences, among them the creation of a national officialdom. The business agents pressed for salaried, full-time national officers and organizers. At the time, only the secretary-treasurer—McGuire—received an income from the national union. For more than a decade, Secretary McGuire used his powerful hold on the rank-and-file to fight off the local professionals. They finally brought him down, old and sick, on charges of malfeasance in office in 1902, and drove him out of the organization. Then at last the carpenters followed the leadership pattern already fixed among national unions in the American movement.[4]

In the formative years, the reform opponents of pure-and-simple unionism seemed typically indifferent to building careers from their labor activities. Their work was selfless and idealistic; or it was accompanied by other ambitions; or, curiously, it combined the two. William Sylvis of the National Labor Union and Peter McGuire exemplified the first attitude. Terence V. Powderly came close to the second. He never conceived of the top post of the Knights of Labor as a permanent career, nor even as a full-time one while he held it. In 1882–83, Powderly served simultaneously as mayor of Scranton, county health officer, the operator of a coffee and tea business, and Grand Master Workman. And he also jockeyed openly for political appointment, an ambition he finally fulfilled after supporting William McKinley in 1896. Eugene Debs combined idealism with an outside career. When he forthrightly attacked craft unionism after many years as secretary of the Locomotive Firemen, Debs also anticipated a comfortable and happier livelihood as writer and lecturer.[5]

After 1900, contrasting attitudes towards career leadership became more sharply defined. The new radical unions abhorred professionalism.

They feared what one member of the Western Federation of Miners called "the peculiar point of view which always comes to a man that occupies an executive position for any length of time." Militancy would shrivel under that influence. So the independent Butte Miners' Union, adopting a constitution in 1914, permitted only one paid officer (the president), compensated him only for days worked, and limited him to a single term of six months.[6] The Industrial Workers of the World incessantly fought careerism. When the organization was one year old, President Charles O. Sherman was ousted and his office abolished. "The labor fakirs," Vincent St. John later explained, "strove to fasten themselves upon the organization that they might continue to exist if the new union was a success." The "decentralizing" faction carried the point to a logical conclusion in 1913 : eliminate all national offices and the national convention as well. "We are ... working to overthrow this [wages] system and we ... claim ... that the rank and file of the proletariat will have to do this themselves." The demand went too far even for the IWW. Still, if organized activity required leadership, the corrupting consequences had to be fought and the careerists constantly rooted out.[7]

So career leadership as a normal and accepted phenomenon was restricted to pure-and-simple unionism. Equally significant, the tendency was especially marked in the American movement. Recently, data has become available that permits a comparison of the extent of professionalism in the trade unions of six countries during the past decade : in the United States, the ratio of full-time officials to union members was one to three hundred; in Denmark, one to seven hundred and seventy-five; in Australia, one to nine hundred; in Sweden, one to one thousand seven hundred; in Norway, one to two thousand two hundred; in Britain, one to close to four thousand.[8] By a wide margin, the American movement maximized the number of career places in its structure. What was there in the American situation that encouraged this distinctive characteristic of American trade-union leadership?

Part of the answer rested in attitudes that American labor shared with the larger society. The sociologist Seymour Lipset has pointed to "the achievement-equalitarian syndrome" of American society. "The emphasis on pecuniary success, combined with the absence of the kind of class consciousness characteristic of more aristocratic societies . . . served to motivate workers to use the labor movement itself as an avenue to financial and status gain." Lipset's thesis finds support in the comparison with English experience. In his illuminating book *Weekend in Dinlock*, Clancy Sigal noted that Yorkshire miners viewed career union leaders with "unbounded, if tolerant and humorous, contempt, the measure being that a man loses worth according to the distance he puts between himself and the coal face." When asked in a recent survey what "social standing" other people ascribed to union officials, English labor leaders revealed a significant contradiction. Most thought a middle-class level or higher. But many also were disturbed by the question, and a few even doubted its propriety : union leaders ought not to be set above the rank and file. "If they 'aspired' to some other 'social standing' they would be betraying the trust put in them by their fellow members," one officer wrote.[9] Such disapproval had little force in a society that demanded everyone rise as far as he could; that denied the importance of class distinctions; and that expected voluntary associations, trade unions included, to pay their functionaries. American social values thus encouraged men to seek, and the labor movement to provide advancement through leadership careers.

The pure-and-simple thrust of American trade unionism, in addition, created a need for career men. From the outset, as Philip Taft has observed, American workingmen organized chiefly to defend their job interests.[10] Their unions assumed economic functions that rapidly professionalized the leadership. In his excellent study of the Carpenters' Union, Robert A. Christie arrived at this explanation for the early appearance of the business agents. The local unions initially undertook to combat the piecework system favored by building contractors, and then to organize and control the local labor market. The Carpenters quickly discovered that only full-time, paid functionaries could handle these demanding tasks.[11] That conclusion followed wherever trade unions allocated jobs, maintained apprenticeship programs, policed agreements, and protected employers against nonunion competition. Collective bargaining—the primary union function—made an especially heavy demand for men skilled in formulating, negotiating, and interpreting contracts. Even at an early point, the issues could

be complex—the sliding scale in the iron industry, for example—
and bargaining itself always called for an experienced, knowledgeable
hand. Hence the plea of the Syracuse butchers' union to the national
office for "someone to help get our Next Contracts signed. There is
no one here who is experienced in this line."[12] Company unions
suffered on this score. Studying the experience of the Colorado Fuel
and Iron Company, one investigator concluded that many steelworkers
"felt that they themselves lacked the training and experience to be
able to meet company officials and other specialists ... on an equal
footing. They needed the aid of union officials who have become expert
in representing the interests of the wage-earners."[13] The relationship
worked in reverse as well. The radical unions, disliking careerists, had
less need for professionalism : they also rejected collective bargaining.

So, in essential ways, career leadership grew from basic characteristics of American labor : its social attitudes and its narrow economic
orientation. The influences, however, ran both ways. Professionalism
affected the nature of the labor movement. The career factor did not
operate alone; it was a contributing, secondary influence. But in that
limited way, assuredly the career needs of labor leaders did serve as a
determinant to the American movement.

Powerful motives were at work. In addition to its avowed function
of representing American workingmen, trade unionism raised a fortunate number entirely out of the blue-collar class. In the mid-1940s
C. Wright Mills made a pioneering study of top labor officials. They
turned out to be predominately working-class in origin. Only one in
ten came from families in the middle class of professionals, executives,
and entrepreneurs. At the time they embarked on trade-union careers,
75 per cent themselves worked at trades.[14] The labor movement gave
them a chance—perhaps the most accessible to American workers—
for steep upward mobility. The sharp break occurred at the first move
into either of the two paid jobs, organizer or business agent, available
to beginning careerists. Job security increased, income rose and, above
all, the white-collar world of offices, suits, and flexible schedules opened
up. Rewards rose commensurate with progress up the ladder. Not
counting expense accounts, salaries reached $9,500 and above for one
third of all union presidents in 1944, and $7,500 and over for the same
proportion of other national officers. Their style of life became, as

C. Wright Mill observed, "like that of any middle-class businessman in an urban area."[15] Nor should the sweet satisfactions of power and influence be discounted. The stakes of office, running as high as they did, could not fail to influence the decisions of American labor leaders.

Radicals grew vociferous on this point. Eugene Debs (who once boasted sardonically of his "modest distinction" as the only national leader ever "to resign his office after being unanimously re-elected and given the privilege of fixing his own salary") explained the AFL reaction to the IWW : "Who is it that is so violently opposed to the Industrial Workers? It is not the rank and file of the trade unions. It is their officers. And why. . . ? For the reason that when the working class are really united a great many labor leaders will be let out of jobs. . . . Let me say to you that their interests are primarily in keeping themselves there."[16] Polemical as the attack was, it rested on a solid respect for the office-holding influence. That partly explained why many radicals preferred dual-union tactics over boring from within. Daniel De Leon warned "that the pure and simple leaders give jobs to Socialists for the purpose of corrupting them. . . ." The IWW agitator Joseph Ettor in 1914 answered the borers from within in the same way.

> The theory that what is needed to save the [American] Federation [of Labor] is the energetic and vigorous men who are now in the I.W.W. is on a par with the "socialist" advice of how to save the nation . . . roll up our sleeves and become active politically within capitalism. . . . We tried, but the more we fooled with the beast the more it *captured us* . . . We learned at an awful cost particularly this : That the most unscrupulous labor fakers now betraying the workers were once our "industrialist," "anarchist," and "socialist" comrades, who . . .were not only lost, but . . . became the supporters of the old and [the] most serious enemies of the new.[17]

What could be more telling testimony to the power of careerism : that it kept radicals at a distance from the trade unions.

The career influence pervaded the American labor movement. The economic orientation itself reflected the inclination of the American worker and, at best, labor leaders could only encourage that powerful bent. It was more important that they directed the economic impulse into channels that best met career needs.

Many union objectives were obtainable through government action. Yet until the 1930s the American Federation of Labor staunchly opposed most labor legislation. Public measures were desired only for defensive reasons—for instance, to curb the courts and immigration—and for groups incapable of acting in their own behalf. Law, Gompers was arguing in 1914, should "free people from the shackles and give them a chance to work out their own salvation." Among its other sources, voluntarism sprang from the career requirements of trade-union leaders. Legislation had this drawback : it minimized the functions of the unions and their officials. Compulsory unemployment insurance, William Green warned, would "pull at our vitals and destroy our trade union structure."[18] When the New York retail butchers' unions finally won a state Sunday closing law in 1901, a prominent official privately warned that they were thereby cutting away their own ground. The butchers soon came to the same conclusion; the regulation of hours, at first pursued through political means, became the subject of collective bargaining.

Economic action, not legislation, satisfied two essentials for professional leadership. First, it built up the permanent, dues-paying membership on which careers depended. Workingmen had to receive "something tangible for their money" that would "induce [them] to join the Union or to keep themselves in good standing after joining."[19] No activity did this better than collective bargaining. (Many trade unions also experimented with insurance benefits and, in the early years, cooperative ventures, but these alternatives received emphasis mainly when collective bargaining failed.) The objective was, in any case, clear enough. As Hardman's hypothetical union president said, "It pays our people to belong to the organization." Second, collective bargaining was the taxing, continuing activity that required a professional hand. By monopolizing the collective-bargaining functions, officials maximized the volume of career-creating work. American unions created no counterpart for the European (particularly German) works councils that handled negotiations at the plant level.[20] Nor, on the other hand, would trade-union leaders share their economic responsibilities either with government agencies or with the American

Federation of Labor (hence its relative unimportance in the American movement).

Nonpartisan politics likewise best fitted the career needs of the leadership. Of course, there were strong practical and ideological reasons not to establish an independent party, but so was the logic of professionalism. A labor party would rest on a broad constituency and create jobs of a different kind and in a different framework. The prospects for political careers would certainly expand for individual trade-union leaders. (Even under nonpartisanship, some unionists did enter public life, more often through appointment than election.) But a regular channel, secure and predictable for career men, could not be erected between the union hierarchies and even a successful labor party. That had proved the case in Great Britain.[21] Nor did a trade-union career provide the kind of base, as did law and business, that would remain secure while a man pursued politics. As in England, a labor party would doubtless be exploited by the middle-class intellectuals and thus violate Gompers' injunction—itself an aspect of professionalism—"that leadership in the labor movement could be safely entrusted only to those ... [with] the experience of earning their bread by daily labor."[22] On the other hand, union officials did go into local politics, through independent organizations and, more regularly, within the established parties.[23] At the local level, no conflict existed between a union career and political involvement; both could occur simultaneously and in fact be connected. Labor's political ends in the state and nation, however, were better pursued through the nonpartisan, lobbying activities that did not force a departure from the career base in the trade unions.

The career influence also played on the internal life of American labor unions. Characteristically, live politics gave way to one-party government as a union matured. The ruling group tended to become permanent and opposition, illegitimate. The formal democratic process remained, but not the substance. This instance of Michel's "iron law of oligarchy" sprang largely from the monopoly of political weapons by the administration and from the indifference and isolation of the rank and file. But it resulted also from the professionalization of leadership.[24]

For one thing, career men acquired the skills of the politician no less than those of negotiator and organizer. Consider, for example, the thoughts of Hardman's President XYZ on his way to an international labor conference in Europe:

> All in all it was not quite easy to put the trip matter straight. Brother A had to be promised the post of representative on the national Advisory Council, and B served notice that he meant to get a seat on the General Executive Board at the next convention. That would mean a good deal of trouble next spring. . . . The Pennsylvania boys would have to be "satisfied," and that would upset the balance of power. . . . It was not easy to sidetrack [B]. Yes, there was that bank possibility for which he was likely to fall and which, if things went right, would take him out of the field. . . . In the meantime one would do well to watch the game very closely.
> XYZ . . . knows of what material human beings are made of. . . . Ambition must be played on. . . . The larger the number of people involved, the more intricate the political game. . . . One must calculate, bargain, gamble, buy, sell. . . . No, XYZ would let no one snatch things from under his hands. And once an issue is raised he will fight it out. . . . In politics only the terms of a deal may be negotiated, not the issue of leadership.[25]

Here, honed by years of experience, was the fine political edge that ensured control of America's trade unions.

Beyond the skills, professionalism created the primary motives for oligarchical rule. The free play of the democratic process could only hinder their job, as labor leaders conceived it. "The administration of labor is an art," said Hardman's hypothetical XYZ, "and it requires knowledge. . . . Centralized action. . . . No open forum exercises."[26] It was not only a leader's sense of competence pitted against aspiring rivals and the uninformed membership. To the professional leader, opposition spelled factionalism. His organisation would lose economic force and, simultaneously, would face irresponsible demands and strikes. Collective bargaining could not be properly directed under those disturbing circumstances. To build a stable relationship with an employer, an astute official might assume the delicate role of mediating union and management interests. If he had broader concerns—for instance, a desire to gain employer support for organizing purposes—he might at times even lean toward the company position on a contested point. As a prerequisite for such a role, of course, he needed the free hand that came only from unquestioned one-party rule.[27]

Finally, a powerful personal factor was at work. The career leader had high stakes in his office. What would defeat mean? To return to a manual job involved an intolerable decline in status and income. In a few unions, such as actors' or printers', the gap between leaders and members remained narrow, and little was lost in the return to the trade. These unions, significantly, retained the democratic process. The International Typographical Union, in fact, evolved a genuine two-party system. The other alternative for the defeated leader, the one usually taken after the early years of the labor movement, was to leave the union.[28] But the labor leader was a political man, not a bureaucrat. Unlike his management counterpart at the bargaining table, he could not circulate without fundamentally altering his future. For his career depended on the support he commanded inside his union—a nontransferable commodity. A post with another union would necessarily be appointive and dependent. A management job signified, in addition, that he was selling out. These hard choices compelled the labor leader to follow a course that would preclude defeat. And the democratic process paid the price.

The leadership view of union members as a dues-paying clientele exerted a broad influence. Jurisdiction, for one thing, naturally became a matter of large importance. Labor unions mapped out their boundaries precisely and exclusively, and even so fought endlessly among themselves over disputed territory. The clientele idea also encouraged the peculiar emphasis on security arrangements—the union shop and the checkoff—which would stabilize and guarantee membership. Finally, it helped shape the approach to organizing the unorganized. The Machinists wanted to send a man into the East because "it would be a profitable investment for us to take earnest efforts to organize that section. . . ."[29] The conception of organizing as a kind of business venture—so much invested, so many members gained—clearly reflected the idea of membership as a clientele. And that narrow calculation, among other things, explained why the attempts to organize the mass-production industries consistently fell short.

Did the influence of career leadership extend to the industrial unions that emerged during the 1930s? A special situation dominated those first years. To a large extent, the unionizing impulse came from the ranks, and with it a marked resistance to outside direction. Control, asserted one CIO man, should rest in "the whole body, in one, acting as one. All of these collectively comprise your leadership."[30] The outlook resulted, among other things, in the spontaneous strikes of the mid-1930s and in the opposition to appointed officials within the Auto Workers, Rubber Workers, and other emerging industrial unions. The recruitment of officers was likewise abnormal. The rank-and-filers and left-wingers catapulted into leadership were motivated— to use Lipset's distinction—more by a calling than by career ambitions. In 1941 a local UAW official who had lost his post wrote:

... I have given serious thought as to whether to accept an organizational job outside of auto at this time, and I don't think it advisable as there is a job to be done and if I leave it means I would be running away from it. It's no use running some place else and losing here. ... I am now back in the shop at $48.00 per with my nose to the grindstone as an electrician and the first week has been a tough one although most of the boys made a large fuss and were glad to see me. My chief Steward resigned so that I could be elected in his place so that I could be in a position to function for the Union immediately [sic]. Boy, did that get the managements [sic] goat.[30]

Although the calling still dominated, clearly the career influence was working among such fresh recruits to labor leadership. There was, moreover, an unusual circulation of professionals into the new unions, mainly from the Mine Workers and Clothing Workers. Their counsel and, where they were able to sustain it, their rule followed closely the standard, professional line. On the whole, however, the career factor was relatively weak in the leadership of the new unions. And, as B. J. Widick has remarked, the CIO then seemed to have the character of a social movement.

Yet from the start it was also in the main line of American trade unionism. The industrial unions always aimed for collective bargaining, and they were fighting for that alone in the bitterest strikes of the 1930s. The CIO was more concerned with political and social issues than the AFL, but by a matter of degree, not kind; and the distance narrowed with the passage of time. The industrial-union leaders similarly functioned as full-time, paid officials. Although some part of the original calling remained, in time they did not differ essentially from their counterparts in the AFL. Here, as earlier, the demands of bargaining unionism forced professionalism on the leadership. Indeed, the pressures intensified because modern problems, centralized negotiations, and the expanded role of government—the National Labor Relations Board and then the wartime regulation of labor relations—required more skills and time from union officers. But, again, becoming professional, they developed the career needs that would influence CIO organization in the same ways as they had the AFL unions.

All historians of American labor eventually come to the fundamental question: why the uniqueness of the American movement? Obviously, the explanation resides in the special character of the American social and economic order. The major interpreters—John R. Commons, Robert Hoxie, Selig Perlman—have suggested the general shaping elements, but they have been less successful in tracing the functional connections between the setting and the movement.[31] Career leadership was one such tie, arising from the characteristics in the society and acting steadily on American organized labor. The career influence never worked alone, nor could it be counted as decisive, but assuredly it contributed in a pervasive way to making American trade unionism what it is today.

NOTES

1. J. B. S. Hardman, "Stakes of Leadership," in Hardman (ed.), *American Labor Dynamics* (New York: Harcourt, Brace and Co., 1928), p. 163.

2. Mark Perlman, *The Machinists* (Cambridge: Harvard University Press, 1961), pp. 21, 187, 294, 297, App. I.

3. Amalgamated Meat Cutters and Butcher Workmen of North America, *Official Journal* (June, 1902), pp. 15–16. Amalgamated Meat Cutters, *Proceedings* (1926), pp. 79–80. *Butcher Workman* (November, 1926), p. 7.

4. Robert A. Christie, *Empire in Wood* (Ithaca: Cornell University Press, 1956), pp. 62–64.

5. Jonathan Grossman, *William Sylvis, Pioneer of American Labor* (New York: Columbia University Press, 1945), pp. 189, 262, and *passim*. N. J. Ware, *The Labor Movement in the United States, 1860–1895* (New York: D. Appleton & Co., 1929), pp. 80–84. Ray Ginger, *The Bending Cross* (New Brunswick: Rutgers University Press, 1949), chaps. 3, 4.

6. Vernon H. Jensen, *Heritage of Conflict* (Ithaca: Cornell University Press, 1950), pp. 182, 343.

7. Paul F. Brissenden, *The I.W.W.: A Study of American Syndicalism* (New York: Columbia University Press, 1928), pp. 137, 308–309.

8. Seymour M. Lipset, *The First New Nation* (New York: Basic Books, 1963), p. 192. In checking Lipset's source for Great Britain, H. A. Clegg, A. J. Killick, and Rex Adams, *Trade Union Officers* (Oxford: B. Blackwell and Co., 1961), p. 38, I found errors in transcription that led Lipset to put the ratio at 1:2000.

9. Lipset, *Nation*, p. 189. Clancy Sigal, *Weekend in Dinlock* (Boston: Houghton Mifflin Co., 1960), p. 73. Clegg, Killick, and Adams, *Officers*, pp. 72–73.

10. Philip Taft, "On the Origins of Business Unionism," *Industrial and Labor Relations Review*, XVII (October, 1963), 20–38.

11. Christie, *Empire*, pp. 61–65.

12. W. R. Satterlee, Local 1, to Patrick Gorman, January 5, 1938, files, Amalgamated Meat Cutters and Butcher Workmen of North America.

13. Ben M. Selekman, *Employes' Representation in Steel Works* (New York: Russell Sage Foundation, 1924), p. 172.

14. C. Wright Mills, *The New Men of Power* (New York: Harcourt, Brace & Co., 1948), pp. 88–95. Mills' survey does show, however, that while labor leaders were drawn from the blue-collar class, they also tended to have relatively more education and to come from skilled jobs.

15. Philip Taft, "Understanding Union Administration," *Harvard Business Review*, XXIV (Winter, 1946), 253–57. Mills, *New Men*, p. 103. On the high status of trade union leaders in the popular estimate—equal to that of executives and proprietors—see C. C. North and P. K. Hatt, "Jobs and Occupations: A Popular Evaluation," in L. Wilson and W. A. Kolb (eds.), *Sociological Analysis* (New York: Harcourt, Brace & Co., 1949), pp. 464–73.

16. *Speeches and Writings of Eugene V. Debs*, introd. by A. M. Schlesinger, Jr. (New York: Hermitage Press, 1948), pp. 181, 444.

17. Quoted in Brissenden, I.W.W., pp. 88, 308–309.

18. Marc Karson, American Labor Unions and Politics, 1900–1918 (Carbondale: Southern Illinois University Press, 1958), p. 130. James O. Morris, Conflict Within the AFL (Ithaca: Cornell University Press, 1958), pp. 139.

19. Amalgamated Meat Cutters, Proceedings (1899), 26, (1902), 31–32, (1904), 16–16a.

20. Adolph Sturmthal (ed.), Contemporary Collective Bargaining in Seven Countries (Ithaca: Cornell University Press, 1957), pp. 174, 181, 183, 312–13. On the English shop-steward movement, see Walter Galenson, Trade Union Democracy in Western Europe (Berkeley: University of California Press, 1961), pp. 45–47. Two distinctions are necessary here. I do not mean that lay members do not participate in the bargaining process, nor that agreements are not subject to rank-and-file ratification, but only that bargaining involves the professional leadership so that its tasks are at a maximum in the process. Second, I am referring to bargaining, not to grievance procedure.

21. Walter Galenson, Comparative Labor Movements (New York: Prentice Hall & Co. 1952), p. 93, also, e.g., on French unions' experience with the Socialists, see ibid., 327.

22. Samuel Gompers, Seventy Years of Life and Labor, ed. P. Taft and J. A. Sessions (New York: E. P. Dutton & Co., 1957), p. 88.

23. See, e.g., Henry David, "One Hundred Years of Labor in Politics," in J. B. S. Hardman and M. F. Neufeld, The House of Labor (New York: Prentice Hall & Co., 1951), pp. 90–112; Michael Rogin, "Voluntarism: The Political Functions of an Antipolitical Doctrine," Industrial and Labor Relations Review, XV (June, 1962), 534–35.

24. See Philip Taft, The Structure and Government of Labor Unions (Cambridge: Harvard University Press, 1956), chap. 2.

25. Hardman, American Labor Dynamics, p. 160.

26. Ibid., pp. 164–65.

27. See, e.g., David Brody, The Butcher Workmen: A Study of Unionization (Cambridge, Harvard University Press, 1964). chap. 6.

28. Seymour M. Lipset, "The Political Process in Trade Unions: A Theoretical Statement," in M. Berger, et al., Freedom and Control in Modern Society (New York: Van Nostrand & Co., 1954), pp. 92ff. Ware, Labor Movement, p. 81. A. J. Muste, "Factions in Trade Unions," in Hardman, American Labor Dynamics, pp. 340–41. Seymour M. Lipset, Union Democracy: the Internal Politics of the International Typographical Union (Glencoe: Free Press, 1956), pp. 239ff.

29. Perlman, *Machinists*, p. 297.

30. Frank D. Manfred to Michael F. Widman, October 9, 1941, CIO Papers, Catholic University of America.

31. See, e.g., C. A. Gulick and M. K. Bers, "Insight and Illusion in Perlman's Theory of the Labor Movement," *Industrial and Labor Relations Review*, VI (July, 1953), 510–31.

10

Horatio Alger, Jr., and the Response to Industrialism

by **RICHARD WEISS**

I

Nations commonly use the names of important figures to designate particular periods in their history. France has its age of Louis XIV; England, its Victorian and Edwardian eras; and in the United States we hear much of the America of Jefferson, Jackson, Wilson, and F.D.R. Americans seem partial to using occupants of the White House to epitomize their times. Yet no presidential symbol exists for the spectacular transformation of our country between the Civil War and 1900. Instead, the popular conception of this period is formed by the image of the millionaire. The use of the business titan to characterize a period marked by industrialization is understandable, even appropriate. The presence of a children's author among the representatives of this era is more curious. American weavers of juvenile tales comprise a long list, but only one has become a national symbol. This unique distinction belongs to Horatio Alger, Jr., whose name has entered the American vocabulary, though his books are scarcely read any longer.

This timid writer of children's stories somehow became identified with the golden age of American plutocracy. A later generation used his name to symbolize the spectacular success that was possible in an era that seemed to spawn millionaires as salmon spawn roe.[1] Those who read the Alger stories with nostalgia envy their simplicity, a simplicity born of "the innocent, hopeful days before the turn of the century."[2] They idealize the certainties of a past time when wealth was regarded as "the direct consequence of honesty, thrift, self-reliance, industry, a cheerful whistle and an open manly face,"[3] and regret that they can no longer share Alger's benign view of the universe. They do not realize that if Alger was an innocent, he was an innocent in Babylon, and that like them he was "a communicant of a dying church" whose doctrine linked "sinlessness to solvency."[4] Correctly understood, Alger is not a representative of his time, but a nostalgic spokesman of a dying order. Of middle-class rural origins, he was always an alien in the industry-dominated society of his adult life.

II

It is ironic that Alger, a timid and lonely man, should have become the symbol that he has. Born on January 15, 1832, he remained a truer spokesman of the era of his birth rather than that of his maturity.[5] He was the eldest of five children and he received special attention from his father. Horatio Alger, Sr., a Unitarian minister, wished his son to follow in his footsteps. He directly supervised his early education and trained him rigorously. Discouraged from taking part in the frivolous activities of his peers, Alger, Jr. became so withdrawn that other youngsters dubbed him "Holy Horatio." His youth was spent with adults and his adulthood, with children.

In 1844, when Alger was twelve years old, his father was called to a church in Marlborough, Massachusetts, where Horatio attended Gates Academy. Marlborough, at this time,

was embarking on a career as an industrial town with shoes as the principal business—made in small, isolated shops which employed in each maybe ten people. As this business prospered, larger shops were erected and attracted many Irish and French-Canadian immigrants. There were two small wool-fabric mills on waterpower of the Assabet River, and several saw and grist mills on lesser streams. . . . In general the town was engaged in agricultural pursuits, and there were large areas of forest, and swamp land.[6]

This was the atmosphere in which Alger passed his adolescence. He frequently used the setting of his youth as a background in his later stories. The pattern of New England life was changing, and it is probable that the shift from commerce to industry was not entirely to the liking of old families like the Algers. While industry increased the wealth of the community, it often placed power and prestige in new hands, upset established social patterns, and brought an influx of immigrants that threatened the homogeneity of the New England countryside.

In Alger's stories, the mill-owner is frequently the villain. He is powerful and often dominates the better elements in the community. Industrial development was also threatening because it undermined the two mainstays of moral control, the farm and the family. Thus in his youth, Alger saw in microcosm the industrial challenge to the rural New England way of life. His sympathies, in his writings, were always with the latter.

While Alger's family was well-to-do, conditions of their life were in many ways rather primitive. Roads were poor, and long-distance travel was by horse-drawn coach. The first railroad to Marlborough opened in 1850, after Alger had left the town. The facilities of Gates Academy, where he received his preparatory education, were meager indeed. There was only one classroom and one instructor. "The classroom was inadequately heated by a wood-burning stove during sessions, and the ink froze at night; it was inadequately lighted by a few windows which in the winter could not be opened for ventilation; there was no artificial lighting; there was no plumbing—there was a well in the yard and also a 'privy.' "[7] From Gates, Alger went on to Harvard. His background was typical of many who had been great figures in the affairs of the nation. Times, however, were changing. Harvard, so long a breeding-ground for the nation's leaders, was now producing what might be called the "alienated generation." Few groups in America before that time lived through as radical a change in the nation's social fabric as these men experienced in their adult years. The change produced shock that manifested itself in a variety of ways: the indignation of the general reformers, the cynicism of Henry Adams, and the romantic nostalgia of a Horatio Alger.

After graduating from Harvard in 1852, Alger spent most of the next five years teaching and writing. He enrolled in the Divinity School at Cambridge in 1857. Completing the three-year course, he left for Europe in the summer of 1860. When he came home in April of 1861, the nation was already at war. Alger tried to enlist in the Union army, but was rejected as physically unfit. He resumed tutoring and writing until he received an offer to fill a pulpit in Brewster, Massachusetts, in the summer of 1865. For reasons that are not quite clear, Alger's pastorate in Brewster—his first and last—was not very successful. He left it after only eight months and went to New York, where he launched his career as a children's author. Ragged Dick, which appeared in book form in 1868, established him as a popular author, and from then on his reputation grew.[8] Alger's works do not rank high by literary standards, but remain classic expressions of the rags-to-riches ideology in post-bellum America.

III

There was little magazine commentary on Alger at the time of his death [1899] and, interestingly, few articles appear until the 1920s, by which time his books were no longer read.[9] Commentary on Alger in the 1920s and 1930s was deprecatory. H. L. Mencken expressed a general belief when he denied that rural origins increased one's chances for success. "The notion that yokels always succeed in the cities," he remarked scathingly, "is a great delusion. The overwhelming majority of our rich men are city-born and city-bred. And the overwhelming majority of our elderly motormen, forlorn corner grocerymen, neighborhood carpenters and such other blank cartridges are country-bred."[10]

In 1932, the centenary of Alger's birth, the Children's Aid Society conducted a poll to determine his popularity among the younger generation. The results showed that the once-famous author had fallen into obscurity. "Less than 20 per cent of the seven thousand members of New York's juvenile proletariat had ever heard of the author of *Tom the Bootblack*; only 14 per cent had read even one of his ... published works. What will be even more alarming to some is the fact that a considerable number dismissed the theory of 'work and win' as a 'lot of bunk.' "[11] A nostalgia for Alger did develop after World War II, but no comparable children's literature ever appeared.[12] The times have too much altered and American children are no longer receptive to Alger's message. Alger wrote one hundred and seven books, the sales of which have been estimated at seventeen million.[13]

IV

An examination of the Alger books belies the Alger myth. If his works reflect the spirit of a particular time, it was not the spirit of the gilded age.

Alger spoke very much as Ben Franklin had. He urged his readers not to smoke or drink, nor to stay up late, not to attend theaters or other places of entertainment. He preached frugality, hard work, and saving. He also told his readers to study and seek refinement and to be good to their mothers.

In one significant way, however, Alger departed from the traditional formulation of the Protestant notion of success. That was in his repeated emphasis on luck, an element that the Protestant ethic did not admit. His heroes all achieve wealth through a stroke of fortune. Either they are left worthless lands that accrete in value, they save rich men's sons or daughters and become wards of generous benefactors, or they achieve wealth and comfort through other chance occurrences. They never make fortunes; they always find them. Alger himself admits that virtue does not always bring material rewards, though luck never comes to the wicked. Luck is always earned by those who have it, though it is not always had by those who have earned it. This resembles the Puritan notion of salvation. The saved are always virtuous, but the virtuous are not always saved. Alger's failures are not always wicked boys, either. Lack of ambition, energy, physical strength often retard the upward movement of his characters, who, while virtuous, will never "make it." According to the author himself, his works had a two-fold purpose: one was "to exert a salutary influence upon the class of whom he was writing, by setting before them inspiring examples of what energy, ambition, and an honest purpose may achieve...."; the other one was to bring to the attention of the public "the life and experiences of the friendless and vagrant children to be found in all our cities, numbering in New York alone over twelve thousand."[14] Notable as an example of the latter is *Phil the Fiddler*, Alger's exposure of the *padrone* system in New York.

In his preface to the book in 1872, he expressed the hope that "revealing for the first time to the American public the hardships and ill-treatment of these wandering musicians, shall excite an active sympathy in their behalf...."[15] The *padrones* would purchase children, usually in southern Italy, and bring them to this country, where they would be sent about the streets playing and singing for money. They were poorly kept and brutally beaten, and they often died before reaching adulthood. This ruthless exploitation Alger called "white slavery—for it merits no better name," and bemoaned the fact that it was "permitted by the law of two great nations," Italy and the United States.[16] At a time when Social Darwinism was being used to justify the elimination, however ruthless, of the unfit, Alger had a teacher in one of his books praise her class because their "sympathies are with the weak and oppressed."[17] Alger's reform work carried on something of a family tradition. His father had been an abolitionist and his sister, Olive Augusta, was active in the temperance and women's rights movements.

Alger's association with the Newsboys' Lodging House in New York was very close. He often lived there and found much of the material for his books in the lives of the newsboys. He took particular pride in the belief that his works were inclining the public toward a more sympathetic attitude to these homeless waifs. In 1879 he expressed gratification at "the warm reception accorded by the public" to his "pictures of humble life in a great metropolis." He was even more pleased that "his labors...awakened a philanthropic interest in the children whose struggles and privations" he described, and asked the public to contribute to the funds of the Children's Aid Society.[18] One receives the impression in reading his books that their inspirational quality springs more from a dread of despair than from a belief in opportunity. Confronted with the horrors of poverty, Alger attempted to give solace. Like other conscience-stricken members of his class, he was unable to view the consequences of industrialization with indifference. Most disturbing of these consequences was the plight of children. Youngsters surrounded by poverty and sickness needed something to sustain them in their early years. Deprived of virtually all material comforts, they must at least be given the hope of a better future. The popular tradition of mobility in American society provided a convenient means of doing so.

Both Alger's distaste for the results of industrialism and his assertion of the Protestant virtues are much more akin to the middle-class reform mentality of the period than to the naked acquisitiveness of the "man on the make." It is interesting to note that in terms of background, Alger fits the pattern of the genteel reformer rather well. He was born into a comfortable New England family, was educated at Harvard, and was the son of a Unitarian minister.[19] He shared other characteristics of genteel reformers, among them a preference for Anglo-Saxons. Frequently, the ne'er-do-wells in his stories are "dark," as is Jasper in Tom the Bootblack, who is also "effeminate in appearance," "smooth, deceitful, and vain, running to dissipation, as far as he had opportunity."[20] This is inconsistent with his attitude toward Italian street urchins in Phil the Fiddler, and it seems his bias sometimes conflicted with his humane inclination. For the most part, however, Alger's heroes are of rural American background, so the conflict is not often evident. Alger avoids dealing with the problem of the immigrants, who rarely appeared in his books.

Another facet of Alger's racial attitudes that appears in some of his works is the implicit belief in a kind of hereditary determinism, which is later found in the eugenics craze of the early twentieth century, and which receives expression in popular novels of the Progressive period. Again, this seems inconsistent with Alger's notions of mobility. American belief in mobility, however, was held at the same time and by the same people who believed that "blood will tell" and attached great importance to family. This inconsistency, though rather widespread, is especially striking in the rags-to-riches context. One of the best examples of this hereditary determinism appears in Jed, *the Poorhouse Boy.*[21] The hero, raised in a home for paupers and subject to all the degradations of such an upbringing, is a perfect gentleman. His manners would be the pride of any mother and his virtue in all things is beyond reproach. The mystery of a boy of such fine breeding, raised in such low circumstances, is finally dispelled by the revelation of his noble origins. Born into a family of high rank, he was shipped across the ocean as an infant by a wicked uncle who coveted his title. The rest of the family think him dead. His innate nobility, however, survives all the years of poverty, and he is finally restored to his rightful estate. This belief in virtue transmitted through the blood provides one of the reasons for all of Alger's characters being orphaned. Poor boys are not likely to be the sons of good men who are alive. The absence of a father conveniently removes the problem of reconciling indigence with virtue.

V

Alger's settings are most often in the New York of the latter half of the nineteenth century, and his accurate descriptions of its streets, hotels, boardinghouses, and restaurants made his books valuable as guides to those unfamiliar with the city. But his attitude toward the city he described so well was one of hostility. While the city was a place of opportunity, it also was a place of unspeakable immorality. Virtue resided in the country. If the country boy could survive the city swindlers ready to prey on his innocence, his chances of success were greater than those of his city-bred equivalents. This was because he was usually stronger morally and had "been brought up to work, and work more earnestly than the city boys."[22] Country boys might come to the city to gain wealth, but city boys could well go to the country for moral regeneration. Alger also warned that "of the tens of thousands who come from the country to seek clerkships, but a very small proportion rise above a small income."[23] For the majority, it would be best to remain home. Charles Loring Brace, a prominent social worker who knew Alger through their common association with the Newsboys' Lodging House, attempted to relocate city waifs in country homes. He hoped to lessen in this way the pauperism resulting from the tremendous influx of people into the cities from rural areas.[24]

Alger's ideal differs in other important respects from the realities of the time. His heroes are never children of workers. They are generally impoverished through the death of their father, who was of the middle class. If their middle-class origins are not known, as in the case of Ragged Dick, their backgrounds are obscured altogether. One commentator has offered a Freudian interpretation of Alger's unvarying use of orphans in his novels.

Alger, who was never freed from emotional bondage to his own father, found a sort of compensation in telling this one story over and over. In each of his novels he punished his father three times. He killed him before the story opened, by making the hero an orphan; he gave Horatio Sr.'s worst traits to the villainous squire; and finally he provided the hero with a new father to cherish him.[25]

The Freudian perspective might be more fruitfully applied from the cultural rather than the personal point of view. The use of the orphan in nineteenth-century literature is too widespread to be ascribed to the psychic structure of a single individual. The orphan was a convenient fictional figure in a society eager to accept change but uneasy about losing its past. Eliminating the father, a symbol of tradition and authority, made the acceptance of change possible without requiring an explicit rejection of tradition. Seen in this light, the orphan reflects the tension between stability and movement that is expressed so frequently in literature with success themes.

Alger's choice of benefactors reveals his nostalgia for the "good old days." They are engaged in mercantile rather than industrial enterprises. The idealization of the benevolent merchant is hardly an accurate reflection of an age where industrial wealth predominated. It does, however, correspond to the widespread belief that the older form of enterprise honed finer character than the new.

None of Alger's heroes exhibits the aggressive acquisitiveness of the time. All are patient and virtuous, akin to the less grasping nature of the ideal man before the Civil War. The moderate fortunes his heroes accumulate are usually measured in five figures. Alger shared the distaste of the genteel middle class, which looked with disdain on the rise of the "New Moguls," whose practice of "Wall Street speculation" was "more dangerous even than extravagant habits of living."[26] Alger never mentions the millionaire in his stories and never urges the accumulation of great wealth as a worthy ambition. Henry A. Wallace correctly perceived Alger's dream when he identified it as a vision which saw America "not as a nation of propertyless workers but rather an America where all can become members of what has been called the 'middle class,' where all can share in the benefits which that class has enjoyed in the past."[27]

Others, less perceptive, made Alger a symbol of the Gilded Age. Implicit in Alger's own work is a critique of the post-Civil War period— of industrialization, urbanization, mammoth fortunes, and the general decline of morals. His stories bespeak a belief in a society where men reaped the fruits of their labor according to their merit. Nothing could have been more alien to Alger than the extremes of wealth and poverty that were characteristic of this period. The social conflict generated by the new order also disturbed him. Alger's work reflects an attempt to recreate the more harmonious society in which he was raised. His heroes come from another time, another society, another reality. Rather than extol the dominant values of his day, he reacted against them. His books exalted a time gone by, when the middle class had played the major role in American life. It is interesting to note, in this connection, that Alger's greatest sales came during the Progressive period. Then nostalgia for an imagined time of equal opportunity ran high and middle-class reformers criticized the consequences of industrialism, on the basis of values that mirrored the rags-to-riches myth.[28]

Straddling the worlds of the rural countryside and the urban metropolis, the Alger stories preserved the purity of the one while conveying the excitement of the other. In these stories, readers might find the reconciliation between different modes of life reality so harshly denied. People uprooted by the eddies of change found a kindred spirit in Alger, who, like them, was a stranger in a new society.

NOTES

1. See Thomas Meehan, "A Forgettable Centenary—Horatio Alger's," *New York Times Magazine*, June 28, 1964.

2. Henry F. Pringle and Katherine Pringle, "The Rebellious Parson," *The Saturday Evening Post*, 223 (February 10, 1951), 30.

3. Clifton Fadiman, "Party of One," *Holiday*, 21 (February, 1957), 6.

4. *Ibid.*, p. 6.

5. There has been some dispute as to the day of Alger's birth. Herbert Mayes in his biography, *Alger: A Biography without a Hero* (New York: Macy-Mesius, Inc., 1928), p. 13, states that Alger was born on Friday, January 13, 1832, pointing to the irony that the American apostle of success was born on an unlucky day. In fact, Alger was born on Sunday, January 15, 1832. A copy of his birth certificate was procured by Ralph D. Gardner, a prominent Alger collector. See "Horatio Alger Books," *Hobbies* (April, 1961), pp 110–11. The January 15 birth date was confirmed in a letter to me from John A. Bigelow, town historian of Marlborough, Mass., dated December 10, 1962.

The Mayes biography is open to question and gives no indication of where the sources of its material are. John Tebbel, in his biography of Alger, *From Rags to Riches: Horatio Alger, Jr. and the American Dream* (New York: The Macmillan Co., 1963), says: "It is a tribute to the research he [Mayes] did at twenty-eight to note that it can hardly be improved upon nearly four decades later," and offers his own book as a new interpretation of Alger's life based on the "facts" provided by Mayes (p.v.). This interpretation consists of a good deal of parlor-Freudianism centering on Alger's supposed sex life or lack of it. Mr. Tebbel's analysis would be of dubious worth even if his facts were certain, but since the only source for them is Mayes' book, it must be discounted altogether.

The latest treatment of Alger's life is Ralph D. Gardner's, *Horatio Alger, or the American Hero Era* (Mendota: The Wayside Press, 1964). This book is written in the style of an Alger romance and suffers from the author's admittedly being "an unabashedly enthusiastic admirer" of Alger (p. 13). Mr. Gardner does, however, provide an excellent and exhaustive bibliography.

6. For this description of the Marlborough of Alger's adolescence, I am indebted to John A. Bigelow in the letter cited above, n. 5.

7. *Ibid.*, Bigelow letter.

8. It was serialized in 1867 in *Student and Schoolmate*, a young people's magazine edited by William T. Adam (Oliver Optic). See Gardner, *Hero Era*, pp. 450–51.

9. For decline of Alger in the 1920s, see W. C. Crosby, "Acres of Diamonds," *The American Mercury*, 14 (May, 1928), 104–13.

10. H. L. Mencken, *Prejudices: Second Series* (New York: Alfred A. Knopf, 1920), p. 223.

11. "The Cynical Youngest Generation," *The Nation*, 134 (February 17, 1932), 186. See also, "A Forgotten Boy's Classic," *The Literary Digest*, 112 (January 30, 1932), 20.

12. See above, footnotes 2, 3. See also the following articles: "Up from Poverty," *The New Yorker*, 29 (May 16, 1953), 23–24; Marshall Fishwick, "The Rise and Fall of Horatio Alger," *The Saturday Review* (November, 17, 1956), p. 42; *Advertising Age* (December 1, 1947), pp. 18–19; Malcolm Cowley, "The Alger Story," *The New Republic* (September 10, 1945), pp. 319–20; Frederick Lewis Allen, "Horatio Alger, Jr.," *Saturday Review of Literature*, 18 (September 17, 1938, pp.3–4.

For the role of historians in perpetuating the myth of "rags-to-riches," see William Miller, "American Historians and the Business Elite," *Journal of Economic History* (November, 1949), pp. 184–208.

For correspondence of some avid collectors of Algeriana see the collection of Alger letters at the Huntington Hartford library.

13. For number of Alger books, see Gardner, *Hero Era*, p. 356. After Alger's death, eleven more books bearing his name were written by Edward Stratemeyer, bringing the total number of books published under Alger's imprint to 118. *Ibid.*

The estimate of Alger's sales is by Frank Luther Mott, *Golden Multitudes* (New York: The Macmillan Co., 1947), p. 158.

14. Horatio Alger, Jr., *Fame and Fortune* (Boston: A. K. Loring, 1868), pp. vii–viii.

15. Horatio Alger, Jr., *Phil the Fiddler* in *Struggling Upward and Other Works*, ed. Russell Crouse (New York: Crown Publishers, 1945), p. 282.

16. *Ibid.*, p. 311.

17. Horatio Alger, Jr., *Only an Irish Boy* (New York: Hurst and Co., n.d.), p. 94.

18. Horatio Alger, Jr., *The Telegraph Boy* (Boston: A. K. Loring, 1879), p. vii.

19. For an excellent description of the backgrounds of "genteel reformers," see James Stuart McLachlan, "The Genteel Reformers: 1865–1884" (Unpublished Master's Thesis, Department of History, Columbia University, 1958), pp. 12–26.

20. Horatio Alger, Jr., *Tom the Bootblack* (New York: New York Book Co.,

1909), p. 122. See also, *Wait and Hope* (New York: New York Book Co., 1908), p. 146 and *Chester Rand* (Philadelphia: John C. Winston Co., 1903), p. 254.

21. Alger, *Jed, the Poorhouse Boy*, in *Struggling Upward*, pp. 401–566. See also, *The Young Acrobat* (New York: American Publisher's Corp., 1890); *A Cousin's Conspiracy* (Chicago: M. A. Donohue and Co., n.d.).

22. Alger, *Chester Rand*, p. 21.

23. Horatio Alger, Jr., *Bound to Rise* (Boston: A. K. Loring, 1873), p. 113.

24. Charles Loring Brace, *The Dangerous Classes of New York* (New York: Wynkoop and Hallenbeck, Pubrs., 1872), pp. 233–70. At the time the book was written, Brace noted that "between twenty and twenty-four thousand" children had been relocated (p. 241).

25. "Holy Horatio," *Time*, 46 (August 13, 1945), 98.

26. Horatio Alger, Jr., *Struggling Upward*, pp. 79–80 (copy in Columbia Library has no imprint). For a perceptive article on Alger's work, see Richard Wohl, "The 'Rags to Riches' Story: An Episode of Secular Idealism," *Class, Status, and Power*, ed. Reinhard Bendix and Seymour Lipset (New York: The Free Press, 1953), pp. 388–95.

27. Henry A. Wallace, *The Century of the Common Man* (New York: Reynal and Hitchcock, 1943), p. 56.

28. Mott, *Golden Multitudes*, pp. 158–59. Mott estimates that by World War I the aggregate sales of Alger books were over sixteen million. Most of these sales came after Alger's death when obituaries placed his total sales at about eight hundred thousand.

11

America on Display: The World's Fairs of 1876, 1893, 1933

by JOHN G. CAWELTI

Mankind loves fairs. In ancient times, periodic religious festivals combined ritual, public entertainment, and opportunities for the exchange of news and goods. Holidays and trade fairs filled some of the same needs in the Middle Ages. In the nineteenth century the great international exposition of arts and sciences became the dominant type of fair in modern industrial societies. The British were first in the field with the epoch-making Crystal Palace Exposition of 1851, but it was not long before most of the major European nations joined them. Before the end of the nineteenth century, seven additional expositions in London, Paris, and Vienna had opened and closed their doors to approximately 116 million people.[1]

The United States was not to be left behind. In 1853, only two years after the opening of the Crystal Palace, and two years before the French had put together a rival attraction, Americans erected a junior crystal palace in New York City. It was not very successful. Attendance of little more than a million visitors led to a $300,000 loss, a reminder that the recent financial difficulties of the New York World's Fair are not without precedent. America tried again in 1876,

317

in celebration of the centennial of the Declaration of Independence. This time the fair, held in the city of Philadelphia, was an outstanding success. It attracted nearly ten million visitors. Philadelphia's example was followed with even greater éclat by Chicago in 1893. In the twentieth century, American World's Fairs were held, with varying success, in Buffalo, St. Louis, San Francisco, Chicago, New York, and Seattle.

Thus, both in Europe and America, the international exposition has become an important cultural institution appealing to many different tastes and filling many different needs. The celebrant city or country points with pride to its industrial know-how and cultural progress, while, at the same time, it hopes to attract large numbers of visitors whose expenditures for housing, food, and local products will greatly stimulate the economy. Moreover, these great expositions sometimes serve important artistic and cultural functions. Several of them have influenced public taste by popularizing new styles of architectural and industrial design, by creating demand for new products, by spreading knowledge about contemporary developments in the arts, and by bringing the art and artifacts of non-European cultures to the public's attention. For example, the Philadelphia Centennial popularized a whole new range of tastes; as Russell Lynes puts it, "nothing on so grand a scale, so exotic, or so euphoric with 'culture' had ever been seen in America before. Americans drank deep of the heady wine of art, and the hangover lasted for at least a quarter of a century, or longer than anyone cares to remember."[2] In particular, the centennial exposition popularized the "Queen Anne" movement in architecture and design and stimulated a new interest in the art and artifacts of Japan and China. The World's Columbian Exposition at Chicago in 1893 had an even greater impact. It not only imported the European academic tradition in the arts into America, it also created a new ideal of urban planning with far-reaching implications.[3] Three decades later, the Chicago Century of Progress exhibition of 1933–34 was the first large-scale presentation of "modernism" in architectural and industrial design in this country, and probably had a major role in popularizing that style.

In this chapter, however, we are primarily concerned with world's fairs from another point of view. Because it brings together many different aspects of civilization under, so to speak, a single roof, a world's fair can give us much insight into how men view the unity of their culture, how they understand the structure of its means, achievements, and aspirations. Of course, expositions are not fully representative of the culture that sponsors them. Even the nineteenth-century observers were well aware of the discrepancy between the beautifully organized and landscaped exposition grounds and the sprawling, chaotic industrial metropolises that surrounded them. Moreover, the men whose job it was to design and construct the fairs did not represent the total population. The fairs' organizers and designers came from a fairly small elite, primarily leading members of the business community together with those architects, engineers, designers, and academicians to whom financiers and industrialists turn for advice on matters outside their competence.[4] Nevertheless, the international exposition unites the various segments of culture as no other institution does. As one writer on the Philadelphia Centennial put it, the exposition's display of industrial art was "the union of two great elements of civilization—Industry, the mere mechanical, manual labor, and Art, the expression of something not taught by nature, the presentation of that ideal, the mere conception of which raises man above the level of savagery."[5] And, though a world's fair is the cultural image of an elite, it is that of a particularly influential elite seeking an image that will be widely understood and approved.

The composition and character of the elites directing American world's fairs underwent some significant changes, though a tentative study shows considerable similarity in the organization and financing of the three fairs discussed in this chapter. In each case, a small informal group of businessmen and politicians initiated the fair organization. Once the project was underway a formal organization was set up, stock was sold, and a board of directors or trustees was elected by the stockholders. Since the majority of stock was held by leading local businessmen, the dominant group on the board of trustees represented these businessmen. As might be expected, the business groups whose representatives stand out are financiers, railroad men, large merchandisers (e.g. Marshall Field) and industrialists. Though I have not been able to get biographical data on all directors or trustees some differences have clearly emerged. In Philadelphia 1876, in addition to the Centennial Board of Finance, the legally responsible corporation, a Centennial Executive Committee, represented the States. This committee evidently had major control over exhibition policies in areas other than finance. In Chicago 1893, a single Board of Directors took the primary responsibility for the exhibition and this board consisted predominantly of Chicago business and financial leaders. In Chicago 1933–34, there was a single Board of Trustees, but it was more representative of the major corporate institutions of industrial society. In addition to business leaders, we find a substantial complement of labor men, politicians, and academicians. These changes in organization seem to bear out the thesis presented here that American culture defined itself in traditional political terms in 1876, in terms of the leadership of a special business-artistic elite in 1893, and as a system of corporate institutions in 1933.

In connection with these changes it is worth noting the changing relationships of architects and landscape designers, and of the executive directors of the fairs. In each case, the Board of Directors appointed an executive director to have primary responsibility for day-to-day management. In Philadelphia 1876, this was General Joseph R. Hawley, a man whose background was more political than industrial. A number of architects contributed to the 1876 fair, in particular the German emigrant Henry Schwarzman, chief engineer of the Centennial grounds, who designed Memorial Hall, Horticultural Hall, and thirty other buildings, but there was apparently no overall artistic direction. Building standards were set by a building committee composed of leading Philadelphia businessmen. In Chicago 1893, the role of artistic direction was greatly enhanced. In fact, the activities of D. H. Burnham as chief of construction and general artistic director seem to have taken the limelight from George R. Davis, the director general and executive officer of the Columbian Exposition. In Chicago 1933–34, the unusual organizational talents of Lenox Lohr, the Fair's director, were so successful in integrating the work of finance, design, and construction that a clear design resulted despite the fact that no single individual occupied anything like Burnham's position of importance.

In this chapter, I hope, by means of a comparative analysis of three of the most important American world's fairs, to show some of the main continuities and changes in America's way of displaying herself, or, more precisely, some of the ways in which the business, political, and cultural leaders who created these expositions viewed the nature and unity of American culture. In the similarities and differences between the Philadelphia Centennial of 1876, the World's Columbian Exposition of 1893, and A Century of Progress of 1933–34, the latter two held in Chicago, some major trends in American culture will become evident.

I

In 1871, Walt Whitman was invited to write a hymn to an industrial arts exhibition in New York City. The main theme of his "Song of the Exposition" was the somewhat embarrassed but ultimately fruitful confrontation of art and technology. Whitman imagines the muse, migrating from "Greece and Ionia" and entering bemused but undismayed into the industrial confusion of the nineteenth century United States.

I say I see, my friends, if you do not, the illustrious emigré . . .
Making directly for this rendezvous, vigorously clearing a path
for herself, striding through the confusion,
By thud of machinery and shrill steam-whistle undismayed,
Bluff'd not a bit by drain-pipe, gasometers, artificial fertilizers.
Smiling and pleas'd with palpable intent to stay,
She's here, install'd amid the kitchen ware!

The initial incongruity of the encounter between the epic splendor of the cultural tradition, symbolized by the muse, and the shrill scream of the factory whistle dissolves in a vision of the cultural diversity, utilitarian progress, and human fulfillment represented by the exposition:

Somewhere within their walls shall all that forwards perfect
human life be started,
Tried, taught, advanced, visibly exhibited . . .
None shall be slighted, none but shall here be honor'd help'd
exampl'd.*

---

* "Song of the Exposition," Walt Whitman, Leaves of Grass (Philadelphia: David McKay, 1891), pp. 158–160.

Whitman's dream of a union of the new forces of industrialism with the great tradition of the arts in a culture dedicated to democratic human values was a dominant theme in all three of the fairs to be considered. Each exposition might have adopted the famous commercial slogan "Progress is our most important product," in both of its senses: that the improvement of human life was man's primary interest, and that this improvement was to be carried out primarily through the production of goods. All three fairs had progress as their main theme. The Philadelphia Centennial celebrated American achievement since the Declaration of Independence; the Columbian Exposition, man's progress since the discovery of the New World; the Chicago fair of 1933–34—explicitly titled "A Century of Progress,"— portrayed advances in science and industry since the founding of Chicago in 1833. Essentially, progress, as defined by the exhibits at these fairs, meant utility and abundance—increasing efficiency in the manufacture and distribution of those goods and services that supported the survival and comfort of the human race. The largest and most elaborate exhibits at all three fairs were those devoted to the products of industry and their technology.

However, the fairs were not limited to manufactures and machinery. Agriculture and the fine arts also played an important role. The categories of exhibits used by the Philadelphia Centennial gives a good idea of the basic material brought together in all three exhibitions, as well as a sense of the ideology of progress that pervaded the displays:

I. Raw Materials—Mineral, Vegetable, and Animal.
II. Materials and Manufactures used for Food, or in the Arts, the result of Extractive or Combining Processes.
III. Textile and Felted Fabrics; Apparel, Costumes, and Ornaments for the person.
IV. Furniture and Manufactures of general use in construction and in dwellings.
V. Tools, Implements, Machines, and Processes.
VI. Motors and Transportation.
VII. Apparatus and Methods for the increase and diffusion of knowledge.

VIII. Engineering, Public Works, Architecture, etc.
IX. Plastic and Graphic Arts.
X. Objects illustrating efforts for the improvement of the Physical, Intellectual, and Moral Condition of Man.[6]

In their ground plans, each of the expositions consisted of a group of temporary buildings erected in a park-like site. The Philadelphia Centennial had five major buildings: the Main Building (for Manufactures), Machinery Hall, Memorial Hall (Fine Arts), Agriculture and Horticulture, and about a hundred smaller ones. The lesser buildings were mainly sponsored by the federal government, by states and foreign countries, and by businesses and trade associations, with a few special pavilions such as the one dedicated to woman's work. Chicago in 1893 followed the same basic pattern, though in a more elaborate, complex, and highly planned fashion. As at Philadelphia, the largest building was for the exhibit of manufactures and industrial arts. The category of machinery and technology had become, by 1893, more complex and specialized. In addition to a machinery hall, there were separate major buildings for electricity, mining, and transportation. Like the Philadelphia pattern, the other major buildings were for fine arts, agriculture, horticulture, and fisheries, and there was, as well, a large collection of buildings sponsored by federal and state governments, foreign countries, trade associations, and women. In 1893, a much more elaborate bazaar and entertainment section developed on the Midway Plaisance. There were other significant changes in 1933, such as the greater importance of buildings erected by corporations and the lesser role of the states, but the main elements were still basically the same: manufactures, science and technology, agricultural products, and the fine arts.[7]

Though the basic continuity of the world's fairs as a linking of industry, science, agriculture, and the arts under the aegis of progress remained constant, the relationship between these elements changed dramatically as the dynamic adaptability of American culture responded to technological change. Specific changes in the technology of living between 1876 and 1933 were vast. At Philadelphia, electricity and the telephone were curiosities. By 1893, they had become an integral part of life. The massive Corliss steam engine, which was the main source of power at Philadelphia had given way by 1893 to the dynamo, which so perplexed Henry Adams. In 1893, the automobile was just beginning to be thought of and the airplane was a fantastic vision. In 1933, automobile manufacturers and their supporting industries were among the major exhibitors while one of the chief heroes of the day was General Italo Balbo, who had led a squadron of seaplanes from Italy to the exhibition grounds. Chicago was so impressed by this gesture that a short boulevard in the "Loop" area was named after General Balbo, though it is doubtful if many Chicagoans still know who Balbo Drive was named after and why. The present writer, who grew up in Chicago, assumed for years that Balbo must have been one of the companions of Columbus, or the discoverer of some important vaccine. To extrapolate into the future, in 1933 the fair was opened by a beam of light from the star Arcturus, which might be taken as a symbol of the opening of the space age.

II

The Philadelphia Centennial exhibition of 1876 opened in the trough of the depression of 1873 and closed shortly before the great railroad strike of 1877, the first outburst of nationwide industrial labor conflict. It was a suitable climax to the first wave of American industrial expansion. After the mid-1870's, things were never quite the same again. The panic and hardship of the depression, the exposure of unsavory profiteering and corruption in high political and business circles, and the crescendo of industrial conflict created strong pressure for a tighter organization and regulation of industrial enterprise. Americans were becoming aware of the dark and problematic side of American industrial growth and gradually, over the next several decades, they would seek means of improving the situation.

Most of this was in the future at Philadelphia in 1876. In the leading themes of that exhibition, we can see why it took most Americans so long to realize that their ebullient expansion was running out of control. The exhibition itself was a rousing success and seemed to be a reaffirmation of optimism and possibility on the hundredth anniversary of the Declaration of Independence. Despite the depression, nearly ten million people thronged to the fair. Gate receipts were close to $4.5 million, while the remaining cost of some $4 million was borne by state and government grants. Many felt that the exhibition itself would go a long way to eliminate the hard times. Shortly after the exhibition closed its doors in the fall of 1876, one sanguine observer wrote, "undoubtedly the setting in motion of millions of people, each with money to spend, has had an effect in breaking the lethargy that has stifled enterprise in the business world and in causing the hopeful beginnings of a revival of trade which we have been witnessing this fall." (1876).[8] This commentator was a bit premature, but his observations do suggest how much the success of the exhibition reaffirmed Americans' faith in themselves and their providential destiny:

> We were regarded as a smart, half-cultured people, of immense energy and remarkable ingenuity, but deficient in the higher graces and achievements of civilization, and depending upon the Old World for all finer grades of manufactures. The reports of foreign commissioners, jurors, journalists, and travellers, all concurring in expressions of surprise and admiration at the excellence of our manufactures, our schools, our railroads, our newspapers, and the soundness of our social life, have greatly modified public opinion abroad, and gone far towards introducing more just views of us. Those who mingled much in foreign circles at the Exhibition know that the astonishment and wonder of our visitors from abroad at our resources and accomplishments was great and universal.[9]

American confidence that everything was getting better in this best of all possible lands made it hard to see clearly the development of American society or to feel the need for greater social control and planning. This confidence was based on the intertwined supports of religion and patriotism, visible everywhere in the exhibition from the profusion of flags, eagles, and other national symbolism which marked the displays to the Roman Catholic Total Abstinence Fountain, a dominant feature of the exhibition grounds. This faith in the divinely ordained progress of the American nation was expressed in the Centennial Hymn written by the venerable poet John Greenleaf Whittier and sung by a chorus of one thousand voices on the exhibition's opening day, May 10, 1876.

Our fathers' God! from out whose hand
The centuries fall like grains of sand,
We meet today, united free,
And loyal to our land and thee,
To thank thee for the era done,
And trust thee for the opening one.

Here, where of old, by thy design,
The fathers spake that word of thine,
Whose echo is the glad refrain
Of rended bolt and falling chain,
To grace our festal time from all
The zones of earth our guests we call. . . .

For art and labor met in truce
For beauty made the bride of use,
We thank thee, while withal we crave
The austere virtues, strong to save;
The honor, proof to place or gold;
The manhood, never bought or sold.

Oh! Make thou us, through centuries long,
In peace secure, in justice strong;
Around our gift of freedom draw
The safeguards of thy righteous law,
And, cast in some diviner mould,
Let the new cycle shame the old![10]

Faith in God and in America as a regenerate society were the organizing symbols of the Philadelphia Exhibition. Probably the Centennial was the last major public event of which this could be said, for as the economic conflict of the 1870s and 1880s shook American confidence in their society, religious and philosophical developments in the same period undercut the unquestioning faith of the first half of the nineteenth century. At Philadelphia, however, the traditional religious patriotism was still sufficiently strong to give those who organized and described the exhibition a sense of order and design amid the confusion and variety.

This ordering principle, however, was a matter of feeling manifested in symbolism rather than a sense of esthetic order embodied in visual and spatial form. From a modern esthetic point of view, the Philadelphia Centennial seems at first to have no form at all.[11] Unlike those of the fairs of 1893 and 1933, the Philadelphia buildings show no unity of architectural style; instead they range from "Persian" to "Renaissance" to "Gothic" to various undefinable combinations of historic styles. Within the buildings, the exhibits are similarly diverse. Each display seems to compete for attention with its neighbors with every crocket, finial, and bracket at its command. Nor did the designers work out an elaborate formal plan for the layout of the grounds. The basic plan was largely determined by the existing natural contours of Fairmount Park, Philadelphia, where the exhibition was held. The park consisted of a level plain with three low hills. The two largest buildings were sited on the plain and the three other major buildings were erected on the hills. Smaller buildings simply proliferated along the avenues between the main buildings. Each building had its own distinctive style. The agricultural building was "Gothic," the art building "Renaissance," the Horticultural Hall "Moorish." However, the use of these styles was anything but historically accurate. The agricultural building, for example, was a large barn whose roof took the shape of a Gothic vault ornamented with spires and buttresses. The horticultural building was a large greenhouse overlaid with Moorish ornamentation. Neither building had the slightest resemblance to an actual Gothic or Moorish structure. This selection and use of styles indicate that the reasoning behind them was neither formal nor historical. It was neither an esthetic sense that particular forms were more pleasurable or beautiful than others, nor a traditional respect for a certain historical period that led to the employment of the Gothic, or classic, or Persian. Rather, the choice grew out of a principle of symbolism.[12] The agricultural building was Gothic because such a style appropriately symbolized the religious piety and closeness to God of the farmers. Greenhouses for the artificial cultivation of flowers and plants in rich profusion suggested the exotic luxury of the Near East and brought the forms of Moorish and Persian architecture into play. For art, the great period was, of course, the Renaissance—one commentator on the fair observed that "the nations compete with each other for a new revival, which seems on the surface, to have more in its favor than had that of the cinque-cento"[13] —and so the art building had more or less the outline and ornament of a Renaissance palace.

Thus, there existed in the design of the Philadelphia Centennial a kind of order difficult to appreciate as we look back, because it was based on a complex of sentimental and historical associations tied to a view of the world few of us hold any longer. This ideology—confidence in the provident intentions of God—also underlay the unregulated enterprise of the first wave of American industrialization. Press, pulpit, and political forum announced that Americans were supremely industrious, patriotic, and pious. Therefore, society had no need to control its entrepreneurs. Insofar as the government acted in the economic sphere at all it should be to foster enterprise. In the same way, in the creation of a great industrial, agricultural, and artistic exhibition, there was no need for a carefully worked-out formal plan. That men were coming together to celebrate the Centennial achievements of divinely guided American society would insure a unity more profound than human art could create.

Despite the confusions of architectural styles, there did emerge a certain similarity of theme, among many of the buildings and exhibits at Philadelphia. Its keynote was Whittier's phrase "art and labor met in truce ... beauty made the bride of use." This way of speaking about the relation of art and industry adumbrates the functionalism later preached by Veblen, Sullivan, and Wright, which is now an accepted principle of architecture and industrial design. Indeed, there was a long tradition of functional or utilitarian esthetics in America, and the emphasis on use in the architecture and design of the Philadelphia Centennial was an outgrowth of this tradition.[14] But there was an important difference between this Philadelphia style and the functionalism of the twentieth century. While Sullivan and Wright sought an organic unity of form, function, and building technology, the Philadelphia style reflected a different way of thinking about the relation between form and function. As the metaphors of Whittier's poem suggest, beauty and use were two independent realms that had to be joined in a balanced relationship, a truce or a marriage rather than an organic unity.

The edifices [of the exhibition] according to the original plan, were to excel their European exemplars not less in elegance and elaborateness than in completeness for their practical purposes, in adaptation and in capacity. The uncertainty, however, of success in raising the necessary funds in time enforced the abandonment of much that was merely ornate—a circumstance which was proved fortunate by the excess in the demands of exhibitors over all calculations, since the means it was at first proposed to bestow upon the artistic finish of the buildings were needed to provide additional space.[15]

In this passage, art and technology are treated as two separate categories, one dedicated to beauty and the other to use. Each category makes its own independent claim and both are necessary for a completely successful building or artifact. The problem is to establish an appropriate balance between them. When the budget was insufficient and the two claims came into conflict, use was generally the victor, but not without a sense of lost beauty. Despite its concern for function, therefore, the Philadelphia esthetic had not fully come to terms with industrialism, as did Sullivan and Wright. Contemporaneous commentary suggests a quite divided attitude toward the primary symbol of industrialism, the machine. On the one hand, the machine represents the vanguard of the nineteenth century, stimulating the mind to new inventions and improvements.

What we see of the advance and position of mechanism is assuring, beyond most other spectacles in the great show of the future of civilization.[16]

But the very same writer viewed with alarm the impact of machinery on the world of beauty. By the turn of the century Frank Lloyd Wright was enthusiastically propagandizing for the fullest use of machine reproduction in architectural design, but in 1876 this critic dolefully observed that

The introduction of mindless automatic machinery has starved out the chisel. Mouldings are run out for us by the mile, like iron from the rolling-mill or tunes from a musical box, as cheap and as soulless.

Forms innately beautiful thus become almost hateful, because hackneyed.[17]

Evidently the machine's purpose, in the mind of such witnesses of the Philadelphia Centennial, was to advance the material well-being of mankind. Yet the advance of machinery threatened to impinge on the traditional and separate realm of beauty. "The esthetic sense does not express itself by steam, and the chisel and the brush will doubtless be its implements thirty centuries hence, as they were thirty centuries ago."[18]

Thus, in 1876 the mechanical principle of industrialism was far from being fully accepted. Many Americans insisted that the other realm of beauty should also have a basic role in their culture. The effect of this way of thinking is evident both in the exhibition buildings and in the displays that filled them. The two major buildings were simple in functional design and elaborately ornate in decoration. Immense in size, Machinery Hall covered 558,550 square feet, while the Main Building, largest in the world at its time, was 1,880 feet long and 464 feet wide, covering 936,008 square feet. Functionally efficient, these buildings embodied new principles of industrial technology in their method of construction. The roofs were supported by iron trusses resting on iron columns, with the intervening wall space largely filled by glass, an early form of the modern steel frame and "curtain wall" type of construction. This iron frame was so designed that it could be readily taken down and used again. Yet this technological efficiency was clearly not enough for the cultural thought of the time. Over this functional framework a skin of beauty had to be fashioned. Even the machinery building, which was felt to be "plain and simple, but little effort having been made at ornament," was provided with such embellishments as the following:

The main entrances at the east and west were finished with handsome facades, consisting of a square tower at each side rising to a height of seventy-eight feet, with a tasteful entrance between them. The central entrance and the towers were each provided with light ornamental galleries, and over the central gallery a large eagle was placed, with a clock immediately beneath it. A similar projection with a similar facade stood at the ends of the transept upon the north and south sides of the building, giving to it a fine and picturesque effect; and in order to further relieve the monotony which would have resulted from the long unbroken lines of the exterior, other projections were introduced upon the north and south sides of the building with tasteful facades. A chime of thirteen bells, representing the thirteen original States, was hung in the northeast tower of the building.[19]

It should be noted that in this quotation, as in the design itself, there is no hint of an attempt to discover ornamental forms that take their character from the function or structure of the buildings. Beauty is another category, something to be added after the basic functional characteristics of the building have been worked out.

The same "truce" between art and technology can be seen in the industrial products exhibited. Among these were such results of American inventiveness as molded veneer chairs and folding beds, the former reflecting a new production technology and the latter an ingenious application of mechanical devices. Then art entered the scene. Elaborate perforated designs were punched into the veneer of the chairs and the folding bed was decked out with the ornaments of a medieval bishop's throne. In the major part of the objects displayed function and method of production created the basic shape of the object; then art uncoiled itself in an exuberant and often fantastic pattern of ornament and historical reference, embellishing the mechanical with a romantic spirit of beauty.

Another instance of the autonomous but balanced roles of art and technology in the culture of the 1870s appears in the mechanical exhibits. Machinery, designed for production rather than public display, was purely functional in form. Even the great Corliss engine which, by an elaborate system of belts and pulleys, operated all the moving devices in Machinery Hall, had very little ornamentation. Almost without exception, the mechanical displays simply followed the form indicated by the machine's operations. No attempt was made to disguise its workings under a steamlined shell in the manner characteristic of the twentieth century. The Philadelphia machinery exhibits bear out John Kouwenhoven's thesis that nineteenth-century

Americans, at least in their technological designs, sought for efficiency, lightness, saving of labor, and rapidity of operation, rather than for beauty, monumentality, and permanence.[20] The designs and examples of bridges, railroad engines, presses, and shop machinery shown at Philadelphia all manifest a striking economy and simplicity of design, so that an eye brought up on twentieth century esthetic principles finds them far more beautiful than the picturesque, fussy confections served up by both the fine and applied artists.

The fine arts display reflects the other side of the equation. Art was dedicated to beauty, sentiment, and idealism. The one building planned for permanence and erected by means of the traditional masonry construction was Memorial Hall, the site of the fine arts exhibit. Aside from the European exhibits—which gave little sense of the revolutionary developments in Paris—the displays ranged from John Rogers' genre scenes to Randolph Rogers' allegorical nude sculptures; from Albert Bierstadt's romantic western landscapes to J. G. Brown's Currier and Ives-like painting of curling in Central Park. It is important to note, however, that the fine arts were not represented as "masterpieces" of the past as was the case in both the Chicago exhibitions of 1893 and 1933. The fine arts were definitely an aspect of the on-going culture rather than a collection of revered old masters.

Two artistic modes dominated the display: narrative and landscape paintings. The narrative paintings concentrated on the traditional verities and pieties: great scenes in the history of America or of Protestant Christianity ("The Trial of Sir Harry Vane", "The Apotheosis of Washington"); sentimental genre scenes expressing the peace and serenity of the traditional rural way of life ("Going to Church in New England in the Olden Time;" "Old Kentucky Home.") The landscapes presented the beauty of the American farmland and wilderness with a sense of the immanent divine presence. Industry, technology, and science had almost no place in the cultural niche represented by the fine arts. When presented at all, they were usually shown in the form of allegorical nudes ("The Genius of Electricity" was a pattable *putti* holding a torch). A revealing incident took place when Thomas Eakins submitted his masterful painting of the Gross Clinic for exhibition in the Fine Arts section. The painting was uncompromising in its straightforward representation of a surgical operation. The exhibition jury judged Eakins' painting unartistic and relegated it to a place in the medical section of the exhibition.

The relationship between art and technology at the Philadelphia exhibition suggests that, at this point of industrial development, tradition and innovation were still rather evenly, if tenuously balanced in the fabric of American culture. The fine arts with their didactic, sentimental, and spiritual content represented the moral, religious, and patriotic tradition of a republican society, centered in small cities, towns, and rural areas, peacefully industrious and temperate, and firmly based on a faith in God's special interest in America. On the foundation of this firm sense of tradition and community, the radical innovations of technology and the new shape of industrial society seemed to represent a measured material progress rather than a threat to traditional institutions and beliefs. That the architects, designers, and manufacturers whose work was exhibited at the fair were able so easily to reconcile the two conflicting forces of technological functionalism and artistic tradition reflected this tenuous cultural balance made possible by the unifying influence of a generally accepted religious and political ideology.

However, the quickening pace of industrial development soon undermined the Philadelphia synthesis. Artists like Eakins began to reject the traditional idealism of the fine arts and to base their work on a naturalistic esthetic directly responsive to the new world of science and technology. Others, like the young architect Richard Morris Hunt invidiously compared the achievements of American art with the esthetic sophistication and technical knowledge of the great tradition of European art. Appointed a government commissioner and judge for the 1876 exhibition, Hunt blasted the Philadelphia style for its "meretricious ornament" and its sacrifice of harmony and repose for novelty of effect. Vigorously, he criticized the "total absence of anything like monumental grandeur" and compared the exhibition buildings with the "more scientific and judicious use of the various building-materials, and . . . higher standard of taste which naturally exists in the Old World."[21] One sign of the great change in American culture between 1876 and 1893 lies in the fact that Hunt, the dean of American architecture in 1893, and others who shared his attitudes toward culture dominated the planning and execution of the World's Columbian Exposition.

III

Evidenced on every side are subordinations of the physical and the enduring supremacy of mind, while ready at hand are all those contrivances of civilization which help to elevate and ennoble man, to refine his tastes, enlarge his ideas, enrich his interests, and further his deliverance from the despotisms of nature. Halos of fresh thought descend and possess us. Questions and ambitions arise, instinct with new powers and new purposes. Objects of beauty meet the eye and illumine the imagination; the aroma of culture fills the air.*

An ironic fatality seemed to dog American world's fairs. The three that are the focus of this chapter all opened to celebrate some aspect of American progress while the country was in the throes of depression and industrial convulsion. The World's Columbian Exposition, which opened at Chicago on Monday, May 1, 1893, honored the four hundredth anniversary of the discovery of America. It was a rich and impressive celebration of American achievement since that time, perhaps the most fantastic spectacle of its type ever produced on the American continent. But it was not long before the fair began to feel the effects of the panic of 1893 and the subsequent depression. Within a year the city of Chicago would be plunged into a maelstrom of violence when the unhappy citizens of George Pullman's paternalistic utopia struck out against their master. This did not prevent nearly 30 million visitors from attending the exhibition, almost three times the attendance of the Philadelphia Centennial. The cost was more than proportionate. The managers of the exposition raised and expended from all sources, including government appropriations, debenture bonds, gate receipts and contributions, a total of $33,248,930.55[22]

The richness and elegance of the spectacle was extraordinary. To transform the meadows, beaches, and swamps of the undeveloped

---

*H. H. Bancroft, Book of the Fair, vol. 1 (Chicago and San Francisco: The Bancroft Co., 1893), p. 3.

Jackson Park on the South Side of Chicago into the great White City of the World's Columbian Exposition was one of the major feats of architectural planning ever undertaken in America. The very size and scope of its unified plan had an incalculable influence on the future development of the American landscape. For example, one immediate result of the fair was the great Chicago plan commissioned by the Commercial Club, a group of leading Chicagoans, many of whom had served on the fair's board of directors, and created by D. H. Burnham, the fair's chief of construction. This plan, published in 1909, has had a world-wide influence on city planning. Even those few perceptive critics like Montgomery Schuyler who saw the essential irrelevance of the White City to the problems of architectural design and urban planning in an industrial society did not deny the splendor of the demonstration. Henry Adams was momentarily perplexed and wondered if the world had temporarily halted on its headlong flight toward perdition. The public was dazzled, stunned, amazed. While the White City lasted, it was magnificent. To walk its pseudo-marble avenues must have been an awe-inspiring revelation of a world of taste and splendor, harmony and beauty, grace and magnificence that was almost totally absent from American life.[23]

The source of this vision is not difficult to trace. In one sense it represented the ideal of a single individual, the dominant figure in the planning and construction of the exposition, Daniel H. Burnham. But Burnham also embodied the ideals and conceptions of a new American social and cultural elite.

This new elite had a complex self-image quite different from that of preceding generations of American entrepreneurs, though in many ways their ideology had been shaped by the traditions of the New York and Bostonian aristocracy.[24] For one thing, these men conceived of themselves as playing a role on a national and even international stage. The picture of Andrew Carnegie bearding the Kaiser on his yacht to tell him that the age of monarchy was passing is extreme, but it suggests the way in which the American business leader's mind had expanded from a concern with production and distribution in a particular area to a feeling of involvement with and responsibility for the world. Because of this involvement, these men developed a new attitude toward the traditions of European culture. Feeling themselves the New-World equivalent of the great mercantile princes of the past, desirous of helping their countrymen share in the cultural wealth of Europe, wanting to immortalize their names by association with the permanent glory of art, and recognizing a good investment when they saw it, the new elite became great collectors and patrons of the arts. Shipload after shipload of their booty flowed across the Atlantic. When William Randolph Hearst took to importing whole palaces and churches to reassemble on the rocky coast of California, he was only surpassing some of his less flamboyant predecessors.[25]

The new elite's art patronage was linked to another aspect of its self-image: a sense of public spirit and upper-class responsibility for cultural leadership. No doubt some magnates were ruthless exploiters of labor and unscrupulous manipulators of stocks, but the most important leaders were also seriously concerned with the state of American culture. It was in the patronage of the arts and sciences that their sense of public accountability found its major outlet. In other words, they were primarily supporters of cultural, rather than social reform. Their capital launched most of the major American cultural institutions—the museums, universities, symphony orchestras, and art schools that still dominate the American cultural scene.

The new elite quickly recognized and affiliated with a new group of architects, painters, writers, critics, and scholars who shared to a considerable extent its conception of cultural reform. The new group of artists and their patrons venerated the great artistic traditions of Europe and desired to recreate in America the institutions and cultural standards of this tradition. Among the artists this attitude frequently resulted from European training and residence, which provided another bond between them and their well-traveled patrons. The close social association and cultural sympathy between the parvenu industrial and financial elite and the artistic leaders was a new force in American culture.[26] It did not outlast the shocks of World War I, but while it did last, certain architects and artists had unprecedented funds at their disposal. The World's Columbian Exposition climaxed the relationship between these two groups. It was the architects' show but its message was also that of the new financial and industrial elite.

The special character of the Columbian Exposition grew out of the fact that it represented a unified plan of landscaping and architecture developed by the leading architectural and landscaping firms of the country. Early in the planning stage, when the Exposition's management faced a choice between free competition or the selection of a few major firms for the prospective buildings, Daniel Burnham fought hard for the elitist alternative. He insisted "that these buildings should be in their design, relationship, and arrangement of the highest possible architectural merit is of importance scarcely less than that of the variety, richness, and comprehensiveness of the various displays within them."[27] He persuaded Lyman Gage and business leaders who were organizing the fair to reject open competition in favor of "choosing each man for such work as would be most nearly parallel with his best achievements."[28] The result was Burnham's selection of the leading architectural firms, led by Richard Morris Hunt—whose commissions had included several great palaces for the Vanderbilts—and Charles F. McKim of the elite New York firm of McKim, Mead and White, architects for J. P. Morgan, among others. Bringing together into one plan buildings by Richard Morris Hunt, Charles Atwood, McKim, Mead and White, George B. Post, and the great Chicago firms of Burnham and Root, Adler and Sullivan, Jenny and Mundie, and S. S. Beman is analogous to some great promoter of the 1950s bringing together Mies van der Rohe, Eero Saarinen, Skidmore, Owings, and Merrill and Frank Lloyd Wright and persuading them to subordinate their own conceptions to a single plan. The remarkable fact is that, with the exception of an articulate and rather dogmatic radical like Louis Sullivan, this group of nineteenth-century architects were able to work with complete unanimity of purpose and concept. Meeting in Chicago, the architects and the sculptor Augustus Saint-Gaudens quickly arrived at an agreement about the ground plan, the basic style of the major buildings, and such esthetic refinements as a common cornice line and a basic module of dimension which would operate to bring their different buildings into splendid and harmonious unity. The sense of excitement and idealism and the rather pretentious air of great accomplishment that pervaded the collaboration of architects, businessmen, landscape planners, and artists is preserved in Burnham's often-quoted narrative of the event, which is worth quoting once more for the cultural style and symbolism it projects:

So the day went on. We had luncheon brought in. Then came the large committee. The winter afternoon was drawing to an end. In the room it was as still as death, save for the low voices of the speakers commenting on their designs. You could feel the thing as a great magnet. Finally, when the last drawing had been shown, Gage [Lyman J. Gage, leading Chicago banker and one of the exposition's directors] drew a long breath, stood up against the window, shut his eyes and said:

"Oh! Gentlemen, this is a dream!" Then, opening his eyes, he smilingly continued, "You have my good wishes, and I hope it can be carried out."

Saint-Gaudens had been in the corner all day, never opening his mouth, and scarcely moving. He came over to me, and taking both my hands, said:

"Look here, old fellow, do you realize that this is the greatest meeting of artists since the Fifteenth Century?"[29]

This remarkable unity of conception and sentiment was partly a result of the fact that most of the leading architects, sculptors, and artists who worked on the fair had a common intellectual, artistic, and ideological background, the Académie des Beaux Arts in Paris. Beaux Arts students shared a rigorous intellectual and artistic training. In scholarly knowledge and training in craftsmanship a Beaux Arts education could not be equalled anywhere in the world. The Columbian Exposition represented the importation of this tradition with its emphasis on monumental design, symmetry, grandeur, and vista; a tradition in harmony with the new elite's aspiration to cultural greatness.

The White City, however, was more than the mere importation of a tradition. It articulated a new cultural symbolism and a new conception of the relationship of art and technology. Leading the parade of new cultural themes was that of America as the home of a new, more glorious Renaissance. As one commentator put it, echoing Augustus Saint-Gaudens' comparison of the meeting of the Ground and Building Committee to a Renaissance symposium, the White City was Venice reborn. "Hither had leaped, across the centuries, across the seas, all that was beautiful and sacred in the Bride of the Adriatic." But he added, as was certainly implicit in the new symbolism, this was a Renaissance without the immoralities and excesses of the past, "a Venice resurrected from its crimes and glorified."[30]

The image of a new, purer Renaissance bursting forth from the chrysalis of American material and moral progress pervaded every aspect of the fair, from its architectural style to its speaker's toasts. Almost equally prominent was a new image of American womanhood. At Philadelphia in 1876, women had begun to appear upon the cultural scene, but they were still largely thought of as restricted to the roles of homemaking, teaching, and certain traditionally feminine agricultural and industrial tasks. A male architect had designed the woman's building at Philadelphia while the theme of its exhibits celebrated not woman's involvement in industrial society, but those achievements specifically identified and approvingly catalogued as "woman's work." By 1933, in the Century of Progress exhibition, the assimilation of women into American society had proceeded far enough that the fair's designers did not even provide for a special display of feminine achievement, and apparently women did not object to this failure to single out their sex. But at Chicago in 1893, the symbols and actuality of womanhood were everywhere. Indeed, the treatment of the theme of woman at the fair suggests a climactic moment between emancipation and assimilation, a cultural phase when women were rapidly becoming important as workers and as consumers but before their uniquely feminine social and cultural position had given way to assimilation into the economy. This was the time of the "new woman," newly vigorous, ambitious, and sophisticated, but still distinctly feminine.

The new woman had her representatives at the fair in Mrs. Potter Palmer and the Board of Lady Managers. Through the active involvement of this group of ladies, many of them wives of the business and artistic elite who designed the fair, women played a significant role in the organization and direction of the fair. The Board of Lady Managers arranged for the erection of a special woman's building, this time designed by a lady architect, Miss Sophia Hayden of Boston. But Mrs. Palmer's group was not satisfied with a separate woman's exhibit:

it was found that the plan adopted at the Centennial Exposition of placing the contributions of women in a woman's department sequestered from the general exhibits, would not answer for the occasion. By those who would furnish the most creditable of these contributions it was insisted that they should be so placed as to challenge competition with the best of classified products, apart from distinction of sex.

In contrast to the Philadelphia fair, therefore, the accomplishments of women "in every branch of industry, science, and art" were spread through the principal buildings, competing for awards with the masculine contingent. Throughout the arrangements of the fair, the Board of Lady Managers insisted that women should be shown in their full involvement in all the work of the world. The Board announced to the public that

one of the cherished ideals is to remove the present erroneous and injurious impression that women are doing little skilled labor, or little steady and valuable work, and that they consequently are not to be taken seriously into consideration when dealing with industrial problems.[31]

It might be noted here that the upper middle-class milieu from which most members of the Board of Lady Managers emerged was also the milieu of Jane Addams and many of her associates and supporters.

Not only did the living and breathing American woman play a central part in the Columbian Exposition, the new woman was the fair's leading symbol of the republic. Harriet Monroe had developed this theme in the ode she read at the dedication ceremonies months before the opening of the exposition:

Columbia ! Men beheld thee rise
    A goddess from the misty sea.
Lady of joy, sent from the skies,
    The nations worshipped the. . . .

Lady of love, whose smile shall bless. . . .

Lady of hope thou art. We wait
    with courage thy serene command. . . .

Lady of beauty! Thou shalt win
  Glory and power and length of days.
The sun and moon shall be thy kin,
  The stars shall sing thy praise.
All hail! We bring thee vows most sweet
  To strew before thy winged feet.
Now onward be thy ways.*

This imagery was also embodied in the great statue of the Republic by Daniel Chester French and in the monumental fountain by Frederick MacMonnies, which stood at opposite ends of the Grand Lagoon, the central point of the fair. It was echoed in statuary from one end of the grounds to the other. To our eyes, these statues look rather like monumental versions of the Gibson Girl and the connection is not an accident. The Gibson Girl also reflected the image of the new woman whose beauty, energy, charm, and sophistication suggested an America that had become more socially and artistically knowing, but whose unambiguous purity and integrity preserved the vision of moral superiority. This was also the image that dominated the fiction of William Dean Howells and Henry James, though James' version of the new woman's fate was far darker and more ambiguous than could have been seen by the clear-sighted goddess who presided over the White City.[32]

The American industrialist and financier as Renaissance prince and the new woman as symbol of the Republic's cultural aspiration and moral purity were hero and heroine, but the White City, itself, was the central symbol of the fair. The White City was a new image of the landscape in which the power of industrial technology had been transmuted into the grandeur of Art. The Philadelphia Centennial had managed a dynamic but uneasy balance between the traditional realm of art and the new world of science and technology. The Columbian Exposition symbolized the great tradition, the belated appearance in the New World of Art, with underscored capital letters. Through the example of the great tradition, the planners of 1893

---

*Harriet Monroe, "Columbia Ode," quoted in The Graphic History of the Fair (Chicago: G. P. Engelhard and Co., 1895), pp. 47–48.

attempted to transform the harsh and ugly world of urban industrialism into a utopian vision of harmonious beauty and monumental
splendor. So successful was the attempt that William Dean Howells
had his traveler from Altruria visit the fair and feel for a moment
that he was back in his utopian homeland. Torn between his fundamental affinity for the cultural vision of the new elite and his
humanitarian sense of social injustice, Howells tried to interpret the
fair as a profound, if only temporary transformation of industrial
society. His utopian traveler proclaims:

> the World's Fair City was not the effect, the fine flower of the
> competition which underlies [the American] economy, but was the
> first fruits of the principle of emulation which animates our happy
> commonwealth [Altruria] and gives men, as no where else on
> earth, a foretaste of heaven.[33]

Few of the fair's designers would have accepted a formulation so
politically colored as this one, but there is no doubt that their conception was a conscious cultural challenge to the chaotic disorganization,
esthetic confusion, and ugliness of the existing industrial metropolis.[34]
There had been nothing like this at the Philadelphia Centennial.
There, the planners had allowed a kind of continuity between
nature, the exposition, and the adjacent city. The existing topography
had largely shaped the ground plan, while the buildings were either
frankly temporary exhibition structures or not unlike the current
architectural style in the surrounding city. The informality and non-
monumentality of the arrangement of buildings was, if anything, less
regular and well-organized than the city streets with their grid
pattern. At Chicago, however, the planners not only created a highly
formal and monumental plan, they undertook to reshape nature in
accordance with it. Under the direction of Frederick Law Olmsted and
his associate Henry S. Codman, the sandy swamps of Jackson Park
were dredged and filled until they became a network of formal lagoons
and canals set off by the calculated "naturalness" of the tree-lined
"Wooded Island." Around the lagoons and canals were erected a series
of monumental buildings, unified by their placement, their similarity
of style and material, and by the formal devices of a uniform cornice

line and a basic module or dimension. As visitor after visitor testified, the effect was a vista of overpowering monumentality. The grand Court of Honor, surrounded by Hunt's Administration Building, Post's Manufactures and Liberal Arts Building, Peabody and Stearns' Machinery Hall, Van Brunt and Howe's Electricity Building, and McKim, Mead and White's Agricultural Building, and dominated by Daniel Chester French's monumental statue of the Republic was one focal point of the Columbian Exposition. Another was Atwood's Fine Arts Building (Now the Chicago Museum of Science and Industry) within which was housed, according to one enthusiast, an exhibition of the fine arts "greater in plan, scope and achievement than any other that has been undertaken in the whole history of the world."[35] In addition to a substantial sampling of contemporary work from the United States, France, Germany, Great Britain, Austria, Spain, Italy, Belgium, Holland, Norway, Sweden, Denmark, Russia, Canada, Mexico, and Japan, the fine arts exhibition featured a major retrospective and historical exhibit of American painting and many casts of the traditional monuments of French architecture and sculpture. At Philadelphia, the fine arts were exhibited as something different from, but not less contemporary than the achievements of science and technology. Here in Chicago, however, the idea of art suggested a realm of human activity not only set apart by its special concern for ideal values, but also related to a permanent tradition of past masterpieces, which set standards and provided sources of inspiration for contemporary life.

The influence of this conception of the great tradition was not confined to the fine arts; the new elite also sought to transform the world of industry. Making the Exposition's architecture monumentally classic in style was not enough. It had to be designed to hide its modern construction behind a gleaming facade of counterfeit marble in the form of staff, a surfacing material composed largely of plaster. While at Philadelphia, the temporary exhibitional character and ironframe construction of the buildings were as apparent as the elaborate decoration that embellished their surfaces, in Chicago, the architects and designers sought the illusion of monumental permanence, the overriding of technology by art. Post's incredible Manufactures Building, the largest in the world up to its time, spanning an area of 732 by 1,687 feet under its twenty arched steel trusses, was a stunning feat in iron and steel technology. But the exterior of the building, masked by colonnades, porticos, arcades, and an oddly hipped roof gave little hint of this achievement. The same artistic ideal shaped the design of many of the exhibits. Whenever possible, articles of manufacture or agriculture were transformed into artistic monuments. Ohio provided an exhibit of its cereal products in the form of a miniature Parthenon with a portico of glass columns filled with grain; Illinois displayed a large landscape painting or, rather, a mosaic constructed out of different colored grains; California erected a monumental Roman column surmounted by an eagle—all but the eagle made out of oranges.

However, the new elite's vision of the dominance of the great artistic tradition was not purchased without cost. To define art by reference to a tradition of masterpieces is to risk setting it apart from the mainstream of life, as something to be honored in the costly and secluded precincts of museums. When this happens, the appreciation and possession of art, always something of a status symbol, can easily become little more than an outworn symbol of aristocratic ostentation. This was one of Thorstein Veblen's great insights and he developed it with bitter and ironic eloquence in The Theory of the Leisure Class, (New York: The Macmillan Co., 1899) which, published six years after the Columbian Exposition, might almost be read as a commentary on it.

Veblen definitively pinned down a fundamental weakness of the new elite's cultural ideology. By rejecting the esthetic potentiality of technology itself and attaching themselves to a preindustrial cultural tradition, the "leisure class" had made art the symbol of their "pecuniary prowess" rather than an integral part of modern life. Veblen's analysis, though it tended to reduce the relation between art and society to an oversimple equation and to ignore the real cultural achievements of the new elite, points up the failures of the Columbian exposition. Despite the remarkable unity of its plan, the White City had all too little relevance to the architectural problems of an industrial age. Montgomery Schuyler justly called it "the most integral, the most extensive, the most illusive piece of scenic architecture that has ever been seen."[36] Even within the White City, the marmoreal magnificence of the main buildings could not quite overpower the tawdry but vivid chaos of the Midway Plaisance, whose shows and rides made it quite evident that in a modern industrial democracy the great artistic tradition was not enough. The Court of Honor, with its monumental vistas and harmonious perspectives, was dedicated to art but it was too grand and awe-inspiring to permit relaxation and fun. For the visitor to recover from the stupendous impact of the White City, an area dedicated to pleasure, excitement, and entertainment was essential and this was provided by the Midway. In the gap between the Midway and the Court of Honor we see the incipient form of that split culture so characteristic of modern industrial society: the "serious" or "high" art of the museums, concert halls, and hardcover books as opposed to the entertainment and excitement of the mass media. Hamlin Garland gives us a moving insight into the gap between the ideal world of the Columbian Exposition and the ordinary world known by his midwestern parents:

> Stunned by the majesty of the vision, my mother sat in her chair, visioning it all yet comprehending little of its meaning. Her life had been spent among homely small things, and these gorgeous scenes dazzled her, overwhelmed her, letting in upon her in one mighty flood a thousand stupefying suggestions of the art and history and poetry of the world.... At last utterly overcome she leaned her head against my arm, closed her eyes and said, "Take me home, I can't stand any more of it."[37]

Yet, those who couldn't take it were evidently in the minority. The fair's unified vision of an esthetic standard for the new industrial society spread rapidly across America, carried mainly by the indefatigable energy and dauntless vision of D. H. Burnham. Louis Sullivan, in his later bitterness, described this influence as a disease and lamented that it had killed American architecture for several decades. It is true that the White City's monumental classicism became the fashionable style in major urban architecture until the late 1930s and that this undoubtedly impeded the development of what we now know as modern architecture in America. But the fair's influence also popularized for the first time the idea of large-scale architectural and landscape planning in American cities. In addition to the superb Chicago Plan of 1909, perhaps the single greatest contribution to our culture of what I have called the new elite of industrial organizers, financiers, and artists, Burnham also worked on plans for Washington, San Francisco, Cleveland, and Manila. Innumerable smaller American cities followed this example. We owe much that is still most beautiful about our cities to the work of Burnham and his followers.

Yet superb as they are, in many respects, most of these plans show the same basic defects as the Columbian Exposition's attempt to transform modern technology with the ideals and conceptions of the great tradition. In consequence, many of our cities are currently in the process of reluctantly, confusedly, and in some instances terribly, dismantling the new elite's creations. In the end, the monumental civic centers and great formal parks that were the focus of most of the new elite's city plans proved incapable of adaptation to the city's changing patterns and needs. With the coming of the automobile, the grand malls and parks were increasingly destroyed by traffic and overrun by parking lots. The monumental buildings turned out to be increasingly inadequate to house the burgeoning bureaucracies of government, yet too expensive to demolish. And, saddest of all, the great formal parks became vacuums into which flowed the tormented and the criminal. Even when twentieth-century man enjoyed the contemplation of vistas, he could not, with the high price of urban real estate and the high crime level in the parks, either afford or risk it.

IV

The men of the nineties, proud of the achievements of the present, still looked to the past for the inspiration of a form in which to house their commemorative festival. . . . In 1933, forty years later, Daniel Burnham's son and his architects look not to the past, but only to the future. They have taken today's materials, and even tomorrow's, and working by the new theorems, have built strange new structures where utility must set the mark of beauty. With modern lighting and ventilation windows are unnecessary. Out with them ! Build sheer blank walls instead. Marble and granite express only one mood. Make synthetic walls and get Joseph Urban from the Follies to splash them with lights, many colored moving lights so that they can express any mood.*

To get some idea of the tremendous change between the World's Columbian Exposition of 1893 and the Century of Progress Exhibition of 1933–34, the curious historian need only pay a visit to Chicago's Museum of Science and Industry. On the exterior, the building still proclaims the vision of 1893: monumental splendor in the great tradition, complete with columns, karyatids, porticoes, and domes. It is, in fact, the one remaining building of the White City, Atwood's Fine Arts Palace, refurbished in more permanent materials. In the interior, we immediately reenter our own world of industrial technology and mass culture, the world of buttons to make things go, of science and movement, of benevolent corporate and government bureaucracies whose loudspeakers baffle the air with continuous explanation, justification, and advertisement. It is the world of now, but its basic shape was already evident in 1933, when many of its first exhibits greeted the crowds at the Century of Progress.

The Century of Progress was officially billed as "the dramatization of the progress of civilization during the hundred years of Chicago's existence."[38] Its organization and exhibits were peculiarly well-suited to the needs of the time, for even though it had to buck the worst years of the great depression, the Century of Progress operated for two summers with a paid attendance of 39 million, (total admission 48 million) largest by far of any American exhibition to that time. Up to World War II, the fair's attendance record was equalled on the world scene only by the great Paris exposition of 1900. Moreover, though it did not have the large public appropriations that had made up the deficits in both 1876 and 1893, the Century of Progress actually made money. After all debts and bonds had been paid and the fair had been dismantled, the management was able to distribute a surplus of $160,000 to the South Park, the Museum of Science and Industry, the Art Institute, and other cultural institutions.[39]

Above all, exhibits at the Century of Progress reflected the new

---

*John and Ruth L. Ashenhurst, All About Chicago (Boston: Houghton Mifflin, 1933), p. 22.

corporate character of American life. Though previous exhibitions had included large displays of the products of American industry, these products were usually displayed by categories in the large exhibit buildings. The exhibitor could proclaim his corporate name only by constructing a large display case or kiosk within the building. But by 1933 corporate identity and image had become so important a consideration that many corporations chose to construct their own buildings. In 1893, only nine out of about 137 buildings were separate exhibitions constructed by business corporations, and four of these were small entertainment booths on the Midway. In 1933, however, out of about the same number of buildings, twenty were erected by business corporations, including Chrysler, Firestone, A & P, General Cigar, General Motors, Goodyear, Sears Roebuck, Sinclair, and Time and Fortune, Inc. Few of these companies had even been in existence in 1893. Several of the corporate buildings were among the larger structures. Moreover, while the number of buildings erected by foreign governments was about the same, the role of state governments had dropped to almost nothing. In 1893 forty-one states had erected their own structures while in 1933, only Illinois, Florida and Alaska had separate buildings, an indication of the political and economic decline of state governments. The large corporation and the purveyor of entertainment for profit dominated the show in 1933. Of the total of about $100 million expended for the construction and operation of the Century of Progress, the exhibitors (mainly corporations) paid out $33 million and the operators of concessions, $24 million.[40]

The outlook and working methods of those who organized and designed the Century of Progress also reflected the changes in American culture that had brought the corporation into a central position in the display. It would be unfair to call them organization men in the pejorative sense, for it took both daring and imagination to pull off the Century of Progress at a time when many Americans did not know where their next meal was coming from. But the creators of the fair, like Lenox Lohr, Louis Skidmore, and Nathaniel Owings were young men, fully acclimated to new conceptions of management, cooperation, teamwork, and organization. (Owings was thirty, Skidmore thirty-six, and Lohr forty-two in 1933.) Just as the established aristocratic giants of 1893 differed from the hustling entrepreneurs of the 1870s, the men of 1933 were more accustomed to operate within the collective terms of corporate bureaucracy than the elite of the 1890s, which associated itself more with the cultural ideology of a class than with the needs of a corporation. The later careers of Lohr, Skidmore, and Owings show their adjustment to the organizational revolution. Skidmore and Owings went on to develop one of the largest and most successful artistic-engineering bureaucracies in American history, the vast architectural organization of Skidmore, Owings and Merrill. Lenox Lohr went on to a career in the management of large organizations devoted to entertainment and education: the National Broadcasting Company, the Chicago Railroad Fair, the Museum of Science and Industry. It is also indicative of the new organizational environment that Lohr's own narrative of the Century of Progress was published in the form of a book on Fair management, a skillfully constructed guide to the organization and operation of such enterprises.

The elite of the 1890s were not organization men. Though they dealt in large organizations, the finance capitalists of the late nineteenth century were most concerned with the consolidation of personal power. Through such devices as interlocking directorates and holding companies, which insured centralized personal control over large enterprises, these men sought to use personal power to reduce the conflict and dislocation of American industrial development. Even industrialists of the period, like Carnegie and Rockefeller, tended to maintain personal control over their far-flung enterprises. In effect, these men sought to bring order into American life by constituting themselves an oligarchy, a small class with large power over American life. Even in the political sphere, Theodore Roosevelt tried to create in government the kind of personal authority that Rockefeller and Morgan had erected in industry and finance. In the arts, this pattern emerged, as we have seen, in the cultural vision that the creators of the Columbian Exposition sought to impose on the country, in the new ideal of city planning, and in the personal authority of men like D. H. Burnham.

But the large corporation, which had been the creature of the new elite's drive to personal power, gradually became the master. Even in the 1920s, leading corporations occupied a more important place in American society than the individuals who directed them. The crash of 1929 and the ensuing depression finally tarnished forever the image of the industrialist and financier as the hero of a new Renaissance. From the opening days of the New Deal, the warm, democratic personality of the new president, and the anonymous government and corporate bureaucracies behind him diminished further the remaining potency of the new elite's oligarchic conception of America.

The cultural vision of the new elite lingered on in certain circles. Its last stand was the construction of the National Gallery in Washington (1938–41), the last major example of the monumental classicism of the Columbian Exposition. But this turned out to be, as a British architectural journal had predicted, "the apotheosis, and the end, of an architectural outlook and endeavor which have had immense influence in this country, as in the U.S.A., for nearly 75 years."[41] By this time, the most important American architects and artists had long since abandoned the ideal of the great tradition. Following the functional esthetic enunciated by Louis Sullivan and Frank Lloyd Wright, they were forging a new relationship between art and technology, in which art became the fulfillment rather than the transformation of technology. Rejecting the relevance of the great tradition as a guide to the artistic problems of an industrial society, these artists and architects tried to take their cue from science and the machine. At Chicago's Hull House, where cultural vision encountered industrial realities, Wright, in a brilliant early paper significantly entitled "The Art and Craft of the Machine" (1901), laid down the main lines of the new functionalist resolution of art and technology. Instead of being opposed to art, he argued, "the Machine is, in fact, the metamorphosis of ancient art and craft . . . [and] is capable of carrying to fruition high ideals in art—higher than the world has yet seen!"[42] But in order to reach these ideals, artists must realize that "the Machine has dealt Art in the grand old sense a deathblow."[43] For Wright, the Renaissance, instead of being the model for a new surge of culture in America, was "this decadence." In turning to the past for its artistic inspiration, the Renaissance had turned away from the only possible source of true art: relevance to human needs, fitness to purpose, harmony between form and use, and simple truth to materials and processes. To recapture these qualities, the artist, instead of imposing his designs upon the machine, should let his forms emerge directly from the human needs his work is to fulfill, from the materials of which it is constructed, and from the processes of its construction.

This functionalist conception of the relationship of art and technology was first popularized in the Century of Progress Exhibition. In the design of the fair, as Lohr later remembered:

it was early decided to cast off the shackles of the past and give a new freedom to design, particularly one which would serve the practical purpose of providing buildings suited in form and size to their primary requirement—the display of exhibits. With architectural requirements based on exhibit demands, the effectiveness would depend on planes and surfaces, as a background for the decorative effects of color and light, and the animated pattern of crowds of people moving at various levels on ramps and terraces. The architecture would find buildings, [sic] designed to create an effect based primarily on usefulness. New elements of construction, the products of science and industry, would be the vehicles of achievement.[44]

In particular, the architects found that they were increasingly concerned with the problems of flexibility, of effective traffic flow, and of rapidity and ease in the construction and dismantling of the exhibition. Consciously rejecting the formal symmetry and balanced vistas off 1893, they embraced an open asymmetrical plan presented by Raymond Hood, which made possible a continuous flow of movement by the vast crowds expected to attend the fair.[45] The same thinking shaped the design of individual buildings. Large stairways, entrances, and spaces that might overawe the visitor and halt his steady passage from point to point gave way to ramps and free-flowing interior designs. Instead of immense individual buildings like the gigantic Manufactures and Liberal Arts Building of 1893, there were groups of smaller buildings like the General Exhibits Pavilions and the complex known as the Hall of Science.

The temporary character of the exhibition was frankly exploited by its planners. In 1893, the architects had sought an illusion of permanence to go along with the commitment to the great tradition, using temporary materials to achieve the effect of monumental stone construction. The designers of 1933 fully accepted the impermanence of their work. Harvey Corbett, chairman of the fair's architectural commission, classed permanence in building with the traditional styles as "just another ... old idea." Architecture in the twentieth century is inevitably ephemeral, he explained to the *Saturday Evening Post*, and it is ridiculous to build structures that might "last as long as the Pyramids," since "we take them down, at the end of twenty-five or thirty years, and replace them with other structures."[46] One of the major planning criteria became the need for materials and methods of construction that would enable rapidity and ease of erection and destruction, as well as maximum salvageability of the component parts. The exhibition itself was conceived as part of a continuing process of change and adaptation, a process that would not be complete with the destruction of the buildings, but would go on as the salvageable materials found new uses.[47]

The principle of change and motion dominated the exhibition. One observer noted that "every exhibit which can possibly include motion of some sort is presented dynamically. Instead of long rows of idle machinery ... the exhibits of the Fair comprise a whole series of mechanically motivated demonstrations, almost theatric in effect."[48] Many science exhibits used working models activated by a button. Several companies provided displays of production lines—Firestone going so far as to set up a complete tire factory. Even the Hall of Social Science, not content with the traditional displays of anthropological relics and charts, had a demonstration school. "The emphasis in the exhibits lies on process. ... There is to be no competition between finished products; the visitor will not be bored to death looking at miles of completed goods. ... Both in the exhibit halls controlled by the fair and in the buildings erected by typical industries, the exhibits have been planned to show the method involved, rather than the end achieved."[49]

The emphasis on process reflected the culture of the new corporate America. For the twentieth-century industrial corporation, the past was nothing but junk and salvageable materials. There was only the

ever-moving future, with its continuous flow of new products discovered by scientific research, produced by changing technologies, distributed by an international organization, sold through mass communications, and consumed by an eager and increasingly affluent
public. In essence, the vision of America offered by the Century
of Progress was of the wonderful changing and abundant world to
come through the advances of science and technology. The success
of the exposition was generally attributed to the tremendous general
appeal of this central theme. "To celebrate the successful union of
science and industry immediately caught the imagination of the foremost citizens of this nation," Lenox Lohr reports. And also notes the
reaction of the general public.

> The public crowded into the Hall of Science. The exhibits seemed
> to satisfy some need of which not even the Exposition was entirely
> aware when they voiced the serious purpose of the project. On
> days of slack attendance which etched worried frowns on the faces
> of concessionaires, the aisles of the Hall of Science were jammed
> with visitors. . . . But what baffled and delighted the men of science,
> the technicians and mechanics, whose industry and ingenuity
> produced the exhibits in this great structure, were the youngsters
> who accepted it as their own.[50]

Thus, "functional" design, scientific progress, and technological
change dominated the planning of the 1933–34 fair. But the Century
of Progress exhibition also reflected a new relationship between
America's business elite and the public. From another point of view,
the fair can be seen as the first major exercise in institutional advertising, shaped by the need of American corporations to communicate
to, to reassure, and to win the approval of the vast heterogeneous mass
of the public. The new elite of 1893 had barely consulted this necessity.
Indeed, they gave the public the Midway Plaisance for its pleasure
and entertainment, but the heart of the World's Columbian Exposition was unalloyed education and uplift. The lighter vein of carnival
amusement was carefully separated from the monumental vistas of
industrial progress shaped by the great tradition. Nor did the creation
of corporate images and the justification of American business enter-

prise play a major role in the fair. As already indicated, few of the buildings and none of the major structures were sponsored by industrial or financial corporations. By 1933, however, both the structure of business and its relation to its public had changed significantly. The 1929 crash and ensuing depression, together with the crescendo of social criticism and reform, had made business leaders increasingly conscious of the need for public understanding and support. They responded by carrying the techniques of institutional advertising and corporate image-making into the erection of individual corporate buildings at the 1933 fair.

In many other ways, the planners of 1933 showed their concern for communicating to and gaining the support of a mass public. They did their best to create a carefully mixed blend of entertainment and education, showmanship and science, public service and corporate advertising. Unlike the 1893 fair, the Century of Progress had several amusement areas, each containing model foreign villages, shops, rides, and shows "so that the casual visitor, no matter where he was, could always turn from his contemplation of the serious side of the Fair to the lighter vein of the Midway."[51] Even in the scientific and industrial exhibits, the planners searched for a formula through which scientific discovery and technological change could be popularized:

> While the theme must have its appeal through those higher concepts of education, science and culture, it was realized that their interpretation must apply showmanship and entertainment of a high order, for people visit an exposition with a carnival spirit, hoping to be amused and diverted from humdrum routine existence by dreams of fantasy. That these could be successfully combined was amply attested by the results.[52]

In the midst of this celebration of science and technology, where was art? It was, to be sure, present on the grounds in the form of architectural and industrial design, but the traditional fine arts that had set the tone of the Columbian Exposition were now a mile away in the Chicago Art Institute, a building that has been constructed at the time of the 1893 exposition. The reason for this was that the art exhibition, no longer primarily concerned with the display of contemporary painting and sculpture, consisted largely of master-pieces of the past, considered too valuable and precious to be housed in a temporary building. By 1933, Art in capital letters had become a realm of static, priceless permanence, appropriate to a museum but symbolically placed outside the cultural stream of the present.

As in 1893, the planners of A Century of Progress strove mightily to create a display that would have a strong impact on American design. It would be nice to be able to report that the fair was as great an artistic as a commercial success. But despite their zeal for new esthetic principles and their successful practical solutions to a number of problems, the chief architects of 1933, including D. H. Burnham's son and one of his partners, were not quite able to resolve the conflict between their academic training and experience and the new functional esthetic. The White City of 1893 was an architectural sea coast of Bohemia, but it possessed a real artistic integrity and impact. Nineteen hundred and thirty-three was an architecture of science-fiction. It had technological efficiency, but the buildings were, as one critic put it:

a pain in color over a medley of chizzle chuzzle forms. A masquerade of jazzed palaces and pylons.[53]

Perhaps the final comment should be Frank Lloyd Wright's. Rather noticeably not engaged by the management of the fair, Wright was invited to a protest meeting at Town Hall in New York City by a group of artists and critics. With his own irrepressible arrogance, Wright rose and spelled out for the assembled protestors three totally different but equally dazzling conceptions for a modern fair. Fantastic though they were, the boldness, integrity, and spirit of these conceptions, fortunately preserved in the pages of Wright's *Autobiography*, reveal by contrast the absence of artistic power, vision, and daring in the work of 1933. Ironically, these conceptions—(1) "a great sky-scraper in which the Empire State Building might stand free in a central interior court-space which would be devoted to all the resources of the modern elevator . . ." (2) "an architectural canopy more beauti-ful and more vast than any ever seen" hung from great pylons, (3) a city of colored glass and plastic tubing floating on pontoons so that the fair would be "a whole world of illuminated illumination, iradiating and irradiated light—an iridescent fair or a fair of iridescent, opalescent 'reeds,"[54] suggest the extent to which Wright's own greatness was dependent on intangibles of artistic vision and cultural insight, which could no more be attributed to the imperatives of functionalism than to the dreams of D. H. Burnham.

V

To define the limits of these two departments of man's activity, which work into one another, and by means of one another, so intricately and inseparably, were by its nature an impossible attempt. Their relative importance ... will vary in different times, according to the special wants and dispositions of those times. Meanwhile, it seems clear enough that only in the right coordination of the two, and the vigorous forwarding of *both*, does our true line of action lie.*

Carlyle was not only the first to name industrialism, at the center of his work was one of the central problems of European and American culture since the industrial revolution : the apparently increasing gap between the artistic and humanistic and the scientific and technological spheres of modern society, the "two cultures" as C. P. Snow has recently defined them. In America, our study of the three fairs of 1876, 1893, and 1933 shows how the relationship between these spheres of human activity has shifted in response to the changing pattern of industrial society and to the cultural visions of business and artistic leaders. At Philadelphia, the exposition was shaped by a balance between a traditional conception of the arts and the dynamic force of technological innovation. Both 1893 and 1933 were more onesided in their structures. The Columbian Exposition was dominated by an artistic ideal of monumental permanence and tradition; the designers of A Century of Progress sought to create a synthesis of science, mass education, and entertainment and to respond to the dynamic of movement and change inherent in twentieth-century

---

*Thomas Carlyle, "Signs of the Times" (1829) in *Critical and Miscellaneous Essays* (Boston: Dana Estes and Co., n.d.), Vol. I, p. 478.

industrial society. In 1876, art, industry, and science were part of a complex pattern in which each element had a distinctive function. In 1893, a cultural elite tried to use the ideals of the great artistic tradition to transform the realities of industrial society. By 1933, industrial corporations and vast governmental and techno-logical bureaucracies had become the dominant social influence and with them, science and industry were the primary shapers of culture. The arts had either enlisted under the functionalist esthetic in the service of industrial design, or, in the form of priceless past master-pieces, had become separated from the mainstream of life.

Perhaps their sense of an increasing cultural fragmentation made the planners in both 1893 and 1933 feel the need for a conscious, highly organized plan in a way that the creators of the Philadelphia Centennial had not. Between 1893 and 1933, however, the concept of planning changed completely. In 1893, planning aimed at the achieve-ment of a fixed, symmetrical, monumental, and static organization based on tradition and reflecting the esthetic ideals of a cultural elite. Though their design was inevitably impermanent, the men of 1893 sought a sense of permanence that would communicate an image of serenity, harmony, and splendor. In 1933, planning meant not only a conscious rejection of the past, but an acceptance of the imper-manence and fluidity of the present. The exposition's designers tried to create a flexible, dynamic, and technologically advanced environ-ment that was capable of continuous change and motion and therefore responsive to the modern imperative of continuous scientific progress and technological development. The future had become the locus of value.

But if the White City of 1893 was an architectural Arcadia with little relevance to the human problems of a modern industrial metro-polis, the future-oriented fair of 1933 failed to establish a coherent and integral relationship between the cultural tradition and the tech-nological future. It did not manage to carry forward into its transient and flowing present anything of the beauty and harmony that the planners of 1893 had so earnestly sought. The 1933 fair was an expres-sion of modern industrial culture, but it also demonstrated with great clarity how that culture had lost contact with many of its own inner needs; within its gates there was no escape from the interminable flow of time, from the undifferentiated round of production and consumption, from the unbreakable stream of traffic. Where was the moment where one could say "Stay! You are so fair!"; where was the still point of the turning wheel?

In the art season of 1965, Robert Rauschenberg, leader of a younger generation of American painters and sculptors tried to give one answer to those questions. This was, of course, not the first time artists and writers had tackled the problem, which has been one of the major provinces of art since the beginning of the industrial revolution. But Rauschenberg's answer was striking enough in the light of the preceding discussion to provide a conclusion to this paper.[55] It was called "Oracle" and it was made from that end product of science and industry, the one thing in the modern world no longer caught up in the process of change: junk. Out of large pieces of junk—an old car door, a discarded window frame, a battered piece of pipe, an old metal tub, and an obsolete control panel—Rauschenberg fashioned five large wheeled objects that could be placed in various positions around a room. Each of these objects was elaborately wired with a special transmitter that would enable it to emit snatches of radio broadcasts and random noises. Ironically, or perhaps appropriately, this required the development of special electronic equipment at a reported cost of $6,000. It was an expensive, seemingly meaningless, ugly, and futile combination of useless objects and incommunicative sound. Yet the striking thing was that as one entered the aura of Rauschenberg's "sculpture" one became caught up in a strangely fascinating mood of stillness and serenity in which junk became charged with a transcendent significance and random noise became momentarily more meaningful than the blur of words that baffles the air in the city of mass communications. The creator of "Oracle" had clearly rejected both the Renaissance esthetic of beauty and permanence and the modern functional canon of form, but there was no doubt that he had made a powerful and haunting work of art. This and similar works of the last decade suggest the emergence of another relationship between art and technology, a relationship that seems to go beyond both traditional estheticism and twentieth-century functionalism. It remains to be seen whether this new vision will strike deep into American culture.

NOTES

1. For a convenient brief history of international exhibitions, with attendance statistics, cf. K. W. Luckhurst, *The Story of Exhibitions* (London and New York: The Studio Publications, 1951).

2. Russell Lynes, *The Tastemakers* (New York: Harper and Row, 1954), p. 112. Lynes' highly critical discussion of the Centennial is on pp. 112–17.

3. The influence of the Columbian Exposition was then and still is a matter of dispute among critics and historians. Louis Sullivan, the great Chicago architect, viewed it as a national disaster that effectually halted the development of modern architecture in America for several decades. Others saw it as a high point of American cultural achievement. Perhaps the majority have now come around to Sullivan's position. However, Carl Condit, the best contemporary scholar of Chicago architecture feels that the truth lies between these extremes: the 1893 fair did confuse the development of a contemporary architectural style, but at the same time it set a high standard for architectural design and planning. The present writer agrees with this judgement. For Condit's doubts about the Sullivan view that the World's Fair "killed" Chicago architecture, cf. *The Chicago School of Architecture* (Chicago: Universiy of Chicago Press, 1964), pp. 160–61. William A. Coles and Henry Hope Reed, Jr., *Architecture in America: A Battle of Styles* (New York: Appleton-Century-Crofts, Inc., 1961), pp. 137–211 give a good representation of the various reactions to the fair.

4. For lists of directors of the fair cf. James D. McCabe, *The Illustrated History of the Centennial Exhibition* (Philadelphia: The National Publishing Co., 1876); H. H. Bancroft, *The Book of the Fair* (Chicago and San Francisco: The Bancroft Co., 1895), 3 vols; Lenox Lohr, *Fair Management* (Chicago: The Cunea Press, Inc., 1952).

5. Walter Smith, *Household Taste*, quoted in Lynes, *Tastemakers*, p. 114.

6. McCabe, *Illustrated History*, pp. 221–22.

7. A note on the evidence for many of the generalizations in this article is necessary here. Because I have been interested in the fairs' structures and designs as they reflect attitudes toward the relation of elements of our culture to one another, much of my evidence is visual. It is derived from the plans, and from engravings and photographs of sites, buildings, and exhibits. Unfortunately it is not possible to reproduce the large number of engravings and photographs that support my analysis. However, I have tried to give some indication of the character of this evidence in the text and, whenever possible, I have sought confirmation of my argument in literary sources such as the speeches and memoirs of organizers of the fairs, the histories and guidebooks published for the occasions, and certain discussions of the fairs in newspapers and magazines. Readers interested in consulting

the visual record will find it rich and fascinating. It is most conveniently accessible in the lavish books of illustrations published at the time. I found the following particularly useful: *The Masterpieces of the Centennial International Exhibition Illustrated* (Philadelphia: Gebhart and Barrie, 1876-78), 3 vols. McCabe, *Illustrated History. World's Fair Photographs* (Chicago: H. W. Hine, 1894). Halsey C. Ives (ed.), *The Dream City* (St. Louis: Thompson Publishing Co., 1893). *The Columbian Gallery* (Chicago: The Werner Co., 1894). Bancroft, *Book of the Fair*. Charles M. Kurtz (ed.), *Illustrations from the Art Gallery of the World's Columbian Exposition* (Philadelphia: G. Barne, 1893). Chicago Century of Progress International Exposition, *Official Guide Book of the Fair* (Chicago: A Century of Progress, Inc., 1932). Lohr, *Fair Management.*

8. McCabe, *Illustrated History*, p. 892.

9. *Ibid.*, p. 893.

10. Quoted in *ibid.*, p. 294.

11. Cf. Russell Lynes' vigorous criticism of the aesthetic confusion and bad taste of the Philadelphia Centennial in Lynes, *Tastemakers*, pp. 112-17. The present writer feels that Lynes fails to grasp the cultural unity that lies behind the exuberant surface, however.

12. I would like to note here that my friend and colleague Joshua C. Taylor, whose conversation has taught me more about art than any other source, suggested to me this explanation for the peculiar use of styles at Philadelphia. The same principle is of course quite evident throughout mid-nineteenth-century American architecture and design. For an example of the theory of one of the leading exponents of the associative principle cf. the works of A. J. Downing.

13. Edward C. Bruce, *The Century: Its Fruits and Its Festival* (Philadelphia: J. B. Lippincott & Co., 1877), p. 21.

14. For examples of mid-nineteenth-century functionalism cf. the works of A. J. Downing and Horatio Greenough. Russell Lynes also points out in *The Tastemakers* how each successive movement in nineteenth-century American architecture had a tendency to proclaim its "functionalism" and to criticize the nonutilitarian character of preceding movements.

15. Bruce, *The Century*, p. 65.

16. *Ibid.*, p. 171. Cf. also pp. 152-53.

17. *Ibid.*, p. 80.

18. *Ibid.*, p. 152. For Wright's conception of "The Art and Craft of the Machine," cf. part IV of this chapter.

19. McCabe, *op. cit.*, p. 471.

20. Cf. John Kouwenhowen, *Made in America* (Garden City: Doubleday and Co., 1948).

21. Francis A. Walker (ed.), *International Exhibition, 1876. Reports and Awards* (Washington: Government Printing Office, 1880), Vol. VII, p. 537.

22. *The Chicago Record's History of the World's Fair* (Chicago: The Chicago Daily News Co., 1893), p. 29.

23. Montgomery Schuyler, *American Architecture and Other Writings*, ed. William H. Jordy and Ralph Coe (New York: Atheneum, 1964), p. 275–93. Henry Adams, *The Education of Henry Adams* (Boston: Houghton Mifflin Co., 1918), pp. 338–42. Examples of other reactions are usefully excerpted in Coles and Reed, *Architecture in America*, pp. 178–211.

24. I have been guided in this conception of the new elite by an unpublished paper, "Aristocracy in America? The Case of the Boston Brahmins" kindly loaned to me by the editor of this volume, Frederic C. Jaher. The formation of a highly cultivated elite is also discussed in Jaher's "Businessman and Gentleman: Nathan and Thomas Gold Appleton—An Exploration in Intergenerational History," *Explorations in Entrepreneurial History*, Second Series, Vol. 4 (Fall, 1966), pp. 17–39. Jaher, "The Boston Brahmins in The Age of Capitalism," chap. 7, this volume.

25. The artistic patronage of the new elite is discussed at length in Aline Saarinen, *The Proud Possessors* (New York: Random House, 1958). Cf. also Stewart Holbrook, *The Age of the Moguls* (Garden City: Doubleday and Co., 1953), pp. 323–63; Wayne Andrews, *Architecture, Ambition and Americans* (New York: Harper and Row, 1955), pp. 152–204; Alan Gowans, *Images of American Living* (Philadelphia and New York: J. B. Lippincott Co., 1964), pp. 366–86.

26. This association was formalized in clubs like the Century Club of New York and in such grand affairs as the testimonial banquet given to D. H. Burnham by the elite of New York. Cf. Charles Moore, *Daniel H. Burnham* (Boston: Houghton Mifflin Co., 1921), vol. I, pp. 68–81. The guest list included Charles Eliot Norton, Joseph Choate, Lyman Gage, Charles Dudley Warner, William Dean Howells, Marshall Field, Abraham Hewitt, Henry Villard, Daniel Coit Gilman, Walter Damrosch, E. L. Godkin, J. Henry Harper, Henry Lee Higginson, and might serve as a partial roster of the new elite and their literary and cultural associates.

27. *Ibid.*, vol. I, p. 38.

28. *Ibid.*, vol. I, p 30. Included on the board of directors of the World's Columbian Exposition were: Owen Aldis, Lyman Gage, Edward Jeffery, Joseph

Medill, Potter Palmer, Ferdinand Peck, M. A. Ryerson, C. H. Schwab, C. H. Wacker, C. T. Yerkes, and Cyrus H. McCormick.

29. D. H. Burnham, quoted in Coles and Reed, *Architecture*, pp. 142–43.

30. Halsey C. Ives, *The Dream City* (St. Louis: N. D. Thompson Publ. Co., 1893), n.p.

31. Bancroft, *Book of the Fair*, vol. I, p. 70.

32. For a survey of this new image of woman in American literature, cf. William Wasserstrom, *Heiress of All the Ages; Sex and Sentiment in the Genteel Tradition* (Minneapolis: University of Minnesota Press, 1959).

33. William Dean Howells, "Letters of an Altrurian Traveller," *The Cosmopolitan*, XVI (December, 1893), 219, quoted in Coles and Reed, *Architecture*, p. 181.

34. Cf. the *Chicago Tribune's* valedictory to the fair as "a little ideal world, a realization of Utopia, in which every night was beautiful and every day a festival, in which for the time all thoughts of the great world of toil, of injustice, of cruelty, and of oppression outside its gates disappeared, and in which this splendid fantasy of the artist and architect seemed to foreshadow some far-away time when all the earth should be as pure, as beautiful, and as joyous as the White City itself." *Chicago Tribune*, November 1, 1893, quoted in Bessie L. Pierce, *A History of Chicago* (New York: Alfred A. Knopf, 1957), vol. III, p. 511.

35. Charles M. Kurtz (ed.), *Official Illustrations From The Art Gallery Of The World's Columbian Exposition* (Philadelphia: George Barrie, 1893), p. 7.

36. Schuyler, *American Architecture*, p. 291.

37. Hamlin Garland, *A Son of the Middle Border* (New York: The Macmillan Co., 1917), p. 459, quoted in Coles and Reed, *Architecture in America*, p. 129.

38. Lohr, *Fair Management*, p. 14. Reprinted with permission from *Fair Management*, by Lohr, General Manager, *Century of Progress Exposition* (1933–1934).

39. *Ibid.*, p. 43.

40. Expenditures from Lohr, p. 44. Number of buildings in different categories compiled from official maps and guides.

41. Quoted in Coles and Reed, *Architecture in America*, p. 236.

42. Edgar Kaufmann and Ben Raclan (eds.), *Frank Lloyd Wright: Writings and Buildings* (Cleveland and New York: Meridian Books, 1960), p. 55.

43. *Ibid.*, p. 56.

44. Lohr, *Fair Management*, p. 62.

45. *Ibid.*, p. 64.

46. F. Crissey, "Why the Century of Progress Architecture?" *Saturday Evening Post*, 205 (June 10, 1933), 63.

47. Cf. Douglas Haskell, "1933: Looking Forward at Chicago," *Nation*, 138 (January 24, 1934), 109–10.

48. John and Ruth L. Ashenhurst, *All About Chicago* (Boston: Houghton Mifflin Co., 1933), p. 23.

49. Paul Hutchinson, "Progress on Parade," *Forum*, 89 (June, 1933), 372.

50. Lohr, *Fair Management*, p. 120.

51. *Ibid.*, p. 168.

52. *Ibid.*, p. 116.

53. Haskell, *1933*, p. 110.

54. Frank Lloyd Wright, *An Autobiography* (New York: Duell, Sloan and Pearce, 1943), pp. 353–57.

55. Rauschenberg was born in 1925 in Port Arthur, Texas. His "Oracle" made in 1965 belongs to the Leo Castelli Gallery in New York. It has been shown in both New York and Chicago, and is reproduced in the catalog of the 68th *American Exhibition* at the Art Institute of Chicago (1966).

12

Protestantism's Response to Social Change: 1890-1930

by **DAVID REIMERS**

For most of her history America has been a Protestant-dominated nation. As late as 1927, André Siegfried remarked: "the civilization of the United States is essentially Protestant. Those who prefer other systems, such as Catholicism, for example, are considered bad Americans and are sure to be frowned on by the purists. Protestantism is the only national religion, and to ignore that fact is to view the country from a false angle."[1]

At the turn of the twentieth century, American Protestants accepted this contention, though they often used the word "Christian" as a synonym for "Protestant." Victor I. Masters, a southern Baptist leader in domestic mission work, expressed it: "As surely as the temple of Jerusalem was built by a sacred patriotism and under the benedictions of a favoring providence, so surely were Christian aspirations and teachings the seed thoughts of our political constitution and Christian evangelism the inspiration of American colonization. . . . We are the only nation that was born Christian."[2] What Masters had in mind, of course, was that the nation's major institutions and origins were derived from Protestantism. To support this view, churchmen cited the Supreme Court, which had declared that the United States was a

Christian nation. In a case involving the Church of the Holy Trinity of New York and the federal contract labor law, the Court said in 1892, "we find everywhere a clear recognition of the same truth ... that this is a Christian nation."[3]

Protestants believed America was a Protestant nation because her origins were Protestant. There can be little doubt that Protestantism, and especially Calvinism, was a motive for the founding of the colonies and a force in bringing many colonists to the New World, but the Protestant apologists exaggerated the role of religion. Nor can there be any doubt that Protestantism influenced the development of certain American institutions. However, churchmen also exaggerated the religious factor in the forging of the public school system and the constitution, the two institutions they most frequently pointed to as Protestant-rooted.

Protestants also claimed that America was a Protestant nation in the sense that the political, moral, and social norms of American life were derived from Protestantism. Basically the churches were identifying Americanism with Protestantism.[4] For example, the difficult concept of separation of church and state, often resisted by Protestants in the colonial period, was one of the American values singled out as Protestant-inspired.

Perhaps at bottom, being a Protestant nation meant to Protestants that the people of the United States were mainly God-fearing Protestants with Protestant ancestors. They were people who professed a simple evangelic faith and who tried to live according to the Protestant moral code. And in so doing, with God behind them, they had reached a high level of civilization.

If Protestantism's position in America seemed secure to many churchmen in the late nineteenth century, changes in American life were threatening it. The industrial revolution and its concomitant technological changes, urbanization, and immigration challenged the Protestant sense of security. An increasing number of church leaders, such as Josiah Strong and Samuel Loomis, warned that the city was the carrier of corruption, vice, secularism, and other evils. The industrial revolution brought unsettling violence and class conflict, and the growing numbers of non-Protestant immigrants added to those already in the population who did not share Protestant concepts.[5]

Around the turn of the century, some factions in the churches responded in a progressive manner to these challenges. The social gospel movement sought to make the modern city and the results of the industrial revolution more Christian and humane, and to accomodate religion to industrialism.

Basically the social-gospel movement was associated with evangelical Protestantism, with its emphasis on individual renewal and revivalism. Of course the major Protestant denominations and leaders in nineteenth-century America, excepting some Unitarians, Universalists, Episcopalians, and a few others, were part of the evangelical movement. The social gospelers were able to combine the traditional emphasis on individual conversion with an attempt to build the Kingdom of God on earth. Thus groups like the Home Missions Council and movements like the Men and Religion Forward Movement of 1911–12 stressed both evangelism and social reform. Eventually evangelicalism suffered, in part due to the growing emphasis on social reform, and a tension developed between those concentrating on personal salvation and those emphasizing social problems.

Most of the social-gospel leaders also adhered to the new liberalism in theology that developed after the Civl War. The conservatives and, to the far right, the fundamentalists, on the whole did not accept the social gospel and were more at home with the gospel of wealth. The correlations were by no means precise, however, for some liberals resisted the social gospel and joined the religious conservatives in upholding political and social conservativism.

The social gospel took root mainly in the northern, middle-class churches: the northern Presbyterians, Baptists, Congregationalists, Methodists, and to an extent, Episcopalians. The social-gospel movement also made headway in the South, but there the Protestant churches were slower to accept it.[6]

The leaders of the social gospel started from the premise that the social teachings of Jesus could be and should be applied to industrial and urban America. Institutional churches, pioneered by men such as the Rev. W. W. Rainsford at Saint George's Episcopal Church in New York City, appeared in the cities in the 1880s and 1890s. These churches expanded their programs to cover the entire life of man.

By their side, the Salvation Army labored in the growing urban areas, and Y.M.-Y.W.C.A.'s enlarged their activities to meet the social needs of youth.[7]

The labor problem loomed as another challenge to the churches. The labor strife of the post-Civil War period shocked many Protestant leaders, and although many were unsympathetic to organized labor, a strain of the social-gospel movement emerged that sought to obtain a better deal for the workingman. Perhaps the most famous of the clergy's labor sympathizers was Washington Gladden. From his pulpit in a Columbus, Ohio, downtown church he defended the rights of labor.[8] In particular, Gladden urged that the workers receive higher wages and work shorter hours. In a day when unions were unpopular and often equated with violence, he defended the right of labor to organize. When the social gospel reached a quasi-official status with the founding of the Federal Council of the Churches of Christ in America, a social creed was adopted. It called for the churches to stand for minimum wages, abolition of child labor, living wages for workers, and conciliation and arbitration in labor disputes.[9]

The large corporation, or "capital" as the proponents of the social gospel usually put it, was another of the issues to face American Protestantism in the late nineteenth century. The growth of monopoly, the unwillingness of the managers and owners of American corporations to grant concessions to labor, and the lack of social responsibility of the capitalists were the problems singled out by social gospelers as associated with "capital."

Basically, Protestantism accommodated itself to the new order and did not urge fundamental changes in American capitalism. Many Protestant ministers and prominent laymen justified the system by preaching the gospel of wealth. Mixing Social Darwinism with certain traditions of Protestantism, these spokesmen equated the activities of the big capitalists with the ways of God.

Yet even social gospel leaders stopped short of economic radicalism. Socialism influenced the churches; but those who embraced Christian socialism, such as Walter Rauschenbusch, were the exception rather than the rule. In insisting that the social teachings of the New Testament be applied to the industrial world, the leaders of social

Christianity generally sought a middle ground between socialism and laissez faire and urged that capital take into consideration its social responsibilities as well as its profits. This meant acceptance of the rights and demands of labor and the community. Protestantism was too deeply committed to the ideological foundations of capitalism to urge radical change. Christian socialists were unable to overcome the belief in competition, the sacredness of private property, individualism, and stewardship.[10]

Part of the problem of the cities, labor, and capital was the problem of immigration. Large numbers of immigrants, increasingly from non-Protestant lands after 1890, entered the cities and joined the ranks of industrial labor. These people were often the workingmen whom the social gospel defended and were sometimes referred to as workers or labor, rather than immigrants.

A few Protestants agreed with Walter Rauschenbusch's statement to a Baptist gathering in 1888:

> I am not in favor of any restriction on immigration. I do not believe it is right to restrict immigration. . . . I believe in throwing open this country to all who will come, for I believe God made it for all. Who are we that we should close this country against the rest of the world? We all came over here sometime; if we did not, our fathers or our grandfathers were all immigrants at one time.[11]

Southern Methodist Warren Candler, writing in 1904, considered Catholic immigration a blessing because, "their coming will save the trouble and expense of sending the gospel to the lands where they live in poverty, ignorance, and national decadence. We can handle the hosts of Romanism better here than in papal lands. Evangelical Christianity has reached and saved millions of them already."[12]

Yet among many Protestants in the 1880s and 1890s a growing uneasiness existed about immigration from Southern and Eastern Europe. In his famous *Our Country*, written in 1885, Josiah Strong listed immigration among the perils facing America: "Thus, immigration complicates our moral and political problems by swelling our dangerous classes. And as immigration will probably increase more rapidly than the population, we may infer that the dangerous classes will probably increase more rapidly than hitherto."[13] Journals such as Lyman Abbott's influential *Outlook* favored some type of restriction.[14] This uneasiness, however, did not lead to loud demands for immigration restriction among Protestant churches, nor did it lead to the churches' association with nativist movements. Some fundamentalists supported the American Protective Association of the 1880s and 1890s, but the A.P.A. had no official endorsement from the churches, and the social gospel leaders generally disapproved of it.[15] Probably most Protestants at the turn of the century fell between Rauschenbusch and the ardent restrictionists, uneasy but hopeful that America could assimilate the newcomers.[16]

In the second decade of the twentieth century, the churches began to respond in a different way to the modern age. By the 1920s, reform sentiment had diminished considerably and intolerance had grown among Protestants. These changes must be viewed in part as the Protestant response to social and economic changes that challenged the concept of a Protestant nation. There were other reasons for the decline of the social gospel, but much can be explained by the fact that the churches believed their dominant position was threatened. A status revolution may have confronted Protestant leaders during the Progressive Era, as Richard Hofstadter has maintained, but the revolution continued to affect the churches and the concept of a Protestant America just as acutely in the third decade of the twentieth century.[17]

Immigration was one of the most perplexing changes facing the churches, and they responded mainly by participation in the Americanization movement. The movement reached its zenith in the 1910s and quickly faded in the early 1920s.

Those who sought to Americanize the immigrant never possessed a precise definition of Americanization. One part of the program was learning English; without knowledge of English one could not be an "American." Hence, the Americanizers devoted much attention to English classes and emphasized the role of the public school. They also established classes to teach the principles of citizenship, focusing on the constitution and voting. And their teaching stressed good moral conduct.[18]

Beyond these programs, Americanization was a vague concept, but for evangelic Protestantism one fundamental aspect of the crusade was the attempt to keep America a Protestant nation. This was a version of what Milton Gordon has called Anglo-conformity.[19] When the Americanization movement reached a peak within Protestantism in 1918–19, the churches labeled it "Christian Americanization." Though they cooperated with one another, they made little effort to work with Roman Catholics. Somewhat suspicious of Catholicism as an alien, un-American religion, the churches directed their efforts at converting Catholics to Protestantism. Hence the slogan "Christian Americanization" could just as easily have been "Protestant Americanization." One could not be truly American without being Protestant.

The domestic outreach of Protestantism predated the Civil War. For decades before the turn of the twentieth century Protestants sought to evangelize America; in the late nineteenth century they directed special attention to immigrant groups. Most of the work centered on the newcomers from lands predominantly Protestant or with a large Protestant influence. The churches labored among German and Scandinavian immigrants before the large immigration from non-Protestant regions began in the 1880s and 1890s. Hence the domestic missionary work among Italians, Russians, Poles, and other Southeastern Europeans was a logical extension of the effort to spread the good news.

Yet there was a difference when Protestants faced immigrants from Southeastern Europe. As they assumed that American values were derived from Protestantism, the immigrants from Southern and Eastern Europe presented a threat to those values. As one Protestant leader in home mission work expressed it in 1903:

It is only in recent years that new, more ignorant and therefore more dangerous elements have entered into the problem of immigration. . . . The Irish and German tides were ebbing, while those of Southern and Eastern Europe were both increasing and threatening. . . . None but an optimist of the purest water can view it without concern. Happily, we are able to count upon our British, German and Scandinavian people for substantial sympathy with American theories of government. . . . They generally believe also, in popular education and in Christian civilization.[20]

The way to counteract this threat was to convert the immigrant to Protestantism.

Northern Presbyterians, Baptists, and Methodists made the greatest efforts among the foreign born, and their work concentrated especially on Catholic immigrants. One student estimated that between 1880 and 1930 American Protestants spent approximately $150 million dollars trying to convert Catholic immigrants, but the results fell far short of expectations. Repeatedly, the churches renewed their efforts and enthusiasm only to encounter failure.[21]

The missions to the Jews were even more futile. Periodically church bodies passed resolutions urging expanded work among Jews, and eager home missionaries insisted that the "Jewish field" represented a vast and growing opportunity because so many Jewish immigrants appeared indifferent to their religion. "If the Jewish young people of to-day are lovingly and wisely dealt with, their children will freely enter our churches tomorrow," optimistically declared the Rev. John R. Henry of the Church of All Nations in New York City.[22] Yet those who worked in the Jewish missions experienced constant disappointment. Jewish immigrants may have been becoming increasingly secular, but few were susceptible to Protestant preaching. Some Protestants could not abandon hope, however. In 1929, Rabbi Israel Goldstein protested to the Home Missions Council, normally associated with liberal and tolerant Protestantism, that the efforts to convert Jewish children were offensive and caused problems between Jewish parents and their children. Basically arguing for religious pluralism, he urged that Protestants concentrate their efforts on fallen-away Christians, of whom there were many, rather than on Jews. The Council replied it was grateful for the rabbi's frank remarks, but:

> The Home Missions Council representing 38 boards of Home Missions of the United States and Canada must insist on not only the right but the duty to present the gospel of Christ in all of its fullness and the service of Christ in all of its implications to every man and woman within the bounds of this Continent, without regard to color, creed or condition.

Though the rabbi, and undoubtedly most Jews, thought otherwise, the Council added, "To do less than this would be false to our faith and unfair to our fellowmen."[23]

The merger of missionary work and Americanization occurred in the second decade of the twentieth century, though there had been overtones of Americanization in earlier missions. Growing immigration from non-Protestant nations and the developing nativism had an impact on Protestantism's attitude. World War I, with its accompanying fear of hyphenated-Americans, prompted intensified Americanization work. From the pulpit and religious press came zealous support for the war effort and appeals for loyalty and Americanism. As the *Christian Advocate* put it in denouncing disloyalty, "There must be nothing and nobody on our soil at this time that is not American."[24] The wartime expressions for Americanism carried over into the immediate postwar period, as the churches gave special support to Americanization in their home missionary groups during 1918 and 1919 under the label "Christian Americanization."

Christian Americanization was not entirely a program to force or persuade non-Protestant immigrants to conform to a Protestant mold. Though some Protestants exhibited suspicion toward Catholic and Jewish immigrants from Southeastern Europe, others pointed out that America was a nation of immigrants, that all groups contributed to the richness and diversity of American life, and that there was no one ideal American type. These Protestant home missionaries published and distributed a number of books on the immigrants' contribution to America. In spite of the fact that their tone was sometimes paternalistic, they preached toleration of diversity, and they were a contrast to the insistence upon conformity that characterized American Protestantism.[25]

Some in the Americanization movement were concerned about the low living standards of many of the immigrants. Those who sympathized with the immigrants' plight maintained that Americanization was a two-way street. In order to assimilate, the immigrant would have to take on some, although not all of the native American's ways; but at the same time native Americans had a responsibility to make the American environment a healthy one. This meant an attack on slums, poor working conditions, exploitation, and other social and economic problems of the immigrant.[26]

Christian Americanization was one way to prevent America from being consumed by alien forces. Another was immigration restriction. When Congress debated the immigration laws in the early 1920s, most major Protestant leaders and denominations remained silent on the racist quota system. Many had previously disapproved of unlimited immigration if it meant creating economic depressions and allowing dangerous radicals to enter the United States. A few statements were issued on the bills themselves. The southern Baptist Social Service Commission, for example declared : "We commend Congress for the passage of the Immigration bill which will greatly reduce the number of aliens admitted to our shores and will admit a larger percentage of the better class from the more enlightened and more advanced nations of northern Europe and a smaller percentage of the lower class from the less enlightened and less advanced nations of southern Europe."[27] The point most frequently discussed by the major denominations was the Japanese Exclusion Bill, which they attacked as discriminatory.[28] The Rev. Sidney Gulick, long-time missionary in the Far East, formed a group that suggested a quota system similar to that finally passed by Congress, but Gulick wanted the Japanese put on the quota and not excluded.[29]

The underlying tone of the discussions of Americanization by Protestants made it clear that most were relieved when Congress passed the restriction acts. The long discussions about unassimilated immigrants and the threats to American or Protestant institutions posed by large pockets of foreigners underscore the point. The mere fact that the churches attacked exclusion of the Japanese and not the quotas suggests their tacit approval. With the quota system, America could remain largely a Protestant nation.[30]

Related to the challenge of immigration was urbanization. The churches made efforts to adjust to the urban scene, especially with the social gospel, but the city increasingly became a threat to the Protestant hegemony.

One reason why the cities threatened Protestantism was the tendency for large numbers of foreigners to settle there. These newcomers were often Catholic or Jewish and unsympathetic to Protantism. "The city problem is a foreign problem," wrote one concerned

Protestant leader in domestic mission work, and he spoke for many others.[31] Josiah Strong's fears received renewed emphasis; the literature on the city problem abounded with worried references to the ghettoes of foreign born. Here was the greatest potential danger to Protestant domination. The city was overtaking the town, village, and farm and non-Protestants were dominating the city. Alva Taylor, a proponent of the social gospel, spoke for many when he noted the connections between the city, immigration, and the opposition to prohibition :

> There is already too much congestion of immigrants in the great cities in the industrial centers. If we are to have an American civilization we must assimilate the stream of newcomers. If we do not assimilate them they will adulterate us with an admixture of old-world morals. A straw in the wind is afforded by the recent referendum in Massachusetts on the liquor issue. The entire state went overwhelmingly dry except the large immigrant filled cities, and they went so overwhelmingly wet as to give the state as a whole a wet majority. National prohibition is the highest mark of distinctively American morality and citizenship. This referendum and many similar instances give us an index of possible adulteration of American ideals through unassimilated masses whose old world or Roman Catholic lack of moral ideals and social standards lower our levels of thinking.[32]

The city was partly responsible for the change in personal morals after World War I. But the city alone did not cause the shift in values. Science, industrialization, and commercialization were also undercutting religious authority and morality. In large measure, the city symbolized these changes, and it seemed to many Protestants that an older, simpler, Protestant America was being destroyed by the modern age.

Many churchmen responded by attempting to legislate against change, and in particular against the carriers of change. In part these attempts were extensions of the prohibition movement, another attempt to legislate morality. Of course the evangelic churches had always been interested in personal morals, but what is noticeable around World War I is the increased interest in legislation about personal morals and the nostalgia for a passing America.

The movies, for example, caused uneasiness. The great growth of the movie industry enabled it to reach into small-town America by the 1920s. Moreover, cinematic themes reflected the change in morality. Though some religious leaders saw the movies' value for religious instruction, their initial response was often hostile. Social action groups within the churches urged that some standards be established for the movies, and some churchmen were willing to have governmental censorship. The northern Methodist General Conference of 1920 attacked certain films for being "vulgar in their so-called humor, loose in their ideas of sex relations, based on the infelicities and infidelities of married life, vicious in their suggestiveness, and inciting our youth to crime by throwing glamor over criminal acts and careers. Such pictures continually repeated through the country cannot fail to have a bad effect." The Methodists concluded by calling for a federal motion picture commission to censor movies in interstate commerce.[33]

The desecration of the Sabbath was another concern of Protestantism. Here, too, the developing modern society and the growing number of non-Protestants were the villains. The expansion of professional and amateur athletics prompted various groups to use the Sabbath for amusement. The continental Sabbath, with its emphasis on enjoyment, was making inroads in America during the first three decades of the twentieth century. The old America of simple church-going and devotion on Sundays seemed increasingly threatened. Whether the eighteenth- and nineteenth-century Sundays were really as holy as the protestors maintained is a moot point; they believed that Sabbath desecration was on the increase and sought to hold it back. The feeling of uneasiness was especially strong among the evangelic and southern churches. The southern Methodist official journal even lamented that the churches were capitulating. Said the Nashville *Christian Advocate* nostalgically:

The United States, once known as a Christian land, is to-day a land where God's law is openly violated and where the sanctity of the day, which is peculiarly the Christian day, is trampled under foot by the consent of the statutes both of nation and State and city. This spirit of reckless disregard for Sunday, finds its voice in the Church, and we hear of churches dispensing with services because so many of their membership are otherwise engaged on Sunday evening. . . . Things are not as they used to be.[34]

Some churchmen pointed out that commercialization and technological changes, such as the movies, were not solely responsible for the decline of the old Sabbath. They noted that influences from Europe were creeping in. During the hysteria of World War I, Germany, with its continental Sunday, was singled out for attack.[35] But Germany had no monopoly on the continental Sunday. Other immigrant groups, especially those from Southern and Eastern Europe, lacked proper respect for the Protestant Sabbath. The field secretary of the Lord's Day Alliance of Pennsylvania declared about a Sunday-law struggle in that state:

Will the Christian, patriotic people of Pennsylvania never realize that our American Christian Sabbath is the point of attack by the masses of foreigners in our land, and that many politicians yield to their demands in order to secure their votes for office? . . . This bill is an attempt by foreigners to foreignize our American Christian Sabbath and establish the European Sunday in Pennsylvania, emanating as it does from the Strip legislative district of Pittsburgh, the population of which is composed of from seventy to eighty per cent of foreigners.[36]

To combat the increasing secularization and commercialization of the Sabbath, the Lord's Day Alliance, originally founded in 1888, renewed its efforts for stricter enforcement of Sunday laws and the enactment of new blue laws. Though some churchmen, such as the editor of the Episcopal *Churchman* of New York, attacked the Alliance and fervent Protestant efforts to pass Sunday legislation, Methodists, Presbyterians, and other sects supported them. Even some Baptists, with a tradition of sensitivity to the touchy problem of separation of church and state, wanted more action. The fundamentalist *Watchman Examiner* remarked:

Slowly but surely the old landmarks are being removed, and the dikes against the tides of secularism are giving way. Unless the church of God and those who stand with it for the general principles upon which our Nation was founded yield themselves to deeper convictions and arouse themselves to more strenuous action it will not be long before the things which have meant so much to us and to our fathers will be little more than cherished memories.[37]

The sporadic efforts to control Sunday were similar in tone to the uneasiness about shifting morals. The increasing divorce rate, the emancipation of American women, the changes in sexual standards and family mores were related to the desecration of the Sabbath. On occasion church bodies singled out culprits, such as the automobile, that were changing social customs. Said a southern Presbyterian committee in 1923, "Another evil threatening the home is unchaperoned automobile riding at night. The matron of a home for unfortunate girls reported lately that a considerable majority of the inmates of her home ascribed their fall to this habit."[38]

Though some of the churches' concern about changing morality was exaggerated, technological changes were undermining nineteenth-century American values. The stable family, considered by Protestants as one of the keys to the Christian and orderly life, was losing some of its responsibility and authority. The schools and the rapidly developing recreational institutions claimed time formerly consumed by family life and parental authority. The Lynds, for example, found Middletown parents worried about the early sophistication of their children that the auto and movies prompted.[39] Church-going and other traditional Sabbath observance were clearly affected by the automobile and motion picture. In short, Protestant values and the churches' position were threatened. As one scholar noted in 1933:

Since 1900 the church has been forced to compete more and more with an ever increasing number of secular agencies and activities. Such recent inventions as the automobile, the radio, and the motion picture, together with outdoor amusements like golf and tennis, now vie with the churches for people's time and interest. The millions of automobiles that crowd our highways on Sunday testify

to the number of persons who use the day for recreation and outings. The old attitude of strict Sabbath observance, which was
generally characteristic of Protestants in all parts of the United
States except the western frontier, has decidedly changed.[40]

It was difficult to legislate against modern technology, but at least
proper instruction in how to cope with change could be given. Hence,
the churches gave increased attention to the role of education in the
first three decades of the twentieth century. They seized upon the
public school as a proper place to teach morals. There was nothing
new in this attitude; proponents of public education in the United
States traditionally had looked to the schools as an instrument of
moral instruction. The matter assumed a new sense of urgency, however, as traditional moral patterns were disrupted by a rapid technological innovations and the large numbers of non-Protestant
immigrants. The public school became one of the bastions of Americanization. Since Protestantism identified Americanization with Christian
or Protestant Americanization, the schools were expected to instill
certain Protestant values. In some cases this meant Bible reading and
prayers in the schools. Thus, Methodists in 1920 praised their Board
of Temperance, Prohibition, and Public Morals for standing for the
reading of the Bible in the public schools, and other churchmen
agreed.[41] In an argument foreshadowing recent discussions about
religion in the public schools, one churchman, speaking for the
Chicago Church Federation, declared:

All Jews, or others, coming to this country should, and in most
cases do, take cognizance of the fact that this is a Christian nation.
Many of them have come consciously or unconsciously because of
the fact that this Christian nation has afforded them a safe asylum.
It is poor gratitude for the hospitality of the nation for these newcomers to undertake to destroy in the nation's life the very element
which has made the nation safe for them.[42]

It would be a mistake to assume that concern over Americanization,
Bible reading in the schools, Sabbath laws, prohibition, motion picture
censorship, and other moral reforms completely swallowed up the

social gospel in the 1920s. The churches were still interested in the problems of labor and peace and race relations and not simply in personal sin and morality. For example, churchmen, and even more, churchwomen demonstrated more concern about the race problem in the 1920s than they did during the Progressive Era. In general, however, interest in the social gospel movement declined in the 1920s.[43] This decline cannot be understood without realizing that many Protestants shifted their interests. The social gospel was the attempt by a large number of Protestants to grapple with the changing world at the turn of the century. In the 1920s churchmen partially pushed aside social Christianity and attempted to legislate and preach against change.

Nor did the attempts to halt social change mean that all the Protestant churches endorsed fundamentalism or the Ku Klux Klan. The major denominations denounced the Klansmen, and although many churchmen supported fundamentalism, many others resisted it. The fight against fundamentalism dissipated the energies of those who supported progressive Christianity, however, and helped account for the weakening of the social gospel and the growth of crusades to legislate personal morality.[44]

Nativism and moral crusades triumphed in the 1920s, but there were other traditions within the churches. One was the acceptance of diversity in American life. Some Protestants were willing to accept cultural and religious pluralism in the early decades of the twentieth century. They did not believe that the United States had to preserve Protestant domination by excluding people of other faiths, by legislating Protestant moral values, or by keeping Catholics out of the White House. These churchmen and women, working through groups such as the National Conference of Christians and Jews, attacked anti-Semitism, anti-Catholicism, and racism in their various forms and were willing to see ethnic changes in the population. Thus, in 1920, a committee of the Federal Council of Churches deplored the use of the term "Americanization" where it was made to mean or imply "that there is no distinction between the words 'Americanization' and 'Christianization,' or carries the implication that Jews, or people of other religions and other races, are not good Americans." "No church," concluded the committee, "should use the term 'Americanization' as a cloak for proselytizing its distinctive religious views."[45] After World War II the carriers of this tradition sang praises to religious pluralism and welcomed the fact that a Catholic could be elected President.

NOTES

1. Andrè Siegfried, *America Comes of Age* (New York: Harcourt Brace and World, 1927), p. 33.

2. Victor I. Masters, *Making America Christian* (Atlanta: Home Mission Board of the Southern Baptist Convention, 1921), pp. 16, 26.

3. Quoted in Anson Phelps Stokes and Leo Pfeffer, *Church and State in the United States* (New York: Harper and Row, 1964), p. 112.

4. For a suggestive study of Protestantism and Americanism after the Civil War, see Sidney Mead, "American Protestantism Since the Civil War: From Denominationalism to Americanism," *Journal of Religion,* 36 (January, 1956), 1–15.

5. See, for example, Samuel Loomis, *Modern Cities* (New York: The Baker and Taylor Co., 1887); Josiah Strong, *The New Era* (New York: The Baker and Taylor Co., 1893).

6. See Charles Hopkins, *The Rise of the Social Gospel in American Protestantism, 1865–1915* (New Haven: Yale University Press, 1940); Aaron Abell, *The Urban Impact on American Protestantism, 1865–1900* (Cambridge: Harvard University Press, 1943); Henry May, *Protestant Churches and Industrial America* (New York: Harper and Row, 1949). For the social gospel in the South, see Kenneth K. Bailey, *Southern White Protestantism in the Twentieth Century* (New York: Harper and Row, 1964), chap. 2.

7. Abell, *Urban Impact.*

8. May, *Protestant Churches.* See also Robert Handy (ed.), *The Social Gospel in America* (New York: Oxford University Press, 1966).

9. Hopkins, *Social Gospel,* chap. 8.

10. Handy, *Gospel in America,* pp. 4–6; Mead, *Protestantism.*

11. *Seventh Annual Session of the Baptist Congress,* 1888, pp. 86–87.

12. Warren Candler, *Great Revivals and the Great Republic* (Nashville: Publishing House of the Methodist Episcopal Church, South, 1904), p. 294.

13. Josiah Strong, *Our Country* (Cambridge: Harvard University Press, 1963), p. 56.

14. *Outlook*, 83 (May 5, 1906), 15–16; *ibid.*, 103 (February 22, 1913), 377–78. See also Sherman Doyle, *Presbyterian Home Missions* (Philadelphia: Presbyterian Board of Publications and Sabbath School Work, 1902), p. 231.

15. Donald Kinzer, *An Episode in Anti-Catholicism: The American Protective Association* (Seattle: University of Washington Press, 1964), pp. 244–45.

16. John Higham, *Strangers in the Land* (New York: Atheneum, 1963), p. 122. For statements of these views, see Charles Stelze, *Christianity's Storm Center* (New York: Fleming H. Revell Co., 1907), pp. 25–26; Howard Grosse, *The Incoming Millions* (New York: Fleming H. Revell Co., 1906); John Henry, *Some Immigrant Neighbors* (New York: Fleming H. Revell Co., 1912).

17. Richard Hofstadter, *The Age of Reform* (New York: Vintage Books, 1960), pp. 151–52. For the decline of the status of the ministry in the 1920s see Paul Carter, *The Decline and Revival of the Social Gospel* (Ithaca: Cornell University Press, 1956), chap. 6. For tension in southern Protestant churches, see Bailey, *Twentieth Century*, esp. chaps. 3–5. For an interesting discussion of social change during the 1920s, see Andrew Sinclair, *Era of Excess: A Social History of the Prohibition Movement* (New York: Harper and Row, 1964).

18. The standard work on the Americanization movement is Edward Hartmann, *The Movement to Americanize the Immigrant* (New York: Columbia University Press, 1948). See also Higham, *Strangers*.

19. Milton Gordon, *Assimilation in American Life* (New York: Oxford University Press, 1964), pp 98–102.

20. Joseph Clark, *Leavening the Nation* (New York: the Baker and Taylor Co., 1903), pp. 263, 266. For other examples of this see Doyle, *Home Missions*; address by the Rev. William C. Roberts, "Momentous Facts and Figures," to the General Assembly of the Presbyterian Church in the U.S.A., in *Annual Report of the Board of Home Missions of the Presbyterian Church in the U.S.A.*, 1892–1893.

21. Theodore Abel, *Protestant Home Missions to Catholic Immigrants* (New York: Institute of Social and Religious Research, 1933), pp. 104–105. See also Gerald Shaughnessy, *Has the Immigrant Kept the Faith?* (New York: The Macmillan Co., 1925), esp. pp. 221–22.

22. *Annual Meeting of the Council of Cities of the Methodist Episcopal Church*, 1917, p. 31.

23. *Annual Report of the Home Missions Council*, 1929, pp. 44–46. Rabbi Goldstein was speaking with the support of the National Conference of Christians and Jews.

24. *Christian Advocate*, 93 (April 25, 1918), 526. See also Roy Abrams, *Preachers Present Arms* (New York: Round Table Press, 1956).

25. Dorothy Giles, *Adventures in Brotherhood* (New York: Council of Women for Home Missions and Missionary Education Movement of the U.S. and Canada, 1924). Georgia E. Harkness, *The Church and the Immigrant* (New York: George H. Doran Co., 1921).

26. See, for example, Robert Handy, *We Witness Together* (New York: Friendship Press, 1956), chap. 3.

27. *Annual of the Southern Baptist Convention, 1924*, p. 117. See also *Moody Monthly*, 21 (July, 1921), 468; *Presbyterian*, 94 (February, 21, 1924), 12–13; *Presbyterian Banner*, 108 (March 2, 1922), 3; *Christian Advocate* (Nashville), 86 (September 11, 1925), 1252.

28. *Quadrennial Report of the Federal Council of the Churches of Christ in America, 1920–1924*, p. 79. *Christian Century*, 41 (May 15, 1924), 619. *Journal of the General Conference of the Methodist Episcopal Church, 1924*, pp. 714–15. *Congregationalist*, 109 (May 1, 1924), 548. *Churchman*, 129 (May 31, 1924), 21. *Christian Advocate* (Nashville), 86 (February 6, 1925), 163.

29. *Christian Century*, 41 (March 27, 1924), 407.

30. For an interesting discussion of the evolution of the term "Americanization" to include Jews and Catholics see Will Herberg, "Religion and Culture in Present-Day America," in Philip Olson (ed.), *America as a Mass Society* (New York: The Free Press, 1963), pp. 373–82.

31. Charles Sears, *The Redemption of the City* (Philadelphia: The Griffith & Rowland Press, 1911), p. 157.

32. Alva Taylor, "Shall We Limit Immigration?" *Christian Century*, 37 (December 30, 1920), 17. For earlier connections Protestants made between immigration and prohibition, see James Timberlake, *Prohibition and the Progressive Movement, 1900–1920* (Cambridge: Harvard University Press, 1963), pp. 14–16, 30–33, 115–19.

33. *Journal of the General Conference of the Methodist Episcopal Church, 1920*, p. 673.

34. *Christian Advocate* (Nashville), 77 (June 16, 1916), 27.

35. *Presbyterian*, 89 (July 31, 1919), 3.

36. *Ibid.*, 92 (May 11, 1922), 10.

37. *Watchman Examiner*, 7 (August 28, 1919), 1225. For the strictures of the *Churchman* see *Churchman*, 123 (January 8, 1921), p. 8; *ibid.* (January 29,

1921), p. 15. See also the *Congregationalist*, 104 (September 18, 1919), 363, for a moderate statement.

38. *Minutes of the General Assembly of the Presbyterian Church in the U.S.*, 1923, p. 84.

39. Helen and Robert Lynd, *Middletown* (New York: Harcourt Brace and World, 1929), chap. 11. See also William F. Ogburn, "The Family and Its Functions," in *Recent Social Trends in the United States* (New York: McGraw-Hill Book Co., 1933), pp. 662–708.

40. C. Luther Fry, "Changes in Religious Organizations," in *Recent Social Trends in the United States*, p. 1012. See also Lynd, *Middletown*, pp. 339–43.

41. *Journal of the General Conference of the Methodist Episcopal Church*, 1920, p. 667. *Minutes of the General Assembly of the Presbyterian Church in the U.S.A.*, 1915, p. 30.

42. E. J. Davis, "The Bible in the Public Schools," *Christian Century*, 37 (March 25, 1920), 13.

43. Robert M. Miller, *American Protestantism and Social Issues* (Chapel Hill: University of North Carolina Press, 1958). Carter, *Social Gospel*. David M. Reimers, *White Protestantism and the Negro* (New York: Oxford University Press, 1965).

44. For the connection between the Klan and Protestantism see Reimers, *Protestantism*, pp. 97–99; Robert M. Miller, "A Note on the Relationship Between the Protestant Churches and the Revived Ku Klux Klan," *Journal of Southern History*, 22 (August, 1956), 355–68. The standard work on the fundamentalists in the 1920s is Norman Furniss, *The Fundamentalist Controversy, 1918–1931* (New Haven: Yale University Press, 1954).

45. *Federal Council Bulletin*, 3 (April, 1920), p. 66.

INDEX

Index

A